A. Kane

Dear Ari,

Thanks for your interest. I hope you find a blessing in this book.

Best wishes,
Pat

# Transgender Good News

D1088714

# Transgender Good News

Pat Conover

*photographs by*
*Mariette Pathy Allen*

New Wineskins Press
Silver Spring, Maryland

New Wineskins Press
12 Wessex Road
Silver Spring, MD 20910-5437
www.newineskinspress.com

© 2002 by Pat Conover

All Rights Reserved.

Printed in the United States of America

Photographs by Mariette Pathy Allen

Book design by Deborah Sokolove

**Publisher's Cataloging-in-Publication Data**
Conover, Pat
   Transgender Good News / Pat Conover ; photographs by
Mariette Pathy Allen. - - 1st ed.
   p. cm.
   Includes bibliographical references.
   ISBN 0-97182563-7
   1. Transsexualism.  2. Transsexuals.  I. Title

HQ77.9.C66 2002      305.9'066
                     QB102-200369

LCCN 2002091981

Dedicated to
Patricia B. Nemore
in appreciation of
soul sharing, gender accompaniment, and
practical support

# Contents

# Preface

This book responds to three basic questions about transgender experience and expression. What is true? What is going on? What really matters? I have tried not merely to answer these questions, but to pay attention to the framing of the questions. After wrestling with transgender questions as an important part of my own life, and after applying the disciplines I have learned as a scientist and a theologian, I believe more than ever that getting the questions right is more important than defending answers.

There are several different ways to read this book and I have tried to provide enough cross-references between chapters to support different reading approaches. I've developed the book in this way with the intention that it will serve diverse reading audiences with an interest in transgender concerns.

For readers working out their personal transgender journeys, a focus on the introductory chapter; a review of Chapter 5, the stories chapter; a review of Chapter 6, my summary and contribution to theory; and then primary attention to Chapter 8, concerning transgender issues, and the first section of the Appendix, may fill your need.

For general and sympathetic readers, perhaps those who love a transgender person, you might begin by reading Chapters 1 and 5 and then picking and choosing topics of interest from Chapters 8 and 9. I also welcome hostile general readers to this book. All the elements of this book are necessarily under development, and this is a good time for lively interchange. I urge hostile readers not to skip Chapters 2, 3, and 4 because you may find that careful attention to the framing of the debates will resolve some concerns before any interchanges.

For readers interested in only the religious aspects of transgender experience and expression, your focused interest may be met by reading the introductory chapter and Chapter 5; then focusing on Chapter 9, where I work with five different approaches to Christian theology; then reviewing the appendix, where I draw out a few implications for local congregations.

For readers who want to understand the causes of transgender experience and expression, I recommend reading at least Chapters 1-7. Chapters 2-4 contain the reviews of relevant physiological, psychological, and sociological scientific contributions. The synthetic integration of these scientific contributions in Chapters 2-4 provides my best posing of the question, What is true? Chapter 7 offers a critique of the clinical professions. The relevant psychological research is reviewed in Chapter 3, and Chapter 7 considers the destructive application of clinical misunderstandings that has been so influential in shaping professional and commonplace views on transgender experience and expression.

I hope that those in the helping professions will read at least chapters 1-8. Thankfully, an increasing number of professional helpers have begun to move beyond medical model concepts. This book offers a lot that can help such professionals to a better grounding of their own practice and encourages a collective effort to free transgender people from clinical oppression, just as gay and lesbian people were freed by the psychiatric declaration that homosexuality is not a disease.

Since language about transgender experience and expression is difficult, and since several key terms are used differently by both transgender and straight writers, readers may want to refer to the glossary provided at the back of the book to understand word usage in this book.

Although this book has been written with diverse reading populations in mind, it was also written to be read straight through. It is important to get a sense of what is true and what is going on before taking up the question, What really matters? I hope that this book will be good news for people who disagree me in one or many ways. I look forward to all well-meant criticism and conversation. I've tried to be clear that I believe that most of the truth about transgender experience and expression is still to be uncovered. I've tried to be clear that there are many kinds of transgender people and that there is a lack of consensus among transgender people on numerous concerns. As the first book of this scope by a transgender Christian, it lacks the benefit of serious dialogue for sharpening many concerns. So I encourage readers to bring along skepticism as well as curiosity. If we can get the questions right, the next book in this line can be stronger.

For those readers who are aware of being on a spiritual quest that involves transgender concerns, I send you my special welcome and best wishes.

# Acknowledgments

This book has been hard to write. Its comprehensiveness is both its strength and weakness. It is the book I wanted to write, and I hope the fact that it is aimed at several audiences will, in the end, prove to be a strength rather than a weakness. Since no agent or publisher would work with me, and since some caused me distractions and delays, there is a temptation to say I did it all myself. But this book could not have lived without the support of my family, friends, and Seekers Church—my local congregation.

My first line of support has been Patricia Nemore, my spouse. Trish is actually published before I am on transgender issues, having written a chapter on her relationship with me for the wonderful book *Trans Forming Families*, edited by Mary Boenke. My daughter Samantha was initially challenged by my coming-out process, but she has worked through her concerns to a deep affirmation of me and a warm relationship. I am thankful.

James Nelson and Virginia Ramey Mollenkott looked at early drafts, and their comments helped my feel that I was on a right track and that the book was worth writing.

I specifically want to thank the librarians at the Long Branch public library, part of the Montgomery County, Maryland, library system. Although the facility is not set up as a research library, the librarians nonetheless proved helpful at an early stage. I profited from a short time in the headquarters of the International Foundation for Gender Education (IFGE), both in finding reference materials and from getting to know Vanessa Murray, who turned out to be a lot of help. She sold me a lot of books, but she also gave me a lot of wise counsel about writing for the transgender community and about dealing with the world of publishers and agents. Alison Laing, Nancy Nangeroni, Linda Buten, Dallas Denny, Yvonne Cook-Riley, and others at IFGE befriended me in various ways and helped me in my own journey and with this book. Several friends in the Trans Gender Education Association, a support group in the Washington, DC, area, have been helpful, and a couple have contributed stories to Chapter 5.

I feel so fortunate to have the friendship and support as well as the wonderful photographs of Mariette Pathy Allen in this book. Mariette has been a photographer at transgender events for a long time. Her book *Transformations* was one of the first major contributions to imaging transgender people as real people rather than as performers—to provide grounding rather than sensationalism.

I'm proud to be a member of the Coalition for Lesbian, Gay, Bisexual and Transgender Concerns, affiliated with the United Church of Christ. The Coalition is the first of the Protestant coalitions to add *transgender* to their name and to start to work at making the participation of transgender Christians an important part of their life. I particularly want to thank Sam Loliger and Mitzi Eilts for their encouragement.

Seekers Church means so much to me. It deserves a book of its own, and I've been threatening to write one after *Transgender Good News* is fully launched. Seekers helped me with the costs of writing this book with a grant from the Growing Edge fund. More importantly, Liz Gould-Leger has been my copy editor. I didn't realize how much I needed her until I began to get copy back with her marks and comments. Deborah Sokolove turned the text into a book and designed the book cover. Her friendship as well as her artistry help me in many ways. Kris Herbst designed the web page for the book, an important contribution, since I have to market the book as well as write it. I am part of the Spirit and Sexuality Mission Group at Seekers, and my several mission group partners have been a continuous source of encouragement and accountability. I particularly want to thank Kate Cudlipp, my spiritual guide for 13 years, for reading my spiritual reports and constantly providing me support, questions, and accountability. Coming out in Seekers would have been infinitely harder without the support of Kate and other mission group members: Jesse Palidofsky, Kevin Ogle, Mollie McMurray, Jane Engle, and Bob Bayer. Seekers isn't a perfect congregation, but it is infinitely interesting and a special embodiment of good news. (You can learn more about Seekers, an independent congregation, at www.seekerschurch.org.)

*"The very process of living is a continual interplay between the individual and his [her] environment and often takes the form of a struggle resulting in injury or disease. The more creative the individual the less he [she] can hope to avoid danger, for the stuff of creation is made up of responses to the forces that impinge on his [her] body and soul."* Rene Dubos[1]

*"We were talking about the space between us all,*
*And the people who hide themselves*
*behind the wall of illusion.*
*We were talking about the love that's gone so cold,*
*And the people who gain the world and lose their souls.*
*They don't know.*
*They can't see.*
*Are you one of them?"* George Harrison[2]

# Chapter 1:
# Definitions, Grounding
# and Confession

I've learned that zippers are the sworn enemies of attractive nails. I've also learned that colleagues can look right past pearly nail polish and pearl earrings and treat me as a man. I've had enough experience and acceptance in presenting my feminine image to feel what I objectively knew: You can draw outside the lines, but it still takes a lot of work to draw a life picture of beauty and responsibility. These are some of the clues I've used to follow the threads of meaning in my experience as a transgender person. The causes and meanings of transgender experience are a bit of a mystery, since the very idea doesn't fit in very well with the English language or with the basic stories about gender we learn early in life. Most of you, my readers, have choices about whether you think there is anything real or significant in transgender phenomena. Since I've been given a transgender path to walk, it hasn't been optional for me to seek to understand the truths I've been given to carry. This book intends to give you a thread to pull on to raise to consciousness something of what transgender experience is about in the rich tapestry of gender experience.

Do I offer a new thing called *transgender consciousness* in this book? I think not. In the first place, it isn't new. More importantly, though I am a bigender person and see things from where I stand, I understand myself as following a not uncommon process of dipping into everyday human consciousness rather than some specialized consciousness. I have merely suspended my judgment that the usual polarized understanding of gender is the best way to understand myself and to accurately see what is going on in others. I know from the inside out that one doesn't have to be either a man or a woman. A lot of people know this in small ways as they choose not to conform to one or another socialized expectation that are elements of the role of man or woman. I merely reconsidered myself and my world with regard to gender and sex using the very best concepts and images available to me from the discourses of several sciences, from the conversations of the transgender community, and from Christian theology.

While I was in the middle of working on the fifth draft of this book, I found myself in prayer during a period of collective silence at Seekers Church, an independent Christian congregation of which I'm a member. I found myself reflecting on a phrase that I wanted to use in this first chapter. I was conflicted because I both liked the phrase and was resistant to using it. As I dwelt with my resistance, I sensed that it was spiritual. I became even more clear that I did not want to write another defense of transgender people, nor did I want to plead my own suffering in search of sympathy or acceptance. Much more is at stake.

I realized that the true theme of this book points to a larger context within which my life, and the lives of my transgender friends, makes sense. To gain the most from reading this book, you may be served well by temporarily setting aside your assumptions about sex and gender, the meanings attached to being a man or a woman. It's not so much that the package concepts of *man* or *woman* are wrong or unhelpful. Rather, gaining a little reflective freedom may help you reconsider the presuppositions that inform your concepts and thus help you use the concepts with greater insight and appreciation. Without such engagement the most you can hope for from this book is learning something about transgender experience and expression. With such engagement, looking through this transgender window at the landscape of sex and gender may help you appreciate your gender journey more fully.

Though I think this book can help anyone better navigate their gender journey, this is not a general book on the subject of sex and gender. I have sought to provide a better overall picture of what is known, as well as greater appreciation of what is not known, about transgender experience and expression. An improved understanding of the available knowledge base is then used to reevaluate several difficult issues that transgender people must face and then as the factual part of the grounding for a Christian assertion that transgender experience and expression can be a channel of God's grace.

I didn't understand at the beginning how hard it was going to be to write this book. There have been plenty of intellectual challenges, including repeated reassessments of my basic categories. The biggest challenge, however, was spiritual. It has been very hard to read most of the dozens of books that have informed me in this writing task. Over and over I've had to put down a book and work with the toxic effects of being told I was sick or sinful, that I was deceptive, or that I was an artifact rather than a human. Some clinicians seems to think they are protecting people like me by explaining to attackers that I'm trivial or harmless. At such moments I have struggled to remember that the flood of negativity tells me things about my oppressors but does not name me. Raising my gaze from such emotional floods, I keep coming back to a few landmarks, some moments of recognition and orientation that help a little. I hope they are useful to you.

So poor an effort. I would prefer to prove everything and convince everyone. But there is no secret revelation here, no revealing of a third sex, no newly discovered brain structure or insight into raising children. Still, my landmarks are precious to me, and I think they can be life-giving for others. You don't have to put on a dress to reconsider the limits of masculine images in this culture. You don't have to play professional football to learn about courage.

The next three chapters offer an extensive review of physiological, psychological and sociological scientific contributions and reasoning relevant to transgender experience and expression. Some of you may wish to skip these chapters. What you would miss is the engagement of the relevant scientific work of others that I have gathered into a fresh synthetic, rather than analytic, summarization. The summarization provides several guiding concepts that clean up the envelope of meaning within which practical and spiritual issues are discussed in the later chapters. These chapters allow a fresh assessment of some of the limits of language, culture and theory that make many transgender discussions so difficult. While scientific work, so far, is short on answers, it can help us find the interesting questions. Knowing that some of you will skip the next three chapters, I've tried to write the last five chapters in a manner that repeatedly makes the fruits of the synthetic summarization available to readers with less taste for scientific argumentation.

The most important questions are about what matters most in life as lived. Such questions are the core subjects of theology. At this point I offer just a taste of where I'm heading in the last chapter. I don't claim to worship a God who is androgynous, or transgender, or a man, or a woman. I'm in no place to define God. Instead, God defines me, and I am just trying to appreciate and understand what is going on. Though it has not come easily, I feel I have been sufficiently open to what God has put before me in my life to accept the good gifts I've been given, including my bigender sense of self. My path has confirmed my hope that I am loved.

This is the first chapter of a whole book of introductions. Conversation about transgender experience and expression is just coming into focus in Western culture. I'm hardly a first explorer of this territory. I join the conversation with those who are knocking on doors, peeking through windows, trying to create interchanges that open up spaces denied by the restricted languages of clinical professions and traditional theologies. One of the introductions in this book is descriptive material that illustrates the diverse phenomena of transgender experience and expression for those less familiar with this material. Another introduction invites readers who are suspicious of Christian theology for scientific reasons to reconsider what contemporary theology can accomplish and invites transgender readers who are appropriately suspicious of Christianity, because of ugly attacks by some Christians, to reconsider what a Christian perspectives can offer when transphobic misconceptions are cleared away.

I've happily given a major part of my life to scientific inquiry. There is no need to write an apology for good science. Unfortunately, not everything presented as science is good science. Within good science the principles of honesty and humility lead to the creations of rules, for example, rules limiting the generalizability of findings from controlled research settings to uncontrolled everyday settings. It is the tightness of focus provided by such rules which releases much of the wonderful power of science. But good science is sometimes ruined when scientists change hats and speak as moralists, or for political purposes, without being disciplined about exactly what they bring with them into the changed discourse. I'm not going to spend much space on the politics and ideologies that have affected the several kinds of scientific discourse reviewed in the early chapters. I understand that such critiques are relevant and appreciate the good work of this kind that has been accomplished by other authors. I'm going to focus on what we can know on scientific grounds from the scientific work that has been done, whatever its motivation.

The problems are even more severe the other way around: religious leaders and clinicians adopt points of view that they think are scientifically grounded when that is not true. Consumers of scientific discourse want to know the facts, and this desire often leads them to skip past the humility of good science. Whether it is scientists going beyond the limits of their disciplines without recognizing the changed discourse, or the misuse of scientific studies by a clinician or religious leader, a key corrective question is repeatedly asked, "How do we know what we know about gender?"

In additions to the many introductions in this book, it seemed impossible to write this without paying attention to the numerous pragmatic challenges facing transgender people living in this oppressive culture. For non-transgender readers, you may nonetheless appreciate the Eighth Chapter and some other elements of this book as "so what" illustrations of the implications of the scientific and theological work. For transgender readers, I want to indicate from the beginning that I'm aware that sometimes my engagements of pragmatic issues are controversial within the transgender community. Some of that is unavoidable since some current divisions seem so deep, so confrontational. On the important policy debates of the day there is no way through except as we learn the paths a step-at-a-time. This part of the book is the most time-bound and contextual and my hope is to merely illuminate some next steps.

Confessions

All of us who write about human concerns are influenced by the social locations we inhabit. What we see depends on where we stand. I am at least standing. It is challenging to live a life that doesn't make sense to many people I care about, to people who care about me. It is challenging to read book after book by socially recognized experts that do not know me but think they do. It is frightening to realize how much some clinicians would have hurt me if I had not stayed hidden when I was young. And it has taken decades of spiritual growth to work with all that my hiding has cost me.

What we see also depends on where we look, what lenses we use, and whether we move around. I am a bigender person, one of the many ways of being a transgender person. I'm also an ordained Christian minister who initially studied psychology and prepared for a career in pastoral counseling. After becoming involved in the civil rights movement and learning about oppression, I changed direction, added sociological skills, and have had a career of ministry, teaching, and public policy advocacy.

My scientific and theological lenses were initially of little help in trying to understand myself as a bigender person. There was little to read in the professional literature in the 1950s and 1960s beyond the Kinsey Report. I remember having to justify my interest in order to gain access to the Kinsey Reports which were held as restricted access volumes in the Florida State University library. The only "literature" that had any vitality was pornography, and after working with that a bit, I found that it wasn't my interest or story. Christianity as well as science had made people like me invisible. I thought I was the only one. But "only one" or not, I knew God loved me, and I escaped the looming alternatives of teenage castration or suicide.

One thread through my academic preparation was an interest in the general philosophy of science.[3] I have been interested not only in *what* we think we know scientifically but in *how* we know it and in the *fairness of our reasoning* based on what we think we know. Such concerns are at the heart of reassessing the transgender experience and expression of everyday people doing their everyday things.

Transgender experience and expression has become more visible as an object of study over the last 30 years. We transgender people are not as hidden as we used to be. We have increasingly found each other, begun conversations, and formed organizations. But we are still mostly hidden, and too much of our public image has been shaped by the popular media. But it is also crucial to note that the sensationalized distortions in the popular media would not stand if our lives were not being measured against the stereotypes created and defended by clinicians, and religious leaders.

Of the many problems transgender people face in becoming known to themselves and society, the most serious is that the professional writing has come overwhelmingly from psychiatrists and clinical psychologists. They have drawn widely varying pathological pictures of me and my community. You might or might not like my bigender commitments and activities but you would have a hard time justifying a picture of me as somehow sick. Indeed, my testimony in this book is that claiming my reality as a bigender person has opened wellsprings in my heart. This book is one way to own and give away all that God has given to me.

As I came to understand why clinical pictures do not fit me, as I figured out why a lot of Christian theology blocked rather than opened the channels of God's grace, it became important to name the misunderstandings and attempt corrections. When I was gifted with a sabbatical in my job, I got a chance to catch up with my reading and write the first draft of this book. There is no point in pretending that I am dispassionate. But, since I trust that God's truth is not separate from God's love, I have let my passion turn my attention to the harder questions and to admit the frustrating limits to my understanding. Sad to tell, a lot of this book is about noticing the limits of scientific work for a well-grounded understanding of transgender experience and expression, as well as about the harm that has flowed from Christendom's attempts to repress gender reform in general and transgender experience and expression in particular. Some of you may be doubtful that my training and commitments as a scientist and a theologian have led to disciplined objectivity. That's fine. This is not a "trust me" book. You will get a chance to see the factual grounding and assumptions of my work.

As part of making clear my sources of potential bias, some may find it relevant to know that I've been working with my personal transgender issues for over four decades. I participate in organizations of transgender people. I have lived out most of my life with a man's appearance and, at the time of writing, live out most of my social interaction with an appearance on the masculine side of androgyny. In some settings I dress in a distinctly feminine image. In all my gender presentations I am trying to pay attention to how my gender-related consciousness is growing, both as an individual and in my multiple human relationships.

I'm trying to explore and affirm all the good things that men and women have carried in this society and to say no to the rest. This really isn't such a radical notion. Many writers have criticized both roles as traditionally defined. What makes my choice seem so radical to others is that I shape my appearance to affirm my identity with both options. I feel this path has led me to more deeply understand and appreciate my whole self. Opening myself to appreciation of all that culture calls masculine and feminine, and bringing it together in an integrated life, has felt like saving grace to me, a gift from God.

In addition to confessing my personal transgender subjectivity and telling you that I have sought to be reflective and analytic from my several intellectual disciplines, it is only fair for me to point out also that the range of transgender experience is so diverse and varied that I cannot claim subjective access to much of it. I stand with the reader in trying to understand experiences of others that I partly share and partly do not share.

I also feel constrained to tell you I'm well aware that I have enjoyed the advantages that come with being white, with claiming the masculine role in my academic and professional life, and with growing up in a middle class family. While I've paid attention to cultural and historic considerations, discipline is always a matter of correcting for limitations.

### Seeing What You Don't Want to See Takes Discipline

Everyday seeing is not a matter of simple or neutral observation since it involves focus and interpretation. Which cues will one notice and which cues will one tactfully avoid? What information will one seek out so that one can understand more deeply? What categories, such as "clean" and "dirty," will be used to link new observations to mental categories and pictures?

When I preached my coming out sermon in my local congregation, where I am an active member, I was very well received by just about everyone. But when I made it clear by showing up that I would sometimes participate in congregational life in my feminine presentation, with dresses and makeup, some became concerned. What would visitors think? What would the children think? The first round of questions and reconsideration was mostly managed by my mission group, which created several organized discussions. I attended one of the three discussions and got very few questions directly. Thankfully, some of the children were willing to ask the obvious questions. Thankfully, things have worked out well, and I continue to preach occasionally, work with the children in various ways, offer adult classes in our School of Christian Living and otherwise participate fully in the social life and ministry of Seekers Church.[4] But this episode confirmed again for me the power of seeing as opposed to just talking about the things that matter in our lives. Though working with my feminine appearance feels to me to be just one part of working with my gender consciousness, it draws a lot of energy and attention because the seeing is so socially provocative. What you see depends a lot on what you are willing to see. People were ready to receive my story as I told it in my sermon and were warm and concerned in response. Seeing me required people to reconsider how to relate to me. Presenting myself as a woman not only causes transitions and adjustments, it challenges the categories themselves, with resulting discomfort and confusion.

Scientific seeing, in contrast to everyday seeing, depends on formal rules of observation so that recorded data can more fairly be compared. What categories and standards are chosen to focus observation? It isn't an automatic process. In the fourth chapter, a lot of the discussion turns on this point. The most distinctive mark of scientific seeing is that by formalizing and reporting one's definitions, categories, and standards, biases may become more visible and the limits of one's factual base more obvious. This process enables additional research and review to be more constructive or corrective. Lacking formal discipline, the reporting of everyday seeing often hides biases hidden from others.

My path to freshly seeing the scientific and theological grounding for transgender experience and expression is illuminated by two opinions. The first is that inadequate science has been linked to misleading theology in Western culture to deny the truth about transgender experience and to oppress transgender expression. The inadequate science is first and foremost the result of clinical studies. The misleading theology goes back to problems in the third and fourth centuries of Christendom, is hostile to the best insights of Hebrew scripture and the teachings of Jesus, and has distorted almost all later versions of historic Christendom.

The second shaping opinion in this book is that people don't have to choose between the limited options of conforming to the roles of man or woman. One *can* choose some of both. Some transgender people go back and forth between traditional roles or make a permanent change from one to the other. Many who pursue a single change are as committed to sustaining traditional gender roles and images as are the defenders of "straight" perspectives. They are just moving their psychological location in a gender landscape that seems fixed. I respect and affirm such choices, but I claim for myself more of the radical freedom implicit in the possibility of movement.

## Definitions

We are stuck with using words for a lot of our communication with each other. Unfortunately, a lot of the words in common usage, words we think we understand very well, are decidedly unhelpful for understanding transgender experience and expression unless we add additional specifications. This book returns repeatedly to definitional issues, because understanding transgender experience and expression is dependent on more carefully attaching words to familiar phenomena and concepts. There are definitional problems with common words like *woman* and the resulting lack of precision is one of the things that messes up research.

Scientific discussions of transgender issues are often burdened with psychological and psychiatric jargon. It is not accidental that such jargon often serves to confuse rather than to clarify important issues. Control of the language is fundamental to control by psychiatric and psychological clinicians of what constitutes professional opinion. Confusing the laity is a major contribution to professional control. Freshly assessing the content and relevance of key words and phrases is a big part of coming to an understanding of transgender issues that initially seem strange or impossibly technical. My fondest hope is that readers will be able to say to themselves "Oh yeah, now that makes sense to me."

Let's start with the common words we use: *male* and *female, man* and *woman, masculine* and *feminine*. I join the convention of discussing physiological differences with the words male and female, psychological and social role differences with the words man and woman, and cultural symbols with the words masculine and feminine.

Some writers move away from a bipolar conceptualization of males and females, men and women. Instead they conceptualize these words as end points of physiological, psychological and social continua. Such usage suggests one may be more or less male or female, masculine or feminine, man or woman. Though I endorse the underlying ideas of complexity, flexibility, and diversity, I am not enamored of the concept of continuum, because it still carries the image of gender as a line between far-apart end points. Instead, because I believe that gender factors are not only complex, flexible, and diverse; but also *interactive*. I have come to see each of the terms: male, female, man, woman, masculine and feminine as *package concepts*. For example, I use the words male and female to describe physiological aspects and contributions to the psychological and social realities identified by the words man and woman. But I'm also aware that social and psychological factors change the physiological realities of people. Thus I use all of these key words to help describe one or another aspect of a complex and interactive whole. Studying the physiological aspects of a person is a powerful analytic simplification, but while it is useful to distinguish the sciences, it is important not to forget that physiological reality is the result of both physiological and non-physiological factors.

When a package fails to fit the contents, it is easy, but wrong, to see the contents as misshapen. Scientific research asks how well the packages fit the contents. For example, the distribution of hair length in any human population is a proper subject for research. It is inaccurate to assert that women have longer hair than men, especially that it is natural for women to have longer hair than men, without doing the relevant research. Such research should properly include the influence of cultural fashion on this physiological reality.

There are some common language usages in transgender writing that can also be over-simplifying or misdirecting. For example, it is common to write of transsexuals that they are either male-to-female or female-to-male (M2F, F2M). This usage emphasizes the physiological changes that are wanted or have been made. In the case of cross-dressers with only modest physiological changes, such as shaving the hair on one's legs, it is even more important to use descriptive words related to gender rather than to sex. The extra care taken with language may sometimes seem clumsy. Perhaps such clumsy moments will remind you that a first challenge in understanding transgender phenomena is the need to learn to communicate across the barriers of mental habits shaped by everyday language.

I use the word *transgender* in a way that is at variance with some other authors when I point to a range of gender issues and not just to appearances.

Violating appearance norms may be the behavior that concerns those who are interested in suppressing such "deviance" with punishments or therapy. Violating appearance norms may be the focus of many who are new in their transgender expressions. In this book I aim at an understanding of transgender experience and expression that takes account of all the varieties and channels of such experience and expression.

Most writers also draw a bright line between the discussion of transgender issues and the discussion of homosexuality. I prefer to treat the issue of whom one chooses as a partner for explicitly sexual expression as just one of many ways to affirm or challenge the traditional role concepts of man and woman, as one expression of identity and desire.

My use of the word *transgender* is not unusual, however. For example, my usage parallels the writing of Leslie Feinberg: "The words cross-dresser, transvestite, and drag convey the sense that these intricate expressions of self revolve solely around clothing." Then, after pointing out the ways this doesn't work, Feinberg concludes, "Because it is our entire spirit—the essence of who we are—that doesn't conform to narrow gender stereotypes, many people who in the past have been referred to as cross-dressers, transvestites, drag queens, and drag kings today define themselves as trans*gender*."[5]

## We Exist

The first scientific point to make about transgender people is that we exist. There has been a lot of writing about issues of sex and gender that leaves out transgender people but presents itself as if it were inclusive. Well, I exist. My community exists. We may not fit into your scientific theory. We may be an embarrassment to your politics or spirituality. But we definitely do exist.

Though appearance issues are but one part of transgender expression, consider some of the different patterns that describe the appearance activities of transgender people. There are:

- Postoperative transsexuals who were assigned the male physiological definition at birth and who assimilate into the role and culture of being women. They become invisible to the transgender community.
- Postoperative transsexuals who were assigned the male physiological definition at birth but now think of themselves as transsexuals, or as transsexual women. They may partly assimilate while also sustaining some connections to other transsexuals and to the transgender community.
- Postoperative transsexuals who were assigned the female physiological definition at birth and who assimilate into the role and culture of being men. They become invisible to the transgender community.
- Postoperative transsexuals who were assigned the female physiological definition at birth but now think of themselves as transsexuals or as transsexual men. They may partly assimilate while also sustaining some

connections to other transsexuals and to the transgender community.

- Repeat all the above distinctions for preoperative transsexuals, with several stages of transition.
- Repeat all the above distinctions for full-time transgender people, who are sometimes called nonoperative transsexuals. These are people who have no intention of undergoing sexual reassignment surgery (SRS) of their gonads. Such people may or may not undergo other kinds of physiological changes by using hormones, by undergoing cosmetic surgery of many kinds, and by electrolysis (hair removal).
- Full-time transgender people who were assigned the female physiological definition at birth but live all the time as men with little or no physiological support.
- Transgender people who were assigned the male physiological definition at birth and who spend a little, a moderate amount, or a lot of time presenting the feminine image of themselves without trying to take on the whole role of a woman. Such people are often called transvestites or cross-dressers. Most people in the transgender community think this is by far the largest category of transgender people. It is also widely considered in the transgender community to be a largely hidden population.

Cross-cutting all the above categories are the distinctions about whom people choose for sexual partners. Further cross-cutting all the above categories is the issue of performance. Drag queens and drag kings have their separate organizations, which also function, in part, as actors' unions for their jobs. There are amateur, part-time, and full-time kings and queens.

The above transgender distinctions are cross-cut by subculture and age group contexts. Further cross-cutting all the above categories is the reality that many transgender people make changes as they grow older. A person who would be defined above as a postoperative transsexual was quoted as follows: "I thought I was a homosexual at one time; then I got married and had a child so I figured I was a heterosexual; then because of cross-dressing I thought I was a transvestite. Now (postoperatively) I see myself as bisexual."[6]

Some people cross transgender lines while resisting the application of transgender language. For example, some people like to dress up for a permissible moment, such as a Halloween party. Others have transgender fantasies or dreams but don't follow them up. Yet others express some androgyny or partial violation of gender appearance norms: a man may wear a single earring.

It is important to remember that people who were assigned the female physiological definition at birth and who sometimes wear masculine clothes face very different labeling circumstances than people who were defined at birth as males and sometimes wear feminine clothes. In the United States at the turn of the millennium, women have a lot of freedom of apparel and appearance without getting labeled as anything by anyone. This means that if social causes are important, and I believe they are, then theories about men cannot be applied to women as if the circumstances of women are some kind of mirror image of the circumstances of men. This is important not only for appearance factors but for other factors as well, such as gender oppression.

Two more definitional issues deserve attention. Those who wish to assign labels based on the subjective claims of the labeled people need to recognize that a lot of transgender people are not ready to claim a particular label or category. This isn't necessarily because of personal confusion, though that too can be an issue. Rather, many transgender people appropriately understand that they have not lived out a lot of their images, questions, and sensitivities in a wide range of everyday experience. Because of oppression and fear, a lot of transgender people are closeted or out only in protected circumstances. With little social support for identity development or confirmation, it isn't surprising that many people express tentativeness or confusion. Instead of pathologizing honesty that reflects a lack of social experience, it might be better to think of many transgender people as going through a delayed childhood or adolescent exploration. Darry Hill has done a small interview study with transsexuals that highlights this dynamic.[7]

Furthermore, as was made clear in several workshops of the 1998 International Foundation for Gender Education Convention, there are more than a few out and experienced transgender people who see themselves in more than one category—for example, intersexual and transsexual, or cross-dressing lesbian. When it was pointed out that claiming two or more labels seems to create some contradictions, one answer is "But it works for me." Another is, "Sure, I'm just living with the contradiction." Yet another is, "It's where I am right now and I hope I'm still a growing person."[8]

Another cut across the issues of definition is offered by Dallas Denney who has offered a brief summary of the kinds of social roles made available to transgender people in other cultures and over time within Western civilization.[9] She names 45 such roles. The fifth chapter further explores the variety of ways transgender people express their feelings, imagery, and selves. Several brief stories are provided there.

## A Scientific Preview

A good deal of the scientific review in the next three chapters is *not* built on specific studies of people with transgender experience. Much of the most relevant work in the context of functioning human beings has been done on gay males who may or may not have transgender experience or engage in transgender expression. Furthermore, a great deal of the research that has been done on any aspect of nontraditional sexual expression, or in comparing men and women, is shaped by the mind set of looking for a needle in a haystack. By this I mean that the studies look for some single factor to explain homosexuality or transgender experience, on the presumption that it is different in kind from everyday expressions of gender or sexual activity. The critique of such studies will repeatedly draw attention to the haystack: that is, research that has been disregarded because it did not find a looked-for needle can tell us a lot by attending to what *was* found. The scientific grounding I point to draws from the same research base that other scientists refer to but emphasizes the larger and contextual truths in such research rather than the focused testing of hypotheses that often failed.

Some aspects of the scientific review in the next three chapters are technical. Attention to the details of the standards of research is important for answering the question "How do we know what we know?" If you read the chapters you will see that answering this question again and again is important to reducing scientific confusion and misunderstanding of transgender experience and expression. In turn, cleaning up the science can contribute to reducing cultural confusion.

Though this book contains some history of the relevant sciences, I am more interested in philosophy of science contributions. My most important goal is not the deconstruction or critique of key scientific concepts for political or ideological purposes. That is good and important work and others are much better at it than I am. I particularly honor and have gained from Anne Fausto-Sterling's *Sexing the Body: Gender Politics and the Construction of Sexuality*. Fausto-Sterling's book extends the feminist critique of science.

If you choose to skip the scientific review chapters you may still want to be aware of the several scientific themes I develop. When I discussed the "haystack" realities of scientific research above I was thinking of *complexity, interactivity* and *flexibility*. I argue against both physiological and psychological essentialism (determinism) by distinguishing between the explanation of biological and psychological *bases* and biological and psychological *determination*. To reconsider what is most real, I emphasize the relevance of *synthetic* thinking as a means of integrating *analytic* studies. My own synthetic theory is available in the sixth chapter, and many readers may find it easier to work with than my reviews and critiques of the research of others.

One of the reasons that the scientific review in this book is difficult is that there is so little direct scientific study of transgender experience and expression. This means that some of the best thinking is based on cognate studies, particularly the study of gay men, the study of lesbians, and studies generally comparing men and women. Perhaps the greatest challenge for my effort to provide a scientific base as part of the grounding for a reconceptualized understanding of transgender experience and expression is that I am interested in explaining everyday experience and expression whereas most of the writing that is currently counted as scientific comes out of clinical analysis based on assumptions of pathology. I don't assert that all transgender people or all non-transgender people are free of pathology, only that we need to understand everyday transgender and gender experience and expression without precategorizing it as pathology.

---

Notes:

1. Rene Dubos (1959), page 13. The bracketed words are mine and are inserted as a correction to the sexist language of Dubos.
2. George Harrison, "Within You Without You" (Song), *Sgt. Peppers Lonely Hearts Club Band*, Capitol Records, (1967).
3. I taught courses in this area at the University of North Carolina at Greensboro, wrote academic papers, and chaired a session of papers at the annual meetings of the American Sociological Association.
4. Those interested in the wonderful and distinctive aspects of Seekers Church can check out the web site: www.seekerschurch.org.
5. Leslie Feinberg (1996), page xi.
6. Dwight Billings and Thomas Urban (1982), in Janice M. Irvine (1990).
7. Darryl Hill (1998).
8. Ibid.
9. Dallas Denney (1997), pages 33-42.

*There are more emotions and phenomena than words.* Magnus Hirschfeld[1]

# Chapter 2:
# Our Bodies

Some Christian theologies are dualistic, separating body and spirit and condemning things of the body as sin. At other points, some Christian theologies have viewed things of the body as immutable gifts of God and therefore not to be disturbed, except for healing that is defined as returning the body to its natural state. This book approaches the body in simpler theological terms. It makes no presuppositions about the inherent goodness or badness of the body except to note that *life* is a good gift of God. Neither is there a presupposition about immutability. Instead, the first thing to note is that the body exists. This means that if we want to say something theological or ethical about the
body, it would be a good idea to understand what the body is and is not. The second step is to ask what the body makes possible and to consider the desirability of the alternatives as measured against Christian standards such as love and responsibility.

There is one theological choice that is worse than dualism or regarding body elements as irresistible psychological, social, or spiritual forces. It is to simply ignore the body. Any of these options earns theology a lot of laughter as a pompous irrelevance. The solution is to remember that Christian theology can trust the truth, with appropriate humility about our grasp of the truth. Respect for scientific sources of truth can help us frame life's most important questions with as much groundedness as we can muster. With God as creator, and Jesus understood as incarnating God's presence in the world, Christians are drawn to an interest in the *embeddedness* of spirit in the midst of life. This is good Christian grounding for both caring about and respecting what science can tell us while remembering what science cannot tell us because of the properly imposed limits of scientific inquiry.

## From Least Parts to Creative Wholes

Many people are most comfortable in scientific discussions of human beings when they reason from body causes to social and cultural effects. In everyday terms, people are prone to say things like "I behave this way because I was born this way." Other people are heavily invested in denying physiological determinism, in making logical space for the causal relevance of environment and nurture. This chapter takes an interactive approach, understanding that our bodies influence our lives and that social forces and personal choices can affect the body. Another way of saying this is that you can't have a life without having a body and that there is more to life than having a body.

Typical scientific theories and research efforts are analytic. The word *analysis* derives from the word *cut*. Analytic thinking cuts the object of study into its constituent parts. When the parts have been identified, and when the processes by which the parts become a whole are identified, analytic science has accomplished what it calls explanation. In physiology this means identifying the parts of the body and how they function together to be a body. When a body part has been identified, and when its effect on the whole body has been identified, then this kind of science has explained the causal impact of this body part.[2]

Analytic thinking, however, is only one alternative for those who want to take science seriously. *Synthetic* scientific thinking works with the same observational base as analytic science but understands what is going on somewhat differently. The key to the corrective power of synthetic thinking has to do with understanding what *is* observed and what *is not* observed.

Whatever the object of observation for any particular science, what is observed in the object is what is *manifest*. What cannot be observed about the same object is its *potential*. When a particular object is observed *as it interacts* with other objects, we can observe a potential that becomes manifest in the interaction. The key point of synthetic thinking is the understanding that this newly realized potential is part of a more complex whole. The interactive potential of an object is realized only *as it interacts* with other objects. Although it is fair to reason that the potential to participate in a more complex manifestation is "in" an object as that objects stands alone, it is equally fair to reason that such potentiality is *not* being accounted for when the object is viewed alone. When an object is considered by itself, its potential is known *inferentially* from previous observation of the object in interaction. Synthetic thinking shows us that any object is more than the sum of what can be observed in its parts when those parts are observed separately. The "more than" is the hidden potential that is revealed as the whole object interacts in a more complex frame of reference. This is the core correction of the common error of scientific reductionism, such as reducing the concept of mind to the physiological base of the brain. Physiological reality is a *basis* for all human activity but not necessarily the most significant *cause* of human activity. This point which will be repeated at several places in the book, is one critical element for understanding why transgender experience and expression should not be understood as pathology.

Consider a synthetic understanding of water. Water is made up of two atoms of hydrogen and one of oxygen, which meld together under certain conditions. Although we know that hydrogen and oxygen can combine to become water, we cannot observe the wetness of water in hydrogen or oxygen in isolation. It is easy to skip over this point, because we "know" it is there.

The core physiological questions to ask about sexuality and gender concern the physiological bases for sexuality and gender: what is limited, what is likely, and what is possible when we observe people in terms of their psychological identity, their social role behavior, and their relationship to cultural symbols. We know that there are physiological limits to life itself. We know that physiological states affect, and in some cases can overwhelm, our consciousness or our feelings. But to point out that there are physiological limits to our sexuality and gender is like pointing out that water can freeze at certain temperatures. It is valuable knowledge, but it doesn't help us understand what is going on when water is in the temperature range of wetness.

Mood altering drugs can profoundly affect human consciousness, human feelings. But this doesn't make the mood equal to the drug. Within usual "temperature" ranges, other factors also affect mood or feelings, and such mood or feelings can take part in a much more complex whole of identity or choice. One can drink too much alcohol and die, less and fall into a drunken stupor, less and be substantially impaired, less and be happily drunk, less and be slightly relaxed. To deny the potential effects of drinking alcohol is dumb. To say that drinking alcohol will kill you, without specifying dosage levels and other circumstances, is a falsehood. It is equally dumb to think that one can fully explain drunken behavior, an intrinsically social observation, by explaining the alcohol level in the blood. The alcohol level in the blood affects the possibilities and limits of human behavior, but it does not explain how people will feel or what they will do within such limits. Different people do not feel the same, or act the same, every time they consume enough alcohol to raise their blood alcohol level to a specific point.

The consideration of the physiological aspects of human behavior in this chapter is important for beginning to build a scientific picture of the phenomena of transgender experience and expression. This consideration is also important because a great deal of contemporary political and spiritual thinking about transgender experience and expression refers to physiological facts and theories. Sadly, it is too often the case that both sides of a political or spiritual argument may grossly misunderstand the science to which they refer and may give far too much importance to physiological factors in the overall picture of scientific explanation. Such mistaken arguments often fail to note the limits to generalization and applicability that are the boiler plate of scientific reporting. Another common error is to reason metaphorically from the scientific base rather than to reason logically. Metaphoric thinking can be quite useful. One just needs to keep clear that it isn't a substitute for analytic or synthetic thinking when a scientific point is being made.

To show the relevance of sharpening our physiological thinking it is worth noting, for example, that many political and spiritual arguments about sexual ethics turn on the scientific understanding of the word *choice*. For example,

Presbyterian ethical statements about homosexuality distinguish between *orientation* and *conduct* and assert that homosexual orientation is acceptable because it is not chosen, whereas homosexual conduct is sinful because it is chosen. This chapter on physiology will try to lay a proper grounding for understanding the issue of choice and similar questions.

## Designer Bodies

People have 23 chromosomes that contain a total of 70,000 to 150,000 pairs of genes.[3] Each chromosome is made up of two genetic strands. In the 23rd chromosome the two strands are markedly different: XX in females, XY in males. Except for the 23rd chromosome in males, in each chromosome a gene is represented on both strands though the paired genes are not identical in form and effect: among other things, one gene may be stronger or weaker in effect than its paired gene.[4]

Our understanding of the complexity of genetics has expanded enormously in recent years. Many of us learned to think of genes as a blue print for our physiological development, and this image still may be compelling. To more adequately understand the blooming complexity in contemporary genetics, consider the following:

- Any gene may have different forms, called alleles. Sometimes, only one allele of a gene is the source of a specific trait.
- There may be several forms of a particular allele, depending on how often certain sub-sequences of genetic chemicals are repeated. Different forms of the allele may have different physiological effects.
- It can matter, in terms of effect, whether a specific gene is inherited from the father or the mother, even though the structure of the two genes appears identical.
- A gene may be dominant or recessive, and some dominant genes are recessive under certain conditions.
- If a gene on one chromosome doesn't work then the matching gene on the other chromosome may kick in, but at a different level of effect.
- Genes work interactively with other genes to shape a particular effect. For example, variation in a single gene can create the unusual shortness identified with an African tribe labeled "Pygmy." But, if that gene is in its most common condition, then many genes will affect height.
- Different alleles may have different penetrance or power in interaction with other genes. For example, you might have the allele for a particular genetic disease, but the disease will not become manifest because the allele's action is suppressed by other genes.
- Genes are considered to act in terms of probabilities, and some genes are never active.
- Many genes that affect development are active only for a limited period of time, except that sometimes, for certain cancers at least, they turn back on.

Some of the most interesting theorizing about the genetic basis for sexual orientation (gay men in particular) concerns genetic action during fetal development.

- A single gene can have several physiological effects: a "negative" effect (sickle cell disease) may be carried along through inheritance as the other side of the coin of a "positive" effect (resistance to malaria).
- Mitochondria, the elements in all cells that release the energy of combining oxygen and carbohydrates, have their own genes which are passed on independently of the chromosomal genes. The mitochondria are also critical in the first stage of the process of converting cholesterol to sex hormones.
- Genes produce their physiological effects by creating amino acids in specific patterns that make up complex proteins. This process can be altered by other physiological factors.[5]

For the above reasons, highly similar genetic structures will not always produce the same physiological outcome. Anne Fausto-Sterling summarizes much of the above argument by pointing out that genes are small bits of organic matter in a cell that interact in enormously complex ways with other elements of the cell and that some of those other elements in the cell enter from the outside.[6] Understanding these multiple complexities has helped us understand why "identical" twins, as close a genetic similarity as occurs naturally, are not really identical. For example, if one twin is left-handed it is more likely that the other twin will be left-handed than a non-twin sibling, but the other twin will be left handed less than half of the time.

The fact that the 23rd chromosome occurs in a female form (XX) and a male form (XY) does not mean that males and females are brightly differentiated genetically. First of all, males and females have 22 pairs of similar chromosomes and only one pair that is XX or XY. The Y chromosome is comparatively short and is currently understood to contain the genes that create male changes in development and very little else.[7] This fact alone should be enough to end the common phrasing about the "opposite" sex. Mary Coombs, a University of Miami law professor, a feminist theorist, and a lesbian theorist, recently wrote, "Frankly, I'm not sure what something the opposite of me would be, but it's not a male human. Perhaps a Brussels sprout?"[8]

A tour through the development of genetic science is one of the several joys to be experienced by reading Chandler Burr's *A Separate Creation: The Search for the Biological Origins of Sexual Orientation*.[9] Burr uses a political analysis of the development of genetics as a scientific discipline to focus on issues of sexual orientation. His work attends primarily to the issues of gay men, and gives only a little attention to transsexuality and none to transgender expression. The central point about genetics that Burr illustrates so superbly and readably, is that genetics is enormously complex and interactive. The several aspects of physiological reality that we label male and female are complexly shaped at the genetic level. This explains why any specific physiological structure may be differently shaped in different people and may be stronger or weaker in its effect on the rest of the body in different people.

Burr tells the story of the first "discovery of a gay gene" by Dean Hamer and his research team. Hamer and his group published their ground-breaking research in 1993, "A Linkage Between DNA Markers on the X Chromosome and Male Sexual Orientation."[10] Hamer and his team did not actually find a specific gene for male homosexuality but rather identified a narrow genetic region where such a gene is likely to reside. Neither did they demonstrate the physiological effect of a gay gene. Neither have they shown the distribution of this gene in human populations. We do not know whether the penetrance of the theorized gene is strong or weak, or whether the physiological effect is strong or weak, or whether the gene might have several strengths in several alleles. Neither do we know how this genetic effect interacts with other genetic effects. Only simplistic blueprint thinking would lead us to conclude that Hamer's research points to a physiological limit, or an overwhelming physiological urge, that overrides all other factors in the explanation of male homosexuality. Hamer does not make such a claim, and Burr is careful to point out the multiple qualifications and caveats that Hamer presents. Although Hamer's research is appropriately cautious, and although he understands that many other causes may be relevant, both sides of the argument about choice quickly jumped to conclusions based on one or another understanding of genetic determinism.[11] This is like arguing that our genetic capacity for language determines whether we will speak French or Chinese.

Hamer's team also spent time doing sociological research in an attempt to identify the trait of male homosexuality so they could specify what they were studying. This research had several methodological problems, which are discussed later. What is important at this point is that Hamer's team ended up recruiting subjects for their genetic research by advertising in gay newspapers. There is nothing scientifically wrong with using such a convenience sample for *genetic* research. The logical problems come from generalizing results about the effects of the presumed gene from a limited sample either to a larger gay sample or to the general population. There may be a lot of difference between males in the general population who have some homosexual experience and those who would answer Hamer's advertisements. While Hamer was careful to note that the gene they are on the verge of identifying may contribute only a small element to the explanation of sexual orientation in some men, popular writers were quick to talk about the discovery of the "gay gene" as if it were dominant and relevant for everyone.

Some of the genetic qualifications relevant to Hamer's study include the following: more than one gene is likely to be involved, which means a genetic base for complexity rather than simplicity. The effect of inheriting a single gene at conception may be radically modified before it in turn affects development. This finding is considered by some a likely explanation for the fact that even a monozygotic (identical) male twin has only a 50% chance of being gay if his brother is gay. Such twin studies are a good reason for arguing against a tight genetic determination. Twin studies show genetic relevance, but they also show that the effect of genetic inheritance is not so simple. If a gay gene is finally differentiated, it will take additional research to show how such a gene influences development.[12]

Hamer's research is directed to finding a specific gene (needle) out of 70,000 or more genes (haystack). He writes, "The overall machine which you could call sexuality, may be, genetically, incredibly complicated, but the directional switch for that machine, straight or gay, may be incredibly simple."[13] The terms *directional switch* and *machine* show that, for Hamer, all the boilerplate qualifications he appropriately included in reporting his research don't really matter to him. At heart he believes in a mechanistic and deterministic genetics. In writing this book I take the boiler plate seriously, both the complexity at the genetic level and the complexity of the experience and behavior to be explained.

Burr follows Hamer and other physiologists and repeatedly argues for "biological essentialism," particularly that a gay sexual orientation is not a matter of choice. Although Burr's essentialist commitments may account for his interest in genetics and anatomy, his book nonetheless makes it abundantly clear that the current state of physiological research cannot support a position of narrow genetic determinism. I salute Burr for his careful report of Hamer's research and follow-up interviews which undermine a deterministic position.

In addition to the impressive achievement of demonstrating a narrow region of a chromosome which may contain a gene that has some influence on gay activity by some men, Hamer also was able to suggest that such a gene is probably recessive and is probably passed through mothers. However, assuming that Hamer and his group have discovered a gene that is statistically more common in a sub-sample of gay males than in the general population, that is still no proof that the gene causes something in a person that affects sexual orientation. Most genes are inactive. They don't do anything at all. If the gene is active in some way that is related to a subsection of the gay male population, there is no proof that the gene is causative rather than a mere corollary of gayness. Even if the gene proves to be active and influential for the sexual orientation of some men, because the gene is recessive and broadly distributed in the population there is no way an antigay eugenics movement could eliminate gayness by controlling reproduction.

## Growing Up

Genesis got its physiology backwards: at conception everyone is on a track to develop as female. Later in fetal development those who have an XY chromosome (males) usually develop high levels of two hormones: testosterone and MIH. The MIH leads to defeminizing development. Thus males usually have only the vestiges of ovaries, uterus and vagina, found near the prostate gland. High levels of testosterone leads to masculinizing development in XY fetuses. Females (XX) also generate testosterone in their ovaries, adrenal glands, and elsewhere, and it is critical for their development. Sometimes XX fetuses also have a masculinized development because of a high level of testosterone.

There are reasons to think that the transition from female to male is not so easy for the developing XY fetus. For one thing, at conception there are 130 XY fetuses to every 100 XX fetuses. At birth the ratio is almost equal. Those scientists who argue that there are physiological causes for gay and lesbian experience and expression, or for bisexuality or transgender experience and expression, often argue that something goes wrong during pre-natal development that either masculinizes the brains of females or feminizes the brains of males. Never mind that such an outcome hasn't been found in adult brains. (See the later section in this chapter on brain development.) Never mind that there is no direct evidence for this theory in human subjects. Never mind that the choosing of sexual partners is only one aspect of being a man or a woman and that no one has demonstrated a general relationship between masculinity or femininity and choice of sexual partners. This theory seems to be so culturally needed that scientific assessment is almost irrelevant.

Just because genetic or physiological determinism hasn't been proved doesn't mean that there is not lots of relevant evidence. Indeed, pre-natal causes of homosexuality is one of the most studied of all research theories in endocrinology. Those who summarize and interpret such research are just unwilling to emphasize the complexity, interactivity, and flexibility that has been found. For example, consider an often referenced study of rats by Roger Gorski which showed that if you cut off a male rats testes at birth they acted like female rats in presenting themselves to be mounted unless they were given rat testosterone within the first five days of life.[14] The surface analysis suggests physiological determinism. Though initially interpreted relative to homosexuality, Burr later interviewed Gorski who agreed that the rat experiment was a "model for transsexuality" rather than homosexuality.[15] However, follow-up research shows a more complex picture. First of all, if one destroys the portion of the rat brain affected by the lack of testosterone nothing changes in the rat's behavior. Secondly, the other rats, that is the rats that mounted the altered rats, were not altered. Are they to be theorized as homosexual or bisexual?

The key point of the Gorski rat studies for transgender concerns is that fetal, or early development, hormones could be relevant for the way one wants to present oneself sexually. In responding to such a theory as it applies to humans, two critical points should be made. First, human sexual activity is far more mediated than rat sexual activity. For example, humans share sexually even when the female is not in heat. More important, human sexual choices are mediated by symbols which means the choices are influenced by cultural realities. Even in the rat studies, the rats that mounted were apparently affected by behavioral signs. To discover that there are physiological referents for human sexuality should not be surprising. What is important to remember is that there is a world of difference between demonstrating a physiological *base* and demonstrating physiological *determination*, or strong *effect*.

Anne Fausto-Sterling provides an extended history of the decades-long traditions of research on the hormonal manipulation of rats and guinea pigs in attempts to support prenatal (or perinatal) theories of sexual development and choice of partner. She points out, for example, that most of the studies are about male sexual differentiation. Before the 1990s little or no consideration was given to female development. She further points out that unaltered rats and guinea pigs show a lot of variability in their sexual expression, such as mounting behavior by females. Perhaps most importantly, Fausto-Sterling points to some studies of sexual expression in rats which show powerful environmental effects that challenge the validity of traditional research models such as the famous Gorski rat studies. After Fausto-Sterling's counter-analyses there is little left of value from decades of rodent studies. Yes, you can alter rodent behavior by cutting off genitals, sewing in new genitals, or giving overriding hormone dosages, but this doesn't eliminate the relevance of experience. Rats raised in isolation are sexually incompetent, for example. Most of all, the research shows that rat sex is not so simple, not so clear-cut, even in radically controlled clinical circumstances.[16] The relevance of hormones to behavior is considered further in a following section of this chapter.

For ethical reasons, there are very few studies of genetically based fetal sexual development in people. June Reinisch has conducted several indirect studies. One example is a study of grown children of mothers who took progestin during pregnancy. It show only weak indications of effect in a methodically difficult research line.[17] Her theoretical summary is that early socialization may increase a physiologically based proclivity for cross-gender identity, but she has done no research on such theorized early socialization.[18] If Reinisch's reasoning is correct despite the weakness of her research base, we would have one more example of physiological influence without physiological determination.

Another line of reflection about fetal hormonal influences comes from reasoning about human intersexual conditions, a matter discussed in the next section. Human intersexual studies are relevant but they do not point to physiological determination of gender behavior. For example, if someone with XY chromosomes (genetically male) nonetheless grows a female body (physiologically female), does one wish to reason from the genetic or the physiological base? Furthermore, in recent decades in the United States and in many other nations, intersexual people are usually altered at birth to conform to an exterior image of being male or female that satisfies the culturally based desires of doctors, and sometimes of parents. This limits the opportunities for studies of surgically uninfluenced intersexuality. It is hard to reason even about the effects of surgical alteration without considering the effects of hidden physiological factors which might, or might not, be influenced by the varying surgeries. Furthermore, intersexual people are assigned to one or another sex and raised accordingly, so the effectiveness of child rearing and socialization still matters. David Carlisle adds the wrinkle that a key hormonal effect may occur just before birth in which a premature breakdown of the mother's placenta subjects a male fetus to maternal steroids.[19] This constitutes a prenatal but not genetic hormone theory.

Reasoning about sexual orientation relies on a comparatively simple dependent variable (choice of sexual partner), whereas reasoning about gender orientation has dozens of dependent variables. Even if one were to assign a lot of weight to hormonal variability in fetal development for explaining the choice of sexual partners—which is not justified by a fair summary of the research—it would not tell us much about the rest of gender orientation.

## Alike and Different

This section moves to a description of adult human bodies as a basis for reasoning about contributions of physiological factors to sexual and gender experience. Most human physiological characteristics are distributed in patterns best described by a bell-shaped curve. Think of the height distribution of people as an example. Some are very short, some very tall, and most are in the middle. Bell-shaped curves have a single average. They are continuous, meaning that there are some people with the characteristic of interest at all the points along the way. The finding that so many human characteristics have bell-shaped distributions has led to the development of a branch of probability statistics based on the mathematical properties of bell-shaped curves, also called normal curves.

However, some genes, or alleles of genes, produce an outcome that is off the charts. In terms of a total distribution of height, for example, it would be most accurate to say that most people can be reasonably described in terms of height by placing them within a bell-shaped curve distribution but that a few people should be distinctively described as dwarfs or giants because their growth pattern is so uncommon. Those who think of same-sex sexual orientation or cross-gender appearance presentations as highly unusual commonly look for a genetic or other physiological needle in the haystack to explain what seems to them the equivalent of dwarfism or giantism. This book argues that we can learn what we need to know from the haystack.

If two groups of people are compared on a single characteristic, such as height, the mid-point (average) is likely to be different between the groups. For example, in the early and middle decades of the 20th century in the United States, younger generations were taller than older generations. On average, 30-year-olds are taller than 60-year-olds. The distributions in height of 30-year-olds and 60-year-olds are both bell shaped. If the two bell-shaped curves are superimposed on each other, you see a two humped compound of bell shaped curves that largely overlap. For example, it would show that even though 30-year-olds are, on average, taller than 60-year-olds, some 60-year-olds are much taller than most 30-year-olds. Reducing the reporting of these overlapping curves to a difference in averages distracts attention from the rest of the information about the distribution. Small differences in averages may be statistically significant, but the larger truth is the overwhelming similarity of the distributions.

Many of the articles about differences between males and females are based on comparing differences in averages between overlapping normal curves. Males, on average, are taller than females. However, some females, without being giants, are taller than most males. If we only considered the difference in averages we would miss the importance of a great deal of overlap of height in male and female populations. On the other hand, there is enough difference that height comparisons are noticeable. The political implications derive from what we make of such differences. At the turn of the millennia in the United States, there is very little legal differentiation of adults based on height.

When people are discussing sex differences, they commonly refer to the distribution of primary sexual organs: penises, vaginas, and clitorises, ovaries and testes. In adult populations, the distribution of the primary sexual organs is U shaped, the opposite of a bell-shaped curve. Most people have either ovaries and vaginas or penises and testes, but not neither or both. But there is more overlap than most people think, as is discussed later in the next section on intersexuality.

How much does it matter that males have penises and testes, whereas females have vaginas, clitorises and ovaries? It is relevant for part of the range of options in sexual intercourse but not definitive for sexual satisfaction in all people. It is determinative for differences in the biological reproduction of children. The secondary sex difference of producing breast milk is important for feeding infants.[20] The influences of testes and ovaries on human development are expressed through hormones. As we shall see in a following section, such hormonal influences are not as sharply differentiated as one might think on the basis of the U-shaped distribution of testes and ovaries.

What is the relationship between primary and secondary sex characteristics? The common idea is that people with vaginas and ovaries will grow breasts, have higher voices, and lack heavy facial hair. People who have penises and testes are expected to have beards and lower voices. But it doesn't always happen this way. Some people have penises and high voices. Others have vaginas, breasts, and beards. If you compared the distribution of people defined as male and female for a characteristic such as weight of breast tissue, you would see a two-humped normal curve based on some overlap between males and females, since fat men commonly have more breast tissue than do thin women. Some of these conditions are associated with specific genetic-based development patterns discussed in the following section on intersexuality. The point I am making is that there is more overlap than people commonly realize.

One significant example of overlap is found in the tone and volume range of male and female voices. Many accomplished transgender people have taken advantage of this reality to train and exhibit convincing voices commonly associated with the sex they were not-assigned at birth. Much of the presumed difference has to do with learned habits of pitch and rhythm. Similarly, the legs of males and females look a lot alike when they are shaved and encased in pantyhose, and racial comparisons show that females (or males) in one racial group have bodies of the general shape associated with males (or females) of another racial group. Although it is common to think and perceive with reference to cultural stereotypes of gender, readers can easily notice that in the United States there are not many men or women who look like fashion models or movie stars.

If we continue to expand our consideration of the physiological characteristics that many assume to be different for males and females - such as musculature, distribution of body fat, athleticism, hair texture, and various brain capacities - the distributions show a great deal of overlap. Take this line of reasoning one more step and consider the distributions of predispositions that some people argue are different for males and females, such as aggression, tenderness, artistry, mechanical aptitude, and choice of sexual partner. If the concepts of sexual differences were to be expanded so far, then, given some degree of overlap for each category, one would have to conclude that trying to designate most people physiologically as either pure male or pure female is a bipolar misstatement of a complex fact. A far more accurate statement is that most people have *some* sex or sex-linked characteristics to degree that is more common in people defined as the other sex. *The physiological base for each element of the culturally created images of masculine and feminine appearance and capacity is related to multiple factors that are influenced by a complex genetic base and physiological development.* Very few women look like Barbie. Very few men look like Ken.

Some writers could look at this same picture and write that most people are male or female except for one or a few deviant characteristics. Such a conceptualization is an attempt to hold onto bipolar thinking as a basis for social standards. It would be more accurate to say that if one is using a broad definition of physiological sex, as is common in our culture, the majority of people are *predominantly* male or female. The same truth is expressed by the comment that most people are at least *partly intersexual.*

### Intersexuality

In this book, the word intersexuality is a physiological term. I prefer *intersexual* to the older term *hermaphrodite* because hermaphrodite suggests a half-and-half balance between male and female, which is misleading for many intersexual people. Though the term hermaphrodite has a medical-sounding connotation, the term is derived from Greek mythology. Eros, better known by the Roman name Cupid, was the child of Hermes and Aphrodite and was commonly pictured as intersexual.[21]

Babies usually have a vagina with a clitoris and ovaries, and not a penis and testes, or vice versa. But some babies are not so simple. Some are born with both penises and vaginas, with testicles and ovaries. Some people are born with male sex organs on one side and female on the other. Some people develop the primary sex organs of one sex but one or more secondary sexual characteristics of the other sex, such as breasts or beards. Some people are born with underdeveloped, impaired, or nonfunctioning primary sex organs. Chromosomal males and females produce both testosterone and estrogen, and some genetic females have as high a testosterone level as males. Genetic females have clitorises, an analog to a penis, and some are large enough to draw surgical attention because many parents are more interested in their babies conforming to cultural standards than in growing up to have an orgasmic sex life.

Medical and gender values lead to changes of primary and secondary sex characteristics and to hormonal changes. Some people lose primary sex organs, for example, by hysterectomies, and are still counted as males or females. Many people, not just transgender people, have had surgeries or other treatments to change their bodies into greater conformity with male and female stereotypes. Infant sexual reassignment surgery is done without the consent of children to solve a cultural crisis for parents or physicians. Transsexual people have had their penises and vaginas radically altered through sexual reassignment surgery. Male eunuchs and women who have had their clitoris ritually removed are part of many cultures. Currently in the United States and some European nations, chemical castration is a legal punishment for some sex offenders. Estrogen is sometimes used to treat prostate cancer and heart disease. Some women choose to replace hormones lost by menopause to avoid menopausal changes. Hormones are provided to some transgender people who do not choose sexual reassignment surgery. The questions of whether people who have changed their primary and secondary sex characteristics or hormonal patterns are more or less male or female, more or less man or woman, are not answered by the details of the medical procedures but by other considerations, especially the cultural meanings given to the different additions and subtractions and whether the subjective identity of the individual in question is accorded weight and value.

Any summary of the amount of intersexuality in human beings can be misleading, because it depends on the definition of intersexuality that is used. If we consider all the physiological features that are sometimes portrayed as sex differentiated in the culture of the United States, then most people are probably at least partly intersexual. If we narrowly focus on intersexuality of the primary sexual organs, Anne Fausto-Sterling estimates that 1.7% of all newborns are intersexual, most commonly as a result of late-onset congenital adrenal hyperplasia (CAH). If CAH is untreated, it leads to masculinization of the genitals, either at birth or during puberty. Fausto-Sterling's reading of the literature also suggests to her that there is significant variability by race and perhaps an overall rising rate of intersexuality.[22] Sheila Kirk is a medical doctor with a long association with the International Foundation for Gender Education. Her reading of the literature finds worldwide studies of intersexuality at birth in the range of 0.5% to 2%. She further reports that the number of intersexual births is apparently decreasing to its genetic base as more mothers are taught to avoid taking gene-altering substances during pregnancy.[23] Another expert, Bo Laurent, believes the number of intersexual births is less than 0.2%.[24] Given definitional disagreements, and considering inconsistencies in patterns of data gathering, such variations in estimates should not be surprising.

To further illuminate the complexity of intersexuality, we might note that *cryptorchidism* is found in 3% of live male births in the United States.[25] Cryptorchidism is the lack of the descent of one or both of the testes into the scrotum. The "wandering" testis may be found in several locations. Sometimes the testes spontaneously descend; by adulthood, only 0.75% of males have this condition. Cryptorchidism is thought to have several physiological effects. Should XY people with cryptorchidism be thought of as male or as intersexual? Assigning either label can be misleading.

How much is intersexuality a cause of transgender experience and expression? Since both the theorized cause and effect are complex phenomena, it will be difficult for anyone to answer that question in a comprehensive way. But we can start. The high rate of cryptorchidism offers some support for the theories that there may be hormone irregularities in the prenatal histories of a significant minority of XY fetuses. However, if one wishes to argue fetal causes of *transsexual* experience and expression, one would have to explain why there is apparently much more fetal intersexuality than there is adult transsexuality. The rate of cryptorchidism, only one kind of intersexuality, is thousands of times higher than the rate of clinically identified transsexuals. A similar argument could be made in terms of Klinefelter's Syndrome, which affects 0.2% of males in the United States. This condition is caused by the presence of an extra X chromosome and causes hypogonadism, or weak gonad activity which produces a body with some pronounced female characteristics, such as breast development.[26]

Does intersexuality account for *transgender* experience and expression? Perhaps there is as much transgender experience as there is intersexuality. The numbers on both ends of such an hypothesis are too little known to justify such reasoning. Some, such as Sheila Kirk, believe that intersexuality does cause transgender experience, particularly if a theorized fetal hormonal intersexuality is included. If one takes this point of view, transgender experience and expression would be an expression of a both/and "brain gender." However, studies of intersexual people do not lead to simple conclusions about the relationship between known intersexual status and gender.[27] The safest theoretical position to take is that some kinds of intersexuality may strongly influence gender identity, whereas other kinds of intersexuality, and variations within the normal range of hormones and other physiological factors, may create weaker urges toward transgender experience and expression. Such theorizing is qualified by just what kind of transgender experience is being considered, such as choice of sexual partner or interest in pursuing a non-traditional career. These considerations are developed further in the sections on hormones and brain anatomy. Given the weak research base on fetal hormones, after decades of attention, it is unreasonable to defend a strong theory of prenatal determinism. It is also important to remember that any physiological causal path is likely to be much mediated by the cultural meanings attached to any results by affected individuals and their audiences. For example, an athletic girl may find it much more fun to match her ability against boys than girls; this preference may have genetic causes—just not genetic causes related to any of the above discussion.

Some writers have responded to one or another aspect of intersexuality and proposed that some people should be considered a "third sex." To defend a third-sex assertion, a distinct characteristic not found in males or females would have to be shown. A more reasonable summary is that there is much more overlap than many people realize.

*Questions About Hormones You Would Have Asked*
*If You'd Known the Answers Would Be So Interesting*

Hormones affect our feelings in general and sexual arousal in particular, so it isn't surprising that hormone studies have attracted substantial attention. Furthermore, many transgender people seek out hormone therapy as part of their gender exploration. Hormone research points to a much more complex reality than is commonly understood. Susan Rako, in *The Hormones of Desire: The Truth about Sexuality, Menopause, and Testosterone*,[28] has recently summarized many studies showing that the level of *testosterone* in *women* is critical to sexual desire and argues that hormone replacement treatment in response to menopause should include testosterone as well as estrogen and progesterone.

Testosterone and estrogen are structurally similar hormones, manufactured by the body from cholesterol and thus called steroid hormones. Both testes and ovaries create both hormones, although in different amounts. One hormone can change into the other. Although both hormones are usually called *sex hormones* they are actually growth hormones that produce effects on many parts of the body. These two hormones are only part of a class of related hormones that are similar in structure and affect each other in complex ways. Some of the hormonal sequences affecting body growth and processes are quite complicated and involve many organs other than the testes and ovaries.[29] Among other things, these facts mean that the genetic base for this complex reality is also complex and that any particular gene, such as Hamer's theorized gay gene, is likely to play only one small part in creating the complex whole.

The range in concentrations of testosterone and estrogen and related steroid hormones in the bloodstream that is considered normal *within* the male or female category is quite large. Depending on which hormone is being considered within a sexual category, one person can have a seven times higher concentration than another person and both can be counted as normal by current clinical standards. For example, some females in the range defined as normal have three and a half times as much testosterone as other females in that range. The same is true for males.[30] This means that there could be hormonal factors affecting transgender experience that are within the range of normality rather than abnormality, a reality which points to the relevance of haystack rather than needle theories in considering genetic and other physiological grounding of transgender experience and expression.

Rako reports on the work of James Dabbs, who studied the distribution and activity of testosterone in males. In a study of 92 men in 8 occupations or unemployed, Dabbs found a higher level of testosterone in professional football players and a lower level in ministers. He also found a higher level in trial lawyers than other lawyers.[31] If testosterone levels have some effect on the choice of professions, it is reasonable to assume that testosterone levels may affect other social choices, including gender experience and expression. Dabbs also found that testosterone levels vary in response to time of day, successfulness in social encounters, and sexual activity. It is also important to remember that there are plenty of women who are great trial lawyers, even though they have testosterone levels that are a small fraction of male levels. The themes of complexity, interactiveness, and flexibility are as important for theories of general gender liberation as they are for this book's focus on transgender concerns.

Although testosterone levels are much lower in most females than in most males, it is still very important for females. In addition to its importance for the sensitivity and vitality of genital tissues and the nipples, testosterone is important for muscles, bones, skin, hair, and many other body processes. Rako reports that Samuel Yen, in *Reproductive Endocrinology*, writes, "Testosterone and other androgens have some biologic activity on virtually every tissue in the body."[32] Females generate testosterone in their ovaries, and most of it is converted to estrogen before entering the bloodstream. About three-quarters of the testosterone available in the blood of females is generated by the adrenal gland and in other diverse locations. The effects of testosterone are also dependent upon the work of receptor elements in cells and mediating chemical processes. The fact that testosterone is generated and used in so many locations, and is significant to so many processes in females, suggests that the genetics of testosterone production and use is enormously complex.

If testosterone and other steroid hormones make causal contributions to psychological identity and social behavior, the above findings suggest that it is most reasonable to assert that such contributions are mediated by many physiological factors and that some of the physiological results are in turn intermediary factors for psychological and social causes. For example, a researcher might conduct a study which showed a correlation between a particular level of a hormone and an emotional capacity for nurturance. This would be interesting, but many other things would have to be considered before a theory of causation would have any weight. Might the emotional activity be causing the hormone level? What is the distribution of this hormone at different levels in the population? What counts as nurturing behavior? How does culture distribute opportunities for different kinds of nurturance between men and women?

Dabbs made a contribution to this kind of research, suggesting that the causal factors are complex, multi-directional and interactive. Doing this kind of research in the analytic tradition requires complex inter-disciplinary theorization and testing. However, viewed in a synthetic context, which emphasizes the release of potential in contrast to seeking out fractions of causative influence in shifting and complex circumstances, it is easy to honor complexity, interactiveness and flexibility as sources of variability in human populations. It is easy to honor psychological and social causal factors without positing them as contradictory to, or overriding of, physiological factors. Such honoring of all scientific contributions is the path to escaping physiological, psychological, or sociological essentialism, to escaping disciplinary hubris, without dismissing useful contributions from each source. It is one thing to try to prove the theory that prenatal hormonal conditions cause transgender experience and expression and quite another to investigate how prenatal and other hormone conditions might contribute to greater or lesser degrees to one or another aspects of transgender experience and expression in interaction with psychological and social factors, and then to consider the relevance of how people respond to their understandings of the spiritual factors discussed in the last chapter. It doesn't matter that any single scientist is likely to check out long before all such complexities are investigated. Each can make a contribution and then theorists, and interdisciplinary theorists, can each have their turns.

During most of childhood, male and female children have similar levels of steroid hormones. Then a surge of testosterone initiates puberty in both males and females. In old age, men and women move back toward having similar levels of estrogen, while most men continue to have higher levels of testosterone. These usual variabilities in hormonal development and change lead to questions that have been given little attention. What does it mean that children become gender differentiated at a time when they have similar hormone levels? Why is our culture more accepting of older women taking sex hormones to reduce or delay the natural condition of menopause, of men taking drugs to improve erections, and much less accepting of transgender and transsexual people taking hormones to achieve a physiological state that they desire? The answers are not to be found in additional endocrinological studies.

Perhaps the most intensely studied physiological cause of adult sexual behavior is comparative levels of testosterone in gay and straight males. Heino Meyer-Bahlburg published a summary of 27 such studies.[33] He found that 20 studies showed no difference in hormone levels between gay and straight men. In three methodologically troubled studies, gay men had lower testosterone levels; in two, their testosterone levels were higher; and in one, bisexual men had higher levels than gay or straight men. Finally, a study of male identical twins, in which one twin was gay and one was straight, found that the twins had similar levels of testosterone. This summary pretty much ended the search for such differences.

In the context of this review it should be pointed out that the studies reviewed by Meyer-Bahlburg concerned choice of sexual partner, not the degree of expressed masculinity or femininity. There is a lot of difference between how one chooses to present oneself for social and sexual encounters and what one looks for in another person. It is quite reasonable that hormones, or other physiological processes, might affect one's sense of identity or pre-ferred activity without affecting the choice of sexual partner. On the other hand, the Meyer-Bahlburg summary suggests that powerful, genetically based hormonal factors are not determinative, or even discernible, in their effect on adult sexual behavior. Two studies of transsexuals showed that "the hormone levels were found to be within the normal range for the individuals' original gender... suggesting that transsexualism does not result from a hormonal imbalance."[34] Perhaps the work by Dabbs, or others, will become more compel-ling. Until that time, the fairest summary of the causal effects of hormonal level on transgender experience and expression is that it has not been shown to be a factor.

If the above summary has not been sufficiently confusing, consider a later study of rat brains by Roger Gorski: "It turns out that much of the work of masculinizing the brain is not actually done by testosterone itself, but instead is carried out by estrogen, which is produced from testosterone by the brain."[35]

Readers looking for a good source of information on the role of hormones in intentional physiological change in transgender people may go to www.savina.com/confluence/hormone/.

*Our Amazing Brains*

Some look for a hidden needle of gender variance in the haystack of the brain because the brain is the physiological base for subjective awareness. Maybe there is a brain factor that occurs only in males that creates masculine subjectivity and/or a distinct factor for females that creates feminine subjectiv-ity. Even before commencing the search for such a factor, one would have to define such a masculine or feminine subjectivity and show that it existed across cultures. Quite a challenge.

Those who do brain research with concerns for sex and gender usually merely assume that there is a difference in male and female subjectivity and that any difference they might find in brain structures is the cause. Even though such thinking is incredibly sloppy, it hasn't slowed down research efforts to find differences between the brains of males and females or differences between the brains of straight people and some sexual minority.

Consider the search for a brain difference that influences the choice of sexual partners. It is one thing to theorize differences between the brains of gay men, lesbians, and straight people and another to demonstrate such a difference. A popular theory at the time of writing is that during the fetal development of some males the MIH hormone defeminizes the primary sex organs but not the brain. Such males, the theory holds, would have masculinized brains because of the effects of testosterone, but not defeminized brains because of the lack of MIH effect. This theoretical approach has not projected specific brain effects that might be observed. Instead, brain anatomists with an interest in this area continue to look for any brain differences, in the hope that such differences will fit with such a theory. In effect, we have a "theory" that cannot be disproved; and a theory that cannot be disproved is not a scientific theory, only speculation.

The research on differences between male and female brains that has drawn the most attention is a possible difference in the corpus callosum, a large brain organ that mediates between the higher brain centers and other parts of the brain. Laura Allen is the best known defender of the theory that there are differences between males and females in the corpus callosum.[36] However, Anne Fausto-Sterling points out that 23 followup studies to Allen's research did not find the proposed difference.[37] Chandler Burr reports an interview with Laura Allen where she points out, presumably in her defense, that she correctly identified the sex of two-thirds of a sample of corpora callosa in a blind test. Even if her theory had not been sunk by the lack of replication, it seems fair to say that if such a highly trained anatomist can find a male versus female difference only two-thirds of the time, her research can be disregarded. Two other eminent brain anatomists sum up the issue of difference in size of the corpus callosum between males and females as measurable, but either as less than the variation in size within populations of males or females, or as largely irrelevant and insignificant.[38] Some experts think that the corpora callosa of males are generally bigger than the corpora callosa of females but that the corpora callosa of females are relatively bigger in comparison to body weight.[39] Overall, this extended research is a classic example of the general point made earlier about the misdirection of emphasizing differences in averages in the distributions of male and female physiological characteristics when the larger truth is significant overlap.

In a later review of the extensive research on proposed male and female differences in the corpus callosum, Fausto-Sterling attends in detail to numerous methodological problems in measuring the corpus callosum. She reviews hundreds of different kinds of measures looking for difference. Little is known about the functioning of a living three-dimensional corpus callosum, and almost all the research has sliced and diced the organ into various sections without asserting a theoretical reason for the relevance of a particular measure. Even before getting to the issue of some mis-constructed statistical work, Fausto-Sterling makes the point that the efforts to find differences have been so unfruitful that more recent research has tried to solve the problems of assessing differences by turning the judgment over to panels of objective observers and then comparing their levels of agreement. Such anatomical research is a very long distance from looking at a corpus callosums, pointing to a difference, and saying, "There it is." Fausto-Sterling asserts that, after a century of looking without any luck for a difference in the corpus callosum between males and females, it is time to point out that they are similar and move on. Science is not served well when culturally driven theories blind researchers to the obvious summary of observations. However, even after several scientists have summarized the overwhelming similarity the drive to find a difference continues.[40]

One current line of research to find differences between the brains of gay, lesbian, and straight people revolves around microscopic somethings called INAHs. In contrast to the big corpora callosa, INAHs are so tiny that some researchers doubt whether some INAHs actually exist.[41] The fairest summary of this research is that it is inconclusive and much challenged. For one thing, even if it were shown that there was something about INAHs that differentiated straight people from gays or lesbians, no one has figured out what INAHs might do. There are a lot of things in the body that don't do much, including most genes.[42]

The failure to find important brain differences could lead us to discount the importance of brain anatomy as a base for gender development. This is like saying "Because we couldn't find the needle, we can forget about the haystack."

Those who have wanted to show a physiological cause of sexual orientation, or of differences between men and women, have been eager not only to show distinctiveness but also to argue that such differences are unchangeable. But the brain is anything but hard-wired in its development. There are about 10 billion neurons in the cerebral cortex, the physiological base for thinking, and the possibilities for their linkage are almost limitless. Quoting Chandler Burr, "Before birth and the final fixing of the brain structure, the neurons roam freely from place to place like nomads..." Quoting Burr further on the connections between neurons, "the bridges, like the dense streets of a medieval city, develop randomly this way and that into a network between cells that happen to meet during their own independent drifting in a sea of neurons, haphazardly growing into the stable circuitry of a mature brain."[43] Such a picture of brain development suggests that the physiological base in the brain for the activity of the mind is highly flexible. We know that the capacity to think and make decisions has some kind of physiological base in the cerebral cortex. Finding such flexibility and complexity, it is not hard to believe that we can think thoughts that are new to us, create sentences we have never heard before, and work out creative responses to gender choices. Anyone who wants to argue some version of a theory of sexual orientation as hard-wired will have to argue that sexual response and gender choices are not mediated by the higher functions of the brain - that the cerebral cortex is irrelevant. Such argumentation would also have to overcome direct evidence based on positron emission tomography of functioning adult brains that shows numerous parts of the cerebral cortex are involved in sexual arousal.[44]

The issues mentioned in this section have not deterred those with deterministic theories. A good example is Joseph LeDoux's 1996 book, *The Emotional Brain: The Mysterious Underpinnings of Emotional Life*. He writes, "The conscious feelings that we know...our emotions by are ...detours in the scientific study of emotions. Feelings of fear, for example, occur as part of the overall reactions to danger and are no more or less central to the reaction than the behavioral and physiological responses that also occur, such as trembling, running away, sweating, and heart palpitations."[45] He later argues that both cognition and emotion are primarily unconscious processes and that only the outcomes of such processes become conscious.

The problems of LeDoux's book are typical of those of any researcher of human behavior whose work is limited to an analytic standpoint. LeDoux tells his readers that most of his work is dependent on research on rat brains. This method has two core problems. The first is that rat brains have some similarities to, and some big differences from, human brains. Humans have a massive cerebral cortex, for example. LeDoux responds to this problem by asserting that for animals with brains and backbones, "the systems underlying fearful, sexual, or feeding behaviors - is pretty similar across species."[46] What he means is that the physiological structures in the brain that are the base for these emotional patterns have some similarities in many species. In effect, LeDoux is arguing that you don't have to pay attention to human differences because many species are similar. He has done important work in identifying specific brain systems that are part of the physiological basis for specific emotions. Nonetheless, as with Hamer's work in genetics, LeDoux has not considered the unobservable potentials of such structures as they interact in more complex wholes and generate phenomena which can only be observed outside of his discipline. LeDoux understands that mental activities, like discipline, can constrain emotions and the effects of emotions on choice and behavior. He admits that higher brain functions affect emotions such as fear. But he still chooses to write as if identifying a physiological base for fear means that he has explained fear.

LeDoux writes, "If we do not need conscious feelings to explain what we would call emotional behavior in some animals, then we do not need them to explain the same behavior in humans."[47] .

Since human have a distinctive and highly developed cerebral cortex to do such mediation, it is illogical to assert that human emotions are not mediated by consciousness because nonhuman animals lack the mediating structures of humans. Neither is it clear that fear is unmediated in nonhuman animals. Just because LeDoux can't talk to a horse about being afraid doesn't mean that horses lack any conscious mediation. Much animal training demonstrates the mediation of fear in nonhuman animals. Put differently, learning affects how human and nonhuman animals respond to various stimuli. The capacity for fearful response to a particular sensory signal does not mean that such a sensory signal will always produce fear as a conscious emotion or the accompanying signals of sweating and the like.

A possible distinction between male, female, and transsexual brains has been reported by Josie Glausiusz, based on a limited study of human brains by a team of Netherlands researchers led by Dick Swaab. They report distinct differences between men and women in the size of a tiny brain region known as the BSTc.[48] Prior study of rat brains suggests that this brain component is critical to sexual activity. Swaab's team compared six brains of male-to-female (M2F) transsexuals in this study and found the BSTc regions were roughly the same size as those found in the brains of females. Before such a study could be evaluated properly, we would need to know the range of variation of BSTcs in male and female brains and whether any difference is a result or a cause of variations in sexual activity. That would include defining a specific human sexual activity, showing that variations in BSTcs were correlated with the specific sexual activity, showing that men and women differed in this sexual activity, and then showing that M2F transsexuals behaved more like women than men in such a sexual activity. This is the kind of study, however small, that keeps raising hope that one or another needle will be found. But, as with other proposed needles, this initial finding is unlikely to be replicated.

So far, the picture drawn by this chapter shows that after substantial effort, no needle of explanation has been found and defended in the physiological haystack of complexity, flexibility, and interactivity. Instead of arguing for or against direct physiological causes of transgender experience and expression, it might be more helpful to consider physiological circumstances that could support or encourage transgender experience and expression. For example, consider a person with Klinefelter's Syndrome, mentioned previously, a condition that results in male genitals and fully developed female breasts. The issue for people with this condition is not so much gender transition as choice of gender when one's body provides mixed signs of cultural significance.

What might be explained with a deterministic physiological theory of gender formation? Are we trying to explain nurturance in men, why women are now commonly wearing pants, or whether there is a gene for attraction to lipstick? Most of those doing research related to transgender experience and expression that I have read would say they want to explain the development of subjective awareness or orientation that, in turn, affects the defining and valuing of transgender experience that, in turn, affects transgender expression.

It may sound simple to name, but transgender related subjectivity is not simple. For example. is muscular strength important to one's subjective sense of gender identity? Perhaps it is for some people. We have seen that the genetic and physiological basis for the development of muscular strength is complex. We have argued that such factors as muscular strength can only be one factor among many in the development of gender identity. One changing cultural factor is that girls are now more often encouraged to become athletes, to think of themselves as strong. The subjective implications of strength for the development of gender identity has changed without any change in genetics or physiology. And whatever the status of such research, those with an eye to the politics of science might also want to remember that slavery wasn't ended by studying slaves.

In reasoning about transgender experience and expression some may point out that there are transgender people who have the kind of bodies that make passing as the other sex relatively easy. On the other hand, there are people (like me) who are challenged to make a respectful feminine presentation. Some clinicians have had the presumption to deny transsexual surgery to people who look like me because we don't meet their stereotypes of femininity. Such denial isn't grounded in a surgeon's expertise on the physiology of health. Feminists properly argue that such decisions reinforce gender stereotypes. The third chapter examines relevant psychological issues and the seventh chapter deals with the development of a clinical movement which has taken advantage of the ambiguity in this area to seize this society's social control of gender conformity.

If those arguing for physiological deterministic causes want to escape from arguing symbolic mediation as an intermediate factor, they must assert some hidden physiological factor. If such a factor exists, this chapter has shown it isn't likely a matter of genetics, hormones, or brain anatomy. It is one thing to talk about relevant physiological factors and predispositions and quite another to argue for a strong specific factor (needle) that explains everything. It seems to me that the contemporary challenge for any physiologists interested in transgender-related research is to help gain more understanding of the complexity, interactivity, and flexibility of physiological factors as they support the possibility of transgender experience and expression.

## Darwinism One More Time

A different kind of physiological determinism is the theory that current cultural standards concerning sexual orientation or gender expression are merely the expression of evolutionary forces in a human context. Such theories name some evolutionary "interest" that has led to our current cultural images and social roles. These theories proceed as if there were some kind of independent evolutionary actor, an idea we will revisit in the section on natural theology in the last chapter. The concept of survival of the fittest easily attaches to an idea of some hidden hand giving direction to human evolution. Such a theology, in turn, gives comfort to those who defend their dominance by arguing it merely proves they are the best fit to dominate.

Neo-Darwinist rationalization about human beings has a long and ugly history in nineteenth and twentieth century thought in the United States. This school of thought has been used mainly by conservatives and reactionaries to avoid social responsibility for the conditions of those who are oppressed, as in slavery, patriarchy and, most recently, those receiving welfare benefits. Richard Hofstadter, after extendedly pointing out that "There was nothing in Darwinism that inevitably made it an apology for competition and force," accounts for the recurrent popularity of NeoDarwinism in the United States as follows: "The answer is that American society saw its own image in the tooth-and-claw version of natural selection, and that its dominant groups were therefore able to dramatize this vision of competition as a good thing in itself. Ruthless business rivalry and unprincipled politics seemed to be justified by the survival philosophy. As long as the dream of personal conquest and individual assertion motivated the middle class, this philosophy seemed tenable, and its critics remained a minority."[49]

Whatever one thinks of neo-Darwinist ideology, it is fair to point out that natural selection is an important part of *biological* reasoning. But evolution also turns out to be complex and interactive.

Contemporary genetics teaches that the process of natural selection does not operate in a simplistic, straight-line fashion. For example, Chandler Burr points out with implicit humor that "maze brightness" in rats is genetic and can be bred for.[50] But, it turns out, this enhanced capacity to run a maze is based not on increased intelligence but on a semiblindness that decreases distractions. Conclusion that could be drawn from this study are that rats are smarter than maze studies can measure, and that rats with the intelligence to seek for alternatives to stupid maze running were too much for the experimenters to cope with.

One way to illustrate the complexity of natural selection as a biological process is to point out that there are inherited, genetic-based traits that are lethal when expressed. They are passed along because the potential lethal expression is linked to something that is positive for natural selection. For example, the gene which contributes to the creation of sickle cells strengthens the body for resisting malaria but also harms the body by creating anemia when it is inherited from both parents. If genes with sometimes lethal effects can be part of natural selection, then neutral traits, or traits that are positive in indirect ways for a human population, can certainly be a part of natural selection and evolution.

One part of getting our evolutionary facts in order begins with realizing that homosexual and transgender people are the biological parents of many children. This doesn't make sense to the stereotypes of the straight world, but it is nonetheless true. Not only do homosexual and transgender people biologically create children, they also are active parents to children, their own and those they adopt. Richard Green did a study of such children and found they were as likely as the children of straight parents to grow up straight.[51] Furthermore, if most writers about transgender issues are correct in their commonly held opinion that male cross-dressers are primarily heterosexual and are typically married and parents, the debate about input to the gene pool is irrelevant. Myself, I'm the biological parent of three children and am currently helping to raise two more in a blended family.

The *biology* of natural selection has to do with the survival and transmission of the gene pool and not of individuals. That is, if an individual is a contributing member of a successful society, then that individual is contributing to the survival of the gene pool of that society. In our current society, many believe that excess population is more of a threat than insufficient population. If that is true, those who contribute to societal success without adding to the "dependency ratio" by creating children might be theorized to be strengthening the gene pool of society. So, even if it were true that homosexual or transgender people have fewer children than average, it would not necessarily hurt the survival of the gene pool of a society, which includes the gene pool basis for gay, lesbian, bisexual, and transgender people in that society.

If we consider the features that are most physiologically distinctive about human beings—the capacities for intellectual reflection, artistic creativity, and the creation of complex social and cultural relationships - it may well be that human freedom from a hard-wired sexuality, expressed in many interesting ways, is a key component of these "highest" human capacities. For example, one distinctive human capacity is the ability to attach passionate commitment to such symbols as flags and crosses and curves. Given the complexity of our culture and society, it might well be that the genes that most contribute to intellectual and emotional complexity and flexibility are the genes that are most valuable for strengthening the genetic pool as a base for future evolution. If any transgender genes are ever discovered, they might be just such valuable genes.

The core logical problem with all kinds of political or spiritual Darwinism is using the concept of natural selection *metaphorically* rather than biologically, then arguing physiological determinism as if that proved the metaphor. Laurette Liesen provides one example of such thinking when she asserts that females are usually more interested in personal bonds, whereas males are more interested in abstract thinking; that this difference is genetically based and derives from an evolutionary advantage; and that this difference accounts for the gender gap in contemporary electoral politics.[52] The previous section on genetics has shown that there is no genetic basis for Liesen's assertion, and a section in Chapter Three on non-clinical psychological research shows that there is no scientific psychological basis for asserting that males are less interested in personal bonds than females. Liesen, as is typical for neo-Darwinists, offers no direct genetic evidence to support her theory. She merely presents her theory, acts as if must be obvious, and then asserts that such a basic difference must be genetic.

All the other neo-Darwinist arguments I have encountered theorize some evolutionary "advantage" or "interest" and are equally grounded in imagination rather than in data. I offered an equally projective theory when I wrote above about the possible advantages of transgender genetic contribution. We are all free to theorize. My own dipping into neo-Darwinist theory was to show that two can play such games. The larger point is that neo-Darwinist thinking is not grounded in science.

The version of neo-Darwinism in recent years that has gained the most prestige is the sociobiology of Edward Wilson.[53] Wilson argues that males are dominant in all known societies and that such universality represents a genetic advantage of males over females. His point about males dominating all known societies is commonly supported in anthropological textbooks.[54] Anne Fausto-Sterling counters with three questions. Is it universal? Does it mean the same thing in all cultures? Even if it is universal, is genetics the cause? Her conclusion is that Wilson's sociobiology is a political attack on women's liberation that boils down to the assertion that "things aren't so bad the way they are...because it's natural."[55]

Ernst Mayr, a leader in the development of evolutionary biology, argues an alternative understanding of the implication of emphasizing a population based, rather an individual based, understanding of biological evolution. "The survival and prosperity of a social group depends to a large extent on the harmonious cooperation of the members of the group, and this behavior must be based on altruism."[56] How is one to choose between these alternatives readings of "sociobiology" when both authors are building on similar readings of the same data? The first thing to remember is that such post-hoc analysis is more akin to history as a discipline than to experimental biology. In reasoning about transgender experience and expression, the important thing to remember is that we are trying to understand the evolution of human beings who demonstrate a great variety of gender expressions rather than trying to explain the selective advantage of a specific physiological trait such as being able to make a tube with one's tongue.

Suppose we were to agree with Wilson that in all societies men are more aggressive and fickle than women, and that the difference is genetically based - two suppositions that I think are unjustified. There would still be two hurdles to pass before assigning weight to such a theory.

The first is that although factors such as size or testosterone levels may make it *possible* for males to get away with aggressiveness and fickleness in social interaction, these behaviors do not show that there is some irresistible, *physiologically based urge* to be aggressive and fickle. Furthermore, even if such an urge were supposed, Freud, Locke, and others have argued that it is the overcoming of such negative animal nature that makes society possible. I do not agree with Freud, Locke, et al, because I do not think the suppositions are justified. But if I did, I would use Wilson's valuable articulation of the importance of thinking of genetics in terms of populations, his emphasis on the survival and enhancement of the gene pool rather than the survival of individuals, to argue that cooperation and trustworthy social relationships are sociocultural advantages that undercut his simplistic sociobiology.

The second point has to do with whether anyone is currently arguing that aggression and fickleness are a good thing, or a social advantage, or a desirable psychological trait. Most of the sociobiologists back off to a position like "Well maybe these are not desirable characteristics, but that is the way things are, and we have to learn to live with them." But "the way things are" is an assertion of fact that doesn't fit very well with the reality in the contemporary United States that churches, schools, and other major institutions support standards of cooperation rather than aggression, support stability rather than fickleness. Although it is important not to give away the factual picture to the neo-Darwinists, it is also important to remember that ubiquity doesn't equal desirability. We have the genetic capacity as males, females, and intersexuals to grow into men, women, and transgender people who can choose how we respond to any urges to aggression or fickleness, whatever their source. We can choose greater personal happiness and greater social benefit instead of sliding down the well-worn slopes of patriarchy, denial, hostility, irresponsibility and war.

In contrast to any who would turn to sociobiology for political and spiritual arguments to oppress transgender people, William Dragoin has advanced a sociobiological theory that links transgender and shamanistic behavior. Dragoin appeals to a fetal hormone theory of brain development as a source of shamanistic talent and argues that shamanistic talent was so valuable to early homo sapiens that it gave an evolutionary advantage to transgender people, primarily through the prestige conferred on close relatives of transgender shamans.[57] Although I find several problems in Dragoin's reasoning, it is nonetheless an excellent example of theorizing that meets sociobiological standards and shows that sociobiological thought can be used to argue for a normal rather than an abnormal understanding of transgender experience and expression.

## Traits and Choices

One of the most common confusions in reasoning from genetics to subjective feelings or human behavior is caught up in the word *trait*. Geneticists commonly use the word to refer to a physiological structure, such as the shape or color of an eye. They also refer to certain behaviors as traits. For example, the capacity to make a tube with one's tongue is genetically based. Some people can and some can't. Part of the confusion in the word *trait* is the difference between *capacity* and *expression*. The expression of a genetic capacity for a behavior named as a trait is thought of as being without choice, just as the color of one's eyes is not a matter of choice. Yet those who can make a tube with their tongue can choose whether they want to do it or not. Mostly they don't, since it gets in the way of talking, eating, and other mouth activities.

Handedness is an interesting trait that is assumed, but not yet demonstrated, to have a genetic basis. Handedness studies show that most people are right-handed, some are left-handed, and very few are truly ambidextrous. This would graph as a J shaped curve: high on one end, lower on the other end, with a trough between. Chandler Burr is interested in handedness because he thinks the observed distribution of handedness is similar in shape to the distribution of sexual orientation.

The general summary of handedness studies is misleading in an important way when we consider how people use their hands in everyday life. Without denying for a minute the scientific accuracy of the handedness studies as summarized above, it is critical to understand what is being said and what isn't. I'm right handed, but I am typing this paper with both hands. I'm hitting about as many key strokes with my left hand as with my right. The handedness studies were not interested in the fact that most people use two hands for two-handed tasks. A more accurate generalization is that for tasks that are commonly one-handed, most people use their right hand, some use their left hand, and a few are truly ambidextrous.

But the improved generalization about handedness is misleading in another important way. I usually hammer nails using my right hand to hold the hammer. But there are some carpentry situations where I hold the hammer with my left hand to get a better angle. Furthermore, when my right arm gets tired, I switch over and hold the hammer in my left hand. Furthermore, in some tasks, like roofing, I find myself relieving boredom by practicing left-handed hammering. And, when I'm hammering a stake into the ground, I may use one or both hands. So a further improved generalization about the human trait of handedness is that for tasks that are commonly one-handed, people typically use a preferred hand but adjust to fit various situations or in pursuit of different purposes.

But even this further improved generalization about handedness is misleading in an important way. If I were to lose my right hand in an accident, I would use my left hand for a lot of tasks I currently prefer to do with my right hand. I would expect to gain strength and skill. Leon Love, father of my best friend in high school, lost his right hand to a fuller's earth grinding machine. He developed so much drafting skill with his left hand that he earned his living as a draftsman for most of his life. Losing his right hand was part of the causal chain to gaining a better-paying job with far better working conditions. What does it mean to say that Leon was right-handed? It means that he preferred to use his right hand when he had the option of using either hand. It also means that he had the genetically generated physiological base for doing left-handed work with a high degree of skill. Like right-handed hitters in baseball who choose to learn to switch hit, the choice of which hand to use may be genetically influenced while still allowing many other possibilities.

There is one more significant correction to the apparently simple generalization about handedness. Some people are apparently more able than others to share tasks, or switch tasks, between hands. Chandler Burr reports a study by Rob Collins of pawedness in mice. Collins found that 50% of mice preferred their right paws and 50% preferred their left paws, and that the trait was very stable when the task of getting a food pellet was equally accessible to either paw. But, when Collins made it hard to get the pellet with either the right paw or the left, most of the mice switched paws. But some mice couldn't, or at least didn't, switch paws.[58] This illustrates the importance of the issue of the *strength* of the trait. It is honest to report that mice preferred either their right or their left paw. It is equally honest to report that the overwhelming majority of mice were willing to use either paw to get a desired result and that those in the small minority might have starved to death if they couldn't adjust and if the experiment was their only opportunity to eat.

With all these qualifications to the generalization based on handedness studies as classic studies of genetically based traits, if one were to support a metaphor based theory that the distribution of handedness in human populations is like the distribution of sexual orientation, one would be arguing in support of complexity and multiple understandings of sexual orientation rather than a sharp distinction with little overlap. Furthermore, relative to the previous section on neo-Darwinism, it is interesting to note that the flexibility that comes from being able to use two hands in similar ways, in complementary ways, and in coordinated ways is an important evolutionary advantage.

The word *trait*, as used in genetics research, isn't inaccurate or misleading. But we must remember that what the word trait means in the context of genetics - in which there is a strong interest in differentiation as part of the research trail for finding genetic locations - can be quite different from the discussion of a trait in psychological or social terms. The difference is that when the reference discipline is psychology or sociology, physiological factors are only one source of causation. When physiological factors are functioning in typical ways, they may be the least interesting factor to be considered. Whether one chooses Japanese or Algonquin as a second language—a choice which might have significant psychological, social and cultural consequences for an individual—is not likely to turn on the physiological base for language, even though such a base is going to be fully involved in responding to the choice.

The gay and lesbian community was quick to celebrate the decision by the American Psychiatric Association in 1973 that homosexuality is not a disease. However, as Chandler Burr exemplifies, much of the gay and lesbian community is eager to hold onto the concept that homosexuality cannot be changed. Burr names the ineffectiveness of all the things done by psychiatrists and psychologists to homosexuals to get them to change as part of his evidence against the theory that homosexuals have a choice about their sexual orientation. But, as we shall see in Chapter Four, survey research suggests that, while it may be true that some homosexuals cannot be changed by clinical intervention, this doesn't mean they don't change on their own as part of their everyday lives. Both truths fit together nicely if one considers how homosexuals were selected for clinical intervention. They were typically forced into clinical settings by homophobic pressures and treatment amounted to attempts to force change. Considering what we learned from a review of genetics and physiology, it is quite plausible that physiological factors are significant for some, but not all, people with homosexual experience. That would indeed fit a J shaped curve but the findings I summarized argue against any genetic determinism.

To point out that the expression of genetically based traits contains choice does not mean that there are no physiological influences on psychological or social traits. Although psychological traits are not wholly determined by physiological considerations, personal choices are not unaffected by physiological considerations. I might like to sing, might want to make my living as a singer, but, if I don't have a good set of "pipes," I'm not going to get very far socially or economically and may be frustrated emotionally. On the other hand, some singers are such great performers that they make a living with quite limited voices.

The point is that choices by human beings in real social settings may be affected a lot or very little by physiological factors. Even when a strong physiological urge is served, such as hunger, it may be done in different ways. I may prepare Chinese food for dinner, but I might go out to my favorite Salvadoran restaurant. If a person chooses a partner for erotic sexual sharing, or presents an image in hopes of being chosen, a complex of physiological, psychological, social, cultural and spiritual factors are relevant. Just because some urges feel powerful, just because some choices are commonly made with little reflection, doesn't mean that the dominant cause is physiological. I have a powerful urge to communicate and I use English without reflection.

## What Our Bodies Contribute to Transgender Experience

There has been very little direct physiological study of people who have transgender experience and engage in transgender expression. Physiological reasoning about transgender experience and expression usually theorizes some simple or distinct physiological cause, skips over all the intervening variables, and oversimplifies or misunderstands the transgender experience or expressions to be explained.

In this chapter on physiology I have emphasized complexity. Many other writers have looked for, or just theorized, a simple physiological irregularity to explain transgender experience and expression. I've suggested that the most reasonable summary of the relevant research is that physiological factors are not likely to be strongly determinative in the explanation of everyday transgender experience and expression. Any simple theory is unlikely to match the complex physiological factors that may be relevant, not to mention the additional complexities of psychological and social factors.

We are each born with whatever mix of physiological characteristics arises from the interaction of our genetic materials and the uterine environment. In this sense each of us is natural. Intersexual people are as much the outcome of natural processes as other people. Instead of beginning by looking for the unusual, the first task of physiologists is to correctly image the usual distributions of various physiological characteristics. If the various kinds of physiological scientists who are interested in issues of sex and gender were to begin by appreciating the complexity, interactiveness, and flexibility indicated by all the forgotten studies which didn't find a simple deterministic cause, perhaps they might begin to focus on the mechanisms by which physiology supports highly diverse sexual and gender realities. At a minimum, such a focus would undercut the simplistic and unsupported physiological reasoning used by some psychiatrists and psychologists who impose sickness theories on transgender people.

---

**Notes:**

1. Magnus Hirschfeld (1910/1991), page 17.
2. Analytic thinking can reflect either Aristotelian or Democritean assumptions. Democritean, or atomistic, thinking, is built on an ontological assertion that a whole is equal to the sum of its parts. Aristotelian thinking is phenomenological rather than ontological, but it also reasons from cause to effect in terms of patterns in data as if a whole were equal to the sum of its parts.
3. We also have genes in our mitochondria, and they are passed on only from mother to daughter.
4. Chandler Burr (1996).
5. Ibid.
6. Anne Fausto-Sterling (2000), pages 236-237.
7. Chandler Burr (1996), page 154.
8. Mary Coombs (1996).
9. Chandler Burr (1996).
10. Dean Hamer (1993).
11. Chandler Burr (1996), page 165 and following.
12. Ibid., page 180 and following, also page 214 and following.
13. Ibid., page 245.
14. Roger Gorski (1978).
15. Chandler Burr (1996), page 46.
16. Anne Fausto-Sterling (2000), Chapter 8.
17. June Reinisch (1983), pages 56-57.
18. Ibid., pages 60-61.
19. David Carlisle (1998), pages 426-427.
20. Even though XY males can produce breast milk after hormonal transitions, few transgender people have emphasized this possibility.
21. Leslie Feinberg (1996), page 65.
22. Anne Fausto-Sterling (2000), pages 52-53. She presents these numbers as best estimates, with the recognition that the research base is not strong for many kinds of intersexuality.

23. Sheila Kirk (1997).
24. Phyllis Burke (1996), page 221.
25. Francis Greenspan (1991), page 425.
26. Ibid., page 421.
27. John Money, (1984).
28. Susan Rako, (1996).
29. Anne Fausto-Sterling (2000), Chapter 7. This is an excellent and readable introduction to contemporary understandings of hormones.
30. Francis Greenspan (1991), pages 417 and 471.
31. James Dabbs (1993).
32. S.S.C. Yen (1991).
33. Heino Meyer-Bahlburg (1984).
34. J. R. Jones (1972) and C. J. Migeon, et al. (1968), quoted in Janet Hyde (1986), pages 389–390.
35. Roger Gorski (1991), quoted in Robert Pool (1994), page 76.
36. Chandler Burr (1996), page 64.
37. Anne Fausto-Sterling (1985), quoted in Chandler Burr (1996), page 41 ff.
38. Larry Kreuger (1995), page 74.
39. Anne Fausto-Sterling (2000), page 131.
40. Ibid., Chapter 5.
41. Chandler Burr (1996), pages 37-41.
42. Ibid., page 144.
43. Ibid., page 213.
44. Irwin Goldstein (2000), page 74.
45. Joseph LeDoux (1996), page 18.
46. Ibid., page 17.
47. Ibid., page 17.
48. The BSTc is the central subdivision of the bed nucleus of the stria terminalis.
49. Richard Hofstadter (1955), page 201.
50. Chandler Burr (1996), page 239.
51. Richard Green (1978).
52. Roger Masters (1995).
53. Edward Wilson (1980).
54. Marvin Harris (1985).
55. Anne Fausto-Sterling (1985), page 204.
56. Ernst Mayr (2000), page 83.
57. William Dragoin (1997), pages 227–247.
58. Chandler Burr (1996), pages 165-166.

*The weight of this sad time we must obey, speak what we feel not what we ought to say.* William Shakespeare[1]

*You who've been on the road*
*Must have a code that you can live by*
*And so, become yourselves,*
*Because the past is just a goodbye.* Graham Nash[2]

# Chapter 3:
# Feeling and Thinking
# About Sex and Gender

This chapter reviews psychological research as it relates to transgender experience and expression. Although this chapter intends to show that the establishment clinical perspective lacks scientific grounding, I do not mean to suggest that professional counselors, including psychiatrists and psychologists, have not sometimes been helpful to transgender people. Some guidance for finding good counsel is included in Chapter 7.

I offered the reader several confessions in the first chapter so that my biases might be taken into account. I should also tell you that I'm angry at many establishment clinicians for the shoddy research work they have done, as well as for serious injuries to transgender people that have resulted from the application of their professional opinions. Many have acted with professional hubris when honesty required that they confess that they didn't know what they were doing and that they were trying to find their way. I'm thankful for the writing of Phyllis Burke, Leslie Feinberg, and Daphne Scholinski, who have shown how much damage establishment psychiatry and psychology can do to transgender people, thankful these authors make their anger so palpable and accessible.[3] They've written the kind of books you can't pick up and can't put down because the hurting is so close. Chapter 7 of this book includes an extended

quote from Burke to provide a taste of this kind of writing. Given their contributions, I feel free to limit the expression of my own anger in this book and to offer a different contribution: an evaluation of the scientific base of establishment psychiatry and psychology with regard to transgender experience and expression.

Although some people in the transgender community are angry at establishment clinicians, others are deeply thankful for the help they have received. Some of the early clinicians—Harry Benjamin comes to mind—were humanitarian in intent toward the transsexual people they were trying to help. Benjamin went out on a limb to establish the practice of sexual reconstructive surgery that has been a blessing to many transsexuals. But being humanitarian is not enough. Truth is also important. Humanitarian intent helps, but uninformed good intentions have contributed to the personal hells described by Burke, Feinberg and Scholinski.

This chapter also points out the traditional goals and values that guide clinicians. Heterosexual men and women, well differentiated from each other, are assumed to be normative. Transgender people are treated as gender and sexual transgressors. The "humanitarian" contribution of clinicians is to offer a medical response to such behavior as contrasted to vigilante or police oppression.

In criticizing the damage done by the medical model, I do not mean to suggest that the criminal justice system is better. Even a quick look at *Prisoner of Gender* by Katherine Johnson and Stephanie Castle reminds us how horrible prisons can be.[4] Neither do I mean to suggest that institutional Christianity has a better track record. Joan of Arc should not have been burned to death by the Inquisition.

The first task for developing a better grounded psychology of transgender experience and expression is clearing away clinical misconceptions. The second task is to start reviewing and building on nonclinical psychological research. In later chapters, contributions from learning theory and from social psychology are added.

## What You Can't Learn in Clinics

Psychology and psychiatry have been interested in sexual variation since the time of Freud and Jung. Vern Bullough has done an excellent job of tracing the early development of transgender concepts in psychology and psychiatry.[0] This chapter settles for assessing the scientific base of contemporary positions.

I offer the following true story to highlight the fundamental clinical bias. During the 1970s, when the American Psychiatric Association and the American Psychological Association were changing their collective minds about whether homosexuality was a mental illness, I had occasion to debate with a psychologist on a local television program about whether homosexuals were sick. My credential in that setting was representing a sociological point of view. The following story line captures the gist of the exchange.

The psychologist said, "They're all sick."
I said, "How do you know?"
He said, "Every homosexual who comes to see me is sick."
I said, "You're a clinical psychologist, right?"
He said, "Yes."

I said, "Do you work with heterosexual people too?"
He said, "Yes."
I said, "And do heterosexual people come to you because they are sick?"
He said, "Yes."
I said, "How come you don't conclude that all heterosexual people
are sick?"
He said, "You don't understand."

A 1990 study of psychotherapists by Benedict Carey suggests that they are as prone to gender stereotyping as the general public. The study asked for clinical evaluations of videotapes of a depressed client. The story line was the same for two videotapes except that in one the client was an engineer with a wife at home and in the other his wife was an engineer and he was at home. Those who saw the tape in which the client was at home rated him as far more severely depressed than those who saw the tape with the wife at home.[6] Although such biases are important, this chapter focuses instead on four scientific problems commonly found in research done in clinical settings.

*Four Common Problems in Clinical Research*

The first scientific problem has to do with *who is seen and when.* Reasoning in clinical studies is based on observations about people who are having problems during the period in their lives when they are having the problems. The selectivity error occurs when the findings are generalized to people who are not having troubles, to people who do not fit the profiles of those who are seen in therapy, and even to the lives of the people with transgender problems at the points in their lives when things are fine.

A second scientific problem concerns *what is seen.* Clinicians try to help the persons who seek out their services. This leads to the bias of looking for problems rather than to general observation. As a result, when writing about transgender people, clinicians try to explain the problems of transgender people – to explain why they hold a transgender conception of themselves that causes them pain when they are subjected to public ridicule or abuse. Locating the problem within the transgender person rather than in social reactions is a powerful reinforcement of the cultural status quo. Looking on transgender experience as a problem blinds one to an appreciation of all that is going on and misses the point that a lot of transgender people like their lives, like the transgender aspects of their lives.

*Data corruption* is a third general problem in clinical studies. It's not that clinical studies are unique in having the problem of data corruption. It's that the clinical process by its very nature is corrupting. Not only do clinicians have an interest in seeing some factors while being inattentive to others; clinicians corrupt the observation process by trying to change the people they are seeing.

The fourth general scientific problem is the use of *revisionist memory* as a source of scientific data. Adults are asked to reconstruct earlier events and feelings in response to leading questions. This is particularly a problem for adults who are asked to remember their childhood. In such an encounter, the clinician and the patient are *jointly* trying to make sense of why the patient is feeling what the patient is feeling. This is about as far away as one can get from objectivity.

Within the United States, the development of establishment clinical thinking can be traced to two overlapping points of view, represented by Harry Benjamin and George Rekers. In 1966, Benjamin published the first scholarly book reviewing the case records of people seeking sexual reassignment surgery. Although Benjamin opposed the notion that transsexualism was a disease that psychotherapy could heal, he needed a disease diagnosis to justify treatment by hormones and surgery. George Rekers, a Harvard-trained clinical psychologist who led a major program at UCLA, represented the view that transgender experience and expression is some kind of psychological disorder that might be healed with psychological interventions. Rekers began reporting in the early 1970s on his "therapy" with children that he defined as having sexual identity problems. His research is much quoted and is used in some training programs.[7] Although there is ongoing debate about the weight of physiological and social causes and about the value of different therapies, Benjamin, Rekers, and the establishment clinicians who have followed them assume there is something wrong that needs correcting and that doctors should be in charge of the correcting.

Rekers' methodology shows three of the common flaws found in clinical research. One example of his research is a case report on a girl named "Becky" who was brought in for therapy by her mother because she refused to wear a dress and act like a girl. Rekers theorized that masculine acting girls grow up to become homosexual, transsexual, neurotic or schizophrenic and are likely to become alcoholics, have bad work records, or commit suicide. Now let's consider what he actually did in his research and what it showed.

Rekers administered several psychological tests, including the IT scale, that presumed to measure Becky's masculinity or femininity. They found out she didn't like to wear dresses and didn't want to act like a girl. Her parents believed this was a serious problem, and so did Rekers. So they tried to change Becky. Becky was subjected to an intense series of clinical interventions in the clinic and at home aimed at trying to get her to change her play habits, her appearance, and her interactional style so that she would appear more feminine. One aspect of the treatment was to make Becky wear a microphone in her ear so that her play could be directed by a psychologist sitting behind a one-way mirror. Then they repeated the psychological measures to see if her scores changed. They did.[8]

What the Rekers' case study proves is that if parents join up with a battery of professionals and put an enormous amount of pressure on an 8 year old to act more like a girl they can sometimes force some outward conformity. Or maybe they can. During followup testing 14 weeks after Becky was pronounced cured, she scored at the highest possible level of masculinity on the IT scale. Rekers nonetheless claimed success because he decided that the IT scale, which he had previously affirmed, was probably invalid.[9]

In evaluating the case study of Becky, it is easy to see clinical biases. First of all Becky was brought in because her parents didn't like her behavior and they could not make her change. Becky, not her parents, was defined as having the "problem." Instead of noticing that he was studying transgender expression in a child with transphobic parents, Rekers wrote as if he were studying one example of any child who gives off transgender expression.

The case report gives limited information about Becky. It reads more like the presentation of a lawyer building a case against a criminal than like an objective style of reporting. She may well have been a terrific kid. She certainly had ego strength. Most importantly, we are not presented with a theory about why Becky liked to play and dress as she did, so there is no way to evaluate a causal theory in terms of data. We also don't know how she turned out.

Rekers' team and the parents didn't merely observe Becky, they brought enormous pressure to bear on her. It is hard to imagine a more data-corrupting research design. The real research is not about understanding Becky's career as a tomboy, but is rather about whether her parents could team up the clinicians to bully her into acting like a traditional girl.

### The Research of Richard Green

If Rekers' work models the worst of clinical research, it is only fair to review the best and most quoted study. The work of Richard Green stands alone in its effort to overcome some of the most scientifically troublesome aspects of clinical research. He published two books on one study of feminine behavior in boys and men. The second was published in 1987 as *The "Sissy Boy Syndrome" and the Development of Homosexuality*. Richard Green follows in the line of research that includes Harry Benjamin, George Rekers, John Money, and Robert Stoller. Like these other establishment clinicians, Green was favored with big grants from the National Institute of Mental Health and other sources. The work of Green and his mentors is broadly quoted in other sources and is a major
basis for the definitions found in the *Diagnostic and Statistical Manual of Mental Disorders* (DSM) of the American Psychiatric Association.[10] These DSM standards became the "expert opinion" that is supposed to guide clinical treatment and is relevant for legal actions related to transgender experience and expression.

Green's book deserves its prominence primarily because he followed his research subjects over 15 years and measured outcomes in adulthood. Green's work is also better than other clinical studies for several additional reasons, including a serious effort to combat the effects of bias in subject selection. But Green's work is still clinical research and is reported as summarized and edited clinical reports designed to illustrate various themes and issues. His study focused on 66 "feminine" boys. In addition to the 12 boys who received intensive clinical attention, there were two control groups: (1) the 54 boys who presented some of the same initial behavior but did not receive heavy clinical intervention, and (2) a group of average boys. Unfortunately, the book tells us very little about the control groups and instead mostly follows the 12 who had therapy.

Green obtained the 66 "feminine" boys by advertising in newspapers and the like. This approach repeats the *who is seen* selectivity problems. The parents brought in their children because at least one of the parents was concerned about, or rejecting of, the child's behavior. The 12 children who received therapy were the 12 whose parents agreed to therapy. Since the book provides very little information about the control group, the selectivity problem is magnified rather than reduced in Green's reporting. For example, I find it fascinating that most of the parents rejected therapy for their boys, and I wish we knew more about that.

As in other clinical studies, Green did not study the everyday childhood behavior of cross-gender play, cross-gender dressing, cross-gender toy selection, or cross-gender identity. He studied clinical relationships with children whose parents responded to a prenamed label – children who had to contend with distressed and disapproving parents.

One of the few bits of information reported for the whole cohort of 66 boys is that, when initially referred, "The 'feminine' boys had few behavioral problems other than sexual identity conflict."[11] The children were happy with their play and otherwise normal. This information is dramatically opposed to a clinical picture of disease or dysphoria. The "problem" that got them into the study was the distress of the *parents*. This finding, by itself, justifies the wiping away of the concept of Gender Identity Disorder from the DSM. Green was well aware of the significance of this issue when he wrote, "the parent's decision to enter our study may have had a profound impact on the son's sexual identity development. (Parental concern)... may be the most marked 'intervention' into the boy's emerging sexual identity."[12]

It appears that the most potentially helpful parts of Green's research were not reported. What was the gender play and experience of the average boys? All we get is a comment by Green that a lot of cross-gender behavior is shown by boys who are not unhappy being boys.[13] Assuming that this comment is based at least in part on the control group in his study, it makes all the more critical the selectivity processes of who is defined as a feminine boy, and who is selected for clinical attention. These two side comments by Green, that the "feminine" boys were happy and otherwise normal and that "average" boys engage in a lot of cross-gender play, opens more of a window on everyday cross-gender expression in boys than does the 99% of Green's reporting that focuses on the 12 case studies. In terms of overall scientific weight, it should be noted that these side comments are powerful evidence *against* the establishment clinical perspective.

Green has a lot of problems with his definitions and they affect what he sees and reports. Green's definitions are not merely inexact. They show systematic misunderstanding of transgender experience and expression. Green's concept of sexual identity is the key concept in his book. What he actually means is gender identity, and he slides back and forth in naming the concept.

For Green, there are three components of sexual (gender) identity. The first is *core morphologic identity*, which amounts to "a person's identity as a male or female." Green is talking about body awareness here. The second is variously named as *gender role behavior, or sex-typed behavior, or masculinity and femininity*. The terms refer to "the culturally fixed signals that discriminate males from females." Green is talking about the degree to which an individual accepts the typical social expectations for gender role behavior. The third is *sexual orientation, or sexual partner preference, or sexual object choice,* which amounts to the distinctions between heterosexuality, bisexuality, and homosexuality.[14]

Since it is at the heart of the subject of his book, Green's sloppiness in his use of the language of sex and gender is surprising. It is important to understand that a person's identity is part of the subject matter of psychology. Awareness of being physiologically male or female is only one important reference for gender self-understanding. The challenge to explain is why some (transgender) people have gender experience that is not in accord with cultural expectations attached to physiological signals of being male or female. Such discontinuity often leads transgender people to wonder whether there might be interior physiological realities that are not in accord with what is visible. Additionally, some people have visible physiological features that are easily seen as not fitting the physiological stereotypes of their assigned genders. The first key to unlocking an understanding of transgender experience is simply facing up to the fact that not all females have a simple psychological identity as women, nor do all males as men. As a student of transsexuals, Green is well aware of this point. Nonetheless, in speaking of "core morphologic identity" he makes it clear that he is refusing to take this distinction seriously.

This profound definitional mistake confuses what is to be explained. Green sets out to explain why some "feminine boys" engage in cross-gender expression and then to examine the relevance of such expression for the child's gender career. Although Green emphasizes the significance of "core morphological identity," he does not argue that these "feminine boys" were unaware of, or denying of, their physiology. The definitional failure suggests that Green doesn't appreciate the core psychological truth these boys were actually presenting. They apparently didn't much care that their imagery and play didn't line up with the expectations of others. Maybe they didn't even know they had transgressed. The psychological truth appears to be that there was no problem in the boys from the point of view of the boys. It seems that the purpose of the therapy, for those "lucky" enough to gain its "blessings," was to teach the boys that they should think of themselves as having a problem so that the parents and therapist could correct it.

A second relevant definitional failure by Green is his assertion that the three definitional elements he identified are distinct and vary independently. Green defines a heterosexual as being culturally typical in all three elements of sexual identity. A homosexual is defined as atypical only in sexual partner preference. A transvestite is defined as atypical only in gender role behavior. A transsexual is defined as atypical in all three elements. This sharp differentiation, which is common in the work of establishment clinicians, misses a lot. First of all, it misses homosexuals who are effeminate or who cross-dress. This is a strange failure, since the main logic of Green's book is to reason from cross-gender identity in children to homosexuality in adults. Once again, Green was aware of the issue. He quoted a survey of 1,500 homosexuals that reports high levels of cross-gender behavior.[15] Green's definitional approach also misses the critical point that the gender role behavior of a transsexual matches that transsexual's sense of *gender* identity. Furthermore, Green fails to understand that transsexuals may choose sexual partners of either sex or gender. These several definitional failures point to the enormous distorting power of the clinical perspective which can overwhelm scientific judgment. It also helps us understand why the clinical perspective is so impervious to scientific correction. Green failed to let his own research correct his own perspectives.

The third problem I see in Green's definitions is his confusion of the concepts of roles, behavior, and cultural images, as found in his second definitional component. Roles, behavior, and images may be congruent for a lot of people, which is probably why Green skipped past such distinctions. But such distinctions are critical in transgender studies for deciding who is counted in which category. The distinctions are also critical to the writing of good theory, because so much theorizing about causation differentiates these concepts. As we shall see in the following chapter on sociological research, the number of people who are included in or excluded from the category homosexual, as found in sample surveys, varies enormously, depending on whether one is measuring role identity, feelings, or behavior.

Green's fourth definitional problem lies in the phrase "culturally fixed signals." Research about cultural definitions suggests that they are not fixed or consistent.[16] This definition also misses issues of subculture variation and family variation. For example, Green argues that parents of feminine boys did not provide appropriate signals to their children about masculinity. The rigidity of this definition by Green—who apparently thinks his sense of culture is definitive for everyone—makes him blind to the variability under his clinical nose. In short, Green used a simplistic stereotype of masculine and feminine behavior, called it traditional (culturally fixed), and then weighed his subjects against it. The same data might be reported as showing that the cultural images are not so fixed or consistent and that "feminine boys" might be conforming rather than transgressing when measured against subcultural or family variations. For example, Green refers to the avoidance of "rough-and-tumble play" by his "sissy boys," with the untested presumption that this is a simple violation of culture. But, if a boy grows up in a setting where rough-and-tumble play is restricted by parents, teachers and other adults, a circumstance that may be common, it would be inaccurate to say the boy is going against culturally fixed signals. We need some solid research on the degree to which cultural signals about gender may be ambivalent and ambiguous for many children.

The fifth definitional problem in Green's book is the overall simplicity of his definition as weighed against the complexity that actually shows up in transgender adults. Such complexity was summarized in the first chapter of this book.

Green's study also shares the third general failing of most clinical research, the data-corrupting effects of his clinical interventions. As a clinician he had hoped to cure the feminine boys. He barely reports that his clinical interventions did not have their intended curative effect. Indeed, though it is counterintuitive, Green's therapy may have had the opposite effect. Social psychology labeling theory shows that attaching a label to someone can be a powerful cause of a person's choosing to exhibit behavior in keeping with the assigned label.[17] Phyllis Burke summarizes this point for Green's book by arguing that he was teaching the boys that they were "pre-homosexual."[18] In Chapter 7 I will present a more complete view of how clinical interventions are social control processes that sometimes produce an effect opposite from what is intended.

The fourth common problem in clinical studies is revisionist memory. Green specifically names it as a problem in other clinical studies and correctly points out the value of getting data during childhood, then getting follow-up data during adulthood.[19] He further notes that transsexual adults are aware of the rules used by psychiatric and psychological gatekeepers when transsexuals apply for sexual reconstructive surgery (SRS). Green suggests that such applicants are likely to tailor their stories to gain approval for surgery.

Although Green's own study is protected against the critique of relying on revisionist memory, he refers to other studies that are not so protected for some of his strongest argumentation. Green asserts that "This linkage between boyhood femininity and manhood homosexuality has long been suspected. Not only do the retrospective data . . . suggest it, but a few prospective studies document it."[20] He cites four such prospective studies, one of them a preliminary study he did with 5 "feminine" boys. The other three studies had groups of 13, 16, and 55 boys and were all follow-up clinical studies. The two smaller studies found that the boys were more likely to grow into heterosexual adults, with traditional gender expression, than into homosexual, transsexual or transvestite adults combined. The study of 55 boys had extra methodological problems. For example, 16 of the boys entered the study as adolescents. It found that two-thirds of the boys became homosexuals.

Despite the numerous methodological and theoretical problems in Green's work, it is still interesting to consider several of his research findings. He reports that 9 of the 12 boys who received treatment grew up to have homosexual or bisexual experience as young men. The proportion was similar for the untreated 54 boys, which led him to conclude that therapy with feminine boys was not likely to stop them from growing up to be homosexual.[21] In considering the relevance of Green's study for transgender experience and expression, his finding is devastating for the clinical establishment's theory of gender identity disorder. *The "feminine boys" in the untreated sample, with one exception, did not grow up to be transvestites or transsexuals.*[22] All the gender identity clinics that have blossomed to treat boys who express feminine behavior are supposed to keep them from growing up to be transvestites or transsexuals. This key research does not justify such an industry, nor does any other. Even if you believe that such clinics are really aimed at preventing homosexuality—which is no longer professionally justified because it isn't seen as an illness—Green's finding is that such therapy is ineffective.

To keep the record clear, for reasons already discussed and for other reasons to follow, I do not believe that Green's research, or any of the other research reviewed in his book, should be counted as scientific evidence for the theory that feminine behavior in boys causes, or is an early indication of, homosexual or bisexual behavior in men. The point made above is merely that the research findings oppose the theory that feminine behavior in boys causes transgender experience or expression in men.

In addition to the common research problems in clinical studies as they relate to Green's work and in addition to the relevance of his research findings in opposition to clinical theories of transgender experience and expression, there are still more major scientific problems found in *The "Sissy Boy Syndrome" and the Development of Homosexuality* which additionally show the limits of clinical thinking and further show that the clinical label of gender identity disorder is unjustified.

Richard Green's study isn't science for the simple reason that *he doesn't actually specify and test a causal theory.* What he provides instead is clinical reflection. There are numerous implicit causes in Green's book, but the failures to define them, to theorize their activity ahead of time, and to specify the research measures of them, makes this work non-scientific. In his concluding chapter, Green talks about causes in a way that ducks and dodges any commitments. Green couldn't even find a causal path after reviewing his findings. Instead he repeats the findings of his original (1974) study of these "feminine" boys: "The disparate patterns presented . . .make it clear that no consistent etiologic pattern exists for extensive boyhood femininity."[23]

Although Green notes his theoretical problems, including a comment that his theory may be more artistic than scientific, and although he notes that his findings do not justify a theoretical statement, he nonetheless proposes an eight-point developmental theory—because, he says, "I am not congenial to reducing all behavioral processes to the ebb and flow of neurotransmitters."[24] His theoretical comments include an unspecified role for predisposing physiological factors, such as hormonal effects in prenatal development, but Green gives primary weight to social factors such as interaction with parents and peers. His strongest emphasis is on what he labels "male affect starvation," which flows, he believes, from alienation of the feminine boy from his father and male peers.[25] But he notes later that male affect starvation could be resolved in many ways other than cross-gender behavior.[26]

My comment that Green didn't test a theory isn't quite accurate. Although his book is not presented as a test of a theory, he does tell us that he *switched theories* in the middle of his study. Green reports this switch as if it hardly mattered. He reports that he started out assuming that he was studying pre-transsexuality in children. But when the adult follow-up study was done, he found much more homosexuality than transsexuality. No problem, says Green, because homosexuals are more likely to report cross-gender play, etc., as children. Such slipperiness is easy for Green because he isn't specific about his causal theories in the first place and doesn't seem to care about the distinction between transsexuality and homosexuality, since he says both are "atypical." The bottom line is that Green was so busy observing the "shouldn't" rather than the "is" that he never got around to the question of why the boys liked girl stuff.

Although Green switched theories when his follow-up study didn't fit his original theory, and despite the fact that his findings don't support the theory that feminine behavior in boys causes transsexual or transvestite behavior in men, he still tries to make a case for his original line of thinking based on the research of others. His strongest argument that others have proved his point of view is his summary of Harry Benjamin's reports on hundreds of cases of transsexuality. Of course all of Benjamin's work is based on revisionist memory methodology which Green criticized as a significant problem. Green states that Benjamin found that "Males seeking transsexual surgery recalled feeling like members of the 'opposite' sex since early childhood."[27]

Then Green reports on his own interviews with 30 candidates seeking SRS. "My interviews of thirty males requesting medical and surgical reassignment at UCLA *confirmed* Benjamin's report."[28] Green continues by reporting on two cases that support Benjamin's view. But, when Green reports his summary statistics for these interviews, it turns out that only 30 % of the 30 candidates reported a childhood self-concept as a girl, while 43 % reported a boy self-concept and 27 percent reported both boy and girl self-concepts.[29] Thus *Green's own research on transsexuality is in opposition to the most basic clinical stereotype of transsexuals,* a stereotype that shows up repeatedly in "learned opinion.[30] This finding by Green is all the more dramatic because Green had reported that he was aware that candidates for SRS knew they had to fit their stories into a particular story line to get the diagnosis of transsexuality so that they could then receive SRS.[31]

For all my dissatisfaction with the scientific quality of Green's work, I actually agree with Green about the most reasonable theoretical posture for explaining the causes of transgender behavior. Green posits some possible physiological predispositions and the importance of family and peers. Similarly, Kenneth Zucker, another establishment clinician, who runs one of the largest clinics in the world dealing with gender identity disorder, names three sources of causation: physiological predisposition, learned behavior and family interaction.[32] In Chapter 6, my own decidedly nonclinical theorizing works with the same kind of variables. There are numerous difference between the way I reason within this theoretical posture and the way they reason, between what I count as data and what they count, but the biggest difference is that instead of looking for a "needle" to explain "abnormal" behavior, I look at the "haystack" of how such causes work in everyday growth and development.

*Summary and Critique of the Medical Model*

Neither George Rekers, Richard Green, nor any other establishment clinician, has shown that there is any line of causation that justifies a picture of transgender experience as "abnormal," as "disease," as "dysphoric," etc. The review of the work of George Rekers and Richard Green shows that having a prestigious degree and getting big grants from the National Institute of Mental Health doesn't make you a scientist. You have to do work that is consistent with the elementary tenets of science before that work deserves the prestige of having the word science attached to it. Instead of thinking of George Rekers as a scientist, try thinking of him as a cultural bully manipulating a little girl against her will. It is ugly behavior. It was probably damaging to Becky. Although Richard Green's work has scientific problems, at least he had the guts to criticize Rekers in print for his "moralistic" biases, and for calling homosexuality "an unfortunate perversion" and "promiscuous and perverted sexual behavior."[33] Green reports that he supported removing homosexuality from the list of disorders in the Diagnostic and Statistical Manual of the American Psychiatric Association (DSM). He has been instrumental in the recent relaxing of some inappropriate standards in the Benjamin guidelines for medical treatment of transsexuals.[34] Perhaps he will someday claim the implications of his own research and oppose the concept of gender identity disorder.

The establishment clinical model, whether hostile to transgender experience and expression, as in the work of Rekers, or humanitarian, as in the work of Benjamin and Green, is based on the classic medical model and is employed first of all for medical purposes. The medical model works pretty well for a host of diseases. For example, a particular strain of flu may be identified as having a specific *cause* (a strain of flu virus), a common *course* (say headache followed by digestive upset followed by 3 days of weakness), and an expected *outcome* (say a 99.4 % recovery rate by the fifth day). An accurate medical model can be very helpful for treating an identified disease. Of course the experience of a specific person with this flu may not match the model: an older and weaker person may die. Such small variations can be handled with a few modest qualifications of a specific medical model for a disease.

When Benjamin applied the medical model to justify hormonal and surgical treatment of those who showed up wanting SRS he hypothesized a specific physiological *cause,* even if it wasn't measured or identified; a traditional *course* (profound feminine sense of self from a very early age, resulting in feminine expression); and an expected *outcome* of profound dissatisfaction and distress, often including suicide, if the condition was not relieved by hormones and surgery. This line of thinking was close enough to traditional medical thinking that Benjamin was able to establish medical clinics in the United States for treating transsexuals.

Once established as a theory, the medical model of transsexuality drew criticism from a host of medical and nonmedical sources. Despite some ups and downs in acceptance, SRS is still available and is still being justified on medical model grounds. I strongly support the availability of SRS and believe many people have profited profoundly from the surgery and that this in turn has benefitted our society. But I don't think the medical model of transsexualism is scientifically defensible for all the reasons presented above. Furthermore, a lot of people seeking SRS don't fit the story line presented by Benjamin, don't fit the medical model of specific cause, expected course,and projected outcome. I've already noted that Richard Green found that many people who were labeled as males at birth and sought SRS had nonclassic elements in their stories. Here I want to point out that in the mid-1970s the concept of secondary transsexualism began to arise.[35]

The concept of secondary transsexualism is applied to people who had been labeled as males at birth and were older than forty when they began to seek SRS. They reported successful career as boys and men but nonetheless wanted to experience life as women, in keeping with their fantasy experiences of themselves as women. These secondary transsexuals were commonly husbands and fathers and reported themselves as occupationally successful. Since I share a lot of such a story line, even though I do not expect to seek SRS, I don't have any problem recognizing that the story can accurately reflect the experience of some people. But such experience is far from the classic clinical course of transsexualism. The only point of agreement is a strong desire to receive SRS.

Once transsexualism was medically accepted as some kind of disease or dysphoria it has apparently been an easy step to assume there are different kinds of transsexualism. But the modification of the medical model of transsexualism is not a small adjustment to a basic model, like accounting for the variable of age in a medical model of flu. The story lines are so markedly different as to require a completely different approach to theorization. Instead of stretching the medical model of transsexualism, a more reasonable assessment is simply that people who want SRS have vastly different story lines and that the *cause* and *course* elements of the medical model, at minimum are not defensible. Of course, those who are committed to medical model thinking can simply decide there are two diseases that require two medical models. Since I've already demonstrated the complexity of transgender experience, I suggest that following this path gets you to a medical model at least as complex as cancer or the common cold—dozens of causes, courses, and outcomes. Those who want to stay with the medical model are going to find themselves saying things that are analogous to,"Most men over 50 have prostate cancer but are non-symptomatic and the cancer is irrelevant to their general health and life-expectancy."

The above critique of the medical model to explain transgender experience and expression, is far more profound than noting a few exceptions to a general rule. Clinicians have not established any of the three components required for a medical model theory for transsexual and transgender expression: neither cause, nor course, nor outcome.

The concept of secondary transsexualism has taken an additional twist with the construction of the concept of autogynephilia, which was initially developed by Ray Blanchard in 1985[36] and more recently promoted by Anne Lawrence in 1998.[37] Blanchard is a clinical psychologist with the Clarke Institute of Psychiatry in Toronto; Lawrence is an M.D. and a transsexual. Lawrence follows Blanchard in conceiving of autogynephilia as a paraphilia—a love or attachment not directed toward another person. The supposed cause of autogynephilia is masturbation fantasies in which the transgender person imagines being a woman. Lawrence's argument is that only sexual energy is powerful enough to cause a male who is reasonably comfortable in the man's role to be willing to go through SRS. But there are two important lines of evidence which don't fit the concept of paraphilia for so-called secondary transsexuals with autogynephilia. First of all, these supposedly autogynephilic people do report erotic attachment and interaction with other people, even though they sustain erotic fantasies about being a woman. Second, Lawrence reports that these supposed autogynephiles want SRS even after there is no longer any erotic fantasy. She accounts for this desire as commitment to a pleasant memory.

Beyond the issues of weak evidence, we return once again to core problems with clinical definitions. Masturbation fantasies have long been treated as signs of disease in psychiatric classification manuals and have a cultural history of religious condemnation[38] . There is a lot of debate about what fantasies are and about what they mean, but the core idea is that a fantasy is imagery linked to an unfulfilled desire or other strong feeling. Assuming that there are people who have been defined as male and as men who get a lot of pleasant feelings in masturbation fantasies from imagining themselves as being female and women, we should ask what is the unfulfilled desire that is at stake.

Why might a man enjoy imaging himself as a woman? The cultural imagery of a woman in the United States commonly includes such things as the ability to feel one's feelings and the ability to receive love and attention. If a man has been socialized in ways that starve access to his own feelings, pursuing a fantasy that opens up such access might best be seen as a movement toward centeredness and wholeness, toward health rather than disease. Then the question for such a man becomes what he wants to do to pursue access to feelings. For such men the following question becomes what to do to give and receive love more easily. There are lots of ways of reforming one's sense of self to incorporate such insight. One of those paths is to seek SRS. This interpretation is the opposite of paraphilia, the opposite of a medical model that assumes a disease has to be explained. Even when masturbation fantasies are part of the story line, it may be important to give primary weight to factors other that sexual feelings to assess what makes SRS attractive. Even if a person is fully identified by the story line that Blanchard and Lawrence propose, if SRS helps one gain greater access to one's erotic feelings, then it may well become part of learning to share a more complete, more satisfying, and more loving interchange with another person. The proper label would still be health.

### Nonclinical Psychological Studies

Vern and Bonnie Bullough have offered an extended nonclinical psychological explanation of transgender experience and expression. Although well aware of clinical writing, the Bulloughs have drawn primarily upon historical and cross-cultural studies for the core of their theory. Taken together, their several recent publications constitute a magnum opus that will influence work on transgender studies for a long time. Their theoretical summary can be found in Chapter 13 of their 1993 book *Cross Dressing, Sex and Gender.*

The Bulloughs theorize the significance of both physiological and social-psychological causes. Their reflections on physiological studies is brief, assumes an admittedly unmeasured genetic predisposition, and emphasizes the untested theory that prenatal hormone abnormalities create abnormal brain development. They refer positively to Pillard and Weinrich, who develop a detailed theory of prenatal hormone influence to explain transgender and homosexual expression.[39] However, when the Bulloughs state their own physiological assumptions, they treat physiological causes as vague and general predispositions to gender transgression that are steered by psychosocial events in the child's life. Such generality is in keeping with their historical and cross-cultural studies, which found wide variation in the ways that gender transgressions have been expressed. It is also in keeping with the finding that feminine boys grow up to become heterosexual, homosexual, transvestite, or transsexual.[40] In short, it seems to me, they want to include a physiological dimension of cause because transgender expression is found in so many places and times. But they do not integrate physiological causation into their essentially psychosocial explanations.

The Bulloughs present their theory of transgender development as a six-step version of a sociological "career of deviance" theory first presented by H.

Taylor Buckner. Buckner collaborated in a survey of transvestites by Bentler and Prince that is discussed in a later chapter.

The first step presumes genetic and physiological factors that produce a boy who is less active and aggressive. This assumption doesn't suggest a needle theory such as prenatal sex hormones, but rather a haystack theory that draws upon complex, interactive, flexible genetic and physiological factors. But this first step has the same problem found in Green's study of feminine boys: boyhood femininity does not lead to adult transgender activity. Furthermore, many transvestites, including me, report an active childhood. Some clinicians, showing their mental "flexibility," call such behavior hypermasculine. Myself, I just enjoyed playing high school varsity basketball and baseball.

The second theoretical step for the Bulloughs lifts up the effects of a wide range of social factors, such as a dominant mother. I agree that many kinds of social causes come into play; I just develop them differently. I would also note that I had a mother who majored in emotional passivity and withdrawal. We seldom touched, but she did at least shake my hand when I went off to basic training in the army at age 17. (Lest anyone think that being in the army was hypermasculinity, I should point out that I was choosing 6 months of active duty training plus reserve duty instead of possibly being drafted for 2 years.)

The third step proposed by the Bulloughs is the discovery of the joys of cross-dressing and masturbation. No one has systematically studied masturbation and cross-dressing, but one main point is that the fantasy content of masturbation is not limited by the clothes one wears. Any good study in this area would have to focus on the fantasy or imagination content rather than on what one is wearing while masturbating. For myself, I think my adolescent fantasies were heavily influenced by wanting to escape the exploitative imagery of men that dominated my subculture. I also remember that I wanted to experience the full range of my feelings and that I wanted to develop a meaningful emotional relationship with a woman. I wanted the girls I dated to know I wasn't like John Wayne, and that helped me have a lot of dates.

The fourth step for the Bulloughs is marriage and the suppression of homosexuality. With regard to this element of the theory, it seems relevant to me that homosexuality is suppressed by our homophobic culture at *every* point in the life cycle, not just marriage. Furthermore, there are people who cross-dress who are at every point on the continuum between heterosexuality and homosexuality. It seems to me that the problem with the Bullough's theory at this point is that they don't give sufficient weight to their own broad historical and cross-cultural studies but were drawn back toward a clinical perspective that transvestites are overwhelmingly heterosexual.[41]

The fifth step that the Bulloughs mention is the response of wives or partners. The Bullough's show their theoretical flexibility by arguing that whether the wife or partner supports, resists or leaves, her action encourages transvestite development. No one has to bother testing this element of the theory since any data will do. I think that partners may support or oppose transgender development but that partner influence is not a primary cause of transgender experience. I also think that many transgender people weigh the costs of transgender expression and that their weighted choices help to shape their careers.

The Bulloughs base the sixth step of their theory on learning theory when they argue that transvestites learn their scripts from transgender support groups before they go public. While I agree with the Bullough's emphasis on learning theory, I need to point out that times have changed. Though transgender support groups might have supported only a single story line in the past, many support groups now include people with great diversity of story lines and social goals.

It should also be pointed out that the Bulloughs focused their theory only on man-to-woman transitions.

Despite my dissatisfaction with their summary theorizing, there is much to affirm in the writing of the Bulloughs. They have made a lot of transgender history and culture available to the transgender community. Most important, they are able to talk about gender transgression without naming it as mental illness. Instead, they write, "The mental illness label ...stigmatizes and lessens human freedom. Since many transsexuals also are very depressed and want sexual reassignment surgery, the illness label, with all its disadvantages, may be reasonable; but in the case of transvestites, who seldom want or need treatment, the label probably only effectively stigmatizes behavior."[42]

### Men and Women Are Alike and Different

How far does one *trans* in transgender experience and expression? How great is the distance between men and women?

Comparing men and women has been a popular activity of learned studies in Western civilization for centuries. Jill Matus lifts up a report by physiologist William Carpenter in 1842 who described a male of African descent, as a "perfect" male with complete genitalia, who had nonetheless developed women's breasts and made his living as a wet nurse."[43]

The feminist revolution, and the antifeminist reaction, have inspired a lot of recent work on differences and similarities between men and women. Some of the scientific work, on both sides, is politicized, which justifies an extra dose of skepticism in relation to scientific value. A lot of the work is simplistic: Pick any psychological attribute. Construct an interview schedule or questionnaire. Give it to a couple of college classes, or print it in a popular magazine, and ask for responses. Publish the results. More substantial work, however, has been done, such as spotting gender bias in standardized tests.

Janet Hyde offers a feminist perspective in a chapter on the differences between men and women in her text, *Understanding Human Sexuality*, Third Edition (1986). Her conclusion is that, with the exceptions of aggressiveness and self-esteem, "for the vast majority of psychological characteristics, there are no gender differences."[44] I see a more qualified picture of such research than Hyde. I would summarize by saying that similarity outweighs dissimilarity. Part of my caution flows from my judgment that so many of the studies of sexual differentiation are so seriously flawed that the main pictorial quality is muddiness. The most pervasive problem of these studies is that differences are presented as differences in the *averages* of measures of men and women. These studies commonly provide data that is distributed in the shape of overlapping normal (bell-shaped) curves of the scores of men and women. Such studies, even if they were otherwise methodologically adequate, show large amounts of similarity, even if there is a statistically significant difference between average scores for men and women.

A widely quoted antifeminist book is *Brain Sex: The Real Difference Between Men and Women*, by Anne Moir and David Jessel.[45] The attractiveness of the book may be that it is written with lots of quotable phrases, which show the writing skills of a television producer and a television journalist. The book is hard to assess on scientific grounds because there are no footnotes or endnotes to link the text to referenced studies. Following are two samples of Moir and Jessel rhetoric: "Men are different from women. . . . To maintain that they are the same in aptitude, skill or behavior is to build a society based on a biological and scientific lie. The sexes are different because their brains are different. [the brain] is differently constructed [and]processes information in a different way."[46] "If women have reason to rage, it is not because science has set at naught their hard-won struggle toward equality; their wrath should rather be directed at those who have sought to misdirect and deny them their very essence."[47]

Moir and Jessel spend a great deal of their time on reporting measured differences between men and women and then in slopping together the explanations. For example, "The truth is that for virtually our entire tenancy on the planet, we have been a sexist species. Our biology assigned separate functions to the male and female of Homo Sapiens. Our evolution strengthened and refined these differences. Our civilization reflected them. Our religion and education reinforced them."[48] This is like saying that because women breast feed they must do the cooking and the laundry. For the sake of brevity I will point to only three of their common scientific errors. These same errors show up in even more popularized defenses of sexual differentiation such as *He and She: 60 Significant Differences Between Men and Women*.[49] These errors are in addition to the already noted problem of comparing averages and suppressing the similarity shown by the overlap of normal distributions.

The first error of Moir and Jessel is their misunderstanding of the methodology of constructing standardized tests. The first evidence they cite for their conclusions is that men typically outscored women in the early Wechsler IQ tests. They then criticize Wechsler and others for substituting male-slanted and female-slanted items to arrive at approximately equal scores. "It is an odd way of conducting a scientific study; if you don't like the result you get from an experiment, you fix the data to produce a more palatable conclusion."[50]

Wechsler was not conducting an experiment in sexual differentiation. He was trying to create a research instrument that accurately measured several kinds of intelligence. Indeed, it is only when a research instrument is free of gender bias in its construction that the results of respondents, differentiated by gender category, can be fairly compared. Biases have been shown in intelligence-testing instruments for a wide range of variables, particularly race, class, and culture. Since there are cultural differences between men and women, it is not surprising that cultural factors would affect scores that are *intended* to be measures of innate difference. Wechsler was not fixing his test to produce equality, he was fixing his test to reduce cultural biases that were already there, which were called to his attention by the sex differentials. With a more gender-neutral list of questions the tests showed more similar scores. That is, a fairer test showed more equivalent scores. Wechsler did not keep adding questions biased in favor of women until he got to equality.

The second basic scientific error of Moir and Jessel is that they discount the cultural effects of *practice.* They write, "On measurement of various aptitude tests, the differences between the sexes in average scores on these tests can be as much as 25 percent. A difference of as little as 5 percent has been found to have a marked impact on the occupation or activities at which men or women will, on average, excel."[51] They note that the biggest of these differences show up in measures of spatial ability. "The fact of the male's superiority in spatial ability is not in dispute. It is confirmed by literally hundreds of studies."[52] They then point out that the typical test of spatial ability is the assembly of three-dimensional mechanical apparatus. They offer no comment about cultural differences in experience with assembling mechanical apparatus. For example, when I went to high school I joined all the other boys in a shop class while all the girls took home economics. This second error is about the issue of practice as it affects test scores. If a difference is innate, it should not be affected greatly by practice. Alternatively stated, if boys start out with more practice, on average, in assembling mechanical apparatus, you would expect them to be better at such activity initially. If girls have similar abilities, you would expect their scores after practice to be like those of the boys. For example, in a study of recognizing "embedded figures," boys did better in the initial testing. This advantage disappeared when the girls got to practice with the blocks used to measure "embedded figures".[53]

The third basic scientific error of Moir and Jessel, belying the title of their book, is that they make no effort to show a direct link between specific findings in aptitude differences and underlying structures in the brain. In separate sections Moir and Jessel talk about genetic differences, differences in early physiological development, etc. They *assume* that physiological differences cause what they count as differences in aptitudes. For example, they make a standard genetic argument in pointing out that males and females have genetic differences that are part of every cell in the body, the difference between the XX and XY versions of the 23rd. chromosome. They conveniently fail to point out that 22 chromosomes are similar and that differences in mathematical or spatial intelligence are probably not related to differences in the 23rd chromosome.[54] Similarly, they argue the importance of the difference between male and female hormones and point out that these hormones also affect brains. They then point out that a burst of testosterone sets off puberty in boys while failing to point out that a burst of testosterone sets off puberty in girls. As argued in the previous chapter of this book, the point is not to deny physiological differences between males and females. Moir and Jessel could have argued more effectively for physiological difference than they did. The key question is, what are the differences and what are the effects of the differences? I offered a review of research on brain anatomy that is based on better and more recent research than that quoted by Moir and Jessel and concluded that such research shows far more similarity than dissimilarity between the brains of men and women. More importantly, Moir and Jessel are reasoning in a way no brain anatomist would reason: that a difference in a performance measure necessarily shows a genetically based difference in brain structure.

Moir and Jessel also make the error of generalizing from the study of rat brains to human brains. They report the work of Roger Gorski and others without troubling themselves with the numerous caveats that the scientists made in interpreting their own studies.[55]

Moir and Jessel also refer to some intersexual case studies that point to the importance of hormonal activity. But these studies do not point to typical XX versus XY differentiation, nor do they measure the factors Moir and Jessel are considering.[56]

Another book that believes in marked sexual differentiation between men and women is Robert Pool's *Eve's Rib: Searching for the Biological Basis of Sex Differences* (1994). It includes a number of arguments based on intersexuality and transsexuality.

Pool argues that transsexuality is not learned. His primary argument is the refutation of a (now infamous) study of one boy that was initially widely quoted in favor of the theory that transsexuality is caused by social learning. The boy was born as a standard XY chromosome male whose penis was damaged in an accident during circumcision. The parents decided on sexual reconstructive surgery to mimic a female body and then gave the child female hormones and raised the child as a girl. John Money reported this case while the child was young and claimed that the socialization to being a girl had worked. He reported that the child's mother said she was surprised at how feminine her daughter was.[57] Pool reports from a later review of the case that the child was indeed raised as a girl but wasn't comfortable. When she was told at 18 what had happened, she insisted on getting reverse sexual reconstruction surgery to become a male again.

An even later and more complete review of the story of the boy with the injured penis is offered by John Colapinto. It exposes a story of clinical mishandling and scientific overstatement that puts Money's work in a very bad light.[58] But Pool's assessment is hardly better than the work of Money. Pool doesn't bother to comment that the child was injured at 7 months, that child rearing changes occurred at 17 months, and that the child only went through partial SRS and didn't have a full vagina.[59] Furthermore, the child was well aware of being special and different because of repeated visits by Money. The child didn't choose the surgery. The child was aware of not having the body of a biological girl, in part because Money pressed the child to undergo additional surgery to create a more realistic vagina. There was a great big secret floating around in this family, and the child figured it out enough to tell a school psychologist about the injured genitals.[60] To assert that there was no social learning is ridiculous. To assert that an example based on a nonchosen accident is equivalent to chosen transsexual SRS is ridiculous. This famous experiment, which propelled Money to sexological stardom, is nearly useless for scientific purposes. If it proves anything, it proves how much human damage can be done by intrusive clinicians. In any case, Pool's error is common for people reviewing scientific work. The fact that one bit of research is inadequate is not evidence in favor of another theory.

Reasoning from the "natural experiment" of doing infant SRS because of a penis damaged during circumcision has taken an additional twist with the publication of a second such study, this one on a Canadian infant. Susan Bradley et al, report that a 27-year-old happily adjusted woman was the subject of SRS at the age of 7 months, a much earlier surgery than in the case reported by Money. They report the case in support of Money's theory that gender is malleable even when there are no indications of intersexuality.[61] Since Bradley and Kenneth Zucker are well known establishment partisans in psychiatric politics, leaders in the creation of the label of gender identity disorder for children, there is reason to greet this report with skepticism. Nonetheless, an argument *for* malleability is an argument *against* the theory that gender identity disorder is a physiologically caused pathology.

Pool also makes much of a study of a natural intersexual experiment that took place in the Caribbean and was reported by Julianne Imperato-McGinley in 1974. Because of inbreeding on an island there was a group of 18 people who all had a genetic problem that created a lack of the 5 alpha-reductase enzyme. These people had XY chromosomes but were born with no signs of penis or testes because of the missing enzyme. They were raised as girls. At puberty, undescended testes began to function, and the external genitals became masculine. 17 of the 18 made then made adjustments to being boys. Despite the lack of a penis or visible testes, these people as children had male bodies, and transgender experience helps us understand that many body signals and images other than genitalia are important for the development of self-concepts. They may have been raised as girls, but that doesn't mean that they didn't notice any differences. Furthermore, the male status is valuable in Caribbean culture, as in most other places. Most important, the choice the 18 faced was not whether they wanted to change sexes but whether they wanted to change their gender to match their new penis. This is a very different kind of choice from the choice facing transsexuals. The boys chose an identity that fit. Although they were raised as girls, like all people they had learned both roles. Most people choose one gender role and stick with it. These people chose to be girls when they were small children and then chose to be boys at puberty. Perhaps the amazing part of this story is that one adolescent chose to remain a girl despite learning the truth about her anatomy. In any case, Pool makes the simplest of logical missteps. He didn't study how people *do* become transsexuals. He studied how people *didn't* become transsexual.

Paula and Jeremy Caplan offer a general critique of studies purporting to show sharply drawn differences between men and women. Such studies, they write, treat a difference as a bipolar rather than a bimodal difference and/or assume that a discovered difference is biologically based and therefore inevitable or unchangeable.[62] One of their contributions to this literature was to take on the widely held belief that boys are more aggressive than girls. First of all they note that it is not so easy to distinguish aggressiveness from the closely related concepts of violence and assertiveness and that almost all operationally developed hypotheses about aggressiveness can be reassessed and seen quite differently. But their most dramatic point from a review of aggressiveness studies is that in studies in which boys thought they were unobserved they were no different from girls in their aggressiveness, but in studies in which they thought they were observed their behavior showed more aggressiveness than did girls behavior.[63]

I am not arguing that all cultural images of gender are totally ungrounded in biological or psychological differences. Rather, I am continuing to make the point of emergence and synthesis. Individually and collectively, we face the human task of making sense of the facets of reality that we know through our senses. Although the idea of gender seems fixed and simple to many people, this book has already shown the complexity, flexibility, and interactivity of physiological and psychological factors that affect the creation, transmission, and changing of gender categories and images.

## Masculinity, Femininity and Androgyny

Sandra Bem set off an interesting line of studies of the differences between men and women in the 1970s.[64] She began by asking college students what traits were desirable for men and women. She was operationalizing the concept of gender stereotypes. She selected 20 masculine items (e.g., "aggressiveness"), 20 feminine items (e.g., "loves children") and 20 neutral items (e.g., "happy"). She created a questionnaire with a 7 point scale for each of the 60 items. She then gave the questionnaire to several college classes and rated the respondents on masculinity and femininity. Her Bem's Sex Role Inventory (BSRI) became popular as an element in numerous studies. Her findings regarding college students have been used as a baseline for comparisons with other populations.

Bem reports that in her initial study one-third of the subjects scored as "androgynous" because they had high masculine and high feminine scores.[65] She interpreted her finding of androgyny positively: "androgynous people have the flexibility to exhibit either masculine or feminine behaviors, depending on what the situation calls for" and "those who are androgynous, and thus transcend gender roles, are better able to function effectively in a wider range of situations." For example, she suggested that androgynous males were better able than traditional men to nurture a sad classmate when that was appropriate. Given its sampling and other limitations, I think it is hard to build very much on the Bem foundation. But it does seem worth noting that in at least one kind of nonclinical population a lot of people chose not to fit into cultural stereotypes about men and women.

Hyde joined others in enthusiastic assessments of androgyny. After reviewing several BSRI studies of androgyny, she wrote, "Probably we should not set our expectations for androgyny too high. It probably will not be the cure to all the sexual woes in our society. But it might help."[66]

June Singer, a Jungian psychoanalyst wrote *Androgyny: Toward a New Theory of Sexuality*. She argued for a single archetype of androgyny to replace the typical Jungian language of anima and animus. But her work nevertheless comes out sounding a lot like anima and animus, since she asserts that men and women are fundamentally different but that each carries internal imagery of the other. Surprisingly, Singer has little to say about transgender experience. Her book is based, like much of Jung's writing on the subject, on an analysis of cross-cultural and cross-religious themes.

Although Hyde praises androgyny, she is not positive about transgender experience. She discusses transsexuals in her chapter on gender roles. There is little scientific reference in Hyde's textbook with regard to the causation of transsexualism. She favors an early-learning theory of transsexualism based on one clinical study of 17 men and the work of Richard Green.[67] As we have seen, Richard Green's study does not defend such a theory. However, Hyde does quote an interesting study by Michael Z. Fleming et al, in which 72 presurgery transsexuals took the BSRI.[68] Fleming reported that the female-to-male preoperative transsexuals had scores that were very similar to Bem's college classes: 35 % scored as masculine, 35 % as androgynous and 30 % as feminine. The male-to-female group scored 60 % feminine, 22 % androgynous and 18 % masculine. The Fleming study can fairly be counted as distinctly counter to clinical establishment theories of transsexualism because it contradicts the theorized course or story line.

Hyde writes about transvestism as a form of fetishism in her chapter on variations in sexual expression. She derives this opinion from Wardell Pomeroy, a clinician who was on the original Kinsey team.[69] However, without noticing the contradiction, she quotes a study of 50 heterosexual transvestites by John Talamini that names four basic motives for men to cross-dress.[70] They include sexual arousal (which is not the same as fetishism), relaxation (escape from the male role), role-playing achievement (success in acting), and adornment (liking pretty things). Perhaps Hyde thinks she is doing transvestites a favor when she dismissively asserts that transvestism is a harmless sexual variation when done in private. It seems that Hyde, Bem, and Singer can praise androgyny only as long as it doesn't mess with appearance norms.

Richard Zuckerberg offers a more explicit challenge to establishment clinicians in his view of androgyny. He writes, "Androgyny speaks to a fundamental issue in all of us. For each of us, it brings up the idea of psychological integration, the notion of being able to explore, develop, bring together, and use all aspects of our humanness, for ourselves and for others. This will lead to a higher level of personal integration, a true joining and a coming together of split-off aspects of ourselves, which will make for a stronger, more resilient structure within."[71] I like the direction of Zuckerberg's comments but find it unfortunate that Zuckerberg, like Hyde, Bem, and Singer, did not take on issues of transgender expression. Many transgender people have been doing exactly the psychological work that Zuckerberg talks about.

In reviewing these nonclinical studies it is important to understand that they are all studies of attitudes. Any study of attitudes should meet multiple methodological standards to be of much scientific value. Bem's work does not meet all these standards. In a later review of her own work she wrote, "By the late 1970's and early 1980's, however, I had begun to see that the concept of androgyny inevitably focused so much more attention on the individual's being both masculine and feminine than on the culture's having created the concepts of masculinity and femininity in the first place. . . ."[72] The core of her later book, *The Lenses of Gender: Transforming the Debate on Sexual Inequality*, is built on calling attention to three cultural lenses about gender that she feels are inherently distorting of underlying human truth. She argues that the lenses affect the everyday processes of learning the roles of men and women and pervade social institutions such as science and the law.

The three cultural lenses that Bem believes distort underlying human reality are androcentrism, gender polarization and biological essentialism. For Bem, androcentrism means the cultural dominance of the masculine perspective. Androcentrism is not merely about social dominance by men. The lens issue is about treating the masculine perspective as normative, or neutral, or natural while treating feminine perspectives as other.

The second distorting lens Bem critiques is gender polarization. She is now unsatisfied with her earlier work, in part, because the problem of false concretization creates gender polarization. It is important to understand this point, because the BSRI is still widely used to measure masculinity, femininity, and androgyny. False concretization is a common problem for social psychological measures of attitudes. In her early work, by asserting that she was measuring masculinity, femininity, and androgyny, she creates the impression that such phenomena are really there and that her BSRI merely points to them. But the "really there" was operationalized by a questionnaire that asked college students to rate items for masculinity, etc. That is, the original measurements were of cultural attitudes, not of some theorized underlying human truth. She reported her finding of androgyny as a new finding that modifies a bipolar picture of gender, when the same data could have been seen as overlap and similarity among people – thus undercutting bipolar conceptualizing.

To understand Bem's reassessment of her work it may help to know that she points to her personal subjectivity about gender as a significant source of her change. She reports this as follows: "Although some of the (very few) individuals to whom I have been attracted during my forty-eight years have been men and some have been women, what those individuals have in common has nothing to do with either their biological sex or mine—from which I conclude, not that I am attracted to both sexes, but that my sexuality is orga- nized around dimensions other than sex."[73] This self-report is another example of confusing choice of sexual partner with the larger category of gender, a concern which will be taken up later in a section on bisexuality.

The issue of whether Bem's concepts of masculine, feminine, and androgy- nous, are falsely concretized depends on the realm of analysis within which one is working. My answer is that, although they may be falsely concretized as *psychological* concepts, they are not falsely concretized as *cultural* concepts. Bem's later concern reflects her awareness that cultural images and stereotypes are not an arithmetic sum of individual experiences. What is going on here is that Bem has become aware that human beings don't always respond to cultural stereotypes in the same way.

Bem criticizes the lens of biological essentialism for undervaluing the creativity shown by individuals and reflected in cultural images. However, although she is able to criticize biological essentialism, Bem shows a psychologi- cal essentialism. This psychological essentialism is shown when she claims that the psychological facet of human truth is somehow more basically meaningful than the cultural facet. I simply repeat that scientific truth is relative to the kinds of questions that are being asked. Instead of thinking of cultural images as a sum of individual experience, we can understand it as individuals sharing in cultural creativity. Once created, the cultural images influence the self-under- standing of individuals. Attention to the creation and change of gender roles and images is addressed in the following chapter.

I value Bem's research from the 1970's more than she does, because I am not interested in reducing all human truth to individually focused truth. The studies she conducted and stimulated point to the complexity, overlap, and ambiguity of the cultural symbols of masculinity and femininity. She has shown that, even though a lot of the rhetoric about masculinity and femininity is bipolar, that doesn't mean that individuals always take on norms and images in bipolar ways. For example, it may go against cultural standards for men to be nurturant, but sometimes they do it just the same.

## Our Freedom Generating and Influential Bodies

One of the important reasons for spending so much time with physiological factors in the second chapter was to lay the groundwork for challenging the misuse of physiological reasoning by some psychologists and psychiatrists. The energy that has gone into studies of physiological and psychological differences between men and women is one measure of how deeply committed our culture is to defending traditional gender relationships. No matter how many studies point to similarity, what continues to be news is another tentative finding of difference.

In the previous chapter I reviewed the studies of an almost microscopic brain aspect (INAH 3) that some think might show a difference between gay and straight males. I pointed out that nobody even knows whether the INAHs are relevant in any way to human behavior. In this chapter, as part of pointing to the difference between the psychological conception of *mind* and the physiological conception of *brain,* I point out that many of the studies of this obscure bit of brain anatomy don't mention that the size of the tiny INAH 3 varies by a factor of 10 in both males and females and that there is great overlap.[74] The constant, although so far unconvincing, search for differences between the brains of males and females distracts greatly from the common finding of a high degree of similarity and overlap in the mind activities of men and women. The brains of males and females support this similarity and overlap. Similarity is the consistent finding of hundreds, probably thousands, of studies. Findings of psychological similarity, complexity, interactiveness, and flexibility do not prove that there are no brain differences that affect mind activities. Despite repeated failures, it is possible that someone will eventually show some difference between the brains of males and females. I've already argued that any such difference may be the result of practice rather than genetically based structure. Here I want to point out that to assert that the brain is the *basis* for mind activity is a very different thing from asserting that a difference in brains *causes* a difference in a specific mental pattern, such as gender identity. This chapter has pointed to the
similarity and overlap of many mind activities in men and women. This means that even if someone discovers a brain difference in males and females, that difference has not created differences in a lot of the mind activities of men and women. Therefore it is not scientifically reasonable for psychologists and psychiatrists to pathologize transgender behavior by saying the equivalent of "Oh, that must be because of some brain, or other physiological, defect." It is far more reasonable to argue that complex, flexible, interactive brains give rise to complex, flexible, and interactive mental activities which include the observed capacity to create complex, flexible, interactive mental constructs, which are

melded together in complex, flexible, and interactive social and cultural activities to create observable complex, flexible, and interactive gender stereotypes and roles.

Roger Gorski has received a lot of attention for his attempts to find and interpret sexual differences in rat brains. Along the way he has trained people like Laura Allen, who studies human brains looking for sexual differences. Phyllis Burke visited the UCLA lab where Gorski, Allen, and others have been dissecting rat brains for 15 years. One major focus of this lab has been the preoptic nucleus in rats. This is interesting to Gorski and his students because the preoptic nucleus is bigger in male rats than in female rats. It hasn't deterred them that they don't know the function of the preoptic nucleus and it hasn't deterred them that there is no similar structure in human brains.[75] After being so often denied in their search for the needle, any difference is interesting.

People pursue physiological changes in response to cultural symbols. Some males take estrogen because they want to feel more feminine or look more feminine. After the estrogen has been taken, they are less distinctively male, and the line of reasoning between physiological and psychological factors gains complexity. Hormonal level becomes not only an initial cause but also an intervening cause in explaining, for example, observable breast development. Breast size is in turn a significant social and cultural symbol that can affect attractiveness to potential sexual partners. Related experience may have a significant impact on self-concept. An important difference between a change in breast size and a change in some aspect of the brain is that the breast change is visible and has symbolic cultural value whereas brain changes are hidden. Such interactivity makes it tricky to sort out causal direction.

As a final warning in this chapter to resist the urge to misuse physiological reasoning to fit psychological theories, I refer to the work of Susan Coates, an establishment clinical psychologist who sat on the committee that created the gender identity disorder (GID) label. She was so eager to suggest a physiological base for her opinions about "GID children" that she wrote that feminine boys "may remark on good odors, such as cookies baking in the oven" (showing a heightened sense of smell) and that "Many boys with GID refuse to wear a new shirt unless the tag is cut out (showing a heightened tactile sensitivity)."[76]

---

**Notes:**

1. William Shakespeare, *King Lear*, concluding speech of Act V.
2. Graham Nash, "Teach Your Children" (song), (1970).
3. Phyllis Burke (1996), Leslie Feinberg (1993), Daphne Scholinski (1997).
4. Katherine Johnson and Stephanie Castle (1997).
5. Vern Bullough (1997).
6. Benedict Carey (1990).
7. cf. George Rekers (1995).
8. Phyllis Burke (1996), page 4.

9. Ibid., page 18.
10. There are important differences in the relevant diagnostic categories regarding transgender expression as found in the several revisions of DSM. They are discussed later in the book.
11. Richard Green (1987), page 13.
12. Ibid., page 387.
13. Ibid., page 388.
14. Ibid.
15. Joseph Harry (1982), quoted in Richard Green (1987), pages 10-11.
16. Marjorie Garber (1992).
17. Pat Conover (1976).
18. Phyllis Burke (1996).
19. Richard Green (1987), page 8.
20. Ibid., page 370.
21. Ibid., page 318.
22. Ibid., page 261.
23. Ibid., page 378.
24. Ibid., page 378
25. Ibid., page 380.
26. Ibid., page 386.
27. Ibid., page 9.
28. Ibid., page 9.
29. Ibid., page 12.
30. For example, Judith Becker, in *The Columbia University College of Physicians and Surgeons Complete Home Guide to Mental Health* (1992) reports the following requirement for a diagnosis of transsexualism: "For a diagnosis to be made, there must be strong evidence that the situation has been continuous for a long period (usually since childhood) and that it is almost certain to continue."
31. Richard Green (1987), page 8.
32. Bonnie Blodgett (1990), page 26.
33. Richard Green (1987), page 262.
34. Anne Lawrence, "The New HBIGDA Standards of Care," a workshop presentation for the 2001 conference of the International Foundation for Gender Education, Arlington Heights, Illinois.
35. Richard Docter, "To Hell With Diagnosis?" A workshop given at the 2001 Conference of the International Foundation for Gender Education, Arlington Heights, Illinois.
36. Ray Blanchard (1985).
37. Anne Lawrence (1998).
38. Genesis 38:9; Nolan Lewis (1943).
39. Richard C. Pillard and James D. Weinrich (1987).
40. Vern and Bonnie Bullough (1993), page 331.
41. Many transgender people also believe that the great majority of cross-dressers are heterosexual, and the Tri Ess sorority, which was historically limited to heterosexuals, has numerous chapters. For a data-based response to this issue, see Chapter 4.
42. Vern and Bonnie Bullough (1993), page 314.
43. William Carpenter (1842), as quoted in Jill Matus (1995), page 35.
44. Janet Hyde (1986), page 381.
45. Anne Moir and David Jessel (1991).

46. Ibid., page 5.
47. Ibid., page 6.
48. Ibid., page 10.
49. Chris Evatt (1992).
50. Anne Moir and David Jessel (1991), page 13.
51. Ibid., page 15.
52. Ibid., page 15.
53. Anne Fausto-Sterling (1985), page 34.
54. The Y version of the 23rd chromosome is short and has relatively few genes.
55. Anne Moir and David Jessel (1991), page 25. I offer a limited discussion of Gorski's work in Chapter 2 as well as later in Chapter 3.
56. Ibid. pages 29-37.
57. Robert Pool (1994), page 70 and following.
58. John Colapinto (1997).
59. Vern and Bonnie Bullough (1977).
60. John Colapinto (1997), page 70.
61. Susan Bradley, et al. (1998).
62. Paula and Jeremy Caplan (1994), page 3.
63. Ibid., page 59.
64. Sandra Bem (1974), for example.
65. Ibid.
66. Janet Hyde (1986), page 386.
67. J. P. Driscoll (1971).
68. Michael Z. Fleming (1980).
69. Wardell Pomeroy (1975).
70. John T. Talamini (1982).
71. Richard Zuckerberg (1989), pages 132-133.
72. Sandra Bem (1993), page viii.
73. Ibid., page vii.
74. Anne Fausto-Sterling (1985).
75. Phyllis Burke (1996), page 209, and Gina Kolata (1995).
76. Susan Coates and Sabrina Wolfe (1995).

*We ought not to under-estimate the psychological effect of the statistical world picture: it displaces the individual in favor of anonymous units that pile up into mass formations.* Carl Jung[1]

*Our statistics show that things would be better than they would be if they were worse than they are.* Anonymous

*All the world's a stage, and all the men and women merely players.*
William Shakespeare[2]

# Chapter 4:
# Gender Identities and
# Gender Relationships

Just as for the sciences of physiology and psychology, there is little directly relevant and scientifically useful sociological or anthropological research on transgender experience and expression. For example, Marvin Harris, in a traditional anthropology textbook, writes, "Very little of a reliable nature is actually known about human sexuality in relation to culture."[3] Harris nonetheless opposes physiological determinism. On the latter subject he writes, "modern anthropology stands opposed to the view that anatomy is destiny. Males are not born with an innate tendency to be hunters or warriors or to be sexually and politically dominant over women."[4]

Even though the late 1990s have witnessed an explosion of writing about transgender phenomena, books continue to be written with a surprising lack of transgender awareness. For example, Roger Horrocks, who wrote *An Introduction to the Study of Sexuality* in 1997, devotes chapters to homosexuality and feminism but not so much as an index reference to anything transgender.[5] Similarly, a large book from the Kinsey Institute, *Researching Sexual Behavior*, gives only two pages to Anke Ehrhardt to comment on gender issues; and although she is a coauthor with John Money of a major work addressing transgender issues, she uses her two pages to comment on traditional gender issues in the construction of interview protocols.[6]

Lack of attention to transgender issues may reveal more than a lack of awareness or interest. There is at least some evidence of suppression of transgender studies. David Carlisle, a biologist, participated in a British study called "Official Commission of Enquiry into 'Homosexuality and Intersexual

States,'" which was completed in 1957. It was officially suppressed for more than 30 years because its findings were judged to be too liberal. Carlisle wrote that after beginning the study "I found the next three years quite stressful, as I gradually realized the degree of discrimination to which transvestites and transsexuals were subjected, a point that had never occurred to me before."[7]

Carlisle's professional direction was changed by the study. He published the results of 40 years of research in 1998. The bulk of his work is a collection of nonclinical case studies such as the story of Belinda. Son of a British diplomat, at age 10 Belinda posed as a sex slave of a wealthy businessman and got herself castrated by a barber in India.[8]

Two main lines of sociological research are relevant to transgender issues. One line is survey research. In addition to the problems mentioned below, survey research faces the challenge of making categories clear enough that survey questions can be constructed. This is tough in dealing with transgender phenomena because, as has been previously discussed in this book, the categories don't sit still and people often don't fit neatly into one category. As Irvine further points out, if one takes sexologist's categories too seriously, they become reified (falsely concretized) into static imperatives.[9] Such imperatives were originally used by transsexual clinics as a basis for providing or withholding hormones and/or surgery to transvestites and transsexuals.

The other approach takes advantage of unfettered subjectivity and tries to provide enough structure in the reporting so that new understanding can emerge. Such qualitative studies, however interesting, are difficult to compare to other studies and are hard to relate to findings from other disciplines.

## What We Can Learn From Surveys

I found only one general survey of sexual attitudes and activity in the United States that meets the scientific standards for survey research. It was conducted by Robert Michael et al, and published in 1994 as *Sex in America: A Definitive Study*.[10] An additional report of the study was written by E. O. Laumann.[11] Beyond the Michael study there are occasional relevant individual questions in other scientifically conducted surveys of the general population. Michael writes, "There have been many sex surveys over the past few decades, of course, but the problem is that until very recently virtually all were methodologically flawed, making their data unreliable, uninterpretable, and impossible to use to understand sexual behavior. The Hite Report, the Redbook survey, the Playboy survey, the Janus Report, all are so flawed and unreliable as to be useless."[12]

The Michael study was initially developed in response to the AIDS epidemic, had federal support for its initial phases, had its federal funding stopped by a vote of the United States Senate on a motion by Jesse Helms (Republican, North Carolina), and was finished with funding from private foundations. The methodology was fully reported and included the details of the random sampling techniques, the pretesting of questionnaires, the professional training of interviewers, etc. Michael and colleagues were able to obtain completed interviews and questionnaires from 3,432 of 4,635 randomly identified households in the United States that had eligible respondents, people between 18 and 59 who spoke English.

The most general finding of the Michael survey was that the United States was "a country with very diverse sexual practices but one that, on the whole, is much less sexually active than we have come to believe."[13]

Unfortunately for the purposes of this book, the Michael survey had no questions about transgender behavior or orientation. However, attention was given to homosexuality. In attempting to measure homosexuality the researchers found that different ways of asking the questions produced sharply different numbers. For women in the general population they reported the following:

- 8.6% had some element of desire, behavior, or self-identification with having sex with other women
- 5.5% found the thought of having sex with another woman appealing or very appealing
- 4.0% were sexually attracted to women
- 4.0% had had sex with another woman since age 18
- 4.0% had had sex with another woman in their lifetime
- 2.0% had had sex with another woman in the last year
- 1.4% identified themselves as homosexual or bisexual
- 1.2% had had exclusively women sexual partners in the last year
- 0.5% had had men and women sexual partners in the last year[14]

The figures for men were equally diverse, higher, and not quite in the same pattern:

- 10.1% had some element of desire, behavior, or self-identification with having sex with other men
- 9.0% had had sex with another man since puberty
- 6.0% were sexually attracted to men
- 5.0% had had sex with another man since age 18
- 2.0% had had sex with another man in the last year
- 2.8% self-identified as homosexual or bisexual
- 2.6% had had exclusively men sexual partners in the last year
- 1.0% had had men and women sexual partners in the last year[15]

These are quite different numbers from those found in the famous Kinsey study. Alfred Kinsey was the lead investigator in the first scientific survey of sexual attitudes and practices. He reported his study on males in 1948 and on females in 1953.[16] The findings set off a cultural firestorm that was so severe that no similarly substantial research was attempted until the Michael study. The Kinsey study was rigorous in many ways and covered a broad range of issues. Data was gathered from 10,000 men and 8,000 women. The big problem in the

Kinsey study was that the sampling was not random. It was convenience sampling of college classes and other targeted populations. The resulting population of respondents was heavily biased toward white and middle-class respondents. Furthermore, it was not random even within the white middle-class population.

Two significant challenges to the relevance of the sample for even the white middle-class population is that the sample contained a substantial number of prisoners and an unreported number of volunteers who were sexual nontraditionalists.[17] At best, we might count the Kinsey numbers as suggestive of the sexual attitudes of a large component of the white middle-class population while remembering that the numbers of nontraditional behaviors are probably overstated.

The Kinsey numbers on homosexuality are certainly higher than the Michael numbers:

- 37% had had at least one sexual encounter with another man in their lifetime, and more had had fantasies of such encounters.
- 8% had had only homosexual experience, for a period of 3 years or more, between ages 16 and 65
- 4% had had sex only with men from adolescence on[18]

Kinsey also reported that 60 % of preadolescent boys had engaged in homosexual behavior.[19] One can question just what "homosexual behavior" was for preadolescent boys. A lot of it may have been of the "I'll show you mine if you'll show me yours" variety. Even so, it seems odd to me that, in the decades following the release of the Kinsey studies clinical psychologists focused so heavily on "feminine" behavior as a cause of adult male homosexuality, when the Kinsey studies suggest that there is a lot of homosexual behavior in children.

In any case, both the Michael and the Kinsey studies show that estimates of the extent of homosexuality are heavily influenced by the kinds of questions asked. Michael notes the continuity of his finding with those of Kinsey in this regard: "Kinsey also emphasized that there is no single measure of homosexuality and that it is impossible to divide the world into two distinct classes_homosexual and heterosexual."[20] This is a critical finding, which provides a very different picture of the phenomena of homosexuality in everyday populations than that found in physiological or psychological research, especially clinical research. Since transgender behavior is even less tightly defined than is homosexual behavior, it seems reasonable to suggest that transgender research is likely to be even more sensitive to the kinds of questions asked.

Stuart Michaels, a theorist who affirms homosexuality, notes two important findings about homosexuality in the Michael research. The first is that a new baseline has been established for estimating gay and lesbian activity in the general population and that that number is lower than previously believed. The second is that "feelings and behavior often exist independently of each other and of a homosexual identity."[21] This last finding weighs against any theories that follow the line that physiological factors lead to noticed feelings, that feelings lead to the development of a gay or lesbian identity and that identity leads to action.

One of the most interesting questions about homosexuality is whether it is immutable. The proper approach for studying immutability or change in homosexual orientation or expression is through panel studies which follow a target sample drawn from the general population over time. This led me to give extended attention to Richard Green's study of feminine boys and their adult identities in Chapter 2. I found Green's work to be severely flawed on several counts and argued that his study, and other clinical studies, are largely irrelevant to understanding homosexual or transgender experience and expression in the general population. I also argued that if any weight is given to Green's research that it should count on the side of change rather than immutability. Since I am unaware of any good panel studies of homosexual or transgender experience or expression, the best basis for theorizing about homosexual or transgender immutability or change is the one-moment-in-time studies of Kinsey and Michael. Both suffer from relying on memory, but at least there is no joint clinical reconstruction of memory. By behavioral measures, perhaps better remembered than feelings or orientation, both the Michael and Kinsey studies show that of all the people who have engaged in sexual activity with same-sex partners, the majority have not continued. The Kinsey study shows that there were twice as many men with a pattern of solely homosexual behavior for a period of at least 3 years as there were men with a lifetime practice of solely homosexual behavior, suggesting some mutability even for some gay men with extended experience.[22]

The findings of the Michael study are similar. He found that a lot of people have urges or desires for sharing sexual experience with same-sex partners but that 59 % of women and 44 % of men do not act on them. This is a strong argument for some elements of choice for at least some people, in contrast to theories that genetic and physiological factors determine behavior in everyone. It is common to respond to such data by arguing that fear and threat inhibit exploration and development. Alternatively, these same data can be used to point to theories of bisexuality. Ronald Fox develops this line of reconsideration of the work of Kinsey and Michael and also looks at some other survey information and some anthropological work.[23]

I have been developing a scientific picture painting the complexity, interactivity, and flexibility of physiological, psychological, and now sociological aspects of the transgender experience. Nonetheless, I have continued to suggest that it is possible that a simpler causal theory, perhaps a particular physiological cause, might explain the transgender experience and expression of some people. No simple theory has yet developed much research support, and I have shown that a lot of research intended to discover a simple cause has instead pointed to complexity. In my first chapter I indicated something of the range of transgen-der experience and expression, a broad reality in contrast to the conceptually simpler dependent variable of choice of sexual partner. In Chapter 5 I provide a few transgender stories that repeat the theme of diversity. Now it is time to close the loop by pointing out that the data pictures developed by Kinsey and Michael fit well with a theory of complexity, interactivity, and flexibility.

*Surveys of the Transgender Community*

Several surveys of the transgender community have been completed. All have been based on convenience samples through contacts made with the visible transgender community instead of random samples of the general population. If it is true that most people with transgender experience are still hidden, as many transgender leaders believe, then the findings of surveys based on convenience may not shed much light on the majority of transgender experience in the United States. They are also likely to undercount the number of gay and lesbian or bisexual people with transgender experience and expression. Nonetheless, it is transgender people who are out and participating in transgender groups and activities, or are known as transgender people in the larger society, who most influence any emerging transgender community as well as influencing societal views of transgender people.

The largest and most valuable of these surveys was reported in 1997 by Docter and Prince and was patterned after a 1972 survey by Prince and Bentler. Virginia Prince helped form the first man-to-woman transvestite group which was called the "Heels and Hose Club." The Virginia Prince award is the most prestigious award given by the International Foundation for Gender Education and recognizes Prince as a major leader in helping the transgender community to gather itself together. Richard Docter, Ph.D., recently retired as a professor in the Department of Psychology at California State University in Northridge.

The 1997 study by Docter and Prince completes work begun in 1983 and is based on written survey responses from 1,032 male periodic cross-dressers gathered from 1990 to 1992.[24] The survey responses were primarily gathered from participants at transgender conventions and other transgender events, and a few were added by advertising in transgender publications. They estimate a return rate of 30%-35% from convention and event participants. The survey is selective within the visible transgender community: participants in conventions and events are likely to be white and financially secure, and the response rate may also have been influenced by the fact that the survey was lengthy. All participation was anonymous and uncompensated. Four percent wrote that they had participated in the 1972 survey. Eighty percent said that they were affiliated with either a cross-dressers club or national organization. The sample did not include female impersonators (drag queens) and included few candidates for sexual reassignment surgery.

*The survey by Docter and Prince documents a picture of normality for people in the visible transgender community.* This finding is equivalent to the work of Evelyn Hooker on homosexuality which became the basis for changing the official position of the American Psychiatric Association and the American Psychological Association from pathology to normality. The following findings were largely similar to the 1972 findings:[25]

- 60 % were currently married and an additional 23 percent were separated, divorced or widowed.
- 65 % had post-graduate educations.
- 12 % had unskilled occupations and 88 % had skilled (16%), business (26%), arts (4%), technical (21%), or professional (21%) occupations.
- 69 % had contributed to the conception of children.
- 87 % reported themselves as having a heterosexual orientation, 7 % bisexual, 5 % asexual and 1 % homosexual. 29 % of the total sample reported that they had had some homosexual experience.

From a similar but smaller (100-plus respondents) survey reported in 1988, Docter also found the following:

- 72 % consumed one alcoholic drink per day or less. 4 % consumed more that 3 drinks per day.
- 65 % of the subjects were nonsmokers.
- 91 % had never used marijuana.
- 46 % said that cross dressing had led to "somewhat" to "extremely" harmful consequences for themselves or someone in their lives, such as losing a job, whereas 23 % said it had not had such harmful consequences.

In his 1988 study, Docter reported that sexual arousal was initially important as part of cross-dressing but that such feelings faded with time. The majority reported that their current transgender interest was gathered around other factors, such as the opportunity to express the "girl within."[26] The 1997 article by Docter and Prince lacks a longitudinal assessment but found that 40 % often or nearly always experienced sexual arousal when they cross-dressed.[27] At the same time, 90 % of the subjects expressed a nonorgasmic pleasure in cross-dressing when orgasm was not feasible.[28] Such findings fit with theories of transgender experience and expression that allow for development and change within transgender people as they gather experience, particularly as they move from isolation to social interaction. I think if is unwise to make very much of statistical relationships between cross-dressing and sexual activities because the social opportunities for transgender expression are so limited. A more telling research effort might compare transgender males and straight females for their sexual experience when they are wearing a sexy nightgown in a private or intimate setting.

For those interested in assessing the contributions of psychological factors to the development of transgender experience and expression, the Docter and Prince article reported the following:

- 76 % were raised by both parents through age 18.
- 76 % reported that their fathers provided a good masculine image.
- 86 % reported that they were raised exclusively as a boy.
- 83 % of wives were reported to be aware of the subjects' cross-dressing. Of these wives, 28 % were reported to be completely accepting, 19 % completely antagonistic, and 47 % had mixed views.[29]

The study by Prince and Bentler, Docter's 1988 study, and four other studies, including British and Australian studies, have been summarized and compared by Vern and Bonnie Bullough. In terms of base line information, the six studies are quite similar in finding high marriage rates, high educational and occupational achievements, and low levels of interaction with psychiatrists.[30] An additional survey by John Talamini, based on 50 transvestites on the East Coast of the United States, draws a similar picture.[31] Talamini also interviewed 50 wives of transvestites and reports that 21 were college graduates, 35 of the couples had children, and 30 of the wives were not told about the transvestite interests of the husbands before marriage. Thirty of the wives were reported as accepting their husbands' cross dressing, and 20 were reported as having difficulty in making adjustments.[32] These surveys, and especially the 1997 survey by Docter and Prince, all support a picture of health rather than disease and thus weigh strongly against the DSM definition of gender identity disorder.[33]

I realize that some gay and lesbian writers and some transsexuals have been heavily invested in theories that emphasize physiological factors and immutability. In particular I want to honor the subjectivity of these writers in their reports that they have experienced the gay, lesbian or transgender aspects of their lives as simple and unvarying, that the only choices they had were about how to respond to the homophobia and transphobia[34] of others. I am impressed by the courage and commitment, the honesty and vulnerability of early leaders in the development of transgender, lesbian, and gay communities and organizations who have argued for simplicity and immutability as a reasonable description of their personal lives. This book merely asserts that the truth they carry is one element of a more diverse and complex reality.

The same themes are further supported in a an excellent interview study of 45 female-to-male transsexuals, published in 1997 by Holly Devor.[35] In dramatic contrast to clinical studies, Devor's study pays attention to the sociological guidelines for such research. She used a research-oriented interview schedule, coded her answers for comparison, and reported all her findings. She admitted her feminist bias and excluded the one respondent who objected to this bias. Her questions and reporting allowed her respondents to speak in their disparate voices on a wide range of subjects and allowed the respondents to illustrate their diversity of subjective experiences, family backgrounds, and paths to and through transitions. A foreword by James Green, head of the largest female-to-male transsexual organization in the world, *Female-to-Male International*[36] confirms the quality and accuracy of her work.

Devor's theoretical review covers much the same material as found in this book, though in much less detail. However, she reverses the path developed in this book and begins with social factors. This approach allows her to begin with clarifying what is to be explained. Transsexual expression is a social act, whatever its physiological and psychological causes or influences. She writes, "remember that transsexualism is a very complex phenomenon. Influences from many different directions have to come into play to result in persons calling themselves transsexual. Also keep in mind that transsexualism actually refers to the condition of desiring certain outcomes—*gender and sex reassignment*—which people want for different reasons . . . people can come to their gender and sex dysphorias from a lot of different directions . . . theories may make it seem as if there were only one road to Rome. History, simple logic, and the facts tell us otherwise."[37] Though she uses the word *dysphoria* she does not intend a pathological meaning of the word but rather defines the word as "extreme dissatisfaction with one's assigned gender and sex."[38]

The core of Devor's assessment of theories focuses on identity development, beginning with dissatisfaction with assigned role identity and ending, for transsexuals, with adoption of a different identity. In sharp contrast to clinical theorization, she notes, for example, that lots of girls are dissatisfied with their assigned role identity but that only a few of them become transsexuals.[39] Beginning from this point it becomes relevant to ask why so many are *diverted* from a transsexual path or other role rebellions. I would also note, relative to the line of synthetic reflection developed in this book, that if we think of diverse physiological factors as making diverse contributions to such feeling of role dissatisfaction then we are drawn to asking the questions, as Devor does, about the range of psychological developments and social expressions that physiological grounding makes possible.

Although Devor makes no case for physiological or psychological essentialism, she does faithfully report the subjective reports of most of the participants in her study that "they really had no other option but to start their lives as females, girls, and women and to complete them as men and males. Whatever else may have transpired in their lives, no matter how difficult their journeys, whatever kind of men they might become, most participants concluded that they had been born destined to traverse a lonely course. Fortunately for them, most participants were able to look back on what they had been through and find far more to be thankful for than not. . . . participants chose to look at their lives as more than survivors: they had faced their most difficult moments with courage and dignity and had emerged victorious."[40]

Anne Bolin made a qualitative anthropological survey and observational study of an unnamed number of male-to-female transsexuals and male cross-dressers people who were out, whom she found through transgender organizations, conferences, newsletters, etc.[41] From my point of view, her most significant finding is that "transsexuals did not begin their transition with fully crystallized feminine personal identities, as is widely reported in the medical literature, but rather gradually acquired a feminine identity."[42] Bolin emphasizes the importance of both medical and transgender culture inputs into the formation of transgender identities. In contrast, in Chapter 6, I emphasize problems in the social construction of the roles and concepts of man and woman and that all children learn the images and expectations of both genders. I regard Bolin's work, and the work of others who emphasize the contributions of medical and transgender cultures, as useful for pointing out some shaping factors for the expression of transgender experience that was initiated long before medical and transgender factors come into play.

## The Social Construction of Transgender Reality

All people develop and then adjust their pictures of reality. Each of us brings direct sensory awareness and emotional, intellectual, and aesthetic capacities to our ongoing development of pictures of the world around us. From our earliest years we are influenced by others, given the gifts of our disparate cultures. We are neither independent individuals nor mere derivatives of our socialization. Our *interactive* capacity to create shared pictures is the foundation for social cooperation and cultural integration. To share a common culture, we need not completely agree with others about what is real. To have a mutually helpful relationship, two individuals need not agree about everything. The crucial social skill is the capacity to make allowances for disagreements while sustaining enough mutuality to recognize common interests and understandings.

A social construction may not accurately point to or analyze an external reality. People's belief in magic doesn't make it true. But the assessment, using reason, that there is no magic, is also a social construction. The difference lies in the grounding, the observations, and the reasoning: all human capacities that contribute to shared constructions. All constructions of gender concepts are real in the sense that people refer to them as part of constructing interactions and relationships. In contrast to deciding about whether magic is real, people can reflect on whether a particular component of a gender concept fits their direct subjective experience. If people feel disjunction rather than fit, they can decide what, if anything, they want to do about it. Out of such experience and interaction come continuity and change in individuals, relationships, societies, and cultures. Considered in the context of individuals, physiological capacities and influences interact with social and cultural influences to form the experiences people use to create their personalities and minds. Considered in the context of relationships and societies, the feelings people have about their experiences, such as comfort or discomfort with gender concepts and expectations, become the raw material for interactions that influence social continuity and change. What happens when such raw material becomes crystallized and mobilized is the subject of biography and history.

The physiological capacity to develop language is fundamental to the development of our partially shared pictures of reality. The psychological work of learning a language is a primary developmental task that fits people for social interaction. But if two people learn only different languages, they have to develop translation skills before their physiological and psychological capacities can be used socially to create language-based interaction. Even within a single language, conversation both communicates the meanings of each participant but also reinforces or changes the usage and meaning of words and phrases.

Individual words and phrases may have reference to perceptual, intellectual, affective, or aesthetic aspects of reality. That is, each word has its reality within a larger envelopes of meaning, whether articulated or not articulated. Not only does conversation allow people to relate words to their personal sense of reality; it also contributes to the development of shared envelopes of meaning. This book has been working with the contributions of several sciences to develop a picture of transgender experience and expression. Along the way we have noticed that different sciences use the same word to mean different things. We noted, for example, important differences in the use of the word *trait* and compared a behavioral study of the handedness trait with the everyday way people use their hands. This was one of several illustrations of the challenge of translating carefully developed scientific language into muddy everyday language use.

In the context of trying to understand how people construct the concept of gender, it is important to note that scientific constructions may have a powerful impact on the everyday use of related words. Scientific theories about gender development influence the way people apply gender concepts to themselves. In this book the most dramatic illustration of this truth is that individuals and civilization had to wait until the latter half of the twentieth century to ask "What is a transsexual? Am I one?" More importantly, the little words *man* and *woman* are constantly under revision as well. Science both creates new concepts for cultures—a radical function—then, by defending its definitions, acts as a defender of the social status quo it helped to generate. Although this kind of language deconstruction is the common fare of some feminists and post-modern thinkers and serves well for undercutting ideological oppressions of various kinds, the challenge at this point is the consideration of how language and other social constructions affect what is true about sex and gender.

A first application of this principle is to notice that languages are different in the ways they incorporate gender. English uses *he* and *she* with regard to people, the Romance languages attach gender differentiations to nonhuman objects, and some African languages do not use gender differentiations at all.[43]

To add yet another mirror to this line of reflection, the word *gender* itself isn't self-generating or obvious. Bernice Hausman argues that the word *gender* was given its current meaning to assist clinicians who were trying to distinguish the social dimension of sex from the physiological. She goes on to make the profound point that language changes both mark and help to make possible "the emergence of new forms of being human."[44] This is important to Hausman because, as a feminist thinker, she is concerned that feminists talk a lot about gender but don't talk much about sex. This book attempts to contribute to a more adequately grounded use of such words as *male* and *female*, *man* and *woman*, by attending both to a careful differentiation of physiology, psychology, and sociology, by trying to recognize and affirm the contribution of each science, and by offering a synthetic integration of these sciences in contrast to any version of essentialism. One important cost of differentiating the sciences is the need to remember with care just what questions can be answered from within a particular science and what questions require the integration of several sciences.

Social construction theory, also called symbolic interaction theory, considers the processes by which people create and revise concepts, expectations, and other social agreements. Symbolic interactionists don't focus on the objective truth value of any socially constructed concepts but rather on the process by which people do their social constructing. If you think clapping your hands will bring Tinker Bell back to life, if you think real men don't eat quiche, your belief is a social fact and has social consequences.

In this book I work with social construction theory a little differently from most symbolic interactionists in that I do not treat social construction as an independent process. I recognize that our bodies put some limits around social constructions and also generate interests or urges that contribute to desires seeking opportunity for expression. I also recognize that bodies give people some of the material around which images and self-concepts are constructed in interaction with culturally based images and expectations. I spent considerable effort in Chapters 2 and 3 to show that physiological and psychological factors serve as a complex, interactive, and flexible grounding for social constructions, though they may be less flexible and complex for some people. I did this work to rebut physiological and psychological essentialists, but also to lay the groundwork for a *qualified social construction theory* made possible by a synthetic integration of the sciences. For example, I can claim to be a woman, but I cannot honestly claim to be a fertile female woman.

When I point out that bodies contribute urges, predispositions, and metaphors that influence our social constructions, I have laid the basis for pointing out that transgender constructions are grounded in our bodies and subjective experience while also claiming the gender freedom that is made visible by social construction theory. Our bodies make possible wide differences in psychological and social development, such as the differences in human languages. Such wide differences of language are nonetheless created within physiological limits and incorporate the urge to communicate. In the last chapter I relate my synthetic development of the sciences to theology when I point out that transgender constructions, like other social constructions, can also incorporate human concerns that arise from awareness of the eternals that we sense but cannot grasp: love, justice, beauty, and truth.

Part of the *interactiveness* of social construction theory with physiological factors points to the social fact that body characteristics have cultural meanings attached to them. For example, many people who understand themselves to be women undergo breast enhancement to more closely match their body images to their gender images, whether they were assigned to be males or females at birth. A common concern of transgender people has to do with whether their mastery of appearance construction will be sufficient to allow "passing." If physiological grounding makes passing easy, it will be easier for such a transgender person to travel a socially visible path.

Formal reasoning on this subject is often traced to *The Social Construction of Reality* by Peter Berger and Thomas Luckmann (1963).[45] Berger and Luckmann explain the creation of cultural symbols, social roles, and social expectations in terms of three concepts. In following this explanation, one might think of the association of the color pink with girls, a social construction that happened about the time of World War I. Previously pink had been associated with boys.[46] The first concept is *externalization,* which draws attention to the fact that once a cultural product is created, it takes on a life of its own. In our example, this would be the beginning of the association of pink with girls. The second concept is *objectification,* which means forgetting. In our example, the culture forgets who first started associating pink with girls, and people just respond to the image without thinking about where it came from. After people have forgotten the source of an image or concept, they becomes carriers of the concept as if it was self-evident or natural. Berger and Luckmann call this last transition *internalization.* After internalization, associating pink with girls was a cultural habit, a habit both exploited and reinforced by manufacturers of baby items. Since not all cultures associate pink with girls, and since our own culture moved to pink about 80 years ago, it is easy to see that the color coding of gender is a cultural construction. The same argument can be made for other features of gender. The Rosie the Riveter image of World War II made it clear that women were able to do heavy factory work that had previously been seen as inappropriate, even impossible, for women.[47]

Another contribution to the concept of social construction comes from Edward Tiryakian. He emphasized that the construction of self-concepts is influenced by the specific location of individuals in time and space, by their physical bodies, and by their spiritual awareness. The integration of these factors into a self-concept is then understood to be expressed by the body and its gestures.[48] Applying this line of thought to transgender experience and expression draws attention to the fact that when transgender people construct their self-concepts, they have to do what other people do: they have to work with their bodies and feelings, their social learning and internalized cultural images, and their spiritual awareness to make sense of their lives. Then they have to try out their self-concepts by making life choices and engaging in social interaction.

When we understand that our pictures of reality are socially constructed, we are prepared to ask deeper questions than "How come people with transgender experience don't just fit in and adjust to the cultural norms?" We can ask questions like "How were our contemporary social norms about gender constructed? What values do they embody? Which cultural symbols have what kind of social meaning, as experienced? What are the inconsistencies, ambiguities, ambivalences in the social construction of the concepts 'man' and 'woman,' or the cultural construction of the concepts 'masculine' and 'feminine?'"

The appearances we present as we enter social relationships are the first cues we offer to others as guidance for interaction. One of the things we are most eager to read in each other is the message of gender. For starters, because the English language is gender influenced, people want to assess gender so that they can construct their conversations accordingly. Furthermore, the estimation of whether one is seen as a man or a woman influences the degree to which a personal appearance is judged to be attractive. At 6 feet 3 inches and 245 pounds, my stature is an advantage when I present as a man and a disadvantage when I present as a woman. When people respond to my image and don't see a woman, it makes it much harder for them to recognize the things in me that make me a woman and that in turn makes it difficult for me to be accepted into social relationships as a woman and that in turn makes it hard for me to gain experience as a woman, experience I need for my further development.

Still, I'm changing. I feel that I am growing in understanding myself as a bigender person. In my earlier decades I mostly suppressed the expression of the aspects of myself that I think of as feminine in terms of appearance cues such as dress and makeup. Even though I'm clearer that it is important to me to claim such appearance cues as an expression of my sense of self, I still have to figure out how and when I want to present myself in a society and culture dominated by bipolar opinions about gender.

My attempts at personal authenticity, as expressed in my appearance, are often not received by others as authentic. In fact, the more believable my presentation, the more the consternation when I am read as having a male physiology while making a feminine presentation of self. It helps a little that I freely concede that I am a bigender person, though that is a meaningless term for most people. On the other hand, in my local congregation, where people have had time to get to know me when I present as a woman, most have worked their way through to treating me with the caring and appreciation I prized before coming out. In short, social reactions to my bigender expression are changing and complex.

Richard Elkins has built the most substantive symbolic interactionist study of transgender phenomena around the issues I have just exemplified. I use the word *built* because Elkins does not do social science in the tradition of testing causal theory. His work can be thought of as the careful development of theories that might be tested. Elkins, based on extensive direct observation as well as the creation and use of an extensive international archive of transgender materials, has sought to provide an ordered understanding of transgender phenomena, using the concept of *ideal types*. An ideal type is not so much the description of an observable social image or pattern that can be counted in various settings as it is the creation of a gestalt (whole) concept that includes many images and patterns. Elkins calls his primary ideal type of transgender expression *male femaling*.[49] Elkins uses the term male femalers to refer to cross-dressers and sex-changers. The several processes by which male femalers cope with the social challenge of gaining acceptance is called masked awareness; and it includes the subprocesses of legitimacy, secrecy, access, and identity.[50] Elkins asserts that male femalers engage in five kinds of masked awareness activities in their efforts to achieve legitimacy, protect their secrets, gain access, and establish an identity as a woman: displaying, disclosing, passing, reading, and pretending.[51]

There are several strengths to Elkins' work which are not found in any other major study. First of all, Elkins followed several key informants over periods as long as 17 years and observed them in a wide variety of social settings. He avoids using clinical language, although he did include consideration of how male femalers, in constructing their identities, responded to clinical language, everyday (lay) language, and language generated by the transgender community.

One of Elkins' most important observations is that male femalers may be significantly differentiated by their degree of concern about issues of body, gender, and sexuality.[52] I think that this particular distinction is overdrawn based on his reports he appealed to for support. Nonetheless, this shortcoming is easily forgiven because Elkins repeatedly makes the point that male femaling is a very fluid process and that individuals move around a lot over the years. I agree with Elkins that his research "showed the proper respect for the ambiguous, ambivalent, multi-contextual, multi-dimensional, emergent nature of much cross-dressing and sex-changing phenomena."[53] Readers who are interested in the nuances and contingencies of constructing a transgender identity and then taking it on the road in a variety of social settings will be well rewarded for the time they give to Elkins' work. His own summary is that "it is the minority who proceed through all the phases of male femaling to a 'consolidated' end state. Most male femalers will circle and cycle all or parts of the phases again and again. They may stop at different points and for different periods, on different occasions."[54]

The variability and fluidity of transgender experience and expression reported by Elkins fit very well with the haystack concepts of complexity and flexibility that I have worked with in this book. It opposes the emphasis of clinical studies on specific disease conditions caused by some specific fault, such as a theorized prenatal hormone failure or a particular pattern of childrearing. Elkins' work counts as strong evidence against clinical theories.

The rigor of his observational methodology, the attention to the everyday settings of transgender people, and its extended time period undergird a piece of research that is strong at all the places where Richard Green's study is weak. Elkins' observations and reporting are every bit as depth oriented as clinical reporting, but Elkins uses neutral and analytic categories for reporting his observations as opposed to assuming pathology and then shaping the clinical reports to defend the assertion of pathology. It is a strength of such symbolic interactionist studies that the researcher constructs his or her categories from within the observation process and thus overcoming the danger of false concretization.[55]

When Elkins does discuss psychiatric perspectives, he makes it clear that clinicians mistakenly interpret cross-dressing or sex-changing as delusional, when the real issue is that many people have been denied access to perspectives that would help them constitute themselves and their gender realities in self-affirming ways, such as the perspectives of the transgender community.[56] Elkins also tells a story of an opposite kind of failing by a clinician who claimed a specialty in working with the transgender community, a clinician who employed a simplistic cookie-cutter analysis of an individual as a transsexual and immediately channeled the person into a preoperative regimen of hormones and gender lessons.[57]

There are, however, several basic problems in Elkins' work. The first is that he dismisses just about every other scientific contribution to the study of transgender phenomena and makes no effort to link his own work to the work of others. Another important limitation is that although one of his core assumptions is that male femalers do what they do in a quest for *meaning* in their lives, he does very little with cultural sources of meaning. In fact, Elkins has almost nothing to say about why males might become interested in male femaling in the first place and settles for working with what male femalers do in response to their interests.

A basic problem for Elkins is that he begins with an unexamined assumption of physiological essentialism to explain transgender desires while giving all his attention to the processes of social construction. He is careful to make the usual distinctions between sex (physiological) and gender (social) but does not take advantage of that distinction in his basic formulations. This is immediately visible in his choice of language to name his primary ideal type: male femaling. He is consistent in using this ideal type to mean social activity although he uses the words of physiology. Furthermore, this unexamined assumption backs him into the assertion that male femalers "coopt" the social world of *females* and their constituent objects.[58] This misses the basic point that his male femalers are trying to enter the *social* world of *women*. Females are the people who usually enter the world of women. When males enter the world of women, they enter it as women, whether their effort is well constructed or poorly constructed. It is a question of empiric fact rather than presupposition whether such an offer to participate in the world of women is accepted. Sometimes it is and sometimes it isn't. Elkins use of the word *coopt* suggests that despite his commitment to symbolic interactionist methodology, he nonetheless views the claims of transgender people as somehow not true in the factual sense or as intrinsically wrong in a values sense. It is just this kind of problem that has led me to emphasize the synthetic integration of the sciences in Chapters 2, 3, and 4, and to assess the values issues in the last chapter.

The reason this last point is so important for an evaluation of Elkins' work derives from his concern about masked awareness. If transgender phenomena are evaluated from a point of view of physiological essentialism, words like *cooptation, pretending* and *deception* will abound in the analysis, and such words are prominent for Elkins. If the same activities are considered in purely social terms, words like *participation, exploration* and *image management* are appropriate. If the issue is whether males should present themselves as women, it is a question of values and deserves to be discussed on that basis. Elkins is on target in emphasizing that transgender people have to cope with potential and actual rejection at some points in their lives. His failing is that he doesn't present this truth as a social contingency for people who are making trans-gender choices but rather as a constituent part of the choice itself. It is an empirical question how much individual transgender people incorporate negative social reactions into a sense of self. Furthermore, those interested in helping transgender people may want to note that a great deal of transgender support group activity is aimed at strengthening self-acceptance so that social reactions will be treated as a contingency rather than as unassailable and disempowering truth. In addition to being one of the keys to claiming indi-vidual psychological health, the point is also central to the politics of transgender people as a stigmatized minority.

Elkins covers a wide range of male femaling activity but makes no mention of two of the most common transgender activities. He doesn't mention partial and hidden cross-dressing such as wearing panties under typical men's pants. Such behavior helps sustain a transgender identity without (usually) exposing one to social sanctions. This highlights the point that the individual cross-dresser is not only an actor but also a critical *audience* to his/her own behavior. It is an actualizing step beyond fantasy, but a protected step. It is a step that claims one's identity in the everyday routines of life, even if it is only a personal claiming.

Neither does Elkins talk about partial cross-dressing or androgynous behavior, such as wearing an earring or developing a unisex hairstyle. It may not be male femaling in Elkins' typology, but it is an important aspect of work-ing with transgender identity for many people, including me. It can be an important step of transgender presentation, even though such presentations are often partially protected by deniability and by the habit of many observers of seeing only the whole—of overlooking specific cues in the interest of simplify-ing interaction to bipolar gender interaction.

## Creating Expectations and Breaking Them

Edwin Lemert applies the idea that our pictures of reality are socially constructed to reassessing the meaning of labels attached to people when they are named as mentally ill. Lemert analyzed 23 cases of people who were committed to mental hospitals with diagnoses that prominently included the clinical label of paranoia. His investigation was based on structured interviews with the families of those who were committed. He found that those who were committed to mental hospitals were people who were generally disliked by their families and others in close social relationships. Within a history of negative interaction between the family and the committed person, Lemert focused on what he called *spurious interaction* with the individual. Simply put, spurious interaction is social interaction that doesn't mean what it says. Some examples are: "patronizing, evasion, humoring, guiding conversations onto selected topics, under reaction, and silence, all calculated either to prevent intense interaction or to protect individual and group values by restricting access to them."[59]

Lemert's genius was to trace the stages of the "deviant's" career. (For Lemert, *deviant* simply meant someone who did not conform to social expectations.) As social relations grew more tense, more active exclusionary conspiracies were developed against the person who was going to be committed to the mental hospital. Lemert discovered misrepresentation and gross misstatements by those in the excluding conspiracy. These lies were believed by the authorities and used to move the individual into psychiatric interviews and preliminary detention. These latter stages are also described by Erving Goffman as a "betrayal funnel."[60] In short, the individual was *accurately* perceiving the processes of social exclusion but was not strong enough to resist the social constructions of the exclusional conspiracies, linked to compliant psychiatrists backed up by the sheriff's office.[61]

An even more sophisticated version of this kind of study is offered by R. D. Laing and Aaron Esterson. They studied 11 young women committed to mental hospitals in England with the label of schizophrenia. This was not a convenience sample but 11 sequential admissions after a starting date. The study focused on the families of the young women and found the same kind of exclusionary dynamics described by Lemert and Goffman. Such exclusionary dynamics can be summarized as scapegoating. They were also able to show from their skillful interviewing, for example, that the girls who claimed to "hear voices," treated by the admitting psychiatrists as "delusions," had in fact heard the voices of the parents saying very ugly things about them from a floor away or through doors, etc. When confronted by the daughters, the parents denied saying such things and told the daughters, and then the psychiatrists, that the daughters were "hearing things."[62]

A fully elaborated analysis of how people are steered into the role of mental illness is offered by John Lofland in his book *Deviance and Identity*.[63] I have defended Lofland's theory with a point-by-point rejection of formal criticisms by summarizing the empirical evidence from studies that tested labeling theory. The summary of my defense was based on 200 sociological studies and applied systems analysis perspectives to trace the multiple paths that people take as they come to accept mental illness labels and sometimes escape from them. In the defense I demonstrate the importance of multiple contingencies, including: behavior, cultural values, social roles, and institutional structures and resources, and show how these contingencies affect the range of outcomes for people who enter the deviance-assigning process.[64] In short, I show that labeling theory is an important theory that lifts up important causes that interact with nonlabeling causes.

The application of labeling theory to the concept of gender and transgender behavior challenges the taken-for-granted idea that social norms are natural or obvious. Asking how gender images and expectations are created and enforced draws our attention to *who* does the defining, and to what *influences and interests* are important to the definer. With such questions in mind, it becomes possible to analyze the formal and informal mechanisms of social control that enforce norms and defend images. This kind of thinking is at the heart, for example, of feminist attacks on patriarchy. In Chapter 7, labeling theory will be further discussed to show the damage done to transgender people when pathological language is used for the purposes of social control even though the surface purpose is just to "explain" transgender experience and expression. At this point, the key implication is that many of the challenges transgender people encounter do not flow from physiological or psychological abnormalities but from the difficulties of claiming and negotiating a transgender status in interaction with a culture committed to a bipolar understanding of sex and gender. This is not merely a problem of interpersonal communication; it is also a process of challenging and negotiating with others who have the support of bipolar language, control of official identity credentials, control of clinical and legal institutions, and control of science and the media.

For transgender people, the construction of self-concepts and gaining access to social relationships is no neutral maturation process. Success requires learning how to defend against stigmatizing attributions and alienating coalitions. For many it has meant learning to cope with job loss, divorce, loss of family connections, and loss of friends. In Chapter 7 we see that for some it has meant the most horrible kinds of physical and psychological abuse and oppression by official institutions acting within the law. Faced with such challenges, it isn't surprising that some transgender people have emotional and intellectual difficulties in accepting themselves and in showing themselves to others. This is a final major argument against pathological clinical assessments such as gender identity disorder and gender dysphoria. Unhappiness, anger, and confusion are not indications of mental disease. Such feelings and thoughts are reasonable as the psychological concomitants of social difficulties in showing and claiming a personal truth that many others find distasteful, of coping with official and unofficial sanctions, of working against lies, wilful misunderstanding, whispering campaigns, and hidden coalitions. Fearfulness is not a sign of paranoia but an awareness of social contingencies.

Taking social constructionist thinking in a different direction, Leslie Feinberg reviews a broad sweep of history and culture to show that many cultures have affirmed transgender experience and expression. Some cultures have given honored roles to transgender people. One of Feinberg's favorite examples is the "two-spirit" people found in many Native American tribes. She argues that the hostility of colonial oppressors to the transgender people they met was "used to justify further genocide, the theft of Native land and resources, and destruction of their culture and religions."[65] In addition to detailing the oppression of transgender people, Feinberg has done foundational work to help transgender people discover that they have a history. Dallas Denny offers a more compact summary of transgender roles across culture and history.[66]

## Choosing Partners for Sexual Sharing

I have been treating the choice of sexual partner as just one aspect of gender-related behavior. Although this is a defensible scientific approach, I'm well aware that the words *gay*, *lesbian* and *bisexual* are more known than the word *transgender*. Gay and lesbian organizations engage a lot more people than do transgender organizations.[67] I'm also aware that although there have been some cooperation, there has also been significant political and interpersonal stresses between transgender people and other sexual minorities. And I'm also aware that there are serious writings by gay, lesbian, and bisexual authors who organize some of the material I've been dealing with quite differently. However, I'm going to leave it to others to compare this book to their work.

The choice of sexual partner, or the choice to be celibate, is a simple concept compared to transgender behavior because transgender behavior includes not only sexual expression but many other activities. Nonetheless, I've shown in previous sections of this chapter that the patterns of choosing sexual partners is not simple for many gay, lesbian, and bisexual people. Such complexities expand geometrically when one considers not merely anatomical pairing but also gender-based pairing.

Dallas Denny and Jamison Green have written a chapter on gender identity and bisexuality in the book, *Bisexuality*, published in 1996.[68] They write, "Any discussion of transsexual sexuality is bound to be very confusing and, we would argue, ultimately very instructive about the nature of sexuality in general and especially bisexuality. Should homosexuality be considered in relation to the individual's natal sex or in relation to their new role? Is a transsexual woman who is still fulfilling the role of husband in a marriage in a lesbian relationship? Certainly it does not seem so to the world, which sees a heterosexual relationship. Yet 5 years later, when the individual has transitioned into the woman's role, the same couple, if publicly affectionate, will be perceived as lesbian. What of a posttransition nonoperative transsexual woman in a sexual relationship with a male? The public sees a heterosexual couple, yet in the bedroom, their genitals match. Should their sexual act be considered heterosexual or homosexual? Does it matter if the feminized partner does or does not take the active role in intercourse? And what if the same individual then has surgery and finds a female partner? Is this relationship homosexual or heterosexual? Finally, what if a nonoperative transsexual man has as a partner a postoperative transsexual man? Is this a gay relationship? A straight one? Are any of these people bisexual? And most significantly, can the term *bisexuality* have any meaning at all when gender is deconstructed?"[69] Denny and Green further compound the complexity by noting the difference between transsexuals, who typically make a lasting transition from one gender identity to another, and other kinds of transgender people who move back and forth between genders.

Denny and Green dig themselves out of this conceptual pit by appealing to social construction theories of the kind discussed earlier in this chapter. They argue that, "For transsexual people at least and perhaps for everyone, it may make more sense to describe relationships as homogenderal or heterogenderal.[70]

In addition to making a contribution to sorting out the language, Denny and Green offer the following substantive summary: "Despite the heterosexist and clinical bias in much of the literature, the balance of the literature and our respective personal experiences suggest that there is a great deal of bisexuality among transsexual persons."[71] They note that this reality does not fit well with the establishment clinical picture of transsexuals. Indeed, it confounds the early justification for sexual reconstructive surgery phrased as "freeing a woman trapped in a man's body," which included the normative assumption that a woman is a heterosexual woman.

Denny and Green end up with an understanding that is similar to the emphasis of this book on complexity, interactiveness, and flexibility. "Like bisexuals who challenge the norm of monosexual orientations, the highly varied transgendered, intersexed, and transsexual people who embody the concepts of fluid, changeable, or contraphysical gender identity also break down a rigid binary system that has been used for centuries to control society."[72]

### Summary

In these three scientific chapters I have not only shown that no evidence in support of clinical theories is based on well-done scientific research; I have also shown that there are important scientific findings that oppose clinical theories. Most importantly, I have shown that a synthetic reconsideration of available scientific work points to a complex, interactive, and flexible grounding for transgender behavior that fits with the complexity and variability of transgender experience and expression.

Although I attempt my own contribution to transgender theory in Chapter 6, the remaining chapters are based not so much on the adequacy of my personal theorizing as on the synthetic integration of the work of others in these three chapters.

---

**Notes:**

1. Carl G. Jung, (1957/1997).
2. William Shakespeare, *As You Like It*, Act II, Scene VII.
3. Marvin Harris (1985), page 507.
4. Ibid.
5. Roger Horrocks (1997).
6. Anke Ehrhardt (1997), pages 361-362.
7. David Carlisle (1998), page i.
8. Ibid., page 384.
9. Janice Irvine (1990), page 267.
10. Robert Michael (1994).
11. E. O. Laumann (1994).
12. Robert Michael (1994), pages 11-12.
13. Ibid., page 25.
14. Ibid., pages 35, 174-175.
15. Ibid., pages 35, 175-176.
16. Alfred Kinsey, et al. (1948 and 1953).
17. Judith Reisman and Edward Eichel (1990), pages 17, 21.
18. Alfred Kinsey (1948), pages 623, 650.
19. Ibid., page 610.
20. Robert Michael (1994), page 173.
21. Ibid., pages 61 and 62.
22. Alfred Kinsey (1948), pages 623 and 650.
23. Ronald Fox (1996), pages 9-17.
24. Richard F. Docter (1988, 1997).
25. Richard F. Docter and Virginia Prince (1997), page 589.
26. Richard F. Docter (1988), page 142.
27. Richard F. Docter and Virginia Prince (1997), page 594.
28. Ibid., page 594.
29. Ibid., pages 595-596.
30. Vern and Bonnie Bullough (1993), pages 292-296.
31. John Talamini (1982), pages 19-22.
32. Ibid., pages 30-34.
33. The Diagnostic and Statistical Manual (DSM) of the American Psychiatric Association has significantly changed the definition of gender identity disorder. This issue is discussed at length in Chapter 7. At this point I point out that the survey research on visible transgender people does not support any of the DSM definitions.
34. Transphobia means fear or strong dislike of transgender people.
35. Holly Devor (1997).
36. Female-To-Male International, 1360 Mission St., Suite 200, San Francisco, CA 94103; web site, www.ftm-intl.org.

37. Holly Devor (1997), page 38.
38. Ibid., page 38.
39. Ibid., pages 43-44.
40. Ibid., page 582.
41. Anne Bolin (1996), pages 447-485.
42. Ibid., page 449.
43. Lavender Linguistics Conference, American University, 1998.
44. Bernice Hausman (1995), page vii.
45. Peter Berger and Thomas Luckmann (1963).
46. Marjorie Garber (1992).
47. Of course many women around the world and in the United States had been doing heavy labor. Though framed in sex or gender terms, Rosie the Riveter can just as well be analyzed in terms of access to economic opportunity and privilege.
48. Edward Tiryakian (1968), page 79.
49. Richard Elkins (1997), page 2.
50. Ibid., page 49.
51. Ibid., pages 48-49.
52. Ibid., page 54.
53. Ibid., page 2.
54. Ibid., page 6.
55. The resulting weakness is the difficulty of replicating such a study, or of generalizing from one study to another, with the result that it is difficult to build a coherent group of studies based on the work of multiple observers.
56. Richard Elkins (1997), pages 109-113.
57. Ibid., pages 116-117.
58. Ibid., page 34.
59. Edwin Lemert (1972), page 253.
60. Erving Goffman (1959), page 127.
61. Edwin Lemert (1972), pages 246-264.
62. R. D. Laing and Aaron Esterson (1964).
63. John Lofland (1969).
64. Patrick Conover (1971).
65. Leslie Feinberg (1996), page 22.
66. Dallas Denny (1997).
67. The National Gay and Lesbian Task Force and GenderPAC are organizations with members who are gay, lesbian, bisexual, or transgender.
68. Beth A. Firestein (1996), pages 84-102.
69. Dallas Denny and Jamison Green (1996), pages 88-89.
70. Ibid., page 90.
71. Ibid., page 92.
72. Ibid., page 95.

*My eyes already touch the sunny hill,*
*going far ahead of the road I have begun.*
*So we are grasped by what we cannot grasp;*
*it has its inner light, even from a distance –*
*and changes us, even if we do not reach it,*
*into something else, which, hardly sensing it, we already are;*
*a gesture waves us on, answering our own wave... .*
*But what we feel is the wind in our faces.* R. M. Rilke[1]

*The hardest years in life are those between ten and seventy.*

Helen Hayes *(at age 73)*

# Chapter 5:
# Images of Transgender People

The "We Exist" section of the first chapter summarizes the many ways in which people experience and express transgender roles. Chapters 2-4 review physiological, psychological, and sociological explanations of transgender experience and expression and point to complex, interactive, and flexible causes of diverse transgender paths and patterns. This chapter illustrates some of the diversity.

Establishment clinicians often simplify and stigmatize transgender experience and expression by focusing on sexual experience and expression, with the assumption that some kind of dysfunction of sexual expression is the driving force of pathological development. Sexual expression is an important subject, but it does not define transgender experience and expression. Consider, for example, the research question "When did you first masturbate and what were your fantasies?" For myself, when I was young and masturbation was an important part of my sexual experience, I was also working away at developing a career line and figuring out how to cope with the demands of a gender-influenced work world. I was thinking about the oppression of women, and I was committed to learning the household skills and following the homemaking "instincts" that were supposed to be beyond my interests as a man. I married at 20, and my sexual interests became focused on my relationship with my wife. Pat Califia notes that the famous Christine Jorgenson complained in her autobiography that "What I slept in, apparently, was considered more important than what I believed in."[2]

At 20 years old I had finished high school in 3 years, playing varsity basketball and baseball along the way; finished college in 6 semesters; and completed

6 months of active duty in the army. I gave my focal energy to attending Chicago Theological Seminary. I wanted to take time for the questions of values that had been unaddressed while I gained my B.S. in psychology. One of the interesting things I learned while attending seminary is that, if you choose to remember that you are in the sight of God while you masturbate, it can create some useful growth questions. Better yet, I learned from Paul Tillich that several things that initially seem incompatible can be true at the same time. During an internship at Elgin State Mental Hospital as an apprentice chaplain, I saw what hell can look like—how much damage is done to people in the name of pursuing mental health.

My Master of Divinity thesis gave me the opportunity to analyze several families of psychological thought in terms of their philosophical underpinnings. I used a typology developed by Richard McKeon, then chair of the Department of Philosophy at the University of Chicago. In addition to reading everything by Sigmund Freud that was translated into English, I also read extensively in Jung, Watson, Sullivan, Horney, and Fromm. From behaviorism to existentialism, I was interested in how psychologists shaped their questions and world views. I concluded my thesis with a constructive chapter that might be thought of as a psychology that Tillich could have written. I began to prepare the questions that, among other things, have guided this book.

This chapter, in addition to the above brief sharing of my story, offers several stories that may help to correct sensationalized or stereotyped mass media images and clinical distortions. For people interested in stories that detail the depth and perversity of the clinical oppression of transgender people, I recommend Daphne Scholinski's *The Last Time I Wore a Dress* and Leslie Feinberg's novel *Stone Butch Blues*.

My own story is about growing up as a boy but learning to value things carried in our culture by women. Most of the stories in this chapter repeat a man-to-woman story line. Furthermore, most of the research discussed in this book focuses on man-to-woman transgender experience and expression. I don't know as much about woman-to-man paths, and this book reflects that deficit. One good way for a reader to gain a better-balanced understanding is to read Holly Devor's 1997 book *FTM: Female-to-Male Transsexuals in Society*. Although it is easy to get the impression that there are many more man-to-woman transgender people, we don't have strong comparative data, particularly when the discussion turns to transgender people who are not transsexuals. It would be hard to create a good study, in part because there is currently greater expressive freedom in appearance for women, compared to traditional appearance norms, than for men. (Women can wear pants, but men can't wear dresses.) For what it's worth, at least one review of the records of those who present themselves for transsexual surgery shows an equal number of male and female applicants.[3] I also want to remind myself and my readers that it is probably not a good idea to think of the woman-to-man experience as a mirror image of the man-to-woman experience.

In addition to the stories below, there are two great story collections available to readers: *Trans Forming Families,* edited by Mary Boenke, and *Out of the Ordinary,* edited by Noelle Howey and Ellen Samuels.

## Stories

### Jeanne

She climbs the stairs of the Queen Mary slowly. Attending the transgender convention was as hard physically as it was financially. Jeanne looks like she doesn't have the financial resources of the more elegant convention goers. But this convention is important for Jeanne. At her age she has outlived a lot of her friends and family. It's hard to find space just to feel at ease.

We talked for awhile. Looking back, I'm feeling cheated that I moved on more quickly than I needed to. Jeanne wasn't going to have her picture taken by the professional photographers and news people that were working the crowd, but her picture is precious just the same.

Jeanne lives by herself in an apartment. When she goes out the door, she presents her masculine appearance. Her only friend lives in the same apartment building – a single mother with one child. Jeanne has become not only a friend but also a source of child care, and both the mother and the child matter to her.

Jeanne would like to tell the mother about her cross-dressing. The mother is the only adult who has real conversations with Jeanne. She had been working up her courage to share this side of her story when they happened to see some cross-dressers on one of the television talk shows. The mother was not pleased. So Jeanne is keeping her story to herself, wondering what fib she will tell if she is asked where she has been over the weekend.

### Delia

Until recently, Delia was a senior officer in the air force. She is used to the discipline of defined ranks and expects a response when she gives an order. Perhaps it should not be so surprising, in a town with a lot of military personnel, that a significant percentage of the participants in the local support group are military people. It makes for a well-ordered security process to find the group and gain admission.

Since I know Delia only on the first Saturdays that are meeting nights, I find it a little hard to imagine her in a military setting. She has the mouth for it, that's for sure. But she is flat-out good-looking, and when she sings a love song on our amateur night, it is easy to be stirred.

Being transgender has cost Delia a lot. The child custody case cost her her military career. Her ex-wife profited mightily from the lost career because now she gets a share of the military pension. Though Delia kept her feminine presentations out of the house, that didn't help much legally. Being transgender is not illegal in most localities, but there are few limits on persons or institutions that discriminate against transgender people.

Keep on singing, Delia. I'm so glad you've found a partner who loves everything you show the world.

*Shelley*

Shelley shared the following story in a transgender support group newsletter.[4]

> It was about 11 pm when I took an exit off of Interstate 10 just outside of Las Cruces, New Mexico. I went north on a gravel road leading seemingly to nowhere. After about a half-mile, the road appeared to end, so I pulled to the side of the road, stopped and turned off the engine and headlights. After my eyes adjusted a bit, through the pale moonlight against a crystal clear night, it appeared that there was no one, nothing in the area.
>
> In the darkness of night, I began to change my clothes in the car. Off with the jeans and shirt and on with the panties, nylons, dress and pumps. I parted my nape-of-the-neck length hair down the middle of my head and brushed it out a bit. It was not as long as I wished. I looked in the mirror at my clean-shaven face and put on my red lipstick, the only makeup with which I had any experience.
>
> Nervously, I stepped out of my car. I had on a cream and lavender narrow-striped ribbed rayon/cotton dress, above knee length, and black pumps. I locked the car door and began walking into the desert—as the woman I was dreaming to be—feeling a bit nervous, but very, very free.
>
> I walked down a small hill and, after a few minutes, my 22-year-old eyes had adjusted to the moonlight. I looked back and eyed my car parked on the road at the top of the hill. I realized that I was walking in a depressed area of the desert encircled by the road above.
>
> I was almost in the middle of the area when I saw the lights of an approaching vehicle above on the road. My heart started pounding and I ducked behind a small mesquite bush. I watched as the vehicle stopped and a person got out and pointed a flashlight into the interior of my car. After a few minutes, the person got back in the vehicle, turned on a bright spotlight attached to the side of the car, pointed it into the area in which I was hiding and began driving around the circular road.
>
> The mesquite bush provided little cover—I was panicked! After all, this was 1972, I was in rural New Mexico near the Mexican border and I had rarely ever gone out dressed, much less ever encountered anyone while dressed. I began to run toward the far

side of the depression where there were larger bushes. By the time I reached these larger bushes, the police car had circled to a point just above on the road. The spotlight shone directly on me as I ran and then ducked to the ground.

The police car stopped and two policemen got out and pointed their flashlights in my general area. My pulse was racing, my mouth was dirt-dry and I was gasping for air as I hugged the dirt behind a large clump of mesquite bushes. They began to descend into the area in which I was hiding and a thousand fears raced through my mind.

Suddenly, they turned around, raced back to their vehicle and sped off.

. . . Surely they took down the license number of my car. Surely they are going to come for me. . .

. . . I went through another purge. I made sure there would not be any evidence, just in case.

. . . I was sure I would never crossdress again.

Recently Shelley had a successful yard sale as part of getting ready to move in with the special woman in her life. A lot of work has gone into building this relationship, and that strength spills over into the community. They've been trying to teach me to line dance, but I don't seem as nimble as my memory says I once was.

*Bubbles*[5]

When Bubbles graduated from junior high school, there was no way she was going to wear a suit and tie. She was going to dress like she always dressed for school, in women's clothes. I cross-dressed all school year – why skip back to male clothes? That's not me," Bubbles insisted, and thus gave her principal, Mr. Hasty, a major headache. Now Ronald Hasty may be a tolerant man, but what would other parents think if they saw Bubbles in drag, bidding farewell to her fellow ninth-graders. Certainly Bubbles, at 16, had every right to be gay, but did she also have the right to be publicly flamboyant?

Bubbles secured a civil rights attorney, and the principal and the D.C. school system relented.

Now consider what a black kid, 6 feet 2, about 240 pounds, who cross-dresses and calls herself Bubbles is up against as she enters high school next week. Yet she intends to cross dress. Like other kids awaiting the delayed opening of D.C.'s schools, she's been shopping – for blouses, jeans, shoes, costume jewelry. She's had her hair and nails done. Says Bubbles:"People are going to accept you or they are going to reject you. You have to be your own person."

Since age 12, Bubbles has lived with Marion Alston, her foster mother, whom she calls "Grandma." Bubbles was different, she knew that from Day One.

Her feminine mannerisms, her desire to wear girls clothes. But, says Alston, "I wasn't going to turn her out from my home because of that. He was a 12-year-old child who needed just as much love as any child."

Her foster child made good grades, sang in the choir, distinguished herself as a cheerleader. She paid for Bubbles's graduation day hair extension because she was so pleased with her success in junior high. She helps her pick out the clothing and patterns that will most flatter her linebacker-like form, and imparts other mother-daughter advice:

"I tell him to portray himself as a lady, not anything else. No loud perfume, no obnoxious lipstick—soft nice colors."

### Zachariah Tourgate[6]

Since October, 8-year-old Zachariah Tourgate has been banished to a dimly lighted, 10-by-13-foot room apart from other classrooms. He is isolated from his third-grade schoolmates during class time and forbidden to join them at recess or in the school cafeteria for lunch.

Zachariah has been placed in an "alternative learning situation," as school authorities call it, because the skinny 9-inch ponytail that he refuses to cut violates a school dress code adopted last summer.

Zachariah has had the "rattail" haircut for all of his 3 years in the public schools of Bastrop, a town of 5,700 people about 30 miles southeast of Austin, Texas. Last September, however, his mother said school officials told her that Zachariah's hairstyle no longer met regulations.

A neighbor said the Tourgates, who also have a daughter, Linzi, 5, are not "flaky parents" using their son for publicity or to make a point. "They are simple, down-to-earth people who have a straightforward way of seeing right or wrong."

### Barbara

It took Barbara a long time to claim what she now calls her "gender blessing." As David, she pursued traditional masculine careers as a Roman Catholic seminarian and as an air force pilot before settling into a long and successful career in public relations. She married and raised three wonderful children. There was no room for Barbara in her marriage or her church, so Barbara was kept deep in her closet. With the children grown, when it was time for retirement, Barbara came out. Though her wife knew about the transgender potential of her husband, when she was asked to relate to Barbara, she quickly moved for separation. Barbara has not disowned her personal history as David and has not turned her back on the values that shaped her life; but she has claimed her deepest sense of self and has found new friends in a new church home—friends and pastors who have supported her journey. Vigorous in her sixties, she is sharing her variety of gifts in volunteer activities.[7]

*Vikki*[8]

MARTHA: (Immediately sensing my problem) You are worried about what other people think about you! Here, let me show you how to find out how others see you.

She took my by the hand and brought me to stand directly in front of Pam.

MARTHA: Now look into Pam's eyes.

I was met immediately with smiling, kindly eyes that stared back at me, full of openness, love and acceptance. I knew immediately that she not only liked me, but was concerned about my feelings, understood how I felt, and was there to support me. I felt the tears well up.

*Jewelia Margueritta Cameroon*

The following is from a letter she wrote to Vice President Al Gore upon the occasion of receiving a Hammer Award for developing computer software in the Occupational Safety and Health Administration.[9]

I am writing in advance to say thank you," Cameroon said in a March 17, 1997, letter to Gore,

> . . . and say that receiving your prestigious award is particularly important for me because it affirms that I, a transgendered (transsexual) woman, am regarded by you as a valuable person.
>
> I am sending copies of the letter to The Post and other papers to advise others in advance of my preference to be regarded, treated, and referred to as the woman, Jewelia Margueritta Cameroon. (I was Richard Green when I wrote the key computer program.) I am in the process of changing my legal name to Jewelia Margueritta Cameroon and my legal gender to female.

Cameroon, a former Navy nuclear submariner for 12 years, when she was a he, said she could "understand how your staff might be wary of allowing America to see an image of you or Ms. Gore touching me. . . ."

*Emily Poher*

The kids in her chemistry class called her Emilio, because they said she wanted to be a boy. They told jokes about her, too. About how she is a lesbian. And everyone would snicker. But it wasn't the name-calling and the laughter that hurt her the most. It was the fact that her teacher heard the comments and didn't intervene.

"The teacher didn't do anything," says Emily Poher, a 16-year-old junior at Annapolis Senior High School. "It got so bad, I had to leave the class. I had to switch. If teachers hear that stuff, they should stop it."[10]

Interestingly, although the title of this article in the *Washington Post* was "Handling Teens' Homosexuality," the lead sentence is a projection about wanting to be a boy and using a boy's name in a derogatory manner.

# Transgender Good News

*Ethel*

Ethel grew up in a Holiness home. Her conservative Christian parents, the rest of her family, and her local congregation couldn't stand her interest in feminine things and wanting to dress in girls' clothes. They beat her. They forced her to pray in a corner on her knees for hours at a time. She learned to speak in tongues and release some of her stress. This pleased her parents, who thought she was saved. But she kept on cross-dressing.

At 14, Ethel was thrown out of the house to live on the street. She learned to provide sexual favors to men to survive. She lived full-time as a woman without any of the support groups of transgender organizations. As a sex worker it didn't take her long to become HIV positive, to develop a drug habit, to go to jail.

In addition to learning how to survive, Ethel continued to care about her family. When her mother developed terminal cancer, Ethel started going home to help care for her mom. She filled a hole that her brothers and father couldn't handle. Her mother had trouble accepting Ethel, but she finally came around to embracing her child. She began to write notes to her husband, encouraging him to look out for Ethel when she was gone. Ethel figured hell would freeze over first.

Ethel went to her mother's funeral. Her grandparents took her out behind the funeral home and whipped her. But she had seen her father at the funeral. They began to rebuild a relationship. Ethel began to develop other sources of income and became an antidrug and anti-AIDS counselor. Her father approved of her good works among people he regarded as the worst of sinners and wrote Ethel into his will as the sole inheritor. Shortly thereafter he had a sudden illness and died. Ethel is out of jail again. She's found a church that can love all of
her. She's fully employed and loves to speak about transgender issues and the redemptive power of love.

*Roberta*

At 82, Robert discovered that he had prostate cancer and that the recommended treatment was female hormones at a level that would produce feminizing side effects.

"Robert left his doctor's office unable to speak. He was thunderstruck. Gasping for air, he sat on a curb and tried to collect himself. Slowly he made his way home, incanting a mantra that stripped his cocoon of denial by its poetic reverberation in his mind—'womanhood.' The doctor's admonition about hormones had been a revelation. For Robert, rather than being horrified at the prospect of developing secondary female sex characteristics, was delighted. For 2 weeks he could think of little else. It was as if some quilter came along, in the

108

winter of his life, to piece together the scraps and fragments, the episodes and decades, and reconfigure them into a recognizable patchwork: womanhood."[11]

Later, in a letter to his therapist on the path to sexual reconstructive surgery, he wrote, "Due to my exceptional vitality, energy, interest in and zest for life I often ask myself these questions: 1.) Is there a connection between the almost incredible condition of my body and mind and that at my age equally incredible, intense transsexual desire? And 2.) Could an unusual condition in my body explain these two equally incredible conditions, like for example, some female gland?"[12]

*Tonye Baretto Neto*

He wears a shiny badge and carries a loaded gun because he is a cop, a transsexual cop. When he volunteered to go on a fact-finding trip to Falls City, Nebraska, concerning the murder of Teena Brandon, he was appalled to find out that the local sheriff had not only failed to arrest the murderers but told Tonye, in essence, that Brandon had "asked for it" by being transgendered. After Teena Brandon was raped, the sheriff provided the *Falls City Journal* with a copy of Brandon's rape complaint. Brandon was stabbed to death by John Lorrer and Marvin Nissen shortly thereafter.

Tonye's distress joined with the outrage of Riki Ann Wilchins, and they created the organization Transgender Officers Protect and Serve (TOPS). They reached out through the Internet, a pathway that provides a lot of security. Now TOPS has 100 members and is taking on its share of the work of supporting transgender officers and educating various police forces about transgender realities.[13]

---

Notes:

1. R. M. Rilke, "A Walk" (1924).
2. Pat Califia (1997), page 25, quoting from Christine Jorgenson (1967), page xvi.
3. Amy Bloom (1994), page 38; refers to Roberto Laura (1983).
4. *Pinnacle* (1997). This is the newsletter of the Transgender Education Association (TGEA), a support group in the Washington, DC, metropolitan area.
5. Richard Leiby (1994). This story quotes extensively from the *Washington Post* article. Pronouns and the way Leiby names her have been corrected to honor Bubbles' gender identity.
6. Elizabeth Hudson (1991). This story quotes extensively from a *Washington Post* article.
7. Barbara Satin (1998). She told her story at the annual meeting of the United Church of Christ Coalition for Gay, Lesbian, Bisexual and Transgender Concerns.
8. Reference lost (1997).
9. Al Kamen (1997).

10. Inara Verzemnieks (1996).
11. Randi Ettner (1996), page 45.
12. Ibid., page 47.
13. R. Scott Gerdes (1996).

## Photos

Mariette Pathy Allen, who provided the photographs for this book, is an award-winning photographer of the transgender community. Her works includes numerous photographs for the cover of *Transgender Tapestry* magazine.

**Roxy Hart**
Roxy is an aspiring female impersonator with a passion for Marilyn Monroe.

**April and Laura**
April and Laura are enjoying their second marriage.

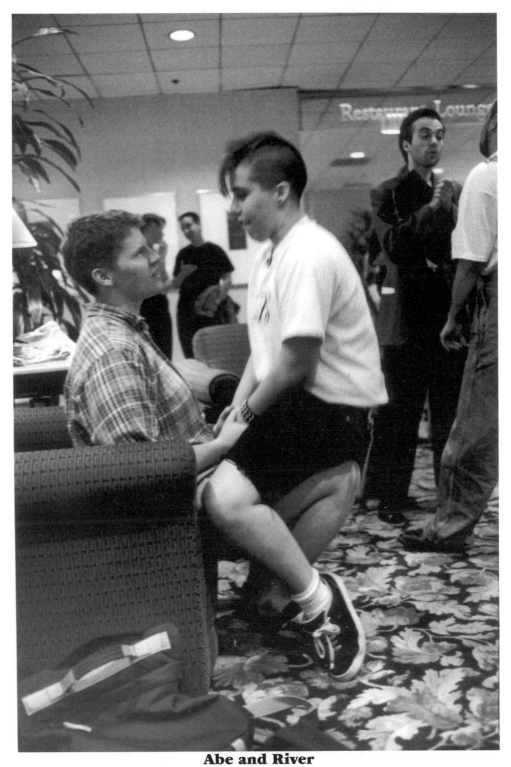

**Abe and River**
Getting to know each other at a True Spirit conference.

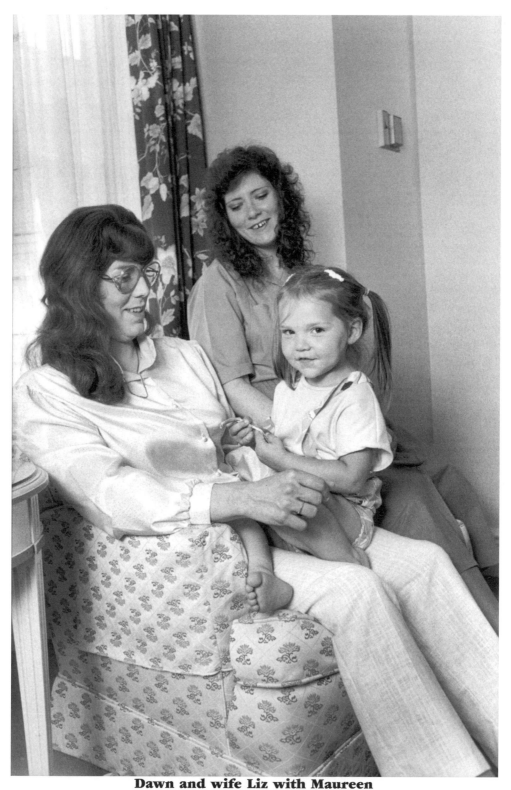

**Dawn and wife Liz with Maureen**

When Maureen sees Don starting to get dressed, she says, "Daddy is going to make himself pretty now."

**Doris and her husband Carol**
Carol is the Executive Director of TRI-ESS, the Society for the Second Self.

**Paula**
An androgynous gay male who loves to dress up.

**Dan Cook Riley**
Dan married Yvonne after they met at a transgender convention.

**Sky and Jamison**
Two transgender men with different sexual orientations.

**Wigstock**
Having fun at the annual New York City festival of drag and music.

**Tori and her nephew**
Voted Prom King in his high school as a Junior and voted Prom Queen in her high school as a Senior.

**Terry**
Attended a university as a man and an all-women nursing school as a woman at
the same time.

**At the Capitol**
Gathered for the annual Lobby Day in 1995.

*They're selling postcards of the hanging.*
*They're painting the passports brown.*
*The beauty parlor is filled with sailors.*
*The circus is in town.*
*Here comes the blind commissioner,*
*They've got him in a trance,*
*One hand is tied to the tightrope walker,*
*The other is in his pants,*
*And the Riot Squad is restless,*
*They need someplace to go,*
*As lady and I look out tonight from Desolation Row.* Bob Dylan[1]

*Choose life, only that and at whatever risk. To let life leak out, to let it wear*
*away by the mere passage of time, to withhold giving it and spending it, is to*
*choose nothing.* Anonymous

*If you can't be a good example, then you'll just have to be a horrible*
*warning.*Catherine Aird[2]

# Chapter 6:
# Understanding Transgender
# Experience and Expression

In this chapter I offer my own contribution to transgender theory as a contribution to future research, to help transgender people work with their life
experiences, and to encourage other readers to understand transgender experience and expression using nontechnical language. Although I believe that the
strength of this book arises from reviews of the work of other writers, I hope
this is a constructive contribution. Up to this point, I have spent considerable
energy to point out the complexity, interactiveness, and flexibility of the physiological and psychological grounding for transgender experience and
expression and have argued for similar complexity, interactiveness, and flexibility in the emergence and development of transgender experience and
expression as social realities. Now it seems only fair that I offer a few naviga-
tional aids to help sort things out a bit. These contributions arise from my own
subjectivity, from my experience with the transgender community, from reading
material generated by the transgender community, from my participation in
transgender activities and conferences, and from consideration of the research
reviewed in earlier sections.

## Theoretical Context

I introduced social construction theory toward the end of the fourth chapter. This chapter works with a qualified version of social construction theory, which considers the contribution of physiological and psychological factors to the material that is gathered into social constructions. My theorizing is focused at the social level because gender is a social fact, a collectively generated, maintained, and changing set of images and expectations relevant to people defined as males and females, boys and girls, women and men. Physiological and psychological realities contribute feelings, limits and constraints, and material for imagery. In the fourth chapter I considered Richard Elkins' summary of transgender patterns, organized by a typology based on the concept of stages of development. I've also profited from the work of Dianna Cicotello who has offered helpful workshops with a six-stage approach to transgender development, but has not yet put her work into print.

In this current chapter I have chosen to work with the simpler idea that there are *contingencies* to be faced in all social settings and that people respond to contingencies with varying self-awareness and varying images and goals. My sense of the complexity, interactiveness, and flexibility of transgender phenomena suggests to me that stage thinking may be more distracting than helpful. Part of this sense of transgender phenomena comes from my interest in all aspects of gender, not only the issues of appearance and sexuality that are so often the focus of conversation in both transgender and scientific circles. I am as interested in men who break the norms of nurturing behavior as I am in men who wear earrings.

Stage thinking can be helpful in calling attention to developmental challenges, and this is important for transgender people who are trying to increase self-understanding and who have to make difficult life choices. However, the very attractiveness of stage thinking is also its danger. Even when one is forewarned, it is tempting to falsely concretize the stages and set oneself a new set of expectations or scripts. One way to break free from developmental theory is to ask oneself the question, "I wonder what it would be like to grow up as a transgender person in an affirming society and culture?" The cross-cultural and historical studies provided by authors like Leslie Feinberg, Gary Kates, Sabrina Ramet, Dallas Denny, and Walter Williams remind us that many kinds of transgender roles and paths are possible.

Sometimes people talk about gender as if it were an aspect of self. At other times, gender is discussed as a role. This differentiation of the context of gender discussions is important, because people usually think of self-concepts as unitary and enduring and of social roles as multiple and changing. I am always Pat, but I have started and stopped being a blackberry farmer. I think of gender as an in-between concept that some call a master role. A master role is a continuous aspect of the self, but it is only one aspect, and it can change.

A person's sense of self (feeling of identity) may be more or less tightly linked to a role. It might seem very important to be a blackberry farmer or not very important at all. It is an empirical question how important particular roles are to a person, how much a role identity is an anchor or base for self-identity. Some people are very much identified with their work roles; others move among work roles easily. Some people feel as if they have lost their identity when they retire; others move along easily to new activities, with a strong sense of continuity and meaning. Although I have not seen survey evidence on this subject, I think the same is true for the master role of gender. Being a man or a woman is very important to some people and not so important to others. Furthermore, being a man or a woman may have stronger social implications in some countries than others. Women in Afghanistan, especially during the rule of the Taliban, work out their roles and sense of self facing dramatically different contingencies than women in the United States. Similarly, the sanctions for transgender expression are far more severe in some countries than in others. Again, my point is that people have to take account of physiological, psychological, and social factors as they construct their gender understanding and expressions. The social construction of gender does not begin with a clean slate.

Gary Kates has written a fascinating biography of the Chevalier(e) d'Eon de Beaumont, a substantial player in the 18th century court of the French king Louis XV. The Chevalier(e) chose to live as a woman and had a successful career in the courts of Europe. As part of his analysis of de Beaumont, Kates challenges the notion that the linkage of a sense of self to a master gender role is automatic in all cultures. He writes, "Before the nineteenth century, educated people had not yet decided that sexual identity was necessarily a key component of human personality. While there may have been homosexual subcultures, for example, few people thought in terms of straight or gay personalities. . . . But such proclivities were regarded as matters of taste and interest. . . not as profound representations of some fundamental feature of the human personality."[3]

Diverse mixes of physiological, psychological, and social factors may influence people to have subjective feelings of gender incongruity. Transgender people offer diverse stories of the first awareness of a lack of fit between their assigned gender and their interests or feelings. Not uncommonly, such feelings and interests include fear or confusion. Confusion is certainly understandable, since the core idea that gender is open to construction and reconstruction feels alien or impossible to many people in a society and culture with strong bipolar images and concepts of gender. It's easier for most people to reconsider being a left tackle or a mid-wife than to reconsider being a man or a woman. Just bringing up the subject for discussion may cause strong negative sanctions, so fear is hardly surprising. When people are uncomfortable with subjective experiences of gender incongruity, they may do some or all of the following things.

*Psychological and Social Options*

One may *deny* the awareness, the feeling, or even the event. Subjective awareness of gender incongruity may be partial and fleeting rather than totally present. The more partial and fleeting the subjective awareness, the easier it is to avoid or deny. To keep from giving a clinical context to the concept of denial, one can think of this process as a sort of internal tact—choosing to overlook some feelings so as to help one's life run more smoothly. Focusing one's attention is the most common of mental activities. You couldn't read this book without such focusing, and that means you are not paying as much attention to other concerns.

If subjective awareness of gender incongruity is pronounced, then decisions of whether to pay attention to such feelings take on more urgency. Gender issues are one territory of questions for self-aware self-development: "What will I pay attention to as I reflect on my life and make my choices?" Feelings of fear and confusion about gender incongruity can be strong enough to lead to the subjective question "Will I pay attention to my gender feeling and interests at all?"

One may *rationalize* an uncomfortable feeling or behavior. To rationalize is to substitute one explanation for another so that one can feel better about what one felt or did. A man-to-woman transgender person might offer the following explanation for occasionally cross-dressing: "I'm not a cross-dresser. It's just that I used to play change with my sister and I like the fun of playing around a little bit." Rationalizing is a cover-up at the feeling level. In the example given, the statement would be a rationalization if the person were covering up feelings of wanting to be the other gender. The critical personal question for people who rationalize is "Do I seek a self-understanding that is in touch with my inner feelings?" The question can become "Will I let go of a powerful web of rationalizations that is keeping me from exploring my real feelings?"

One may resist or avoid an uncomfortable feeling or behavior by *reinforcing the alternative.* In gender terms this would mean reinforcing one's sense of being a man or a woman by emphasizing masculine or feminine styles and activities in keeping with one's assigned gender. Such reinforcement may be continuous or episodic and enlists social support for one's preferred consciousness.

One may acknowledge transgender feelings or interests but *resist exploring* them. Such resistance may not matter much to a person with weak feelings or interests. For people with stronger desires such resistance can be frustrating. Identifying the sources of resistance, whether they be general self-acceptance, morality, or consideration of interpersonal commitments and responsibilities, can sharpen one's inner-growth agendas. Some of these concerns are addressed in the last chapter of this book. A related group of questions has to do with facing up to oppression. For such questions, insight is not an adequate solution.

One's personal courage and one's willingness to bear potentially negative social responses matter. Even expression that is intended to be private might become known. Since social threats are real, it is reasonable for people to ask themselves whether it is worth it to explore transgender feelings and activities. All of these questions may lead one into counseling and many counselors are trained to help one clarify such questions and to sort out feelings and options. Issues in seeking help and avoiding being hurt by the helpers are addressed in the next chapter.

There are social as well as psychological alternatives for working with feelings of gender incongruity. One may *explore "safe" transgender expressions.* For example, a man might become a more nurturing parent even though such activity does not fit his original concept of "being a man." Such a choice may win more positive than negative social reinforcements in some social settings, because gender stereotypes may not be as rigid in some settings as in others. When positively rewarded, such a strategy is likely to produce emotional satisfaction and comfort if the transgender feeling is limited to a desire to nurture children. Although an internal gender transition was made, such safe transitions can be seen as stretching the role of "being a man" rather than as taking on a womanly attribute.

If a transgender interest or feeling is different from, or more than, participation in such "safe" expressions, then a "safe" solution is only partially satisfying. Part of what is at stake here is the psychological issue of *sublimation.* Some feelings, such as the desire to nurture, may be expressed in many ways. If caring for children is a sufficient outlet for expressing a sense of nurturance, then the individual has indeed found a relatively safe solution. All that is lost is the opportunity for other nurturing expression that isn't so safe. But, for this example, if caring for children does not feel like an adequate expression of one's desire to nurture, or if the social opportunity to nurture children is limited, then the individual is back to the choices between denial, rationalization, etc., and more broadly exploring transgender experience.

One may *pursue androgynous alternatives.* The acceptability of androgynous expressions varies widely within subgroups and subcultures. For example, a famous portrait of Louis XIV of France, intended to show his male virility, portrays him with long curly locks and intentionally exposed pretty legs (and no leg hair).[4] What counts as androgynous expression shifts over time in a single culture. Furthermore, an act or appearance that might feel like androgynous expression for some individuals might feel like merely an extension of traditional gender expression for others. Wearing an earring or two might have a transgender emotional charge for some men but not others. Wearing conservative earring studs in one setting may be intended to keep the ear holes open for dangling earrings in another setting. However expressed, androgyny allows some self-expression that does not conform to traditional gender definitions but that does not publicly claim the role of the other gender. The personal question is whether such partial expression of feelings is emotionally satisfying or whether a bolder claiming is wanted. In any case, when one begins to experiment with appearance cues, one is beginning to show other people a lack of full congruity with at least the most conservative gender appearance norms. The importance of changing appearance cues, as contrasted to other gender changes, is that such cues call attention to the issue of gender identification rather than to mere expansions or exceptions to the master role of man or woman.

One may *express transgender feelings or interests in a private or socially protected setting.* Many people who are intentionally working with a transgender sense of self use this strategy. Direct, but protected, expressions of transgender interests through changing appearance cues may be limited to solitary activity or shared with a trusted partner or transgender support group. If the current common wisdom of the transgender community is right, the majority of transgender people who have come out of the closet express themselves primarily in protected settings. Individual decisions are commonly influenced both by the felt need for expression and the levels of risk regarding a specific group, family, or subculture. The "out but protected" choice may be a sufficient lifetime solution for some and only a stage of development for others. Personal questions cluster around whether a half-hidden life is satisfying and around the anticipated social costs of public expression. Coming out of the closet, even if only in protected settings, presents two concerns for transgender identity. The first is that a person has to respond to what they look like in contrast to their imagined appearance. The second is that sharing one's expression with even one other person brings up issues of social acceptance.

One may engage in *part-time open transgender expression.* In this option, people openly express masculine and feminine appearances in some, but not all, social activities. For example, a birth-assigned male might work all day as a man, come home, and dress as a woman to go out to dinner with her spouse. The critical personal questions in this option include finding and adjusting to a continuously moving internal balance, coping with the confusion of others, and the various financial and practical costs.

One may make a *full-time transition* to the other traditional gender. The critical personal question is one's comfort level in moving from one's assigned gender identity to the other gender option. Many transsexuals, and some transgender people who make little or no physiological change, say they always had an identity with their nonassigned gender and are therefore just bringing their gender expression into conformity with their sense of identity. With or without substantial physiological alterations, they settle for living within their nonassigned gender identity as a best choice in terms of emotional, conceptual, and social comfort. For such people, gender change is subjectively sensed not as "moving out" but as "coming home." Other transgender people who make a full-time transition lack such fundamental clarity but are still making the most comfortable choice. A full-time transition has the advantages of cutting down on the emotional and practical wear and tear of repeated transitions. Transition time and financial cost are reduced, and the challenges of one's social world are simplified. One set of personal questions in this choice revolves around whether memories from the time of living in one's originally assigned gender are being denied, rationalized, or sublimated.

One may engage in part-time or full-time *claiming of a transgender identity.* My bigender choice fits here. Those who make this choice often feel unique, although this may be changing with the increasing emergence of transgender organizations. Whatever an individual's access to the status and supports of the transgender community, everyday social life is still predominantly bipolar in terms of gender for most people in the United States. Personal questions about social acceptance are common. Some subcultures, such as some Native American tribes, have established some kind of transgender role. Then the personal questions are around how well the subculture role fits, as well as how it feels to function in multicultural settings.

Finally, one may *reduce one's attention to gender roles* and just do what one wants to do. A man might reason as follows: I feel nurturing. I am a man. Therefore I feel the kind of nurturing men feel, so it must be acceptable. A more rebellious version projects any stress onto others. "If you don't like to see me wearing lipstick that's your problem." If there isn't much negative sanctioning, that may be the end of it. If there is a lot of negative sanctioning, the man in the example can try a variety of coping skills and strategies without necessarily feeling any gender challenge. In some cases, such psychological habits may allow one to press the limits of traditional gender roles without much consciousness or discomfort. If discomfort grows, one can choose some of the psychological or social options described above.

The options described in this section can also be taken as a description of alternative aspects of transgender experience and expression. These options, in addition to being individual paths and choices for people who claim a transgender identity, or the identity of the nonassigned gender, are also contributions to social change around the meaning of the words *man* and *woman.* Following is one description of such change observed in a high-achieving subset of the current college student generation.

> It was only recently that Princeton went coed, but one wouldn't know it. The male students are modern, enlightened men, sensitized since the first grade to apologize for their testosterone. The women are assertive and make a show of self-confidence, especially the athletes."[5]

Changes in the definitions of man and woman change the distance and direction of whatever is "transed" in transgender experience and expression.

Whatever one's path through the options just discussed, every circumstance presents challenges and questions for personal development that incorporates concerns about feelings of gender incongruity. But how do such feelings arise in the first place?

## Building Blocks for Understanding Transgender Experience and Expression

This section lists a variety of potential sources contributing to feelings of gender incongruity. At this point no suggestions are made about the number of factors, their strength, or their sequence in generating one or another kind of gender incongruity feeling or interest.

- Possible physiological predispositions
- Physiological aptitudes, such as hand-eye coordination
- Physiological grounding for appearance
- Physiological alterations
- Parental role models (many issues here)
- Sibling and extended family relations
- Relationships with spouses and significant others and with children
- Moral and political dissatisfactions with birth-assigned gender roles and images
- Intentional reflection, play, exploration
- Social opportunities
- Social sanctions and pressures
- Cultural and subcultural images and values
- Access to transgender individuals and the transgender community
- Access to gay, lesbian, and bisexual individuals and communities
- Direct spiritual experience of the eternals such as beauty, goodness, truth

These causes may fit into a specific research paradigm as independent, interactive, or intervening variables, depending on just what is to be explained in what setting.

My theoretical beginning point is that people with initial transgender feelings or interests use the response strategies discussed in the previous section to begin diverse transgender careers. For many people such careers are brief and perhaps only marginally conscious. Once transgender feelings and interests become fully conscious, I think that social factors and individual choices probably account for most career variability, including the choice to stop. I further think that the mix of these factors is different for different individuals. Richard Docter has done factor analysis of his survey of transgender people and has identified five relatively independent factors. I'm not following in Docter's path because I use a more diverse concept of transgender experience and expression and consider more aspects of causation.

Given the complexity of gender identities; given the complexity of initial, interactive, and intervening causes; given the hiddenness and fearfulness of much of the relevant population, which makes good research difficult; and given the change in many individuals over time, it seems to me extremely unlikely that anyone will be able to create and scientifically defend a single causal path that is adequate for explaining most of the variability in transgender experience. My alternative is a multipath theory, which works with the range of causes just identified to explain part of transgender experience and expression.

## A Theory of Everyday Transgender Identity Development

In the third chapter I review and critique the work of Richard Green and other establishment psychologists and psychiatrists. After pointing out the inadequacy of their scientific work, and after showing that some of their findings actually oppose the clinical definition of gender identity disorder they helped to create, I note that I agree with the *framework* of those establishment clinicians whose thinking about transgender experience was multicausal and multipathed. I would like also to note my agreement with Muriel Dimen, who has taken feminism an additional step as it relates to this issue. She writes that after rejecting Freud's theory of penis envy (female inadequacy), feminists gathered behind ideas that were first presented in the psychiatric realm by Karen Horney. Horney located women's difficulties in their economic and political inequities instead of in some kind of biological inferiority. Dimen then favors taking a third step. "The third step promotes the theory that gender identity is ambiguous and conflicted. Women and men differ among themselves and within themselves. The stereotypes do not allow for the real ambiguity that exists."[6]

Although I use a theoretical framework similar to that of clinicians, I differ radically by considering everyday kinds of transgender experience and expression and by emphasizing "haystack" rather than "needle" factors. Instead of assuming that transgender behavior is so unusual that it requires a distinct kind of theoretical explanation, I emphasize that common physiological, psychological, and social factors and processes can cause and shape transgender experience and expression. By no means do I think there is an adequate research base to defend my theory. But my following theory is better grounded than clinical theory and has the advantage of focusing on general transgender experience and expression rather than only on some experiences and expressions of some transgender people who are troubled enough to seek help from a clinician.

### Common Gender Role Learning

Almost everyone who has grown up in the United States has learned about girl and boy roles, man and woman roles, masculine and feminine images. Girls learn what is expected of men and women even though they are expected to identify with the woman role. Boys learn what is expected of women as well as men. I do not mean that females commonly learn as much as males about the skill and expectations linked to the roles of boys and men. I do mean that we all learn, or learn about, the images, skills, and expectations primarily linked to the gender we were not assigned.

I realize that some writers think there is a clear difference between the growing-up worlds of boys and girls. The kinds and degrees of such difference deserve more objective analysis. My point here is that, although there may be differences in what boys and girls are *supposed* to respond to (*and I intend both meanings of supposed*), the images and modeling of both genders are usually available to both boys and girls in the contemporary United States. I grew up with the common socialization that boys were supposed to be active, to be subjects, and that girls were supposed to be responsive, to be objects. Boys look. Girls are looked at. Forgetting for the moment that the stereotypes I learned were not universal even in the 1950s, not even in the white middle-class culture of the 1950s, I nonetheless did learn that girls are supposed to be looked at. I didn't practice the skills of presenting myself as "attractive," but I knew the category existed and I chose to date "attractive" girls. When I later thought about the importance of feeling my own feelings as a positive element of claiming my general psychological health, I was able to connect to the feeling that I wanted to be attractive, to be desired, to be wanted. The images that came to me for claiming such feelings were the feminine images I grew up with but was not allowed to explore.

### *Lack of Fit Between Traditional Gender Stereotypes and Physiological Reality*

In Chapters 2 and 3 the case is made that males and females both have physiologically based capacities or predispositions to nurture and to fight, to think abstractly and concretely, and so forth. The distributions of such physiologically based capacities and predispositions between males and females overlap, and that led me to assert that most people have some elements of intersexuality in the sense of having some degree of predisposition or capacity that is not named as appropriate for their birth-assigned gender. Conceptual and emotional disjunctions are created when elements of an individual's capacities or predispositions don't fit traditional gender roles. For example, male children with little capacity for rough-and-tumble play are less likely to experience positive rewards from trying to live up to this traditional expectation of being a boy. Whether this factor is felt to be conceptually or emotionally weighty depends on numerous factors, including the weightiness and direction of reactions from parents, siblings, friends, teachers, and other important actors.

### *Noticing that One's Interests or Feelings Fit Better with the Stereotypes of the Other Gender*

If it is true that many people feel some lack of fit between elements of their life experience and their assigned gender roles, and given the reality that we all learn both traditional gender roles, it would be *common* for persons to notice that they have some interests or feelings that fit with the gender role or images they were not assigned. Traditional socialization presses individuals to deny or reject such interests or feelings in pursuit of gender role conformity. I distinctly remember an elementary school teacher who trashed my interests in art, and I got the message that boys were expected not to be good at art.

Emotional reactions to negative social sanctions may shut down awareness and create inattention to feelings. If a boy is feeling nurturing feelings, it would be common for him to explore nurturing feelings in his play. But if the boy is negatively sanctioned by parents or peers, an emotional conflict is created. Later, perhaps much later, the feelings or interests may reemerge with links to accumulated confusion or distress. The linking of these three points suggests that some feelings of gender incongruity may be *usual* in the United States at the beginning of the 21st century. The list of psychological habits and social contingencies presented in the previous section suggests many paths by which transgender experience and identity may develop or be blocked. If feelings of gender incongruity are common, and if most people deny or resist naming their feelings with transgender language, then the existing hostility of some people to transgender expression may be the result of a felt need for social reinforcement to assist in denying or resisting feelings that are stimulated by seeing transgender expression.

It is may be interesting to some readers to point out that this line of theory is compatible with a feminist deconstruction of patriarchy. My theory applies such deconstructive thinking to both genders and incorporates a complex understanding of physiological factors.

*Transgender Careers*

For some people, transgender feelings and concepts may be a motive to explore transgender expression. Once expressed, especially when such expression brings social responses, such expression may develop a pattern appropriately discussed as a transgender career, however transitory. When stereotypic visual images of gender are noticeably challenged, as contrasted to the previous example of men nurturing children at home, more internal awareness of not meeting gender expectations and more sanctioning from others is likely. Many factors influence the development of psychological and social habits that advance or repress transgender career lines. At this point many people who later make connection to the transgender community report fear, confusion, and the hurt of rejections.

In response to such discomfort and disruption, individuals may take one of three paths. They may stay stuck in discomfort with limited awareness and exploration and perhaps fill up their lives with other activities and concerns. They may deepen their denial and other habits to reduce awareness of disruptive feelings. Some clinicians choose to discuss some versions of this option as neurosis or psychosis.

Other people, when they become aware of a lack of fit of their feelings and interests with their assigned gender roles, particularly when the transgender interest includes exploration of cross-gender appearance, may choose alternatives that lead to a conscious and personally organized transgender career. For people initiating such transgender careers, personal questions begin to revolve around how much to explore, how much to get in touch with feelings, how much to share with others, etc. Clinicians misapply the language of gender dysphoria or of gender identity disorder at this point. Sociologists are prone to discuss such behavior as deviance, in the formal sense of breaking cultural gender norms and social expectations. *The same reality can be named as a path to personal wholeness which overcomes distorting limits in traditional gender roles and cultural images.* By *distorting limits* I mean limits to the awareness and expression of personal feelings that arise in many people from common physiological, psychological, and social factors. Transgender support groups are now available in most cities in the United States, and their stock-in-trade activity is helping transgender people name and claim the healthy grounding of their exploration and expression.

Sometimes audiences of transgender expression try to stop the expression. Several clinically coached versions of such oppression are discussed in the next chapter. Transgender people tell some very sad stories of the punishments they have received for their transgender expression: lost family relationships, lost jobs, and physical or verbal abuse. However, some transgender people report only modest negative sanctions. Formal and informal punishments may be effective in stopping or delaying behavior and in encouraging the repression of awareness. The effectiveness of social repression depends not only on the power of the sanctions but also on the personal and social resources of the transgender person. The emergence of the transgender community is an important social resource. The effort to end the tyranny of the gender identity disorder label is a specific social change effort aimed at reducing professional support for the oppression of transgender people.

In the face of powerful negative social sanctions of transgender expression, sometimes including an array of clinical and legal powers, the transgender community is nonetheless awash with stories of the courage to claim feelings and the right to self-expression. Some of the stories show so much strength as to raise the question whether significant transgender feelings can ever be repressed or controlled by social and cultural authorities. On the other hand, the fact that the organized transgender community has been visible for only about 20 years reminds us that the forces of oppression used to be more dominant. It is also important to remember that some transgender people have received significant support from spouses, families, coworkers, and friends.

The theory I have developed in this chapter builds on the repeated emphasis in earlier chapters on the complexity, flexibility, and interactivity of physiological, psychological, and social factors. Such factors, joined with the multiple habits and paths identified in this chapter, fit well with a picture of highly diverse transgender experience and expression, as identified in the first and fifth Chapters. My theory also fits well with the multiple ways in which people with "straight" self-concepts live out gender roles and identities. As pointed out above, one does not have to have a transgender identity to engage in transgender expression. The research by Bem, though problematic for other purposes, certainly documents this complexity.[7] One good reason to avoid social construction theories based on stages of development is that such constructions draw attention away from transgender expressions of straight people.

Notes:

1. Bob Dylan, "Desolation Row" (Song), *Highway 66 Revisited.* Columbia Records (1965).
2. Catherine Aird, from a privately circulated list of unreferenced quotations.
3. Gary Kates (1995), page xviii.
4. Ibid., page vii.
5. David Brooks (2001), page 48.
6. Muriel Dimen (1995), page 303.
7. Sandra Bem (1979, 1993).

*Sometimes I aint so sho who's got ere a right to say when a man is crazy and when he aint. Sometimes I think it aint none of us pure crazy and aint none of us pure sane until the balance of us talks him that-a-way. It's like it aint so much what a fellow does, but it's the way the majority of the folks is looking at him when he does it.* William Faulkner[1]

*If there is anything we wish to change in the child, we should first examine it and see whether it is not something that could better be changed in ourselves.*
Carl Jung[2]

# Chapter 7:
# Getting Help and Getting Hurt

Counseling can be helpful for transgender people for the same kinds of reasons it can be helpful to others. Later on in this chapter are some suggestions to transgender people for finding good counselors. The first sections prepare transgender people for dealing with clinicians who base their work on establishment orientations and American Psychiatric Association diagnoses and definitions. The chapter offers grounding for resisting such diagnoses and definitions and offers guidance for counselors and other helpers who want to offer assistance without applying illness definitions.

### A Review of Why Clinical Studies Lack Scientific Credibility

The third chapter of this book included evaluation of the scientific basis of clinical studies by establishment therapists. My summary of clinical research is that it lacks scientific credibility and should not be counted in favor of vague clinical theories. Such research should specifically not be counted in favor of the current psychiatric definitions and presumed etiology of gender identity disorder (GID) as found in the *Diagnostic and Statistical Manuel of Mental Disorders* of the American Psychiatric Association, 4th Edition, Text Revision (DSM-IV-TR), published in 2000. I pointed out that Richard Green, at least, has somewhat conceded this point.

To prepare for the issues addressed in this chapter, I offer a summary list of the scientific problems in clinical studies.

- Failure to study the subject in everyday settings
- Studying only those people who are seeking clinical help
- Failure to account for the distortions of therapeutic interest
- The limitations of any study based on memories of childhood

- Failure to clearly define what is being studied, including the distinctions between feelings, self-identification and the many kinds of behavior
- Failure to adequately define or measure many presumed causes, such as parental influence
- Failure to consider or measure alternative explanations of transgender experience
- Failure to theorize links between theorized early childhood causes and adult outcomes
- Failure in most studies to measure whether children actually develop into the kinds of adults they are theorized to become
- Failure to consider the influence of clinical intrusions, particularly labeling, which has been shown to be a powerful source of unintended consequences
- Failure to consider obvious physiological factors, such as hormonal variation over the life cycle, including the effects of puberty, while appealing to vague or unmeasurable possible physiological sources
- Failure to consider cross-cultural factors such as differing definitions of what it means to be a man or a woman in different families, classes, races, ethnicities, and religions

The beginning point for this chapter is that, despite the lack of scientific support for clinical theories in general and gender identity disorder in particular, and despite several kinds of opposing evidence, the psychiatric diagnosis of gender identity disorder exists and is used. Clinical psychologists and psychiatrists pathologize transgender experience as they once pathologized homosexuality. This diagnosis is a powerful social reality, a damaging injustice to me and my diverse transgender friends.

Some clinicians, although they take advantage of the diagnosis of gender identity disorder, are going easy on assertions of mental illness or psychological disorder. I've read comments, including those of Richard Green, that boil down to "Of course we don't know what we're doing, but we are helpers and we are helping. People with transgender experience face great social and cultural rejection, and we want to save them from such pain. Even though what we do shows no signs of being effective, we are still doing the best we can to help." Some add, "And besides, parents have the right to socialize their children in any way they wish, and it is our duty to respond when they seek our help." This chapter shows that despite whatever good the establishment clinicians have done, they have also done a great deal of harm.

There is direct harm to people, especially children, who are subjected to pressures to change their transgender ways. Such "therapy" inevitably teaches the therapeutic target that something is wrong with them, something so wrong that it has generated reaction from the therapists. But the harm that comes from pathologizing transgender experience spreads far beyond therapeutic encounters. It stands as a powerful referent for the law and supports the hostile stereotypes that shape everyday interaction. It is not enough that some clinicians describe cross-dressing as a "harmless fetish." That is still pathological thinking that derogates transgender experience and expression. Even though pathologizing language may be used in a mild form, that doesn't mean less has to be proved to justify such statements.

The transgender community will not succeed in claiming a human rights basis for social acceptance as long as clinical definitions sideline discussions of transgender concerns as discussions of abnormality. Furthermore, claiming transgender experience as experience that can lead to positive social contributions is critical for people who are trying to make sense of their own lives and to develop feelings of self-worth. Additionally, an escape from pathological self-labeling is critical for developing self-conceptions that include accepting responsibility for one's behavior and being open to the possibilities of human growth.

## How Professional Opinions Are Created and What They're Worth

Despite the lack of scientific grounding, many psychiatrists and psychologists have assumed their clinical theories to be true and have acted on them. They have acted as if training in science, rather than actually practicing science, was sufficient grounding for their profession. The real grounding of the establishment clinicians is their professional opinions. That is, they are paid members of professions and they have opinions. The clinicians not only have personal professional opinions, their professions have official collective opinions.

### Labels Don't Fall From the Sky

Early efforts to categorize mental illnesses were heavily influenced by an intent to clarify Freudian perspectives. The goal was to clarify the language of psychiatrists so that they could know what they were talking about when they used various phrases. This was a highly confusing and complex business. The original definition of schizophrenia, for example, boiled down to "mental illness that isn't like any of the above categories." We see this same kind of labeling strategy a century later in such titles as gender identity disorder not otherwise specified.

In the 19th-century intellectual world of Freud, a lot of the diverse phenomena considered in this book were named in the single concept of sexual inversion. Sexual inversion meant feminism, homosexuality, transgender expression, and any other kind of challenge to patriarchal control. Sandra Bem quotes D'Emilio and Freedman on this point: sexual inversion "was conceptualized not as homosexuality, but as. . .a complete change of gender identity of which erotic behavior was but one small part."[3] Whatever sexual inversion might mean in scientific terms, there was no doubt that it was a *perversion,* and there is no doubt that the core meaning of perversion is attached to concepts of wrong, dirty, unnatural and disgusting.

Homosexuality was not named as a separate mental illness in early 20th -century attempts at categorizing. However, homosexuality, masturbation, and a variety of fantasies were taken as symptoms of other mental illnesses. There was a lot of talk about nontraditional sexual practices as immature or undeveloped in some way as compared to vaginal intercourse between men and women.

As one element of the development of selection criteria for soldiers in World War II, Harry Stack Sullivan led the American Psychiatric Association to define homosexuality as an illness. The label was part of the "Classification of Mental Disorders" in the 1942 edition of the *Standard Nomenclature of Disease* as approved by the American Psychiatric Association and the American Medical Association.[4] One could be labeled a psychopathic personality with pathologic sexuality, with or without psychosis, if one was a homosexual. Other pathological labels included: "erotomania" (too much sexuality), "sexual perversion" (including fetishism and transvestism), and "sexual immaturity," meaning primarily masturbation. The impact of such labeling was brought home to me when I was part of a group touring a Florida juvenile delinquency facility in the 1970s. The tour leader explained during our tour of a dormitory that they kept the lights on all night in the dormitory so that an attendant could watch to make sure the boys didn't masturbate under the covers.

Masturbation was a target of clinical control, but the behaviors most likely to get one labeled "with psychosis" were "hallucinations" or "delusions." The common claim of transsexuals—that one is a man trapped in a female body or a woman trapped in a male body, was a claim likely to be labeled a delusion. It would also be easy to label such transsexuals as psychopaths. Following is the official 1942 description of the concept of psychopathy: "Psychopathic personalities are characterized largely by emotional immaturity or childishness with marked defects of judgment and without evidence of learning by experience."[5]

One way of exposing the scientific quality underlying the 1942 *Standard Nomenclature of Disease* is to point out that the psychiatric profession was still holding onto the now laughable concept of somatotyping. Somatotyping tried to explain mental illness on the basis of whether one was thin, fat, or athletic. The summary statement on somatotyping was, "In general, conclusions are that Kretschmer's formulations add a valuable and often a practical viewpoint in the study of clinical psychiatry."[6]

Questions in the standardized psychiatric examination of that day show the pitiful quality of psychiatry at that time. They included the following: Divide 63 by 7. Pronounce "imperturbable." Why did the Pilgrims come to this country? What is foolish or absurd about the following statement: The angry hen chased the duck to the other side of the river.

Some terrible things were done to people who were given labels under the above system. Some were given lobotomies. Lobotomy is surgery performed by sticking an ice pick like instrument through the eye socket into the brain and moving the instrument around to turn the prefrontal lobes, the highest thinking centers, to organic mush. Researchers found you can make a person totally passive by doing a lobotomy.[7] The horrible things done to people labeled mentally ill exceed the standard outlawing cruel and unusual punishment that is supposed to protect people found guilty of crimes.

One professional outcome of such clinical activity was that psychiatry eventually became discouraged because lobotomies, castration, electric and chemical shock treatment, and a host of more benign therapies had little effect in "curing" homosexuality. Because the professions of psychiatry were powerless to force change on homosexuals, practitioners concluded that the disease was incurable and that anyone who became a homosexual never changed. This conclusion was based not on any independent studies but on professional hubris: "If we can't change it, it must be unchangeable."

Then Evelyn Hooker carried out a study of homosexuals in everyday settings. She didn't find anything that looked like pathology.[8] After years of debate the American Psychiatric Association finally concluded in 1973 that homosexuality was not a disease. The change was published in the third edition of the *Diagnostic and Statistical Manual* (DSM III) in 1980. The American Psychological Association, The American Medical Association, and the American Academy of Pediatrics have since formally joined the consensus that homosexuality is not a disease.

At the end of the 20th century we were privileged to watch the radical Christian right join with some clinicians who had lost the debate over the disease status of homosexuality to launch a large advertising campaign in an attempt to reinvigorate the theme that homosexuals are sinful and sick. The advertising campaign showed the Madison Avenue touches that a lot of money can buy. The ads emphasized a soft appeal to homosexuals to give up their sin and sickness by taking advantage of ex-gay ministries and reparative therapies. When challenged, the proponents of this approach could offer not a single documented study in a refereed journal which defended their theories or showed the effectiveness of their treatments.[9] The National Association for Research and Therapy of Homosexuality (NARTH) was supposed to supply the scientific grounding. NARTH has some leaders with academic positions, but none has published an article in a refereed journal that defends their claims. In addition to the lack of scientific grounding, the NARTH report also has at least the following major faults: 63 % of the respondents who claimed to have found help were still in therapy, there was no differentiation of homosexuality from bisexuality, and there was no follow-up study to show that whatever was changed was stable over time.[10] The lack of a follow-up study is particularly telling, since people who submitted to ex-gay ministries and reparative therapy report that they were able to repress their feelings for awhile but later recovered their sense of themselves as gay or lesbian people and claimed their full health by throwing off the pressures of such ministries and therapy.[11]

In the 1970s, the profession of psychiatry came under sharp attack in general. The general critique of psychiatric labeling discussed in the Chapter 4 of this book was one of several intellectual contributions that led to the process of deinstitutionalization which closed many mental hospitals across the nation. The sharpest critique, by Thomas Szasz, summarized why the profession of psychiatry had been unable to establish itself in universities. It wasn't scientific.[12]

Eminent sociological theorists, like Talcott Parsons, pointed out the social control aspects of "illness": "the primary criteria for mental illness must be defined with reference to the social role performance of the individual."[13] Thomas Sheff set forward what became the standard position of sociologists of mental illness when he defined mental illness as "residual social deviance," the violation of informal social norms. Given this perspective, the treatment of mental illness, especially the hospitalization of mental patients, is most appropriately understood as social control.[14] Following Sheff's lead, a raft of sociological studies showed such things as the inability of psychiatrists to agree on analyses of specific cases, the performance of mental patients to meet the expectations of hospital staff that they were "crazy," race and class discrimination in the admitting processes of state mental hospitals, the critical importance of being represented by a lawyer in incompetency hearings, the common violation of the law by those bringing charges in incompetency hearings, and the most critical finding of all, that practically all incompetency hearings were initiated by people who had been insulted, injured, or upset by the accused.[15]

In incompetency hearings it was commonly the case that the testimony of the accused was not allowed because of the need to "protect" the accused. Some people were given the equivalent of life sentences, including assault by psychotropic drugs or worse on the basis of a one-minute court trial. Other sociologists have shown that, once labeled and institutionalized, people were taught the role of being mentally ill; further, they showed the rewards and punishments attached to adequate performance in that role. Many of these studies can be found in *The Mental Patient: Studies in the Sociology of Deviance*.[16] A review of labeling theory was included in Chapter 4.[17]

### Gender Identity Disorder: So Convenient, So Lucrative

The word *transvestite* was coined by a German sexologist named Magnus Hirschfeld in 1910. At about the same time, Havelock Ellis described cross-dressing as eonism after the story of the Chevalier(e) d'Eon de Beaumont, who presented as a woman on diplomatic assignments to the courts of Europe and then returned to France to live full-time as a woman. The terms of Hirschfield and Ellis, though differentiated from sexual inversion, were still within the category of perversion.[18]

Harry Benjamin began to use the word *transsexual* in 1953 at a point when sexual reconstructive surgery (SRS), based on earlier work with hermaphrodites and in response to war injuries, was becoming effective.[19] In that same year Christine Jorgenson became the first widely publicized transsexual (the surgery was done at a clinic in Denmark). Perhaps in the best interest of his patients, and perhaps to spread the legal risks, Benjamin required extensive psychological workups to justify the decision that surgery was appropriate. At that point psychiatry began developing a separate diagnostic category for transsexuals. The Benjamin Standards still require a pass from a clinician before SRS can be obtained. That is, *a definition of psychiatric disorder was created in response to technical advances in urological surgery, and the transsexual pattern, which clinicians had never noticed before, was reified as a new disease.*

In the same 1980 *Diagnostic and Statistical Manual of Mental Disorder* (DSM-III) that ended the definition of homosexuality as a disease, the disease category gender identity disorder—children (GID-C) was created for the first time. The child psychologists who had been treating gender-nonconforming children as prehomosexual conveniently decided that they would now be treated as pretranssexual, since homosexuality was no longer a justification for their professional involvement. In this new label of GID-C for DSM-III, the American Psychiatric Association emphasized the idea of self-identification with the other sex from an early age as the core issue for diagnosis. This diagnosis fit with the clinical stereotype of adult transsexuals who seek sexual reassignment surgery.

Phyllis Burke gives substantial detail about the initial definition of GID-C and how it changed in DSM-IIIR and again in DSM-IV.[20] Additional criteria were added, and the key word *may* was strategically inserted with regard to the criteria of recognition. The loosening up of the definition was justified by asserting that children knew what psychiatrists were driving at but were too smart to admit it. The result was that, to receive the GID-C label, children no longer had to say that they thought they were a member of the other sex.

Susan Bradley and Kenneth Zucker, who were on the APA committee that expanded the GID definition, wrote in 1990, "One could argue, that GID-C or its subclinical variants may occur in two percent to five percent of children in the general population."[21] I find this a most interesting number since the highest projected ratio of transsexuals in a population by any study is 1/12,000.[22] The number offered in DSM -IV is 1/30,000. Later on, under the section "Course," the authors of DSM-IV note that "Only a very small number of children with Gender Identity Disorder will continue to have symptoms that meet criteria for Gender Identity Disorder in later adolescence or adulthood."[23] Knowing this, what justification does the APA have for listing children and adults under the same heading? The only continuity is *social*—that is, the violation of social norms. Even if one believed that adult transsexuals have a mental disorder, there is no defense for using prevention of transsexuality as a justification for treating children under the phantasm of the GID-C label. Sandra Bem offers a similarly critical perspective on the process of the construction of the GID label.[24]

The most recent twist is that in DSM-IV the distinctive designation of gender identity disorder – children was dropped, and children were defined with adults in a single GID category. Although there is no scientific justification for this approach either, it has the distinct political advantage for psychiatrists of tying a label to children that some transsexuals want to maintain. Currently, adult transsexuals need the GID diagnosis as a door to qualifying for sexual reassignment surgery (SRS). Sometimes the GID label will even justify insurance payments for some of the medical costs. Dividing the transgender community might be politically astute, but it is another moral disaster for the profession of psychiatry. Perhaps Richard Green is backing off from this travesty. His voice could make a difference. In the meantime, his research counts against the position of the APA. At least he has been willing to argue that transsexuals should not be denied SRS on a variety of procedural grounds. In support of this position he pointed out that some transsexuals who have been denied treatment have committed suicide rather than continue with the psychic strain of feeling trapped in the wrong body.[25]

The section on GID in DSM-IV follows sections on voyeurism and on paraphilias such as copulating with corpses and animals. Following is a quote from the section on the diagnostic features of GID:

There are two components of Gender Identity Disorder, both of which must be present to make the diagnosis. There must be evidence of a strong and persistent cross-gender identification, which is the desire to be, or the insistence that one is, of the other sex (Criterion A). This cross-gender identification must not merely be a desire for any perceived cultural advantages of being of the other sex. There must also be evidence of persistent discomfort about one's assigned sex or a sense of inappropriateness in the gender role of that sex. (Criterion B) The diagnosis is not made if the individual has a concurrent physical intersex condition (e.g. androgen insensitivity syndrome or congenital adrenal hyperplasia) (Criterion C). To make the diagnosis, there must be evidence of clinically significant distress or impairment in social, occupational, or other important areas of functioning (Criterion D). The second component is "persistent discomfort" with his or her sex or "sense of inappropriateness" with his or her gender role.[26]

Instead of maintaining a separate diagnosis of Gender Identity Disorder—Children, DSM-IV provides descriptions of what this disorder looks like in boys, girls, adolescents, and adults.

> In boys, the cross-gender identification is manifested by a marked preoccupation with traditionally feminine activities. They may have a preference for dressing in girl's or women's clothes. . . . There is a strong attraction for the stereotypical games and pastimes of girls. . . Stereotypical female-type dolls, such as Barbie, are often their favorite toys, and girls are their preferred playmates. . . . They avoid rough and tumble play and competitive sports and have little

interest in cars and trucks. . . . They may express a wish to be a girl and assert that they will grow up to be a woman.[27]

Girls with Gender Identity Disorder display intense negative reaction to parental expectations or attempts to have them wear dresses or other feminine attire. . . . They prefer boys clothing and short hair, are often misidentified by strangers as boys, and may ask to be called by a boy's name. . . . These girls prefer boys as play-mates, with whom they share interest in contact sports, rough and tumble play, and traditional boyhood games. A girl with this disorder may occasionally refuse to urinate in a sitting position. She may claim that she has or will grow a penis and may not want to grow breasts or to menstruate. She may assert she will grow up to be a man.[28]

Adults with Gender Identity Disorder are preoccupied with their wish to live as members of the opposite sex. This preoccupation may be manifested as an intense desire to adopt the social role of the other sex or to acquire the physical appearance of the other sex through hormonal or surgical manipulation. . . . To varying degrees they adopt behavior, dress, and mannerisms of the other sex.[29]

DSM-IV notes that it may be hard to diagnose adolescents because of their guardedness: ". . . the diagnosis should be reserved for those adolescents who appear quite cross-gender identified in their dress and who engage in behaviors that suggest significant cross-gender identification (e.g., shaving legs in males)."[30]

The basic adult diagnosis of GID is tailored to the concept of trans-sexualism. However, this does not stop DSM-IV from working in the diagnosis of "transvestic fetishism." Such transvestic fetishism is supposed to "occur in heterosexual or bisexual men for whom the cross-dressing behavior is for the purpose of sexual excitement." One can also be labeled as having Gender Identity Disorder and Transvestic Fetishism, or as having Transvestic Fetishism with Gender Dysphoria. If this doesn't do it, one can also be labeled as Gender Identity Disorder Not Otherwise Specified on the basis of exhibiting "transient, stress related cross-dressing behavior."[31] Despite Criterion C, one can also receive the diagnosis of Gender Identity Disorder Not Otherwise Specified for having an intersexual condition, even though there is no psychological distress. There are also some qualifier words like persistent or severe that relate to the diagnoses above.

In addition to the general lack of scientific grounding identified in earlier chapters, the details of the GID diagnostic category quoted above reveal more reasons to disrespect the label. First, the DSM authors deny the GID diagnosis to homosexuals, even though much of the anxiety about childhood GID is over the possibility that it might lead to homosexuality. Perhaps the authors think that transgender behavior is pathological for heterosexuals but not for homosexuals. Second, no justification is offered for the language about fetishism; it is merely clinical stereotyping, maintaining that transgender experience as an aspect of one's sexuality must be fetishistic. Third, there is an implication that if transgender experience is upsetting to the people having the experience, it deserves a psychiatric label, whereas if people like their experience, it is just fine. This almost amounts to a confession that there is nothing intrinsically pathological about the condition. (*Dysphoria* is a psychiatric word for *discomfort*, the kind of technical word that would lead us to believe that only a psychiatrist can understand what is going on.)

The last paragraph in the GID diagnostic section is particularly telling for what is at stake in this diagnosis:

> Distress or disability in individuals with Gender Identity Disorder is manifested differently across the life cycle. In young children, distress is manifested by the stated unhappiness about their assigned sex. Preoccupation with cross-gender wishes often interferes with ordinary activities. In older children, failure to develop the age-appropriate same-sex peer relationships and skills often leads to isolation and distress, and some children may refuse to attend school because of teasing or pressure to dress in attire stereotypical to their assigned sex. In adolescents and adults, preoccupation with cross-gender wishes often interferes with ordinary activities. Relationship difficulties are common and functioning at school or at work may be impaired.[32]

This last paragraph makes it very clear that the DSM-IV definition of gender identity disorder is not based on phenomena that are usually thought of as components of mental illnesses. We are not talking about depression, anxiety, hallucinations, or confusion. We are talking about people who do not meet conventional cultural standards or social role expectations related to gender. Instead of giving in and conforming to social expectations, transgender people are punished for their resistance to traditional social roles and cultural stereotypes. GID is not about psychological disorder. It is about social nonconformity. Let's make this simple. If you go to a psychiatrist with concerns about your transgender experience, or if your parents take you because you don't or do like trucks, there is so much slippery language, and there are so many diverse alternatives that you can be tagged with the GID label. As I used to tell my students, "All students who come to class early are showing anxiety, all students who come on time are displaying compulsiveness, and all students who come late are resistive."

*Living Off Clinical Momentum*

Despite the lack of a scientific base, the social reality of the GID diagnosis will continue for awhile. What constitutes a "disease," a "disorder," or "dysphoria"? The legal answer is that the courts tend to defer to the people they recognize as professionals: the psychiatrists and clinical psychologists. A legal disease, disorder, or dysphoria is whatever the recognized professionals say it is. Distasteful or not, this is one important reason why it is important to understand the latest generation of nomenclature.

In DSM-III-R, transvestism is listed as a paraphilia. In DSM-IV it is listed next to the section on paraphilia but is not called paraphilia. Timothy and Joseph Costello (1992), in a textbook of abnormal psychology, explain that the last version of DSM-III-R changed the name *sexual deviations* to *paraphilias* because it is a less pejorative word. (I guess they think it is less pejorative because it is a Greek word people don't understand.) They explain that paraphilia means "beside or beyond what is preferred." Such comments make it additionally clear that transgender diagnosis is about social control. In DSM-III-R there are two kinds of paraphilias: fetishism and transvestism. Since the concept of transvestic fetishism is alive and well in DSM-IV, but it is no longer called a paraphilia, just what is going on?

In one sense, I rather like the way the Costellos try to explain transvestism. They talk about two kinds of transvestism. In the first, they argue that males seek enhanced pleasure from heterosexual coitus by partially dressing as women. In the second, males "move around" in the "full regalia" of a women, suggesting "some kind of gender identity problem but not necessarily homosexuality. Transvestites usually report less frequent homosexual urges than do average American males."[33] Of course there is no scientific base for these assertions either. What I like, although it may be unintended, is the suggestion by the Costellos that the sexual aspects of transvestism are not fetishistic. A fetish-oriented sexual act is one in which sexual energy is in attached to an object, such as a shoe, rather than to a person. At least the Costellos are willing to allow that transgender expression as part of sexual activity can be part of a person-to-person relationship. I also like the fact that they appear to realize that there may be more to transgender behavior than sexuality. Although they are clueless about what that might mean, they at least recognize the possibility.

In discussing causal factors in transvestism, the Costellos acknowledge that "Psychological testing of transvestites indicates that they show no more evidence of psychiatric disorder than would be found in the rest of the population. Their problem is more likely to be marital conflict and divorce because of a spouse's objection to someone who dresses up like a woman."[34] They then theorize about the mother who allows or encourages early cross dressing and the father, who, if present, ". . . must be very weak or not very interested in his son's upbringing."[35] For any scientist to fill in the theoretical blanks with "must be" statements rather than observations is ridiculous. However, when the Costellos say there is no evidence of increased psychiatric disorders in transvestites, one can fairly ask why this group shows up in a textbook on abnormal psychology or in DSM.

When the Costellos write about sexual identity disorder, meaning gender identity disorder, they define the issue in terms of psychological identity, but then assert that "There is a sharp struggle between the individual's anatomical sex gender and subjective feeling about choosing a masculine or feminine style of living."[36] Several confusions are evident. First, there is a failure to distinguish between style of living (androgyny) and the violation of appearance norms. Second, the Costellos assert that the struggle is between the person's sexuality and masculinity or femininity when the struggle is actually between the person's appearance presentation and those who respond to it. Third, they confuse subjective feelings, which do not cause social reaction as long as they are only subjective, and transgender expression. As we have seen in the fourth chapter of this book, such confusion makes a big difference in terms of who is in or out of these categories and slops lots of different things together without appreciating that some people have identity and not behavior, etc.

One way to appreciate the damage done by the inclusion of gender identity disorder in DSMs, and then by interpretive efforts by psychiatrists such as the Costellos, is to trace how it shows up in popular books. In *Dr. Ruth's Encyclopedia of Sex* (1994), for example, transvestism is named "an extreme form of fetishism."[37] Once clinical ideas are established, popular authorities like Dr. Ruth help sell them to the general population, and they gather force as if they were true.

One particularly ugly version of popular advice is offered by Eva Margolies in *Undressing the American Male: Men with Sexual Problems and What You Can Do to Help Them*. In her chapter on unusual sex, she begins with a rhetorical question about the strangest case she had ever seen. She exemplified "Jenny," "who was 6' 2" and wore a tiny pill box hat with a veil. . . and had the hairiest face I had ever seen on a woman."[38] Not only is her description intentionally insulting to cross-dressers; she was also indirectly insulting hirsute women. Margolies goes on to discuss transvestism as a paraphilia, which she calls a "technical word for kinky behavior." She further calls this behavior "sexually addictive" and warns women that regardless of what a partner might think, transvestites are really sexual addicts who are out of control, who lack the capacity for mutuality, and who are driven by shame.[39]

Although popularizers might be dismissed as unprofessional, the same toxic comments also show up in reference books with more prestige. *The American Medical Association's Encyclopedia of Medicine*, for example, calls transsexuality a "rare psychiatric disorder" and asserts that it is often associated with a disturbed parent-child relationship. It does not name transvestism as an illness or disorder and describes the phenomenon as "A persistent desire by a man to dress in women's clothing. . . ."[40] In addition to blindness about female-to-male behavior, the AMA book is not in keeping with the view of the Costellos and draws a sharp line between transvestite and transsexual behavior—a line that is fuzzed by DSM-IV.

These several references show that once a psychiatric disorder label has been created, it develops a life of its own, and the fine points of recategorization within DSM never catch up with the use of the concept in society.[41] Only a very public change of heart by the clinical professions, as occurred for homo-sexuality, will begin to reverse the damage that is still going on.

In his 1987 book, Richard Green stayed away from using "disorder" lan-guage in justifying his clinical intrusions with feminine boys. Instead he simply argued that the boys were uncomfortable.[42] But his own reports are that the kids liked their cross-gender play and were, by Green's own assessment, other-wise normal and happy. Green simply sided with the parents and ended up defending parental attitudes: parents have the right to bring children in for treatment. They have the right to try to foster gender conformity. But the issue is not parental rights. The issue is the ethics and honesty of a profession that unjustifiably trades on its prestige to pathologize children, to guide parental response, and to offer expert witness to the courts and other institutions. If one wanted to help a boy who really was uncomfortable, as well as his parents, one might help them bond around strategies to resist the oppression of a society that is currently stuck with rigid gender standards.

Psychological and psychiatric "helpers" who operate out of sickness theories about transgender people do not draw their mandate from science but rather from a defense of current cultural traditions. They wrap themselves in the mantle of science to justify their professional status, their control, and their fees. This misuse of funds is bad enough. Far worse is the damage to some people these professionals are supposed to help. The issue is not the intent of the helpers or their personal integrity. I've read enough praise of the humanity of some medical leaders such as Harry Benjamin and Robert Stoller to assume good intentions and personal caring. My challenge to the clinical establishment is to their willful ignorance about the limits of their theories and their unwill-ingness to challenge their theories when the lives of their "patients" don't fit. If we can get clear that what the clinical establishment delivers in its "clinical" interactions is about conformity rather than health, we can begin to shake off these professional deceptions.

## A Case Study of Clinical Oppression

Some may feel that all this analysis is interesting but not very substantial. After all, what is so bad about a psychotherapist working with parents to help a child become more gender conforming? Richard Green says at the end of his book that he hopes he hasn't hurt anyone. Certainly his therapies were not as gruesome as those of others. The following story needs to be told to help clear away any generosity towards the psychiatric definitions.

Phyllis Burke learned the story of Jamie from an interview in 1995 and tells it in *Gender Shock*.[43] The story begins with Jamie as 6 years old.

> Mother and Father left Jamie in the hospital admitting area. They went outside and did not return. They had spoken to a doctor about Jamie's troubles with being a boy, and the doctor had told them to take Jamie to the hospital. It was because of dolls, and tea sets, and

feeling too sad to move, that Jamie was there. . . . Jamie knew what this was all about, and said, "I'm a girl," even when they said, "No. You're a boy." Jamie did not do boy things and wouldn't lie about it.

. . . The nurse said, "This way," motioning for Jamie to follow, to step inside, across the threshold into a child's nightmare. The children Jamie heard and saw moved more slowly than other children do, and only later would Jamie understand that they were all drugged. . . . One nurse handed a paper cup to Jamie. There was a pill in it to swallow, and Jamie recalled that it looked like an M&M.

. . . Surely Mother and Father will come back, Jamie thought. Surely they will see that this is not good, and that I am not bad.

. . . Jamie awakened, mouth dry from medication and nerves. Some days had passed, but it was hard to count. Mother and Father had not returned. . . . On this morning, a nurse stopped at the foot of Jamie's bed. "Do not eat breakfast," she said.

. . . The children who could not have breakfast formed a line, and they all wore the paper slippers which were green. . . . Jamie was not the first in line, and did not even know where the line was going. It inched forward, the slippers rustling like paper wings. It was not so long before Jamie was next.

. . . Placed upon a hospital bed, Jamie's wrists and ankles were then tied with restraint cords against the metal rails. There was a large black box, on wheels, and there were wires coming out of it. No one said anything. No one said what was going to happen.

The technician spread cream on Jamie's forehead, and attached two electrodes to his temples. It was quiet. This was the first time Jamie had been gently touched since arriving at the hospital. The technician put something in Jamie's mouth that separated the teeth and the tongue. The technician nodded, and then there was sudden pain that could not be coming from anything human as the switch was flipped and electricity flowed through the wires into Jamie's brain, throwing the child into grand mal seizure. . . . Shock treatment would always be the same for Jamie: imagine your eyes falling apart inside your head, imagine an arc of pain splitting your skull into pieces.

The next morning, Jamie was awakened by the sound of the nurses walking through the ward. The sunlight was cold and yellow. The nurse stopped at the foot of Jamie's bed. "Do not eat breakfast today," she said.

And the nurse did it the next day. 'Do not eat breakfast.' And the next day. And the next. The next. The next.

Jamie understood that Mother and Father were not coming back. The season changed, and changed again. . . . Jamie was now nine years old. . . . The children formed their line, the paper slippers shuffled out onto the ward corridor, toward the door of the shock room. The Black boy, now ten or eleven years old, so full of light went into the room. He was always smiling. They brought him out of the shock room, past the day room, toward the nurses station and its big window without the glass behind which the nurses stood with clipboards and tiny paper cups. Jamie saw something suddenly happen. The boy went into seizure, and his convulsions were so violent that, through no will of his own, he leaped up into the air through the open window frame, and into the nurse's station, as if he were flying. But his body fell with a thud back to the floor, to the linoleum, and the clipboards and paper cups came raining down from the nurses' hands. Again, he convulsed, and then he stopped, and as Jamie and the other children watched, he died. There were no more shocks for the children that day, and there were no explanations.

Burke finished the story, telling how Jamie was hospitalized for 15 years, how he was trained to be an assistant in the hospital beauty parlor. . . and how he escaped. Miraculously he survived, wandering and homeless. Finally he got a job as a singer, earned enough for a bus ride to San Francisco, and, years later, became a transsexual woman.

Electroshock is a less common treatment now. Burke says it is mostly reserved for older women. But there are hundred of institutions, according to Burke, including 100 in Texas alone, that advertise treatment for feminine boys. Such treatment can include heavy drug therapy and behaviorist therapy. Behaviorist treatment can include attaching electrodes to the penis and providing electroshock if the boy shows any physiological response to pictures of men making love. For those with the stomach for it, I suggest reading additional Burke stories about life in such hospitals.

The story of how psychiatrists and mental hospitals stole the childhood and adolescence of Daphne Scholinski, making the problems of a badly parented child far worse, is told in the pain-filled book, *The Last Time I Wore A Dress*.[44] She found her healing from such things as noticing the beauty of a sunset, the courage of a handicapped person who made a living as a gas station manager, and an untrained aide who broke the "Master Plan of Treatment" by telling her she was sane. One power of this book is in the repeated examples of the stupidity and blindness induced in hospital authorities and psychiatrists by their multiple labels and plans, including the label of gender identity disorder. Daphne's well-told story offers us a terrible beauty, a Guernica of psychiatry, in which the mental limits of the "healers" are exceeded only by the limits of their compassion. Over and over, the pathos of Daphne's story is denied as she is repeatedly reduced to an object of treatment. A real hug, instead of treatment-required hugs—a little honest conversation, instead of checking out the treatment categories and plans—a little friendship, instead of professionalism, could have made so much difference. As Pete Seeger has noted, you can't sing very well when you are maintaining your professional objectivity.

## Professions Gone Wrong

Any profession in the United States at the beginning of the 21st century has prestige, in part, because it is presumed to be grounded in science and logic. It is presumed that professions are self-correcting as a result of ongoing informed conversation. If old theories cannot stand up to review, they are supposed to be changed, whether the profession is metallurgy or psychiatry. It is time for the American Psychiatric Association, the American Psychological Association, and others to take responsibility for the outrages being performed by their members, within their standards, against children and adults who are gender nonconforming.

At their annual meeting in 1993, the American Psychiatric Association began to debate the proposal that "well adjusted transsexuals not automatically be considered to have a mental disorder."[45] Making such a change would be helpful indeed, particularly if they don't keep transgender people in DSMs under another of their slippery categories. Eight years later no action has been taken. But such a change, if it comes, is not nearly enough. I call on each of these professions to offer public apologies for the thousands of people they have hurt. I call on them to make reparation for the breach of their public trust by taking the lead in helping our society move to greater acceptance of variety in gender expression, and to value the positive gifts of every person, whatever the gender design of the wrappings.

To further bring the enormity of the outrage home, I suggest that the reader consider whether any punishment of juvenile delinquents comes close to such barbarity as was visited upon Jamie. Notice that gender-nonconforming children are found guilty of the charge of masculinity or femininity without due process and with no defense attorney. Homosexuality is not a crime, and it is not a disease within the legal standards of the United States. But showing masculinity or femininity to the wrong parents can get you injured in ways that are hard to imagine.

Let me be personally clear. I am a transgender person. By my own subjectivity and by any reasonable measure of social functioning, I am about as healthy as you can get. I regard it as a social threat when anyone tries to define me as unnatural or sick.

In the first part of the 20th century, millions of people were given indeterminate "sentences" of forced stays in mental hospitals. Some had needles stuck into their brains to produce a dreamlike conformity; others were electrically and chemically attacked over and over again with a thoroughness that rivals the worst tortures of the Spanish Inquisition. Some people received lifelong sentences that were initiated by nonconforming behaviors far milder than those that lead to criminal sentencing. When some of the legal protections allowed to criminals were granted to mental patients, and when the standard was established that you couldn't keep someone in a hospital unless there was a treatment plan, the inpatient population of mental hospitals plummeted to a small fraction of its previous size.

Despite some reformed opinions, such as declaring homosexuality not to be a mental illness, and despite having to adjust to legally forced reforms, such as deinstitutionalization, the clinical professions are not in retreat. For example, in 1995, George Rekers published his *Handbook of Childhood and Adolescent Sexual Disorders,* which pushes the traditional cultural agenda while falsely claiming a scientific base. In short, as I pointed out in Chapter 3, we still allow cultural bullies like George Rekers to abuse children like Becky. It has got to stop.

But the larger issue is not the ugliness of individuals like Rekers. Some therapists who work with transsexuals are nice people and even win awards from the transgender community for their service. Randi Ettner, for example, wrote a first-person account of her psychotherapy with transsexual clients. She learned to like and appreciate some of her clients. She realized that some of her clients were healthy and wholesome people. In addition to showing the world that she is a caring therapist and doing something helpful, she gives a picture of transsexuals that is mostly positive. On the other hand, she also lets her prejudice show. She describes Carla as having garish-looking makeup and being "a tad peculiar looking, like a woman who might be of slightly below normal intelligence."[46] Later she chooses to describe Rochelle as looking like a "sausage coming out of its casing."[47] But the really dangerous thing is that she defends all the clinical theories and labels, even when they do not come close to describing her patients. For example, one of her patients was an 82-year-old man who suddenly discovered his transsexuality in response to being told about estrogenic treatment for prostate cancer.[48] It's nice to have Randi Ettner as a friend and a personal advocate, at least as long as you are physically attractive. What we need are professionals who are also reformers—clinicians who will take responsibility for ending the damage done by their profession, even when the profession wears a pretty smiling face.

## Clinical Parenting

George Rekers (1982) and Peter and Barbara Wyden (1986) have written books that attempt to build on clinical research for the purpose of helping parents teach masculinity to boys as a way of avoiding homosexuality. It is bad enough that the scientific basis for such books are lacking. Studies reviewed in an earlier chapter show that clinical interventions do not redirect children from a homosexual career. But the worst aspect of such work is the caricature of culture that such an approach purports to defend. As a counter caricature, I share Phyllis Burke's report of a psychoanalyst who began treatment with a boy at 3 years old and declared him cured of his femininity at 8 when "Stanley" joined him in a word fantasy and murdered President and Mrs. Reagan. The drumbeat of masculine socialization that fills the reports of establishment "therapies" is that boys should not be nurturing and boys should not engage in household domestic activities. This amounts to teaching boys to be terrible parents, and then blaming stereotypical fathers for being emotionally distant and uninvolved, which clinicians then theorize is a cause of the children's problems.

## Changing Bodies

This section deals with the desire of some transgender people to get medical help to change their bodies to more closely fit their personal images and self-concepts. Some of the changes sought are of the same sort sought by straight people wanting to change their bodies to more closely fit their personal images and self-concepts.

Our bodies, in addition to bringing capacities, limits, and predispositions into every moment, are also potent symbols. In person-to-person interactions our appearances begin the informational interchange before a word is spoken. Even when we intend no specific message by our appearances, we are nonetheless providing signals to which others respond. The book that helped me understand the social-psychological issues of appearance is the *Presentation of Self in Everyday Life*, by Erving Goffman.[49] An important book about more specialized presentations is Goffman's *Stigma: Notes on the Management of Spoiled Identity*.[50] The great book on transgender cultural images is Marjorie Garber's *Vested Interests: Cross Dressing and Cultural Anxiety*.[51]

Everyone who combs their hair alters their appearance. This section considers more permanent transgender alterations of the body. Most of these changes are for symbolic purposes. In seeking changed body imagery, transgender people are acting as audiences to their own bodies although the image goals are subjectively sensed as internal. Seeking such changes is presented in Chapter 6 as one possible development of transgender careers.

The "shapes" of gender imagery have cultural roots. Some body changes focus considerable emotional energy as gender signs and as status signs within genders. Claiming, paying for and experiencing changes in gender-related appearance cues can be a strong reinforcement of individual transgender commitments, a landmark in transgender careers.

A substantially changed body can give a transgender person a crucial sense of personal permission to see himself or herself as a transformed person—that is, when one wants to apply alternative gender expectations to himself or herself, it helps when such expectations *appear* to be appropriate. For those who have a goal of assimilation into the other gender, permanent body changes can be an important aspect of emotional and conceptual self-acceptance. Such changes are also important because they make it easier to complete the time-consuming practicalities of sustaining the appearance of the other gender.

Thwarting such appearance changes with social, legal and medical roadblocks is severe punishment for people who feel an intense personal need to live out of an alternative gender self-conception. It is cruel to block someone from attaining a whole and healthy sense of self. The transgender community is filled with stories of the agony such blockages sometimes bring. Such personal costs have social implications as well: from lowered job performance to disrupted marital and parental relationships.

The formal reference for clinicians in acting as gatekeeper to hormonal therapy and SRS is the *Harry Benjamin Standards of Care,* published by the Harry Benjamin International Dysphoria Association. The Benjamin Standards were created in 1979 and continued with only small changes until 1998, when the Fifth Version was published. The Fifth Version was created by a committee with significant internal lack of consensus. The committee stress was so severe that after nine drafts there was still significant disagreement. To end the process, the Association decided to publish the last draft in draft format. Richard Green then appointed a new 17 member committee, which included some transgender people and some nonclinicians. Despite greater diversity, this committee was able to achieve much greater consensus which led to the publication of the Sixth Version in 2001.[52]

The Sixth Version is considerably more friendly to transgender people. For example, it allows for hormonal therapy for people not seeking SRS and not seeking a full-time transition. Nonetheless, the Sixth Version strongly reaffirms the medical model and the DSM-IV diagnosis of gender identity disorder. It makes the case that SRS is medically necessary for people with severe GID and is not experimental, elective, cosmetic, or optional. SRS is claimed to be the effective and appropriate treatment for transsexuals or for people with profound GID. Such language makes it clear that one of the important purposes of the Sixth Version is to lay the groundwork for insurance-based reimbursement for the costs of SRS and hormonal therapies.[53]

One alternative to the Benjamin Standards is offered in the *Health Law Standards of Care for Transsexualism*, created and adopted by a gathering of transgender lawyers and activists. The first standard reads, "Physicians participating in transsexual health care shall provide hormonal sex reassignment therapy to patients requesting a change in their sexual appearance subject only to (1) the physician's reasonable belief that the therapy will not aggravate a patient's health conditions, (2) the patient's compliance with periodic blood chemistry checks to ensure a continued healthy condition, and (3) the patient's signature on a form providing informed consent and waiving liability. If a patient is married, the physician may not require divorce but may also require the spouse to sign a waiver of liability form." A third standard makes sexual reassignment surgery contingent on completing 1 year of hormone treatments.[54]

Perhaps the most disheartening defense of the GID diagnosis and the Benjamin Standards of Care is that of David Seil.[55] He is a clinician who has had responsibility for over 100 cases of transsexuals seeking SRS. He offers the usual clinical defenses, discussed in previous sections, and messes up definitional issues in ways already discussed. He may have helped many of his clients, but there is no doubt that he is intent on sustaining clinical control as gatekeeper to the transsexual process.[56] He writes that he wants every transsexual to be funneled through one of the 19 gender identity clinics in the Western world that "provide sound medical and psychiatric care."[57]

What makes Seil's chapter so disheartening is that it is found in a textbook on homosexuality edited by active proponents of ending the illness definition of homosexuality. The introductory sections and chapters of the text are a model of gay affirmative psychiatry. Robert Cabaj and Terry Stein put their perspective up front, and they note that the text is "written and edited from the perspective that homosexuality is not an illness and is not pathological. . . . homosexuality is a normal but less frequent expression of human sexual desire and behavior."[58] It surprises and saddens me that Cabaj and Stein accepted a chapter from David Seil that repeats every element of bad science and clinical oppression that they have fought against for homosexuals.

Charles Silverstein adds an additional unfortunate element to the Cabaj and Stein book. "The new forms of treatment reject concepts of etiology with their emphasis on abnormality. Newer therapeutic techniques assume that same-sex desire is an *acceptable* variation of human sexuality and that attempts to identify the 'cause' of homosexuality can lead to political, social, and legal efforts to repress it."[59] Such an antiscientific bias will serve the gay, lesbian, and bisexual communities badly over the long haul: it weakens any minority to present itself as hiding from the truth.

Hormonal therapy and sexual reconstructive surgery are invasive medical procedures and need the support of well-prepared medical professionals. The transgender community in general, and the transsexual community in particular, has much to be thankful for to Harry Benjamin and other courageous medical leaders. But such thankfulness is for their ground-breaking work in a period of cultural resistance. Now that hormonal and surgical procedures are well established, it is time to ask the policy questions freshly so as to lay down a proper basis for the next decades.

Paul Walker analyzes the history of the second stage of transsexual services. In the late 1970s and early 1980s there was substantial reconsideration of the desirability of SRS and many clinics withdrew from the business, including the Johns Hopkins University Hospital, where Harry Benjamin did his pioneer work.[60] Although several studies showed generally positive results from SRS, a study by Meyer and Reter provided a negative analysis, arguing that those who had had the surgery were no more well adjusted that those who had not.[61] This study, however, was quickly criticized for errors in the research design, in statistics, and in logic.[62] Although some may attribute the decline in SRS services to the negative research by Meyer and Reter, the decline began before the appearance of Meyer and Reter's article, and a survey of clinicians who had stopped doing SRS work found that the clinicians thought SRS was effective but quit for other reasons, including burnout, inadequate funding, and lack of research grants.[63] Walker also notes that the official explanation from Johns Hopkins Hospital was that the clinic stopped doing SRS because the staff felt they had completed their research on the subject and had shown that it was effective.[64] A check of the Gender Education and Advocacy website in 2001 generated a list of as many as 17 surgeons in the United States who perform SRS and additional surgeons providing related surgeries.[65]

Although the most recent changes in the Benjamin Standards have had the benefit of respectful interaction between transsexuals and establishment clinicians, the legal, theoretical, and power aspects of relationships between transgender people and their therapists remain unchanged. Forcing transsexuals to accept pathological labels to obtain care is hurtful. Responding to cross-dressers with the presumption that fetishism is the defining characteristic is hurtful. The typical "clinical" encounter still has the basic script: "I will help you if you will first agree that you are deviant or abnormal and need special consideration." This is ugly. This is antihealth ideology. It has to stop. The American Psychiatric Association cannot claim it hasn't gotten the message. Substantial picketing of their headquarters and annual meeting in 1996 by such groups as the Transsexual Menace, The National Gay and Lesbian Task Force, Bi-Net USA, the International Gay and Human Rights Commission, It's Time America, and others makes it clear that there is substantial opposition to this diagnosis—that it hurts.[66]

*Paying for Transgender Care*

The agonizing issue within the transgender community is not definitions or standards of care. The consensus is widespread in this regard. We want good medical care. We know some of our transgender friends need substantial counseling. We want our transgender friends to carefully think through what they are doing before undergoing invasive medical procedures. We know we don't want to be pathologized. We know we don't want to play the games, tell the lies, that will convince the gatekeepers to give us what we want.

For many transsexual people, counseling, hormone therapy and SRS are agonizingly expensive—compounded for some by job loss because of transgender oppression. Some transsexuals and other transgender people have gotten financial help from Medicaid[67] or private insurance[68] for some aspects of medical and psychological transitions. In 2001, the San Francisco Board of Supervisors voted 9-2 to provide SRS coverage as part of their employee health care package.[69] Many have not received any assistance because of policy barriers in private and public insurance standards. For example, SRS is often defined as cosmetic and therefore not eligible for reimbursement. Proponents of such restrictions argue that plastic surgery for the image enhancement of straight people is usually treated as cosmetic and ineligible. This has encouraged some transsexuals to join with some clinicians in defending the gender identity disorder diagnosis so that SRS can be defined as medically necessary rather than cosmetic. In contrast to the fractured system in the United States, Canada and the nations of the European Union provide full coverage for the medical needs of transgender patients, including SRS.[70]

This book emphasizes depathologizing transgender experience and expression. If transgender or transsexual status is not defined as a disease if will be hard to assert the principle of medical necessity as a bias for claiming insurance based financial support for treatment. It upsets me to take a position that may make it more difficult for some transgender people to get the financial support they need. One alternative, argued in the most recent changes in the Benjamin Standards, is to emphasize the principle of harm reduction. This principle was important in legalizing abortions and is still important in defending a woman's right to choose. It is sadly true that some transgender people injure themselves by taking hormones without monitoring by a doctor. Worse, some transsexuals have committed suicide after being denied treatment.

Clinicians have offered an approach for gaining insurance reimbursement that modifies the pathological label. It is based on the clinical definition of dystonia. Only 17 people in the world think they know what dystonia means. Since I'm one of them, no more than 16 support the concept. Humor aside, the concept of dystonia builds on the idea that the choice of violating traditional cultural standards in choice of sexual partner or choice of gender presentation is not itself pathological, but that people making such choices may believe what society says about the choices and become internally conflicted. Dystonia is discomfort based on introjected transphobia or homophobia based on enculturation. Some therapists love to pick on religion at this point and talk about homosexuals who think their orientation is sinful. Although I agree that improved theology is needed, (a topic addressed in the last chapter of this book), it is equally fair to say in response to the clinical establishment that their insistence on pathologizing transgender experience and expression is a major source of dystonia. To be blunt, "Therapists make us sick." But not to worry. Now that I am sick from dystonia—now that I am sick because I've been taught that I'm sick (or sinful)—I might be able to qualify for financial support for my medical condition.

Although I toss the word *dystonia* on the scrap heap with the long list of other now obsolete pathologizing words, there is an underlying truth that deserves attention. Transgender people, like other people, may have difficulty using the cultural landmarks of sexuality and gender to navigate their sexual and gender journeys. Many kinds of efforts to deconstruct and improve images and concepts of sexuality and gender are needed, and a variety of perspectives, from feminism to fundamentalism, are making contributions to such changes. This book argues that transgender people are also pointing to needed changes but have to pay high personal prices for such contributions. My argument for providing financial assistance to transgender people for counseling and other medical help is that society should help transgender people stabilize their lives in the face of cultural oppression, just as it is has helped others adjust to divorce, rape, or job loss.

One current practice that provides some financial assistance for some transgender people takes advantage of the ambiguities of many non-transgender psychological categories and diagnoses to qualify for services under other labels.[71] Such tactics may help with getting financial support for some counseling costs but is less likely to help with hormonal or surgical costs. Transgender people pursuing the stretching strategy need to be warned that some of the other labels used can have just as negative effects on employment or health insurance applications as does the GID label. Such considerations make medical privacy a big deal for transgender people and transgender people need to know that, despite numerous assurances, medical privacy is not currently well-protected.

Transgender activists can join others who are making the case that some mental health support should be available to everyone, without any diagnosis or labeling. This is a difficult policy argument to win because there has been so much abuse—so much expensive gaming of the systems for providing mental health care. Nonetheless, it is fair to argue that there are significant social benefits, and potential cost savings, in providing private and public insurance-based support for initial orientation and mental health planning to anyone who is emotionally upset or mentally confused and to anyone who needs help in making difficult life choices. Such assistance should be available before any diagnosis is made. Then, when any psychotropic drugs (including hormones) are believed to be warranted in order to reduce emotional discomfort or to improve social functioning, such drugs should be provided to everyone on an equal basis to improve both individual functioning and the general functioning of society. This general reform is needed by many groups abused by current clinical practices and insurance standards, and transgender people can join others in creating a relevant reform movement. Such an approach requires coalition building and a focus on larger social purposes rather than on special transgender problems.

Public health thinking can also be applied to seeking financial assistance for SRS, although it is more of a special-case agenda. The terms of such assistance could also recognize that there should be a sufficient copayment to reinforce the importance of personal responsibility for initiating such a major change. Because some transgender and transsexual people are poor as a result of oppression, such copayments should be on a sliding scale. One good way to provide such support would be to create a few national public health clinics with an appropriate sliding fee scale to serve transsexuals. Such a clinic or program could be linked to a training program. Currently, a free clinic in San Francisco offers counseling and hormone assistance and there is active debate about providing SRS.[72]

*Therapy and Intersexuality*

The issues around SRS look very different when one considers the imposition of SRS on intersexual infants. Thousands of people are subjected to such surgeries. James Monteleone, who performs such surgeries, makes it clear that the physician should exert a strong influence on the decision to operate because "A child with ambiguous genitalia represents an emergency situation. . . . While awaiting test results, the child should remain hospitalized and not sent home until the sex of rearing has been decided and a name given. If possible, corrective surgery should be completed so there is no sexual ambiguity when the child is home."[73] He goes on to note that it may be difficult to convince parents of a child with a micropenis to go ahead with SRS.[74] Monteleone makes it clear that though there are 31 different intersexual conditions, with 8 causes of just one (micropenis), the motive to operate is cultural. "The decision on the most appropriate gender should not be influenced by the karotype (genetic sex) nor the gonadal sex, but is based mainly on the appearance of the external genitalia and their adult potential or the likely pattern of sexual development at puberty."[75]

As an aside, relative to the focus of this section, it is interesting to note that the medical standard used by Monteleone and others assumes that gender is *not* determined by chromosomal or gonadic sex—a sharp challenge to those who theorize that gender identity disorder is significantly caused by a theorized but unmeasured fetal hormonal development. The larger point is that physicians who are defending bipolar gender standards injure both children and adults. They force their therapies on infants without knowing the need for or appropriateness of their actions while resisting similar therapies to adults who are very clear about their need.

In about 90 % of the cases of infant SRS, the intended outcome is a female infant. These surgeries are not always simple or satisfactory. In many cases sexual sensation is lost or reduced. This justifies applying the term *genital mutilation* to this practice. One intersexual was conformed to male status with 22 separate operations over many years. The result was a scarred penis which felt like a piece of wood to the owner.[76]

Anne Fausto-Sterling studied case histories of intersexuals in the 1930 - 1960 period, before infant SRS became routine. Her summary is that intersexual people adjusted to their conditions and there was not a psychotic or suicide in the lot. For intersexual children there is no "emergency" other than cultural control aimed at defending a bipolar definition of sex. Reports from the Intersex Society of North America are full of deep distress caused by infant SRS, not only from the genital mutilation, but from the shame of their parents, from being treated like a freak, and from having a secret in one's body that was known or suspected but that was denied by the parents the child loved.[77] The Society argues that if SRS is desirable, then let the child have a say in it, fill the child with love and acceptance, and do any surgery after puberty when the result is more likely to be surgically satisfying. How painful an irony that infant SRS, which is often unwanted later, is covered by public and private insurance, whereas SRS that is wanted by fully informed adults is not covered.

### Transgender Friendly Counsel

Many transgender people need some good counseling as they come to grips with their transgender experience. Some seek help to work with emotional discomfort or confusion as they begin to work with transgender feelings and images. This kind of counseling, although specific in content, is not different in kind from counseling for other kinds of emotional discomfort and confusion. The initiating need for counseling may be prompted by any of the common life crises that transgender people share with everyone else. A lost job or the death of a parent can be hard to handle for anyone. Or moving away from home to go to college may create a bit of psychic freedom that allows an interest to come to consciousness. How can transgender people find a counselor who will just focus on helping out rather than loading the person down with clinical labels?

There are at least three paths to finding a good counselor. You can seek help within the transgender community. There are 250 transgender support groups in the United States. They might be found through the local gay and lesbian press. They can be found through the International Foundation for Gender Education, either through the magazine *Transgender Tapestry* or at their website: www.ifge.org. Most of the local groups can offer advice and referrals.

A second path to getting good counsel is to offer transgender education to a minister, social worker, or counselor one already knows and trusts. You might share an introductory pamphlet from one of the national organizations. A good introductory book is Niela Miller's *Counseling in Genderland: a Guide for You and Your Transgendered Client.*[78] You might also want to provide this book as a reference.

Fortunately, the world of social work is developing a much more engaged and sensitive understanding of transgender issues. For those working in, or seeking help from social service programs, a good place to start reading is Gary Mallon's *Social Services With Transgendered Youth.*[79]

A third path is to shop around for a counselor. That's what I did when I was working through a divorce. Although transgender expression was not important in my second divorce because I was suppressing it, as I started looking forward to life after divorce I felt it was time for me to clarify my transgender path. I was fortunate to find a good counselor on my first try. She was not knowledgeable about transgender issues. Neither was she a friend. Nonetheless, she was helpful for several reasons that might be thought of as the minimum requirements for a good therapist:

- She kept the sessions focused on my needs and didn't ask a lot of questions that would have amounted to charging me for educating her about transgender issues.

- She was nonjudgmental and didn't set forth an agenda of helping me adjust to traditional roles and images.
- She was good at helping me clarify several issues, attending to both their distinctness and their interaction.
- She didn't try to draw me into an effort to reconstruct my personality going back to early childhood. We stayed focused on the issues I needed to deal with and brought up memories as they were relevant.
- Best of all, she did not talk about my "symptoms" in a sickness model but accompanied me, and challenged me, as I prepared for several important decisions.
- She created safe space for the release and acceptance of some long-carried feelings.

If you are a person needing good counsel, I wish you good heart and perseverance in finding a helpful counselor to share with, both in claiming all your experience and in giving yourself to all that is meaningful.

---

## Notes

1. William Faulkner (1930).
2. Carl Jung, quoted in *Poverty and Race*, Vol. 6, No.4, page 7 (July 1997).
3. Sandra Bem (1993), page 82. John D'Emilio and Estelle Freedman (1988), page 226.
4. Nolan Lewis (1943).
5. Ibid., page 140.
6. Ibid., page 157.
7. Chandler Burr (1996), page 124.
8. Evelyn Hooker (1957).
9. Kim Mills (1998), pages 2-12.
10. Ibid., page 6.
11. Tracey St. Pierre, 1998.
12. Thomas Szasz (1970), page 167.
13. Talcott Parsons (1957), reprinted in E. Gartly Jaco (1972), page 107.
14. Thomas Sheff (1963).
15. Patrick Conover (1976).
16. Stephan Spitzer and Norman Denzin (1968).
17. Patrick Conover (1976).
18. Vern and Bonnie Bullough (1977), page 76.
19. Ibid., page 83.
20. Phyllis Burke (1996).
21. Ibid., page 66.
22. A. Bakker et al. (1993).
23. Ibid., page 536.
24. Sandra Bem (1993), pages 106-111.
25. Richard Green (1985).
26. DSM-IV (1994), page 533.

27. Ibid.
28. Ibid.
29. Ibid.
30. Ibid., page 534.
31. Ibid., pages 536-538.
32. Ibid., page 534.
33. Timothy and Joseph Costello (1992), page 267.
34. Ibid.
35. Ibid., page 268.
36. Ibid., page 273.
37. Ruth Westheimer (1994).
38. Eva Margolies (1994), page 127.
39. Ibid., page 130.
40. Charles Clayman (1989), page 106.
41. Janice Irvine (1990) extended this analysis to sexologists. "Moored within the scientific establishment, [by which she meant establishment clinicians] gender sexologists were seemingly untouched by the social movements in the 1960s and 1970s that called for a loosening of rigid gender strictures. Rather, by aligning the profession with the dominant ideology, the gender industry reified normative, oppressive constructions of gender roles, and encouraged these values in the individuals they treated."(page 278) And again, "sexology as an institution seems impervious to critiques of the limitations of science."(page 285)
42. Richard Green (1987), page 274.
43. Phyllis Burke (1996), pages 75 ff.
44. Daphne Scholinski and Jane Meredith Adams (1997).
45. Richard Green (1985) cited in Ruth Colker (1996), pages 116, 265.
46. Randy Ettner (1996), pages 24-25.
47. Ibid., pages 78-79.
48. See Roberta's story in Chapter 5.
49. Erving Goffman (1959).
50. Erving Goffman (1963).
51. Marjorie Garber (1992).
52. Anne Lawrence (2001).
53. Ibid.
54. Health Law Standards (1993).
55. David Seil (1996).
56. Ibid., pages 750.
57. Ibid., page 755-756.
58. Robert Cabaj and Terry Stein (1996).
59. Charles Silverstein (1996).
60. Paul Walker (1983), page 281.
61. J. Meyer and D. Reter (1979).
62. M. Fleming, et al. (1980).
63. N. Fisk and J. VanMaasdam (1981).
64. Paul Walker (1983), page 281.
65. www.gender.org.
66. News item from *In Your Face,* No.4, Spring, 1997 (274 W. 11th St., #4R, New York, NY 10014).

67. At least four states have paid for SRS through Medicaid under some circumstances. The four relevant cases turned on related issues, but framed in different ways. The four states are Georgia, Iowa, Minnesota, and California. Case citations and additional references are available from the Gender Education and Advocacy website:http://www.gender.org. www.gender.org. A particularly helpful decision that recreated the right to Medicaid funding in Iowa is reported in *Lesbian/Gay Law Notes* December 1998.

68. Private insurance provided by employers can change quickly with regard to specific benefits. A 1998 survey done by It's Time America turned up the following corporations and insurance companies that have provided SRS in at least some cases: American Airlines, AT&T, IBM, Microsoft, Motorola, Upjohn, US West, United Healthcare, The Guardian Insurance Company, Unicare, and Blue Cross/Blue Shield.

69. Rachel Gordon (2001).

70. Web communication by Miranda of It's Time Illinois.

71. Category stretching is an insurance application strategy used in numerous medical circumstances. The transgender strategy is just a specific application of a common practice.

72. Evelyn Nieves (2001).

73. James Monteleone (1983), pages 65, 67.

74. Ibid., page 68.

75. Ibid., pages 67, 76-77.

76. Phyllis Burke (1996), page 222.

77. Ibid., page 227.

78. Niela Miller (1996).

79. Gary Mallon (1999).

*As ridiculous or quixotic as it may sound these days, one thing seems certain to me: that it is my responsibility to emphasize the moral origin of all genuine politics, to stress the significance of moral values and standards in all spheres of social life, . . . and to explain that if we don't try, within ourselves, to discover or rediscover or cultivate what I call "higher responsibility," things will turn out very badly indeed for our country.* Vaclav Haval[1]

*The first thing you have to do if you're going to do anything about changing the world. . . you have to buy it for perfect and become responsible for it in the condition that it is now in . . . not say, Hey let's get it neat and then I'll be responsible for it, but responsible for it in the condition that it is now in.*

Stephen Gaskin

# Chapter 8:
# Transgender Issues

I noted in Chapter 4 that institutions and societies are more than a sum of the social relations within them, just as a relationship between two people is more than the sum of the individuals involved. Each of us brings potentials to interpersonal, institutional and societal relationships. Some of these potentials are unknown to us before we enter relationships and learn from them. As we interact with each other and with our environment, as we reflect on our interaction and notice the needs and possibilities that are accessible to us, as we notice our rising questions and curiosity, and as we are touched by the lures of what is eternal (love, beauty, truth, and more), we gather awareness of the possibilities of our lives as human creatures. Responding with appreciation is considered in the next chapter. Earlier chapters consider the source of transgender potentials, name the range of transgender options, and tell some transgender stories. Here we consider contingencies that affect our choices of engaging in or avoiding activities with transgender aspects.

Individuals estimate likely and potential social responses when they plan their actions. Sometimes, people with transgender experience may estimate that negative responses to transgender expression are so likely and so strong that they feel their only reasonable choice is to conform to traditional gender expectations or take up a hopeless rebellion that would bring the punishments of lost social relationships and positions—and maybe worse. But when we switch to a social or historical frame of reference, it is easy to see that institutions and societies change. The causes of such change include the needs and values of individuals that they bring with them into social relationships. In the previous section we noted how a change in the law led to a large decrease in the number of people forced into mental hospitals by court orders. This practical and political chapter considers how transgender people and their friends can encourage relationships, institutions, and society to be more supportive and more fair.

Although there is a section in this chapter on legal issues, many transgender people are most concerned about informal social reactions and sanctions. George Rekers justified his professional abuse of Becky, discussed in Chapter 7, by arguing that society is very harsh on masculine girls as they grow up. Rekers' professional power was legally backed, but his appeal is that he was helping Becky because of the threat of informal social sanctions. Becky defied informal expectations about how little girls should look and how they should play and her parents gained legally backed clinical support for heavy-handed punishments to try to force conformity. Gary Mallon tells the story of gender-transgressing kids who are thrown out of their homes and end up on the streets as sex workers. Fortunately for the kids, he not only tells their stories but offers them a full-time residence program to get a new start.[2]

## Transgender Sexual Relations

For me, and for many in the "out" transgender community, explicitly sexual interaction is an important part of transgender awareness and feelings. This usual behavior parallels the explicitly sexual interaction of people expressing bipolar sex and gender conceptions. I know of no useful data-based answers regarding whether transgender people are more interested or less interested in sexuality than other people. The Robert Michael study, discussed in Chapter 4, while lacking a focus on transgender people, shows that questions addressing such issues are highly sensitive to nuances of definition and question construction.

Many writers have focused on whether transgender people are homosexual or straight. The surface answer is that they can be gay or lesbian or bisexual or straight, with reference to the preferred physiology of partners chosen for sexual sharing. Said alternatively, gay, lesbian, bisexual, and straight people may present transgender or typical gender behavior as part of their sexuality.

A focus on the physiology of partners chosen for sexual sharing misses the point that transgender expression is about crossing gender lines in attracting the interest of partners. Focus on the physiology of sexual sharing undervalues the importance of emotional satisfaction, the formation of social bonds between the partners as a basis for marriage and family relationships, the artistic (esthetic) aspects of sexual activity, and love as a spiritual issue. Kate Bornstein is fond of answering the question about why people choose others for sexual activity by pointing out that they may choose others for particular kinds and styles of sexual activity and intimate relationships as opposed to choosing the physiological equipment of the partner.[3] I'm not sure most people have thought things through as carefully as Kate Bornstein has, but I do think that people respond sexually to symbols of masculinity and femininity.

Transgender people are constantly confronted with the charge of fetishism as a description of their sexual activity. Previous chapters have given partial answers to this challenge. Here, the concept of fetishism is placed in the context of common experience.

An enormous amount of advertisement aims at reinforcing masculine and feminine symbols and at linking all kinds of extraneous objects to such symbols. At the time of writing there is a television ad that is working hard to make a connection of feminine imagery to the curves in a cola bottle, a curve you can hold in your hand. I've never seen or heard a description of the buying of soft drinks as fetishistic. But think how the fashion industry creates and uses cultural images to lure people into spending ridiculous amounts of money to buy fashionable clothes. This work of the advertising industry could easily be described as fetishistic, since it is aimed at creating links between sexual feelings and objects to be purchased.

Transgender people respond to the same kinds of symbols and interests as other people but make their choices across gender lines. This isn't all that unusual. Over my lifetime, many straight women have started choosing clothing across gender lines, even buying fly-front pants that are anatomically irrelevant and recently illegal.[4] There are still gender standards for women's clothing and appearance, but they are not what they were when I was a child. To cap the irony, advertisements that do so much to encourage gender conformity often appeal to transgender themes for fashion changes. It is apparently lucrative to encourage a little transgender tasting within the acceptability standards of changing fashion expectations.

It is not gender nonconformity that defines fetishism. Fetishism concerns the degree to which one's sexuality is attached to an object rather than to people.[5] Gender fashions are an important part of the process by which people assign emotional significance to objects, and this is as true for straight people as for transgender people. Just because transgender people attach emotional and sexual feelings to clothing and other appearance props across gender lines, it doesn't mean that their choices are fetishistic.

There are at least five nonfetishistic reasons why transgender people may choose clothing and appearance props associated with the other gender. It's been commonly noted in transgender literature that when a person who has been socialized to be a man is just getting started with cross-dressing, the first purchases and uses of feminine clothing and makeup may feel scary. Adrenalin can produce a lot of endorphins, a physiological mechanism of pleasure. The feelings of rebellion and release can be pretty exciting. On the other hand, as noted earlier in the research of Richard Docter, most transgender people lose a lot of the feelings of sexy stimulation from cross-dressing after awhile. This certainly fits a fear-as-aphrodisiac theory. When a male transvestite shaves his legs, it may be fun the first few times. For many it becomes an onerous task that is part of offering a feminine presentation—a more onerous task than for women because there is more hair to shave more often.

A second reason is that transgender people choose clothing for the same reasons as do straight people. Transgender people can be thought of as responding to the same ads in the same way, wanting to experience the same *feelings* associated with the objects. It is because a straight audience feels a man *shouldn't* want to feel the feelings associated with wearing lipstick that there arises the over-reaction of charges of fetishism. Indeed, wearing lipstick may be an encouragement for a transgender person to open up feelings in sexual interaction that would otherwise be repressed, thus enhancing the person-to-person quality of the interaction.

A different entry point into this discussion points to a third nonfetishistic explanation of cross-gender appearance expression. If a person is physiologically male and wants to wear lipstick, it may be because of a male physiological urge that has been squelched by social oppression. Consider the straight-line reasoning. I was defined as biologically male at birth. I choose to wear lipstick sometimes to express or claim one of my feelings. To the extent that physiological urges are involved, I am choosing lipstick to express a male urge. Although this book argues heavily against such straight-line reasoning in general, I have carefully preserved some room for the argument that physiological factors may have some influence on behavior. In this example, pointing to physiological influence seems strange only because it doesn't fit cultural stereotypes about how physiological factors work. This third reason proposes that there are male physiological urges which are not given room for expression by a restrictive culture. There might be a male urge to feel attractive, and a male might learn from all the lipstick ads that people can feel attractive by wearing lipstick. See Chapter 6 for more discussion of this kind of thinking.

This third line of reasoning is no more, *and no less,* provable than the anti-transgender theories based on other assumptions about physiological causes. It does make the ironic point that those who believe in physiological essentialism and who claim that transgender expression is unnatural can have such thinking turned against them.

A fourth line of nonfetishistic explanation of transgender sexual expression is like Max Weber's classic explanation of charisma. Weber notes that the subjective feeling that another person has charisma is the feeling that this other person is extraordinarily powerful or appealing. Weber goes on to point out that this feeling arises because the charismatic leader has touched a significant unmet need that is mostly unconscious in the person attributing the charisma to the other. Charisma is a strong source of emotional bonding. But, Weber notes, true freedom and power come when people claim their unmet needs and develop the capacity and relationships to meet those needs. Relative to the issue of transgender imagery as part of sexual sharing, transgender people, like straight people, face the challenge of claiming any unmet needs so that they can develop the capacity and relationships to meet those needs. As for straight people, transgender people may be strengthened in breaking any compulsive attachments to specific objects or images by recognizing and breaking free from the commercialization of fetishism found in contemporary advertisements. Part of that breaking free can include direct experience so that an individual has something to evaluate other than imagination. Ironically, it is by playing with— by experiencing—the wearing of lipstick that it becomes clear that the magic isn't in the lipstick but in the release of feelings. Stopping such play can arrest the development of such psychological maturity. For people who continue transgender expression, such maturity merely provides additional flexibility for their expressions and sharing of sexual exchanges.

A fifth nonfetishistic explanation for a felt excitement in purchasing and wearing clothes of the nonassigned gender is that it may express a longing for psychological wholeness. Transgender expression may open direct channels to denied feelings, express a courage to claim oneself in the face of oppression, and help to integrate fantasies and unexpressed energies into a whole self—a more creative and adaptive self, because more energy and imagination are accessible in everyday moments. Chapter 6 also speaks to this possibility. One bit of evidence for this theory is that first-timers at transgender support groups commonly express a great sense of relief when they have a safe place to talk about how their transgender journey has been emotionally healing and how being able to claim such healing as part of human relationships is empowering.

In offering these five nonfetishistic lines of reasoning to explain why some people include transgender expression in sexual interaction, I don't mean to deny that some transgender people have fetishistic attachments. J. J. Allen tells a story of a cross-dresser who bought 2,100 pairs of women's panties.[6] Most transgender people, however, buy panties to *wear* them. In the wearing, any feelings attached to the panties become only a part of the range of everyday experience, not just sexual expression. Such everyday normalization can be one of the best cures for a specific fetishistic feeling. When you wear panties every day and give your attention to the wide range of daily activities, you build up a lot of experience in which wearing panties is not associated with sexual arousal. Anyone interested in helping a transgender (or straight) person overcome a fetishistic attachment to an object might want to consider such a desensitization strategy. In short, the problem of fetishistic blockage to fully human interaction during sexual activity begins to be relieved when people begin to claim their feelings and start to work with them. Purging a transgender wardrobe is an expression of denial and blocks the path to working with one's feelings. Any fetishism that exists for transgender people can be thought of as a failure to complete the claiming of a transgender sense of self. Of course, claiming a transgender sense of self doesn't mean that one has to express such a sense of self in any particular way.

In addition to the charge of fetishism, transgender people also face the charge that their sexual behavior is narcissistic. The grounds for such a charge are twofold: a lot of transgender sexuality is expressed through masturbation and some transgender people who were defined as males at birth report sustaining an image of themselves as a woman or a female during intercourse.

Evaluating transgender masturbation as narcissism is problematic for several reasons. Given the oppression of transgender sexuality, it may be the only sexual outlet available to a transgender person. When interactive sexual sharing is available, carrying transgender imagery into intercourse may be a first step toward integrating one's fantasy life into social interaction as a sexual partner. A second step would be letting a trusted partner in on the secret so that the integrative process can be mutually supported. Habits can be powerful, but a commitment to growth and paying the price of full attention in sexual interaction can make a lot of difference. Sometimes, simply slowing down makes room for growth.

For man-to-woman transgender people, another issue is relevant to the charge of narcissism. In the culture I grew up in there were some strong messages to boys and men not to feel their feelings and to avoid emotional entanglements. Men were also taught to objectify women—to see them as sexual objects. Such messages taught me that feeling my feelings, including my feelings during sexual interaction, is a feminine activity. Against such a standard, it is easy to define as narcissistic any attention by a man to feeling his feelings. Whether or not one links feeling one's feeling to feminine imagery as I have, the labeling of men as narcissistic because they dare to claim their feelings, must give way to encouraging access to feelings, even when such vulnerability brings pain as well as joy. Different expressions of the men's movement are focusing on this very task. This task is important, not only for emotional health and psychological wholeness, but also for improved relations between men and women.

After clearing away the charges of fetishism and narcissism, there is room to notice that many transgender people and their partners report that transgender aspects of the expression of sexuality can be emotionally satisfying for both partners, and strongly bonding as a basis for marriage and family relationships. It can be a door to expanded awareness, sensuality, passion, and erotic love. Many transgender people and their partners have made this testimony. My treasured version of this story was written by my spouse, Trish Nemore, and can be found in Mary Boenke's wonderful book of stories *Trans Forming Families*.[7] Such testimony should stand as a sufficient rebuttal to all the efforts of the clinical professions to pathologize transgender sexual experience. I hope that clinicians who read this chapter, as well as Chapter 7, will choose to reconsider their "tolerant" insults that transgender expression is a "harmless fetish."

Although some transgender sexual relationships work beautifully, there are plenty of sad stories as well. When transgender sexual expression is part of a relational problem, and if there is a common goal of saving the relationship and a commitment to honesty, one or more of the following strategies might be helpful. A couple can negotiate limits to transgender expression in sexual activity that allows both partners to get some satisfaction. The transgender person can agree to keep transgender expression out of sexual interaction but can ask for acceptance, or at least tolerance, of other forms of transgender expression. A couple can accept that the transgender person should seek support and affirmation outside the couple relationship. A couple can agree on mutual celibacy. A couple can also work for relational transformation, with some room for transgender expression. Peggy Rudd has written usefully about such tranformational possibilities and strategies.[8]

If a couple chooses to pursue transformation, they may find it helpful to begin on the positive note of becoming clear about what really matters in the relationship. This helps create a deeper grounding than does a negotiation strategy. Focusing on what really matters is an invitation to include spiritual reflection in the conversation. Some may find Chapter 9 interesting in this regard. Transformation is a more attractive option when the goal is clarified as the enhancement of all that is emotionally satisfying, bonding, and loving.

Transformation might or might not be a realistic goal in a specific relationship. For some people the traditional social and cultural signals that frame sexual interaction feel so important and immovable that there seems little hope in pursuing a transformational course. Realizing that such signals are socially constructed might open a path to deeper reflection but that doesn't mean a person will want to walk that path. Whatever a partner's flexibility or rigidity, human relationships are worked out in the middle of complex lives with cross-cutting agendas. However creative and responsible the process, honesty and caring remain the keys either to transforming a relationship or to transitioning out of a relationship and moving on. When the doors are open, transgender people and their partners can walk out of the small room of specialness and into the big rooms of experience, communication, growth, and love.

### Transgender Parenting

Transgender people are often parents for part of their life journey. I've been blessed to give life to three children and I'm helped in raising two more in a blended family. I also have six grandchildren.

Parental gender presentations influence children. But such influences are probably not explained by simple learning theory. One study by Richard Green of 37 children raised by homosexual or transsexual parents found that the children grew up to be as straight as the general population.[9] This shouldn't seem surprising, since, after all, many straight parents end up with gay, lesbian, bisexual, or transgender children.

Transgender people who are parents who often carry the burden of being stigmatized. Sometimes the hostile characterizations come from close family members: a spouse, a former spouse, in-laws, parents, and siblings. It can be hard to work through one's own feelings of rejection. It's worse when relatives and friends intrude on relationships with your own child. Sometimes the intrusion is a hostile divorce with denial of rights of visitation. Sometimes the intrusion requires cutting off relations with family members who have been important to your children. In addition to family influences, children are also influenced by friends, school, church, and or other relationships. Sadly, some of those who shout the loudest about family values do the most to damage families with a transgender member. Fortunately, there are transgender people like me who have had better luck with finding and helping to create more affirmative situations for child-rearing. I have no special insight for transgender people who are parents. My advice is just to work hard at being a good parent and trust that, over time, it is the good parenting that will be remembered. Sustain your confidence and positive sense of self. If you know you are modeling love and responsibility, you can let unfair criticisms pass by without absorbing them. Just keep building on the positive relationships you have with your kids in the space and time you have to work with.

I write the following few paragraphs on a parent-to-parent basis. I'll bet many of you love your children as much as I love mine.

If you are a parent who strongly values and desires traditional gender expression in your children and have raised your children to be gender con-forming, you may nevertheless be faced with a child who has developed cross-gender interests and styles of self-presentation. You may have to decide whether you are more committed to your gender expectations or to your child. Good parenting means different things for different children. You may like or dislike different things about any particular child. Doesn't matter. You still have to figure out how to be a good parent to the children you have. If you have a gender nonconforming child, a child that may be hard for you to understand, a child you don't like very much, there are still several things you can do to be a good parent. Fortunately, elementary good parenting, rather than special knowledge or understanding, is what is critical. Whatever the issues your child has, you can help to create a safe space for your child to explore his or her feelings—safe space to develop the gifts and follow the callings that each has been given. Reducing the need to rebel, reducing the secrets, and positive modeling give children the greatest opportunity to find their best paths, the best grounding for active reflection and ongoing change. If you are having trouble with your transgender child, or any other child, your positive contribu-tion depends first of all on working with your own issues and discomforts.

Just as for children challenged by other issues, children who are showing visible transgender interests need space and experience, need support for feeling their feelings, need an understanding of the larger world, need to feel valued and appreciated, and need support when the world is oppressive. If you feel the proper parenting goal is the avoidance of transgender and homosexual identities in your children, a couple of reflections may prove helpful. The first to keep in mind is that a lot of children show some transgender elements in their play, but only a few end up as transgender, bisexual, lesbian, or gay adults. The second is that experience is a great antidote to fantasy.

Perhaps the most important guideline to remember if you want your child to avoid a transgender adult identity is the general good parenting practice of helping your child not to get stuck in rebellion because of fear. Fear can be a good thing, because there are certainly some things in children's lives that hurt. The growing-up trick for a transgender child is to not be paralyzed by fear, whether or not the fear is grounded in reality. Fear can create blindness, which blocks growth and change. The best way to help your child avoid being stuck in fear is to get beyond your own fear.

Good parenting starts with working on your own issues, whether fear or something else, and not working them out through your children. If you feel shame or embarrassment because you have a child expressing transgender interests, your starting point is your own feelings. In addition to working on any issues of shame or embarrassment, you may find that your child's transgender expression stirs up some discomfort with your own gender choices. Such a discovery may feel decidedly unwelcome, yet a path to your own growth. Maybe you're a mother and want to feel physically strong. Maybe you're a father and want to develop a repressed artistic interest.

Try not to get too excited by the rhetoric of the guardians of gender conformity, even if you value gender conformity yourself. For years, George Rekers has been pasting the label of gender identity disorder on girls if they show too much skill in throwing a football or shooting a basketball.[10] But think about it: if your daughter learns to play basketball, loves to play basketball, loves the pushing and shoving that comes with learning interior defense in basketball, she is not doing anything wrong. Instead of taking the girl to a therapist, cheer for her team and help her perfect her spinning jump shot. Your caring and support give her the guidance and modeling of a gender-conforming adult who is not intimidated by social pressures.

Even if your child enjoys the most explicit kinds of transgender behavior, such as cross-dressing, and even if you really don't like it, the problem isn't *in* the child. The child is having fun. The child is exploring. The child is getting in touch with inner feelings. You don't have to subject such a child to therapy for the purpose of helping the child get in touch with inner feelings. Your child is already doing that! If you can continue to demonstrate your respect and caring for your child, you have a lot better chance of working with your child to develop social strategies that respect your feelings and meet your child's needs.

An example of what I consider helpful advice for parents of children who are expressing transgender interests is offered by Stanley Greenspan, M.D., and Jacqueline Salmon. They note that prepubertal children commonly try out gender roles.

> Keep in mind that at this age (and at later ones too) children try on many different identities before they settle on a more permanent

one. . . .There are always girls who are considered tomboys, who want to play on the boys' team because boys are faster and tougher. . . .Some boys on the other hand may not like some of the other boys' roughhousing and may want to play some of the girls' more gentle games. *Respect that child's need to play out different roles in the peer group. Be supportive and empathetic.* [My italics] If you're understanding about the pink bows and the cowboy boots and the sudden shyness you are ultimately giving your child flexibility so that when he gets older he can put all the pieces together for himself and make a rational decision.[11]

It may help you to know that if you have a child with a deeply seated cross-gender commitment, you probably can't change it. If your child has the potential to grow out of a transgender commitment, and you want that to happen, you need to consider that it could be counterproductive to force a child to defend cross-gender commitments from your pressures at a time when that is what they know about themselves. If your child remains committed to cross-gender expression, your real choice is whether you want to raise a child who is transgender and alienated or a child who is transgender and supported. It may not be your favorite choice, but it is a choice that will matter a lot to your child. If you are still reading at this point, I hope you will also read Chapter 9 and see that raising a transgender child may open surprising channels of God's grace.

I do want to post one warning signal for parents of a child who is showing transgender interests or behavior. Be cautious about seeking clinical help for your child. A transgender child, like any child facing potentially hostile social reactions, needs strong parental support. Be warned that many therapists believe theories that parents, in one way or another, are the cause of the "abnormal" behavior in the child. The fact that there is no research supporting this theory does not deter therapists from acting on it. Psychiatrists are prone to think that a feminine boy should be separated from strong female influences, like a loving mother. Some psychiatrists are arrogant enough to think that a feminine boy should also be emotionally separated from his father and should transfer parental love to a proper father figure, the psychiatrist himself. Psychologists working out of learning theories are also likely to intrude on parent-child relationships. If you are considering hospitalization to try to break a child of cross-gender interests and behavior, remember that the hospital may try to totally isolate the child from you, may lie to you about what they are doing with your child, and may build on the child's feeling of abandonment by the parent to gain psychological control of the child.

I think that parental influence may be a contributing factor in stimulating cross-gender interests in some children. I don't think there is clear research supporting my thinking, but this line of thought fits within my general perspective of modified social-construction theory as developed in Chapter 6.

Since my own story doesn't reflect clinical stereotypes about what my parents must have been like, I suspect that parental influences are either not dominant or far more complex than previously theorized. In any case, if parents are important, then I suggest that it is far better to work with a therapist who is committed to strengthening and transforming family systems, than to work with an establishment clinician who can injure your child the way Jamie was injured in the story repeated in Chapter 7.

### Transgender Law

In addition to considering how parents, lovers, or other individuals respond to transgender expression, transgender people also have to take account of the opportunities, limits and pressures of relevant laws. Transgender expression that violates informal expectations may also initiate a process that leads to formal reactions by institutions and the question of whether those formal reactions are legal, or should be legal. Even if people have never thought about the legal aspects of transgender expression, the law is still in the background as a frame of reference for informal responses and as one basis for formal responses.

It is a commonplace to say that the United States is a society ruled by law. Most nations have legal frameworks, and many also have strong social patterns based on ethnicity or religion. The United States, in contrast, is distinctive for its history of using respect for the law as a basis for creating societal unity across many kinds of diversity. I don't mean to suggest that the process of creating unity was or is easy or that mutual respect has been fully accomplished. Still, the importance of respect for law as a basis for such societal unity as we have achieved would be hard to overstate. While being a nation "under law" does not of itself make the United States a just nation, understanding and changing the law is an important part of the path to becoming more just. The civil rights movement, the movement for equality for women, and the movement to improve life for the disabled have each had diverse social and cultural effects; but it was the legislative changes and the enforcement of altered laws that most clearly signaled to society that new days had come. Although race, gender, and ability discrimination continue, the terms of engagement have been changed. I consider it one of the greatest of all my privileges that I have done my small part in a generation that completed landmark legal changes in these three cultural transformations. Before I die I hope to see a real breakthrough for transgender people as well.

In addition to the direct effects of passing and enforcing laws, the legal processes also affect the ways we talk about issues in everyday interaction. The Civil Rights Act, for example, is probably more important for its shaping effect on informal expectations and everyday discourse than for its direct coercive power. (It is not easy to win antidiscrimination cases in court, and many people who suffer discrimination don't have effective access to the courts.) Whatever the technicalities of the law, legal reference influences a lot of the discussions of values in the United States. For example, the role of law is a hidden factor behind the apparently informal standard of wearing a necktie to work.[12]

Sister Mary Elizabeth summarized a series of cases in the 1970's and 1980's in which transgender people were arrested for the simple act of cross-dressing.[13] Many of the municipal codes made it illegal to wear three items associated with the "opposite" sex. It was the enforcement of such a law that led to the famed Stonewall riots in New York City, often credited as the beginning of the open gay and lesbian movement in the United States. John D'Emilio and Estelle Friedman tell the Stonewall story, with the instigators named simply as lesbians. This telling represses the transgender (and multiracial) aspects of the story.[14] Gay, lesbian, and transgender groups need to more explicitly recognize and affirm drag queens, and that includes defending their legal rights.

No one was convicted in the cases Sister Mary Elizabeth reported. Some statutes were disallowed as unconstitutionally vague. Cases based on a charge of impersonation were dropped because the transgender persons were understood to be expressing themselves. In other cases the special status of transsexuals was recognized.[15] Although it is likely that there are some jurisdictions where laws against cross-dressing are still on the books, the transgender community is no longer reporting much action resulting from such laws. But cross-gender appearance issues are still part of more complex legal situations and may be an important source of mistreatment by some law enforcement officers. I follow the advice of my local transgender support group and carry a transgender identity card with a distinctly feminine picture in case I am stopped by the police. This might help to protect me against a charge of impersonation or might help me if I'm put in jail.

### The Problem With Categories

Ruth Colker has provided commentary on the issue of how legal categories are formed, on the issues in categorization schemas in general, and on how legal categories are applied with relation to race, sexual orientation, gender, and disability.[16] After demonstrating that legal categories oversimplify the multiple ambiguities in human phenomena, she argues that categories inevitably lead to misapplication of the law. She nonetheless parts company with those who would try to eliminate categorical thinking: "Categorization under the law, however, is inevitable."[17]

Colker's agenda is the improvement of categories. Understanding the issues underlying categories can help to improve sensitivities, which in turn will help to shape better laws. Colker makes the point that legal categories are used to help as well as to punish. Affirmative action strategies are category-based efforts to gain legal redress for past injustices. Her conclusion is that "We must find ways to allow individuals to identify as multiracial, transgendered, bisexual and bi-abled without the fear that moving off of one polar point on the traditional bipolar scheme will subject them to subordination and necessarily preclude them from taking advantage of ameliorative programs."[18] One potential application of the reassessment of scientific thinking in this book is its relevance for reconsidering the legal categories used with regard to transgender experience and expression. A related purpose is to contribute to the general social conversation from which law and custom arise.

Legal decisions are based not only on the law but also on what happened. In turn, legal categories are one important frame for discussions of what happened in an event of interest to a court. Sometimes legal decisions, such as the decision in the case of Renee Richards, discussed in a later section, turn on the willingness of a judge to redefine categories. Such redefinitions commonly turn on a fresh understanding of relevant scientific findings. This can be troubling for scientists who are aware that they are critiquing and testing *theories,* and who are appropriately cautious about the generalizability of their findings. Scientific discipline assumes an openness to repeated reconsideration of theories and facts, a mental habit that does not mesh well with the legal need to make a determination of truth. Sometimes, all the scientific niceties, such as methodology, sampling, the construction and testing of indicators, bias in the researcher, and other factors are brought before the court. Although a court would like to deal with *established facts,* it commonly has to settle for *professional opinion* when the underlying science is called into question. When a judge or jury pay attention to this distinction, they show admirable humility— an awareness that they are lay people in regard to much of scientific complexity.

In the case between Renee Richards and the United States Tennis Association, the judge listened to competing professional opinions and ruled that Richards' side had made the more compelling case. The judge made a scientific judgment without being a scientist. Although such judgments have to be made, they also have to be unmade as the quality of the scientific base improves. This book has repeatedly shown that there is lots of room for improvement with regard to issues of transgender experience and expression. I hope that the next stages of transgender research will be in keeping with the revised grounding offered in previous chapters, particularly Chapter 6. In the meantime, and it could be a long meantime, the scientific critique in this book, as well as the alternative theorizing, may be useful for appropriate legal reasoning and social reforms. This does not mean that I think my theorizing has adequate scientific grounding, only that I believe it to be the most plausible approach within a field of study that is in its infancy.

Colker helpfully draws out one issue in the relationship of legal categories to the phenomena categorized that has been painful for the human rights community.

> Exposing the pervasive ambiguity of all categorization schemes,
> including racial ones, will help destroy some of the distinctions

between 'genuine' racial civil rights claims and 'inappropriate' homosexual civil rights claims. We need to understand that categorization schemes have been developed to pursue political and social policies ranging from the perpetuation of Jim Crow laws to the institutionalization of people with disabilities. No categorization scheme should be accepted as natural and inevitable. . . . Undoubtedly, the categories typically used to describe sexual orientation, gender, race, and bodies have perpetuated subordination."[19]

In the area of race, Colker makes the usual biological and anthropological judgments that races are not really pure and that, for example, most African Americans in the United States are genetically multiracial. She then points out that racial identity and its meaning are social constructions—that people attach values and cultural symbols, based on history and experience, to the concept of race. In her discussion of racial issues she addresses the special needs of people who understand themselves to be multiracial and of those who can pass. Some people, for example, may discover unknown racial connections late in life. Such people have some choice about how they will identify with racial categories, and how they will name themselves in various legal documents. On the other hand, some people clearly do not like any of the choices that are socially available or required by various documents. Colker then affirms the development of a multiracial identity movement because it "emphasizes the constructed aspects of racial identity."[20] That is, Colker emphasizes that racial identity is an important social reality even if there is no clear physiological basis for racial categorization.

Colker notes a few of the many complexities in transgender, sexual orientation, and intersexual definitions that are discussed earlier in this book. She points out the many ways in which laws try to force people into bipolar categories. One example is the support for surgical work done on intersexual infants before they have any choice in the matter. She also points out the cultural inconsistencies and mixed messages of punishing a lot of cross-gender behavior while at the same time greatly rewarding Michael Jackson for cross-gender expression as an entertainer. Colker discusses the oppressive results of current legal suppression of transgender expression (even though cross-dressing may not be in itself illegal). Some examples include the enforcement of employer dress codes, denial of visitation rights to a divorced father, loss of custody of a child by a lesbian mother that was justified in part on gender grounds, the loss of jobs, and issues affecting bathroom usage.

*Legal Identity*

The most fundamental issue of legal categories for transgender people is the establishment of identity. Since the transgender world is more complex than are legal categories, there are likely to be inequities for the foreseeable future. Institutions are not used to distinguishing between sex and gender. The legal ambiguities show up in the practical questions of what sex should be listed on such documents as birth certificates, driver's licenses, and passports. Changing one's legal sex designation on such documents can also affects things like the cost of medical insurance and the right to marry.

The current reality in the United States is that, at least in some jurisdictions, all official documents can be changed in terms of designated sex. Sometimes the relevant institution considers medical or psychiatric opinion to be legally relevant for such changes—a factor that gives additional social significance to physiological and psychological theories. Should legal sexual identity be a physiologically based determination, or should psychological and social factors be considered? One relevant question that can help improve justice in varying situations is to ask about the purposes that frame the situations within which issues of legally designated sex or gender arise. For example, men's and women's bathrooms are equally adequate for physiological relief. In that context it would seem fair to work out the issues of justice within the context of gender rather than sex.

So far as I know, no legal consideration has been given to the creation of a third legal status for those who do not want to be named as either male or female. This last consideration, by the way, parallels legal questions about the racial designation of interracial people.

Martine Rothblatt provides an excellent summary of the case that established the right of an individual to legally change sex, *Richards v. the United States Tennis Association* (USTA) in 1975. Renee Richards had competed as a male professional tennis player. After undergoing hormonal treatment and sexual reconstructive surgery (SRS), she began to compete as a woman. When she sought to compete in the USTA championships and was challenged by the USTA, She took her case to court.

The USTA lawyer argued that "Sexual identity is a complex pattern of which some features are immutable (the nuclear and chromosomal); some can be effaced but not converted to the opposite (the gonadal and ductal structures); some are alterable by surgery and drugs (the external genitalia and hormonal balance); and some are largely subjective (the psychological and social sex)."[21] The USTA lawyer would not claim that Richards was either male or female but argued that if she failed the Barr body test (a chromosomal test) Richards should be judged to be a woman.[22]

Renee Richards had several experts testify in her behalf. John Money testified that "The Barr test would work an injustice since by all other known indicators of sex, Dr. Richards is a female, e.g., external genital appearance is that of a female, her internal sex is that of a female who has been hysterectomized and ovariectomized; Dr. Richards is psychologically a woman; endocrinological female; somatically (muscular tone, height, weight, breast, physique) Dr. Richards is female and muscular and fat composition has been transformed to that of a female; socially Dr. Richards is female; Dr. Richards' gonadal status is that of an ovariectomized female." Judge Ascione decided that

"Dr. Renee Richards should be classified as female and for anyone in the medical or legal field to find otherwise is completely unjustified."[23] Richards competed in the tournament and was a doubles finalist.

The following points could be added to any further physiological guidelines for legal sex changes:

- Males and females are more similar in genetic composition than different. Any genetic differentiation is part of a larger similarity. Measurement of most physiological and psychological features shows overlap between males and females, men and women. An additional factor, which might be relevant in some cases, is that after an initial burst of differentiating hormone activity, boys and girls grow until puberty with similar hormonal patterns.

- More importantly, chromosomes have their effect on the body through intermediary mechanisms. For issues of sexual differentiation the most important intermediary mechanism is the endocrine system. Hormone treatment can dramatically change hormone levels and thus override chromosomal factors.

- Although SRS and hormonal therapy may not reverse some of the effects of fetal development, fetal development theory should not be applied to the legal designation of sex because the "shape" of such theorized difference, if any, is unknown and therefore cannot be measured. If anything, the fetal development theory justifies flexibility in legal sexual designations, because the theory was created to explain transgender *differences*. If, in the absence of convincing evidence, people nonetheless believe that fetal development theory is true, then people with a transgender identity would be intersexual with regard to this component.[24]

It is fair for the USTA, for example, to be concerned about males' taking advantage of some average differences in physique or musculature. But such concern should be mitigated for transsexuals like Renee Richards, because any chromosome-based initial advantage is largely reversed by transsexual procedures. The issue here is sex much more than gender. What is fair for transsexuals is not necessarily fair for other transgender people. The ambiguity of such distinctions, shown in earlier chapters, extends Colker's point about the intrinsic difficulty of category-based law. A further extension of this discussion comes with noting that SRS is hard on the body, so it may be reasonable to assert that any postoperative transsexual is competing at a disadvantage rather than an advantage. Additional complexities arise regarding intersexuality and distinguishing the legal relevance of changes made in infancy without the individual's consent from intentional changes made in adulthood. In generalizing from a sports-based case to all issues of legal identity, it is important to note that most legal issues do not revolve around competitive physiological advantages. Repeating the review completed in Chapter 3, the long record of research on sexual differentiation of a variety of mental capacities has shown far more similarity and overlap than difference. The fair conclusion is that there is no general physiological reason to deny legal change of sexual status to transsexuals. If some specific fairness issue is demonstrated concerning trans-sexual men or women, let that issue create a limited and appropriate legal differentiation rather than distinguishing access to the broad assignment of sex or gender.

The Richards case does not speak to the issue of people who have a transgender identity but have not gone through both hormonal and SRS transi-tions. There is at least one case in which a person was granted a change of sex designation on a driver's license on the sole basis of a hormonal transition.[25] As a basis for arguing that legal gender identity might be changed solely on gender grounds, I would point out that the primary purpose of driver's licenses and passports is recognition and identity. That purpose would best be served by gender rather that sexual definitions. An accurate picture and the legal name are the best resources for such identification purposes. Since some transgender people present strikingly different appearances at different times, any docu-ment with one picture is going to be inadequate. If an identification document allows only a single picture, it is likely that the individual is in the best position to know which image is most representative.

Although the Richards case made the changing of sex legally possible, the practical accomplishment of that right boils down to the specific rules for changing the designation of sex for each document. At least 17 states have passed laws making it generally legal for transsexuals to change their sex desig-nation on their birth certificate.[26] Other states also allow such changes under various circumstances. An additional issue is whether a state will not only allow such a change but will also issue a clear certificate indicating only the new status rather than a certificate showing the change. Since, for some transgender people, an important reason for changing the legal designation of their sex is to assimilate into their chosen gender, a certificate that names the change defeats this purpose. It seems reasonable to ask what state interest, other than oppress-ing transgender people, is served by refusing to provide a clean document. Staying focused on desirable social goals, whether arguing for a clean certificate for transsexual people or for a complex document or record for other transgender people, gives the best hope of refining and managing the legal categories of sex and gender.

*Discrimination*

Political and legal issues concerning the protection of transgender people from discrimination are complex, changing, and hotly debated at the time of writing. However, discrimination against transgender people is often treated as a derivative or a corollary to gay and lesbian rights.[27] Whereas 12 states have passed laws aimed at protecting gay and lesbian people from discrimination, only Minnesota, Connecticut, and Rhode Island have passed laws aimed at protecting transgender people as well.[28] At least 20 cities and 3 counties have also passed laws aimed at protecting transgender people from discrimination.[29] A good example is an amendment to the Cambridge, Massachusetts, Human Rights Ordinance. The ordinance now reads as follows:

> Discrimination on the basis of race, color, sex, age, religious creed, disability, national origin or ancestry, sexual orientation, gender, marital status, family status, military status or source of income is unlawful in the City of Cambridge.

In the above ordinance, gender is defined as follows:

> "Gender" means the actual or perceived appearance, expression, or identity of a person with respect to masculinity or femininity.[30]

The Cambridge ordinance has been challenged by Sky Publishing Corporation on the ground that an antidiscrimination law should be state law and not the law of cities.

Until recently there has been very little protection under federal law for transsexual or other transgender people. Numerous courts have ruled against claims of discrimination brought by transgender people, whether the claim was brought under the due process protections of the 14th Amendment to the Constitution, Title VII of the Civil Rights Act of 1964, or the Americans With Disabilities Act.[31]

A useful summary of political and legal realities as of the year 2000 has been provided by Chai Feldblum, Professor of Law and Director of the Federal Legislation Clinic at the Georgetown University Law Center.[32] One of her core arguments is that, whether or not the Employment Non-Discrimination Act (ENDA), is ever passed, there is a reasonable chance that additional nondiscrimination protection for transgender people can be obtained by judicial reinterpretation of current law, particularly of Title VII. This article also presents a fascinating and detailed report of her transition from initially opposing the inclusion of transgender protection in ENDA to supporting such inclusion. Such a change is particularly noteworthy since Feldblum was a primary drafter of the original ENDA.

Feldblum's assessment is that "courts are increasingly interpreting sex discrimination laws to apply to cases of gender nonconformity and transgender status."[33] Courts originally refused to accept transgender discrimination claims based on Title VII, on the premise that Congress did not *intend* Title VII to be applied to transgender issues. Considering that the status of sex was added to Title VII by an amendment intended to bring about defeat of the overall bill, it seems to me to be pretty hard to reason about intent in this case.

Things began to turn around for transgender rights in 1989, when the Supreme Court ruled in the *Price Waterhouse v. Hopkins* case that Price Waterhouse was wrong to deny partnership to Ann Hopkins because she failed to act in a sufficiently feminine manner. There was testimony that Hopkins' supervisor had told her to "walk more femininely, talk more femininely, dress more femininely, wear makeup, have her hair styled, and wear jewelry."[34] Although there was no assertion of any transgender aspects to this case, an important blow was struck against sex stereotyping. Justice Brennan, who wrote the majority opinion, included the following comment: "In the specific context of sex stereotyping, an employer who acts on the basis of a belief that a woman cannot be aggressive, or that she must not be, has acted on the basis of gender."[35] This opinion substantially broadened the court's understanding of the meaning of "because of... sex." in Title VII. Furthermore, the court took a step away from repeated reference to the intent of Congress.

In the second Supreme Court case emphasized by Feldblum, *Oncale v. Sundowner*, Justice Scalia specifically applied his common emphasis on the importance of what the text says as trumping whatever intent Congress may have had: "It is ultimately the provision of our laws rather than the principal concerns of our legislators by which we are governed."[36] *Oncale* was about a male employee who was harassed by male supervisors and co-workers. It carries additional weight because the decision was unanimous. The important point is the assertion by Justice Scalia in writing the unanimous opinion that "statutory prohibitions often go beyond the principal evil to cover reasonably comparable evils."[37] Feldblum summarizes the convergence of *Price Waterhouse* and *Oncale* as follows: "Courts are increasingly acknowledging that adverse action taken against an individual because that individual does not conform to societal expectations of how a 'real man' or 'real woman' should look or act *are* actions taken 'because of sex.'"[38] The Ninth Circuit has applied this line of logic in *Schwenk v. Hartford* in which a transgender person was sexually harassed and assaulted by a prison guard. The court asserted that "discrimination because one fails to act in the way expected of a man or a woman is forbidden under Title VII."[39] Other cases have been won using this line of logic, including a case about the denial of a bank loan application and the effort of a school to stop a male from wearing girls' clothes or accessories. Feldblum cites a number of other cases and notes that the Hawaii Supreme Court and the Court of
Appeals in Oregon have grounded their opinions on marriage for same-sex couples and on the denial of benefits to same-sex domestic partners in sex discrimination law.

Although there is still significant remembered pain for the transgender community in the Human Rights Campaign's (HRC) efforts to block transgender concerns in the original ENDA bill, this pain has been significantly moderated by the revised stance taken by HRC, and especially by the active support provided by the National Gay and Lesbian Task Force. Such coming together was highly visible at the 2001 Conference of Gender PAC in Washington, D.C. With Professor Feldblum's help, it may be possible to pull together a more coherent litigation strategy that works well for transgender people as well as lesbian, gay and bisexual people. The realization that may facilitate increased cooperation is that lesbian, gay, and bisexual people are often punished for appearance and other gender transgressions and that transgender people are often punished because the public thinks transgender people are all homosexuals. New public support for increased cooperation by groups like the Lambda Defense and Education Fund and employee groups like GLOBE (with Verizon) make it even more likely that more solid lesbian, gay, bisexual, and transgender cooperation is becoming possible.

No discrimination is more immediate than direct verbal harassment, assault, and murder. Although it is hard to assess the hate factor in some cases, the transgender community reports a dozen or more murders a year. In the famous Brandon Teena case, after years of litigation, the Nebraska State Supreme Court ruled that Sheriff Charles Laux's failure to protect Brandon Teena led to her death.[40] As her mother said, "because of this case, fewer parents will find their children abused and exposed to danger by law enforcement officials."[41]

Lillian Potter tells a more common story of harassment. Potter, a straight woman high school athlete, had the temerity to challenge the illegal discrimination against women's athletics at Walt Whitman High School in Bethesda, Maryland, one of the most privileged communities in the United States. Her courage and perseverance eventually led to systemwide changes in Montgomery County school athletics, but at a significant personal price. Following is part of her testimony:

> During my senior year of high school, it was impossible for me to walk down the halls of my high school without being called a "dyke" or, my personal favorite, "man-woman." The harassment followed me everywhere — to class, in the parking lot, at the McDonald's at lunch, at the mall, and at parties on the weekend. During every class period, at least one student would interrupt class with some epithet or insult directed at me. Sadly, teachers did nothing to discourage the conduct. The athletic director, who was also my history teacher, managed on a daily basis to segue from American history into a discussion on gender equity, which inevitably descended into an ad hominem attack on me by both him and other students. . . . The principal in particular enjoyed arguing with me in public. . . . I was spit upon, received threatening phone calls, had threatening letters and notes left on my car, locker, and mailbox, was shoved and pushed into walls, and had my car spit upon.[42]

Ironically, one of the reasons we need to include gender issues in the expansion of hate crime laws is for protection of straight people who are treated as if they were gay, lesbian, bisexual, or transgender people. For the last decade we have made no more progress with federal hate crimes legislation than we have made with ENDA. Homophobia and transphobia still rule but progress has been made. Significant minorities of Representatives and Senators support expansion of the definitions of hate crimes and the passage of ENDA.

Some are even beginning to understand the relevance of transgender issues and speak out.[43] Given the political invisibility of the transgender community, this is quite remarkable.

### Getting and Keeping a Job

The issue of legal discrimination in employment against transgender people is discussed above. For the moment, the best possibilities for legislative improvement are at the local level. For example, in Santa Cruz, California, the Municipal Ordinance Pertaining to the Prohibition of Discrimination was specifically broadened to include the word *gender* with an explanatory note that this is intended to ". . . be broadly interpreted to include transgendered individuals."[44] Perhaps more importantly, some large employers have reviewed transgender issues and become inclusive. Even with these changes, however, the distance to go is longer than the distance already come.

The employment issue is more complex than merely adding the word *transgender* at key points in existing antidiscrimination laws. It is reasonable for some employers to have concerns about the appearance of some of their employees. Whatever the law is, and however it may change, working out appropriate accommodations in real work settings, with the variety of people who have transgender experience and identity, will be complex. Although the law is an important framework for resolving social conflicts, resorting to formal legal action is a signal of the breakdown of institutional relationships and interpersonal processes. Many courses of action are possible within existing law, as witnessed by the accommodations already being made by some employers. Suggested employment guidelines and helpful hints are available from the International Foundation for Gender Education.[45] Dianna Cicotello has written a helpful book on transgender employment issues.[46]

The bad news is that some transgender people have been unfairly fired for transgender expression and have difficulty in finding comparable work, or any work at all. The good news is that some transgender people have transitioned from one gender to the other at work, are well accepted, and are valued employees. While some transgender youth are thrown out of their homes, abandoned to the streets, and recruited to become sex workers, other transgender youth grow up to be highly successful in their professions, even wealthy. How long will it be before even conservatives realize that our society will be strengthened by ending all destructive discrimination and making space for everyone to contribute to society through employment?

### Marriage

Marriage is a fundamental contract in the United States, with multiple social and legal implications, including tax benefits, a right to inherit, criminal testimony protections in certain circumstances, and right-of-access issues. A study by the General Accounting Office found 1,049 federal laws in which marital status is relevant.[47] Governments have created marriage as a fundamental contract because marriage supports stable family relations, responsibility and accountability for raising children, the channeling of sexual relations into stable emotional relationships, and ordering relationships between families. Many religious traditions have long recognized the value of marriage for these societal reasons while also wanting to protect marriage relationships as possible channels for God's presence. Within a social frame of reference, the critical question is whether society benefits or loses by denying the advantage of marriage to same-sex couples.

Unless one thinks that there is a social advantage to homophobic or transphobic oppression, it is hard to imagine a reason why society would not benefit from encouraging same-sex couples to enter into marriage contracts. I understand the critique of the history of marriage as a patriarchal institution, and I agree with the historical reading behind that critique. But current civil marriage laws in the United States are not narrowly patriarchal. In fact, divorce laws do a lot to protect the weaker party in a marriage, usually a woman. Social Security laws do a lot to help spouses, including divorced spouses, and this primarily benefits women. When children are involved in a marriage, providing for such children is a primary interest of the court. Since long-term committed relationships have substantial financial implications, since marriage is a contract aimed in part at creating financial fairness for both spouses and dependent children, and since marriage helps to equalize power relationships, it appears that positive antipatriarchal social purposes are served by contemporary marriage contracts. Drawing same-sex couples into marriage has the same social purposes for society and the same protections for individuals as does marriage for different-sex couples.

In responding to the challenge that gay and lesbian people shouldn't marry because it supports a heterosexual institution, Mitzi Eilts, Coordinator for the United Church of Christ Coalition for Gay, Lesbian, Bisexual and Transgender Concerns, comments, "Fighting for the right to marry is fighting against heterosexual privilege."[48] I agree.

Marriage is a lived relationship as well as a legal contract. A lot of marriages don't work out and transgender issues make some marriages more difficult. There are issues of personal identity, issues of interpersonal encouragement and accountability, issues of sexual sharing, issues of financial sharing, and issues of religious perspective. Despite a lot of legal support and political rhetoric in support of marriage and families, the increasing dominance of business and professional values has put great pressure on marriages which is only partly ameliorated by protections like the Family and Medical Leave Act and increasing support for child care services. Gay, bisexual, lesbian, and transgender people have extra challenges to face when working out extended committed relationships with a life partner, including caring for children. Before the marriage laws become fair, other institutions can start doing their part to help things work out. As a Christian, I pray that more congregations will recognize the opportunities for encouragement and support of bisexual, lesbian, gay, and transgender families, however legally structured, as the kind of ministry Jesus would appreciate.

In 1996, the Defense of Marriage Act (DOMA) was signed into federal law. The act prohibits distributing certain federal benefits to people in same-sex marriages and allows states to choose not to recognize same-sex marriages performed in other states. The passage of DOMA was a coup for the Christian Coalition and its allies, who presented their homophobic agenda as a *defense* of marriage when in fact it was an *attack* on the right of people of the same sex to marry. The right of same-sex couples to marry and remain married is under active consideration in state legislatures and court actions. The religious conflict over the right to marry calls attention to the impact of cultural and spiritual issues on social change and continuity, with a resulting impact on identity and relational issues.

One minor reason that DOMA sailed through Congress is that there was a common misperception that there are no existing same-sex marriages in the United States. This misperception is easy to understand, since, at the time of passage, no state allowed the *contracting* of same-sex marriage. The excitement that led to DOMA was the possibility that the Hawaii Supreme Court might start to allow same-sex marriages. However, because some people have legally changed their designated sex after becoming married, there are at least dozens of currently legal same-sex marriages in existence. A legally constructed contract continues until it is broken, so, unless there is a divorce, the marriage remains in force. Whether intentional or not, the "defense" of marriage by the Christian Coalition may actually destroy some existing marriages, and is thus an anti-family law. The testimony of Dianna Cicatello before the Colorado legislature in 1997, along with the support and witness of her daughter, may well have been pivotal in that state's rejection of a law to ban same-sex marriage. Dianna is a Roman Catholic and has been married to one partner for 28 years, most of them in a same-sex marriage.[49] To complete the reporting in this area, it is worth noting one case in Ohio in which a transsexual woman was denied a license to marry a man.[50] Other transsexuals have contracted legal heterosexual marriages. New Jersey has case law dating back to 1976 that recognizes a transsexual in the changed legal gender for the purpose of marriage.[51]

The fact that an organization with the name *Christian* in its title led a homophobic attack on same-sex marriage begs for attention and response from other Christians. As a transgender spouse and parent, I am outraged that the response from official church structures to DOMA was so weak. Some did the best they could from limited policy bases, but many just ducked. Such silence condones an attack on me and my friends, particularly my gay and lesbian friends, and it hurts.

I found Ruth Colker's discussion of legal categories to be particularly interesting when applied to the work of the Hawaii Supreme Court. In considering the issue of whether same-sex marriage should be made legal, she points out that the Hawaii Supreme Court carefully made the distinction between *sex* and *sexual orientation*. The efforts to stop homosexual marriage are written in terms of sex and not sexual orientation. DOMA, for example makes it illegal for two males or two females to marry, whatever their sexual orientation. The Hawaii court pointed out that no one makes assumptions about sexual orientation when a male and a female marry, even though one or both may be bisexual or completely homosexual. The couple in the test case were careful not to state their sexual orientation, and it mattered to the court that it was the state that raised the issue.

When the issue of marriage is considered as it relates to transgender people, it is important to remember that the right to become married, or remain married, also involves the rights of spouses and children. Although the Christian Coalition and its allies aim at oppressing homosexuals and transgender people, when they shoot at such targets they also hurt spouses and children. Clarification of this point is a good example of the reason this book has given so much attention to definition and to distinguishing physiological, psychological, social-psychological, social, cultural, and spiritual dimensions of transgender experience and expression. The Christian Coalition has been so interested in imposing its misunderstanding of biblical mandates on others that it has not stopped to consider the social purposes of secular marriage contracts or the harm it is doing to existing families.

Christian churches and other religious bodies are not bound by the laws about secular marriages. These bodies have the right to recognize same-sex marriages even though such marriages have no secular standing. The proper reference for Christians for celebrating and recognizing sacred marriage is God's guidance. If same-sex partners truly love each other, want to form a lasting, committed relationship, and want to be known and accountable in a congregation for their commitments in the same way heterosexuals are known and accountable, why should this recognition be denied? Most of the reasons offered to deny it do not speak to this core reason for recognizing and celebrating sacred marriage. Chapter 9 of this book offers a fresh grounding for such considerations.

## Transgender Activism

Transgender people are increasingly organizing to seek favorable legal treatment. Five meetings of the International Conference on Transgender Law and Employment Policy have been held in Houston, Texas. The five books of proceedings from the conferences are a useful contribution to legal theory and practice.[52] Several national and local organizations are carrying forward transgender activism.[53]

Some activist writing in the transgender community includes: Leslie Feinberg's *Transgender Warrior*, Kate Bornstein's *Gender Outlaw*, and Martine Rothblatt's *The Apartheid of Sex*. Though Phyllis Burke writes as a lesbian, her book *Gender Shock*, makes an important contribution. *Transgender Tapestry* provides periodic activist news and more up-to-the-minute information is regularly available on the World Wide Web.[54]

There are several other indicators of increasing transgender activity, including 6,000 search sites on the Internet and 250 local transgender support groups.[55] Another measure of transgender activism is transgender conferences. There are about four regional or national conferences a year, spread across the United States. They typically run for several days at a time and include a mix of social, practical, and organizational activities. They commonly draw a couple of hundred people each.

Since the early 1990s the transgender community has been fitfully gathering itself to undertake more organized political advocacy. This has led to some traditional political activities as well as a variety of "movement" activities, and direct-action confrontations. In addition to the growing pains that are common to many areas of political organizing, there are three major problems that are likely to challenge transgender organizing efforts for some time to come.

First, if the transgender community's perception is correct—that most people with transgender experience are deeply closeted—and if it is also true that the goal of a large proportion of transsexuals is assimilation into the world of the other gender, it is going to be difficult to move a substantial number of the people who have transgender experience into open political activity. A further factor that disempowers transgender organizations is that many of its members are financially poor, in part because of employment discrimination. The anonymity of the Internet helps to reach closeted people, but it remains to be seen how much political organizing can be accomplished in this faceless medium.

A second organizing challenge is the reality of divisions within the visible transgender community. Many of the distinctions discussed in this book are the source of diverging interests. For example, issues of legal identity are not the same for transsexual people as they are for other transgender people. Diverging interests are reflected in a plethora of small caucuses and small organizations. Good communication skills, the habits of positive political organizing, and the personal growth of some of our new leaders can help to overcome divisions. In addition to improving our habits, the transgender community needs to become clear about the difference between friendship, organizing, coalition building, and cooperation. Too much of what is currently called organizing is really just interlocking friendships, which often produces alienation from those on the outside. Friendship is terrific. We need it. But political organizing builds on the basis of shared ideas and interests with people we hardly know at all, and some people we don't like. Elementary civility and respect, even when one is angry, is critical.

Some transgender leaders are holding up a vision of growing into a movement with a participation base in the tens of thousands. Climbing that hill depends, first of all, on understanding the difference between *similar* interests and *overlapping* interests. Specific organizations are built on the cooperation made possible by similar interests, whereas coalitions are formed on the basis of mutual advantage from recognizing overlapping interests. To create a beginning political base, it is important to have some leaders and organizations that build bridges between the diverse transgender groups and individuals. Such holistic vision would challenge some groups to broaden their strategies enough to work in coalitions.

The core of coalition building is not about loyalty and friendship; it is about moving in and out of coalitions gracefully with the will to make the coalition effective while it exists. After 16 years of employment as a public policy advocate, I believe that learning to work together in the midst of unfinished arguments is the most precious of all political skills. Coalitions are sometimes reduced to temporary and uncomfortable alliances based on a limited and specific deal. On the other hand, working together can be a path to recognizing additional common interests and to creating more effective coalitions.

The third ongoing political challenge for the transgender community is to correctly identify its potential political strength. In analogy, I am thinking of how feminists identified their common interest in expanding the role definition of woman so that it could include construction workers, real estate agents, and military pilots without giving up what it wanted to keep from the traditional role of woman. Organizing for political purposes is enhanced by identifying the differences between *what* we want and *why* we want it. People concerned about different *whys* can sometimes join together for common *whats*. Chapter 9 takes up some *why* concerns.

Moving from coalition building to movement building requires more consensus about *why* transgender rights and protections are important. Trust comes, in part, from sensing a shared vision. Sometimes, however, shared vision can blind individuals and organizations to the pragmatism of practical politics. Mature political organizing holds *what* and *why* in tension. The transgender community needs a lot more of such maturity. We are blessed with some vibrant prophets—but we are currently short on transformative listening.

After getting our own act together, the next most important agenda for transgender political activism is building coalitional relationships with gay, lesbian, bisexual, and intersexual groups. Accurately remembering two stories can give a little referential grounding.

The Stonewall riots in New York City were set off by the harassment of drag queens in a bar by police—for the most part racial and ethnic minority drag queens. Such people are not much loved by straight society and not loved much more by elements of the gay, lesbian, and transgender communities. In fact, as pointed out earlier, some gay histories skip over the transgender and racial and ethnic designation of the Stonewall heroines. Loved or not, some drag queens in the bar decided that they were not going to treat themselves as expendable or as scapegoats. For at least one night, they chose not to be fodder for oppression. It made a difference.

John D'Emilio has preserved the story of Jose Sarria, an ethnic minority waiter at the Black Cat bar in San Francisco. His contribution was to bridge the gap between the bar culture and the activist culture, and when the gay community walked over that bridge, they had a movement. "Sarria often dressed in drag and enlivened evenings at the Black Cat....But Sarria's act departed dramatically from the female impersonation found in some gay male circles." He developed protest songs and then got his audience involved in singing "God save us Nelly Queens." Sarria's performances drew increased oppression of the bar culture by the police, but Sarria kept talking about the rights of homosexuals.[56] Though D'Emilio did not emphasize the point that Sarria was crossing gender boundaries in his act, the Black Cat story, as well as the Stonewall story, point to common beginnings of political consciousness for transgender people as well as gay and lesbian people.

I read current relationships between the several communities as ambivalent. There are now plenty of examples of organizations that include the words *gay*, *lesbian*, *bisexual* and *transgender* in their titles; and plenty of local events, such as pride marches, that include everyone. At the same time, there are plenty of gay and lesbian people who see transgender people as a political liability or embarrassment. Beren de Motier, a lesbian, was quoted in a 1998 story in the New York Blade as follows: "It's this merging of 'trans' with 'lesbian, gay and bisexual.' I hate it with greater fervor everyday....My skeptical side says that transgender activism is yet another attempt by extremists (identified as gay before this whole 'trans' deal became the latest thing) to shoot our movement in the foot—for who knows what reason."[57] Despite the discomfort of some gay and lesbian people, the National Gay and Lesbian Task Force, the second largest organization working on gay and lesbian political issues, now proudly announces itself as "the Nation's leading organization fighting for gay, lesbian, bisexual and transgender civil rights."[58]

Progress has been made in building friendship and alliances, but there is still a long way to go. Two preliminary things need to happen. Gay and lesbian people need to build transgender bridges within their own communities. (One foundation for that bridge would be a better understanding of why drag shows are entertaining.) The transgender community needs to keep building bridges of communication and appreciation between participants who identify themselves as heterosexual and those who name themselves as gay, lesbian, or bisexual.

Transgender, gay, bisexual, and lesbian people can learn similar lessons from the Stonewall and Black Cat stories. Freedom doesn't start just from books, visions, political skills, or organizing. It comes down, again and again, to people deciding they've had enough and taking next steps before the end of the road is visible. The voice may be inarticulate, the action impractical, but we find each other at such points of risks and vulnerability. Fortunately, the transgender community is not short of risk and vulnerability.

## Cultural Oppression

In this book, the word *culture* means the values, symbols, and stories that provide reference and direction for the formation of societies and institutions, guidance for social relationships, and grounding references for identity formation. The relevant disciplines are anthropology and history. We are not likely to improve the stories we live within unless we know their beginnings and transformations.

Standards of fairness and honesty are as important for history and anthropology as for any other discipline. Both disciplines have been challenged for homophobic bias, and I add the charge of transphobic blindness and bias. Fortunately, in the last few years, some historical and anthropological work is helping transgender people learn that they have existed across cultures and over time. Leslie Feinberg's *Transgender Warrior* is the best single book. A more scholarly effort is edited by Sabrina Ramet, *Gender Reversals and Gender Culture*. *Vested Interests* by Marjorie Gerber provides an excellent encyclopedia of transgender cultural images in recent Western culture, primarily in the United States.

Walter Williams has summarized anthropological contributions to the study of third gender roles in different cultures and described his own work on the berdache role that has been part of some Native American tribes in his book *The Spirit and the Flesh.*[59] While well aware of homosexual concerns, Williams is unwilling to discuss transgender phenomena in transgender terms. Nonetheless, I learned from Williams that many tribes created ceremonial roles and shaman roles for their transgender (berdache) members and generally kept berdache members as full participants in tribal life. Such anthropological work is water for questing spirits that are thirsty for additional intellectual grounding beyond the punitive work of clinical theorists.

In addition to its scriptural significance, the Bible is also a valuable historical and cross-cultural source. In this regard I did a word search through my computer Bible and found that the Hebrew and Greek words for *eunuch* appear at least 49 times in the available texts. However, the King James Version uses the word *eunuch* only 7 times and the New Revised Standard Version only 11 times. Other versions are only slightly better. The translations substitute such words as *officer* and other nongender words. Whatever else eunuchs were, some were people who were given valued social roles in ancient societies because they had a gender status that was neither man nor woman.

The first grounding point is that the above references show that transgender people live in a lot of cultures and that this has been true for a long time. Such beginnings of transgender-relevant research show that transgender experience is not unique to modern society. *This means that transgender experience cannot be explained by some special cause that is unique to our day and time,* such as a theorized parenting style. Some writers suggest that a cross-cultural, cross-historical perspective argues in favor of the importance of physiological influences, such as a reappearing genetic fault. A direct assessment of physiological issues was presented in Chapter 2. Limited as the above references are, they are sufficient to warn us against dependence on a culture-bound standpoint in reasoning about transgender experience. Such dependence was demonstrated in the Chapter 4, using an illustration provided by Marjorie Gerber—that color-coded gender identification of blue for boys and pink for girls is a post-World War I development.

A second grounding point from anthropological and historical studies is to remember that at least some cultures made nonstigmatized room for transgender people without becoming destabilized. Statements by some apologists for the status quo, that allowing transgender expression would destroy the fabric of society and culture, are thus shown to be unjustified. All that would be lost is their transphobic pattern for such fabric. Transgender experience and expression are not intrinsically antisocial or anticultural. They may not fit the cultural standards of powerful groups in the contemporary United States, but such groups are defending *their* cultural values, not some universal or natural standard. It should also be noted that some subcultures in the United States are more accepting of transgender expression.

There has been substantial attention to transgender people in the popular media in the last few years, including films and popular television talk shows. Such exposure has been a mixed blessing for the transgender community. On the one hand, it helps with the "we exist" theme. On the other hand, the movies never show a simple affirmation of people claiming a transgender reality for themselves. In the films, attention is directed primarily to man-to-woman changes, and there is almost always some excuse for the men who put on female appearances, such as getting a job or hiding out. The transgender people on the talk shows are often treated as curiosities. Of course this is the way many talk show guests are treated. But perhaps the times are changing. Nancy Nangeroni now has her own transgender talk show and maybe we will see more of that.[60]

It would be helpful for someone to do a content analysis study of transgender cultural presentations. Unfortunately, the transgender community is as invisible in such studies as they are in other academic places. For example, in a 1995 book, *Gender, Race and Class in the Media,* none of the 61 articles touched on transgender expression.[61] A content analysis study in the general media would provide an interesting contrast to the content analysis done on transgender fantasy books.[62]

One biographical work deserves special mention. Gary Kates, in his book, *Monsieur d'Eon Is a Woman,* not only makes this interesting life available to readers but also talks about early feminism as it relates to the French Enlightenment. Readers may want to familiarize themselves with this story, in part, because Havelock Ellis introduced the concept of "eonism" (transvestism) into English language scholarship with the Chevalier(e) in mind.

Kates asserts that the life of Chevalier(e) d'Eon does not fit the clinical concepts of transvestism or transsexuality. "As we shall see, d'Eon did not cross dress at any time during the years before England and France declared him to be a woman; even after that, he went through a two-year struggle with Louis XVI to retain the right to wear his (male) military uniform. . . .Again, there is simply no indication that d'Eon hated his own body or that he wanted, or even imagined he would be better off with, the body of a woman."[63] Kates accounts for d'Eon's decision as follows: "He chose to become a woman because he deeply admired the moral character of women and wanted to live as one of them. . . .during the thirty-two years that he lived as a woman, he developed a fascinating and pioneering ideology of gender identity that I call a 'Christian feminism.'"[64] When Havelock Ellis influenced the memory of such an interesting and courageous person by attaching his/her name to a pathological category, he demonstrated a clinical oppression and historic ignorance that we suffer from to this day.

Limited attempts have been made to survey transgender presence and rights in the contemporary world outside the United States. At least some transgender presence has been found in many countries. Some nations are at least as transphobic as the United States, and some are more violently oppressive. For example, Phaedra Kelly tells of transvestites being burned in Greece, of transvestites beaten to a pulp by police batons, and of the persecution of Aloma Haralambos in prison on trumped up charges.[65] An Associated Press story tells of 9 young Saudi Arabian men who each were sentenced to 2,000 lashes and at least 5 years in prison for deviant sexual behavior including dressing in women's clothes.[66] On the other hand, the European Supreme Court has granted to transgender people employment rights people that are still lacking in the United States.[67] One positive note is that, in 1998, Amnesty International Australia formally voted to include abuses of transgender people as one element of their work on human rights abuses.[68]

## Transgender Culture?

Is there a transgender subculture in the United States? I would say that there is not. Perhaps there are some microcultures. The close relationships, organizations, and events created by drag queens in New York City come to mind. San Francisco is more tolerant of transgender presence than are many places. But a coherent subculture with a distinctive set of values and images? I don't see it. Someone else will have to make that case.

I see a fragmented and mostly hidden community. I see that many transgender people want to assimilate into the other gender, that a lot of transgender people put immense energy into "passing." I see homophobia and expressions of transphobia between different groupings of transgender people.

I see race and class divisions, religious divisions, and a lot of small organizations. I see divisions over the use of language and debate about standards of appearance.

On the other hand, transgender organizations are new and are just beginning to work on common projects. Fifteen years ago it was hard to form even a mutual support club; now transgender organizations are dipping their toes into the waters of political activism.[69] The current conversations, however contentious, however personalized, are part of community formation. It isn't easy to create community when we have had so little to work with in terms of history, religion, and culture, so few stories that are not stories of oppression.

There is no natural requirement that transgender people form a transgender culture. The fact of our common oppression is not enough glue to stick such a culture together. It is not clear that there are many people who are willing to risk exposure as part of the process of creating a visible community, something more than the semihidden safe spaces of support groups and conventions. Perhaps my pessimism reflects the reality that creating a distinct transgender culture is not a high priority for me. If there were such a culture, I'm not sure how I would relate to it. I'm clear that my transgender experience and expression are not the basis of my identity. I am first of all a Christian. I hope to help strengthen any emergence of transgender community, but I think that, at least for a while, its best hope is to be a decidedly multicultural community. It isn't likely that we shall see the emergence of a transgender lifestyle in the United States when so many transgender people simply want to be a man or a woman.

Mariette Pathy Allen, who has provided the photographs for this book, has been photographing the transgender community for years. In addition to her excellent photojournalist book *Transformations*, she has created excellent slide shows reviewing transgender gatherings. She believes that a gathering of the transgender community is under way.[70] If a true transgender culture is forming, one major element will be the kind of attitude modeled by Dallas Denny, editor of *Transgender Tapestry*, when she writes: "For many years, transsexualism was considered a 'condition' that was 'cured' by sex reassignment....I have called assimilation 'the closet at the end of the rainbow.' ... More and more transsexual people are accepting their transgendered condition as a permanent state of being; this has opened the door for political and scientific activism...."[71] Another bridge that could help to draw a possibly emergent transgender community into a more coherent subculture is the attitude expressed by Nancy Nangeroni when she recognizes the internal validity of many versions of transgender expression and then calls on the helping professions to take "an active role in promoting transsexualism and transgenderism without SRS."[72] For anyone interested in doing research on the possible formation of a transgender culture, several valuable archives are available.[73]

## Notes:

1. Vaclav Haval (1992).
2. Gary Mallon (1999), pages 8-13. Mallon's program is the Green Chimneys Gramercy Residence program in Manhatten, New York City.
3. Kate Bornstein (1994).
4. Laws regarding appearance, sometimes called sumptuary laws, are part of the United States' cultural inheritance from England. Leslie Feinberg writes about the oppression of butch lesbians based on determinations of the gender of clothes, such as fly-front pants, in *Stone Butch Blues*. For additional discussion, see the transgender law section of Chapter 8.
5. Max Weber developed his famous conceptualization of charisma in a similar manner (1968), pages 1111-1157. He points out that while charisma appears to be a quality of a charismatic leader, since the followers of charismatic leaders strongly feel that the charismatic power is an attribute of the leader, in reality the source of power is in the primarily unconscious needs of the followers that is addressed by the leaders' words and actions. When a follower becomes conscious of this reality, the follower can take control of his or her own opportunities and responsibilities for meeting his or her needs. The follower may still respect the leader but the power of the unconscious bond to the leader is moderated.
6. J. J. Allen (1996), pages 44-49.
7. Trish Nemore (1999).
8. Peggy Rudd. See References for access information for her four books.
9. Richard Green (1978).
10. George Rekers and Shasta Money (1990).
11. Stanley Greenspan and Jacqueline Salmon (1993), pages 234-235.
12. *Fountain v. Safeway Stores, Inc.*, 555 F.2d (Ninth Circuit 1977) quoted in Ruth Colker (1996).
13. Sister Mary Elizabeth (1990).
14. John D'Emilio and Estelle Freedman (1988).
15. Sister Mary Elizabeth (1990), pages 15-20. Also see, Spencer Bergstedt (1997).
16. Ruth Colker (1996).
17. Ibid., page xiii.
18. Ibid., page 9.
19. Ibid., pages 5-6.
20. Ibid., page 31.
21. Sheila Kirk and Martine Rothblatt (1995), page 97.
22. Ibid., page 97.
23. Ibid., page 98.
24. See Chapter 2 for an extended discussion of this issue.
25. Phyllis Frye, commenting on her own change of status at the International Conference on Law and Employment Policy, Houston, Texas, 1996.
26. John Cloud (1998).
27. Wallace K. Swan (1997). In this book, which purports in its title to deal with transgender as well as gay, lesbian, and bisexual public policy issues, the only direct mention of transgender public policy is two paragraphs, which lament the failure of Minnesota to adequately fund an existing transgender health care program. No mention is made of transgender issues in chapters on public schools, the workplace, marriage, and other important concerns.

28. Abigail S. Clough (2000). Also, In May of 2001 Maryland became the 12th state to pass a law aimed at protecting lesbian and gay people. A petition to create a referendum to repeal the law was declared to lack the necessary signatures and the law went into effect on November 21, 2001. The reference for Connecticut and Rhode Island is a reprint of an Associated Press story as reprinted in *Pinnacle*, July 2001, a transgender newsletter, which may be obtained from P.O. Box 16036, Arlington, VA 22215.

**29.** National Gay and Lesbian Task Force Press Release (2000).

30. Cambridge Municipal Code, Section 2.76.110 and Section 2.76.030, Definitions.

31. Abigail S. Clough (2000).

32. Chai Feldblum (2000).

33. Ibid., page 15.

34. *Price Waterhouse v. Hopkins*, 490 U.S. 228 (1989) (plurality opinion), as noted in Chai Feldblum (2000).

35. Ibid., page 17.

36. Ibid., page 18.

37. Ibid., page 19.

38. Ibid., page 19. Emphasis in the original.

39. Ibid., page 20.

40. GenderPAC press release (April 2001).

41. Ibid.

42. Lillian Potter (1999).

43. For example, Rep. Barney Frank (D-MA) has made comments for the record so that even though the proposed legislative expansion of the definition of hate crimes doesn't explicitly name gender orientation, the intent of Congress to include transgender concerns will be clear. Noted by Dana Priesing, a lawyer working with Gender PAC, in "A Note on Federal Hate Crimes Legislation," *Transgender Pinnacle*, December 2000.

44. Ordinance 983.

45. International Foundation for Gender Education. Box 540229, Waltham, MA 02154-0229; telephone 617-894-8340; web site, www.ifge.org.

46. Dianna Cicotello (1992).

47. General Accounting Office (1997).

48. Mitzi Eilts (2000).

49. Personal Communication, 1997.

50. Colker (1996), page 265.

51. *M.T. v J. T.*, 140 N.J. Super. 77, 355 A.2d204 (N.J.Super.A.D., Mar 22, 1976). This citation was made available on the Internet by Angela Bridgeman.

52. Proceedings, Volumes 1–5, 1992-1996.

53. Access to transgender activist organizations is available through many channels including the International Foundation for Gender Education. Web site, www.ifge.org.

54. Some good locations on the web for transgender activist news include www.ifge.org, www.tgforum.org, www.genderpac.org, and www.ngltf.org.

55. A list of these groups is provided in every copy of *Transgender Tapestry*. Other lists are available on the Internet.

56. John D'Emilio (1983), pages 187–188.

57. Beren de Motier (1998).

58. Fund-raising letter, National Gay and Lesbian Task Force, July 16, 1998.

59. Walter L. Williams (1992). Within the way I use language in this book, it is reasonable to talk about a third gender but not a third sex. I have discussed gender as a master role, more stable and important than other roles, but less inclusive than the concept of self. Since a master role is a social construction that may or may not be claimed by an individual, it is reasonable to note the social reality of berdache roles, for example. A berdache role is a distinct set of social expectations attached to an individual who is then understood to be neither a man nor a woman. A berdache person was allowed to move freely within both gender groups in societies with clearly differentiated gender groups that have distinctive social expectations.

60. You can contact Nancy Nangeroni at Nancy@gendertalk.com.

61. Gail Dines and Jean Humez (1995).

62. Vern and Bonnie Bullough (1993), pages 286–292.

63. Gary Kates (1995), page xxii.

64. Ibid., page xxiii.

65. Phaedra Kelly (1997).

66. Associated Press story in the San Francisco Chronicle, April 17, 2000.

67. Comment, Fourth Annual International Conference on Transgender Law and Employment Policy, Houston, Texas, 1996.

68. Resolution, National Annual General Meeting of Amnesty International Australia, May 22- 24, 1998. Reported in GAIN, an Internet news summary for the transgender community.

69. Alison Laing (1996), page 48.

70. Mariette Pathy Allen (1997), pages 311–315.

71. Dallas Denny (1997), page 39.

72. Nancy Nangeroni (1997), page 349.

73. The National Transgender Library and Archive is available in the Hatcher Graduate Library at the University of Michigan. Julie Herrada is the current curator and is available at jherrada@umich.edu. California State University–Northridge has a special collection that includes extensive material from Vern Bullough and Virginia Prince. The Rikki Swin Institute has a library and archives that includes materials from the International Foundation for Gender Education and other valuable sources. The Institute's web site is www.RSInstitute.org.

*When Trish and I visited Hawaii, we found several wonderful surprises. One was a night rainbow. Rainbows are plentiful in Hawaii: fragments of rainbows and full-arch rainbows. Sunny days are punctuated by mountain-ripped clouds that trade some of their water for a change in altitude. The rainbows are beautiful in themselves and additionally beautiful to Jews and Christians for exciting biblical memories of a God who can forgive and will not always destroy.*

*Who pays the wages of sin for us so that we do not always reap what has been sown in unkindness and injustice? Maybe an answer is in the night rainbow. I had never seen a night rainbow before I went to Hawaii and have never seen one since. The sweep of the ocean gives a lot of room for moonlight to have its full effect. Although I would not have believed before seeing one that there was such a thing as a night rainbow, it fortunately did not depend upon the puny powers of my belief. Though lacking the prismatic display of its daytime counterpart, the night rainbow more than compensates with surprise—the recasting of the night as a time that can also hold the light in arched beauty and promise.*

*If we look to Hebrew scripture for a story of the promise of the daytime rainbow, where shall we look for the story of the promise that comes at night? Native Hawaiians have a worthy story to share.*

> *A great queen, Liliokalani, was so highly venerated that she was treated almost as if she were a god. Her charisma was sensed as so great that if her shadow were to touch a loyal subject, the subject would be killed.*
>
> *Queen Liliokalani might have acted like a superstar, running around and watching the people scatter. Instead, she stayed within her house during the day to protect her subjects. What a sacrifice—to give up daytime movement. She swallowed her brightest colors in compassion.*
>
> *But oh how she shone when she went out at night. Her compassion changed the night, and her loyal subjects could gather close to her and show their faces free of fear.*

*Such stories stand on their own and also help us appreciate a specifically Christian story.* Pat Conover

# Chapter 9:
# Transgender Channels of Grace

Previous chapters have been devoted to building the best possible scientific basis for understanding transgender experience and expression. A consistent theme in my review of the scientific literature has been the emergence of possibilities for transgender experience and expression, given the contributions and limitations of our bodies, the development of psychological identities, and social relationships. This chapter turns the corner to consider what can be *good* about choosing gender possibilities that don't conform to either general cultural stereotypes or the specific mix of gender messages a person grows up with. Along the way, this chapter responds to hostile critiques of transgender expression and offers an alternative grounding for Christian theological, ethical, and spiritual concerns. Although this chapter is explicitly Christian, it is my hope and intent that non-Christians might find good news here as well.

Science, when it is well done, declines to discuss the personal or religious *meaning* of phenomena, but rather focuses on what *is* and *how* what is came to be. Phyllis Burke, Chandler Burr, and Anne Fausto-Sterling have spent considerable energy to point out that, when many scientists work with issues of sexuality and gender, they often stray from the standard of value neutrality.[1] Here, however, we take on a different challenge. When science studies individual people and social relationships, it is studying people who assign meaning to their choices and relationships. In studying the development of gender identities and expectations, it is appropriate for science to consider how people learn and incorporate meanings. While well-done science should not evaluate *values in themselves* it appropriately studies the formation and acquisition of *meanings as held.* When people *reflect* on the meanings they have assigned to objects, images, experiences, and relationships, and especially when people contemplate their direct experience of values, the discourse moves to theological, spiritual, and ethical considerations.

The first challenge of this book has been to point out that there really are people who have transgender subjectivity—who do not fit smoothly into bipolar gender stereotypes of man or woman. The second challenge has been to point out that this is a natural rather than a pathological process by showing that transgender experience and expression arise from common physiological, psychological, and social potentials and influences, not some special cause. Seen in this light, the issues of the value and the meaning of transgender experience and expression are appropriately discussed in general, rather than special case, terms. Such general framing supports a discussion of transgender experience and expression that is very different from discussions focused on helping (health) or controlling (legal) perspectives. Clinical and legal discussions have assumed that transgender experience and expression are highly unusual, pathological, disordered, or some other kind of special-case phenomena. However, I am *not* arguing that just because transgender experience and expression arise as a natural or normal or common possibility, it is therefore good.

For any readers who skipped the earlier scientific chapters, here is one more brief restatement of my understanding of the causation of transgender experience and expression. Gender roles and identities, including transgender roles and identities, are social constructions, which may be influenced by, but are not simply caused by, physiological and psychological factors. Instead of thinking of any physiological or psychological factor as an overwhelming urge that dominates gender constructions, the synthetic approach in this book directs attention to a range of possible outcomes that emerge from the interaction of common physiological, psychological and social factors. The importance of any single factor as a cause of transgender experience, as a cause of subjectively sensed urgency to engage in transgender expression, is an issue for empirical investigation, not a matter of ideological declaration. Whatever the degree of sensed urgency to engage in transgender expression, choices to engage in different kinds of transgender expression are influenced by an individuals awareness of, and projection of, social contingencies. [2]

Earlier chapters gave substantial attention to what a physiological *trait* is and what a psychological *choice* is, and they presented a more complex picture of gender and transgender development than is seen by many people. Chapter 4 makes it clear that different people feel different degrees of urgency about gender concerns, and it points out that some people have complex rather than simple gender careers. The picture developed in earlier chapters is that some adults feel strong and unrelenting urges to express themselves as men, although they were defined at birth as female; or as women, although defined at birth as male. Other adults have less general, less strong, and more complex feelings and expressive desires. My emphasis on the development of transgender expression should not be reduced to the development of psychological choices. Many straight and transgender adults experience themselves as having little or no choice about their gender identification; others have more sense of choice. In addition to factors of psychological orientation and sensed urgency, people with transgender experience consider their social circumstances in making action choices. At this point it is important to remember that, whatever the urgency or complexity of transgender experience and expression, it is only the masculine and feminine experience and expression of people who are not expected to have such experience or the desire to offer such expression. That is all there is to the "surprise" of transgender experience and expression.

Previous chapters show how difficult life can be for transgender people who have to contend with the formal and informal sanctions of people and institutions that defend bipolar gender conceptions and standards. The intellectual grounding of legal and clinical professionals who defend such conceptions and standards is shown to be based on unjustified appeals to physiological or psychological essentialism. The first four chapters show why physiological and psychological essentialism is not scientifically justified. The seventh chapter appeals to the clinical professions to reconsider and restate their official opinions. Here I point out that some clinical professionals have appealed to the grounding of religious authority to justify their views. This chapter makes clear that claiming a Christian basis for transgender oppression is unjustified.

I offer my own contribution to scientific theory about transgender experience and expression in the Chapter 6. Here is my summary of my thinking, as exemplified by my own story: I am a transgender person. Although I was identified as a male at birth and raised as a boy, I nonetheless learned about the social role of woman and about cultural images of femininity from what was shown to me as I grew up. I came to claim the self-concept of woman as my best and most honest way to identify and share my sense of some aspects of myself. By making such a claim I realize that I am not meeting the expectations assigned to me as a male, and I recognize that I am not meeting the common expectation that I be either a man or a woman. Other people follow quite different transgender paths than I have followed. I believe, however, that most transgender people could summarize their stories within the theories developed in this book in general and within Chapter 6 in particular.

Few straight Christian writers have commented on transgender concerns. Those who have addressed transgender issues have mostly wanted to address the ethics of transgender expression or to raise pastoral concerns for transgender people. This chapter touches on such issues, but the larger purpose is to point to the good news that can flow through transgender experience and expression: good news for transgender people, good news for everyone. In addition to celebrating such good news, I hope this chapter is helpful to those who want to understand their relationships with transgender people, including those who are concerned about the place of transgender people in the life of the church.

## A Theological Introduction

Developing a scientifically accurate picture of transgender experience and expression is an end in itself. Christians are hardly alone in valuing truth as a guide for pictures of reality. Indeed, those of us who are aware Christians need to continue to confess that we carry a story that has had too many antiscientific chapters. Christianity at its best welcomes the truth wherever it takes us. But Christianity has not always been at its best. Since we Christians believe that God is the creator, we have nothing to fear from the truths about creation. I can testify that appreciating creation, and trying to understand how it works, can be a spiritual path to coming close to God.

In earlier chapters I not only emphasized a synthetic reconstruction of what we scientifically know but also pointed out that there is a lot we don't know. Christian theology cannot live on the thin gruel of trying to fill in with faith the dwindling territory of what is not known. That approach misapplies theology to a scientific agenda. Instead, we need to ground ourselves in the most accurate scientific picture of transgender experience and expression, while remembering with humility, just as good scientists do, that our picture is inadequate and incomplete; and then do the best we can to live well.

We do not all need to be scientists, but we do need elementary honesty about the groundings of our opinions and beliefs to sustain more constructive conversations. Garry Wills has done a magnificent job of making this point in the realm of Roman Catholic discourse with his book *Papal Sin*.[3] Protestant leaders also need to be reminded of this point, since many have also engaged in strategies that subordinate truth to other purposes. [4] One wonderful example of Christian confession has been offered by Gil Alexander-Moegerle, the co-founder with James Dobson of Focus on the Family: "I apologize to lesbian and gay Americans who are demeaned and dehumanized on a regular basis by the false, irresponsible, and inflammatory rhetoric of James Dobson's anti-gay radio and print materials. "[5] Confession and humility are not merely Christian virtues and scientific values; they are also critical to the development of social institutions and cultural images that empower mutuality of understanding. Confession and humility make transformative conversation possible, and that, in turn, makes possible the development of common goals and expectations aligned with the best we are capable of as human beings. To contribute to such conversation, this chapter asks how gender understandings might be reconstructed to better embody the eternals that all of us can touch but not grasp: love, justice, responsibility, truth, and beauty. We do not define the eternal realities. They define us. We can only point to them, celebrate them, and try to embody them.

Our knowing of the eternals involves cognition, but it is a knowing by the whole self. It includes the subjectivity of self-knowing as we participate in valued relationships. It starts with the sense that some things are important, really important. We know such things by participating in them, even if only by anticipation or imagination. The sciences can help us understand the possibilities that are open to us; theology helps us figure out what to choose. For example, even people identified at birth as females who urgently feel they must live their lives as men still have choices about what kind of men they want to be. My understanding of Christian theology begins with an appreciation of my life and world as God's creation, and with thankfulness for the redemptive presence of God, which lures me to turn away from what is ugly, false, and hurtful. I am interested in spirituality and theology as they inform and give direction to my life, my relations with others, my engagement of this marvelous creation. I leave it to others to lift up speculations outside of human experience.

Theology needs the sciences for grounding its pictures of reality as accurately as possible, while remembering that the sciences have grown and changed. One key element in achieving a rapprochement between theology and science in general, and in creating the best possible theology of transgender experience and expression in particular, is to remember that theology has no privileged grounding for truth assertions that are properly a focus of science. Although good theology helps to ground science as a valuable human activity because it is a search for truth, theology is a corrective to science only at those points where science overreaches its proper discourse and makes de facto theological statements. As whole people, scientists might be great theologians, and vice versa, but it is still important to keep the realms of discourse clear.

Theology is built from contemplation and reflection about what is important in life. Appreciation of what is most important is the spiritual work of private prayer and corporate liturgy. Applied theology offers guidance to culture, to society, and to individuals by grounding evangelism, stewardship, and ethics. Theology is about how people work with the things that are eternal—that are expressed in the midst of life but are not defined by limited human expression.

The core theological assertion in this book is that transgender experience and expression can be an expression of and an incarnation of love, truth , justice – just as much, and just as little, as other human experiences and expressions. Working with transgender experience and expression can sensitize a person to one or another theological issue, but neither transgender experience, nor any other kind of experience, is special for expressing what is eternal, what is precious. Just as "haystack," rather than "needle," facts and theories are emphasized in other chapters for understanding what we can learn from the sciences, this chapter treats transgender experience and expression as merely one more life path.

Some writers do theology as if they had a privileged grounding for declaring spiritual truth to others. As one who has experienced the love of God, I too feel that I have something precious to share. But I am aware that my personal sharing is testimony for the reader to evaluate rather than a privileged grounding for declaration. I will point as well as I can, but it is up to the reader to do the seeing.

As this chapter unfolds, several theological perspectives will be developed. But it seems only fair to the reader that my core testimonial should be clear from the beginning. As a person with my identity centered in a Christian understanding of salvation, I want to claim and express all the Christian virtues in my life without regard to whether our culture has named them as masculine or feminine. Because of my theological critique of United States culture, I am not willing to settle for life answers that uncritically accept cultural images and values—that simply adjust to social roles and expectations. I accept, and I want to explore, all the good gifts God has given me, rather than hide some away because I've been told they do not fit. I have chosen to violate traditional gender expectations in order to honor what seem to me to be more important values. I seek to express myself, and be open in my interaction with others, by using common cultural symbols and images to express my commitments, which are culturally defined as masculine or feminine. Others may judge my gender expressions to be clumsy or ugly or immature. From the inside out, what I can say is that I'm doing the best I can.

Other Christians have written to share their transgender experience. I particularly thank Vanessa S. , Kathryn Helms, Frances Cormier, Karyn Kroll, Dana Cole and Dianna for their witness. [6] I've been most moved recently by reading the sharing of Chris Paige. [7] Those interested in Internet-based dialogue might want to take a look at www. whosoever. org.

Some nontransgender Christians have sought to respond affirmatively to the transgender community. David Horton, for example, offers a compromise with transgender people. On the one hand, he doesn't want transgender people to feel guilty for their existence, and he offers some limited biblical and ethical reasoning to that end. On the other hand, he repeatedly points to the selfishness of transgender people and urges them to stay in the closet as much as possible to protect the sensibilities of spouses, children, and church congregations. The saving grace to his pamphlet is an unanswered question written as the last sentence: "Do we represent Christian values to those who are different, or do we merely seek their conformity to our patterns of behavior to save ourselves from embarrassment?"[8] It is much easier to affirm his pamphlet as a resource for the church than to affirm it as a resource for transgender people. Although I am concerned about the tone of his writing, I am thankful for the ministry and witness he has offered in Great Britain. In the United States, the earliest clear support from a church leader came from Rev. Clinton Jones, Episcopal canon, Christ Church Cathedral, in Hartford, Connecticut. In 1978 he wrote, "I see no reason for determining that transvestism is ethically immoral." He went on to call for sympathy and support rather than prejudice.[9]

I began this chapter by setting the theological stage. Next comes a section contrasting a positive Christian natural theology to the antinatural theology that is such an embarrassment for Roman Catholicism. The biblical section considers biblical passages used by some Christians to attack transgender experience and expression, then claims the core Judeo-Christian themes that can help one appreciate transgender experience and expression. The section on doctrinal theology responds to those who are concerned about transgender experience and expression as sin. A section on liberation theology responds to some feminists who have attacked transgender experience and expression, then shows how liberationist thinking can appreciate and elucidate transgender experience and expression, with reference to other feminist authors. The final dialectic and constructive section aims at engaging the saving truths of Christianity as they relate to transgender experience.

Finally, before proceeding to these specific theological approaches, it is important to me to share my Christian understanding that the saving love of God can come through many channels, including non-Christian channels. This is good news, since Christendom has hurt so many transgender people so badly. As a result, many transgender people who grew up in the church have turned away to other religious expressions. The following sections are written with this hurting much in mind. Even though I write as a transgender person, I join the confession of aware Christians that we share in the sin and alienation done in our common name. We can do better.

# Transgender Good News

## Gaining Perspective Before Picking Up the Work

*Oh the history books tell it, they tell it so well;*
*The cavalry charged and the Indians fell,*
*The cavalry charged and the Indians died,*
*Now the cavalry too had God on its side.* Bob Dylan[10]

The Dylan lyrics remind us that theology books as well as history books are mostly written by the victors. The witness of Jesus, revelation in the midst of oppression, is different from the witness of later centuries, when Christendom had gained power and consolidated that power in the hands of church patriarchs.

Convoluted and misogynist theology in the early church, and its repetition and extension in the Middle Ages, helped shape some examples of transgender behavior. In the 4th century, Jerome, following the Greek philosopher Philo, said that "[so] long as woman is for birth and children, she is different from man as body is from soul. But when she wishes to serve Christ more than the world, then she will cease to be a woman and will be called man."[11] This may well have been a common attitude, since Ambrose in the same century agreed. "she who does not believe is a woman and should be designated by the name of her sex, whereas she who believes progresses to perfect manhood, to the measures of the adulthood of Christ. She then dispenses with the name of her sex, the seductiveness of youth, the garrulousness of age."[12]

Later, Thomas Aquinas helped to set the patriarchal cast of Roman Catholic tradition in stone, writing, "good order would have been wanting in the human family if some were not governed by others wiser than themselves. So by such a kind of subjection woman is naturally subject to man, because in man the discretion of reason predominates."[13] Although it is common to note that some church authorities continue to preach such woman-oppressing theology, it is interesting to note in the context of this book that a number of Catholic saints began their lives as women but came to sainthood as men. When, at death, their sex was discovered, their cross-gender behavior was counted as further proof of their saintliness. Pelagia is one of the best known of these saints.[14] The Roman Catholic Church once welcomed transgender leadership and has precedents it could use to justify supporting transgender leadership today.[15]

Issues of the clergy standing of transgender people are beginning to show up within several denominations. Dr. Erin Swenson prevailed in a trial with the Presbytery of Greater Atlanta and will be allowed to retain her ordination as a male-to female transsexual.[16] Transgender people are named in the new By-Laws of the United Church of Christ as one element of a coalition that is authorized to participate in the guidance of the denomination.[17] I have had standing as an ordained minister within the United Church of Christ for 37 years and officially explained my transgender status to the Association in which I have my standing in the mid-1990s. But the larger story is a story of rejection.[18] It is time, past time, for change.

## Seeing the Hand of the Creator in the Creation

*Natural Theology and the Sciences*

In earlier chapters I take a synthetic approach to the sciences that honors and responds to the range of analytic studies that make up science, arranged within different disciplines. Instead of dividing a whole into parts, as does analytic science, the synthetic approach focuses on what is gained when parts are integrated into a whole. Aspects of reality that are only potential in the parts, and are therefore unobservable when only the parts are examined, become manifest when the parts are joined together. For example, human bodies can be analyzed in terms of the physical particles that make up the body, but many of the most interesting realities of human beings can be observed only when such particles are integrated in the marvelously complex ways in which the human body comes together. Similarly, it is only when human beings join together in social relationships that the hidden potentials of civilization begin to come into view.

Such a synthetic approach to the sciences makes the interface between science and theology much easier to understand and work with. In contrast, analytic science defines the parts that make up a whole and shows how they come together, without addressing what is gained (what potential is released) by the coming together. Analytic science draws its enormous power from focusing on what can be observed; and potential, by definition, cannot be observed. When analytic science considers the whole, in turn, as a part of a yet larger whole, what was merely potential has become manifest and can be observed. Analytic science assumes that the potential, which was released by the joining of parts into a whole, was caused by the joining of the parts. But, when the whole is a human being, the whole has some choice about the integration of its parts and more choice about how it wants to fit into larger social wholes. Things become infinitely more complex because human beings take account of social factors in shaping themselves. A tennis player practices tennis and builds up some muscles rather than others. Human beings, by taking account of the wholes of which they are a part, are thus shaped not only by the influence of their parts but also by the influence of larger wholes (social relationships) of which they are parts. Human beings choose among the potentials, and that means that analytic science cannot assume that human beings are simply caused by their parts. Theology enters the picture by considering the intrinsic values, such as goodness, beauty, justice. These intrinsic values can be perceived, but not manipulated or defined by human beings. If one acts in an ugly fashion, that does not change beauty. Although we human beings cannot define the eternals, we can perceive them and measure our actions and products against them. Indeed, instead of always pursuing survival as we assume other animals pursue survival, sometimes humans decide not merely to shape their lives to perceptions of the eternals, but to give up their lives to express their valuation of an eternal.

Analytic science has the appearance of completely explaining reality because there is a scientific discipline assigned to each higher level of integration: physics, chemistry, physiology, psychology and sociology. But there are two consistent problems with this approach. The first, and for this book the least interesting, shows up in internal debates within any single discipline. Some physiologists focus on the elements of cells, such as their genome, and others are interested in the interaction of cells in a body. You can study the human genome as if it existed as a separate reality, but the genome of a cell can and does change because of interactions of the cell with its environment. The genes in a cell help to create a cellular reality, which, in turn, introduces environmental effects into the cell and changes the genes. Thus, although it is possible to study the human genome as a separate reality, such a study is not a complete study, because it does not consider how a genome is affected by its environment but only how it is affected by its parts. Whenever scientists reason from a part, or a collection of parts, to the whole and argue that some element of the part determines the activity of the whole, they are making the essentialist mistake of disregarding the potentials for interaction that were hidden in the parts but become manifest in a joined whole.[19] Synthetic science is interested in the variety and complexity of a whole, in and of itself, instead of focusing on how the whole contributes to the next larger reality of which it is a part.

The second, and more important, problem is that an analytic scientist may easily correct the essentialism of scientists working with less complex wholes but may become an essentialist about his or her own object of study. Psychologists may correct physiologists by asserting that transgender experience cannot be explained by merely physiological factors, but the psychologists may in turn fail to give sufficient weight to the significance of social factors. My analysis in Chapter 3 of Sandra Bem's work is an example of why this failing can matter a lot. An additional way to make this second point is to remind readers that the complexities and potentials of brains make possible the complexities and potentials of minds. The complexities and potentials of minds in turn make possible the further complexities of societies and cultures. When societies and cultures make the impact of the eternals more manifest, it is easier for individuals to perceive the eternals.

I've emphasized that sociology can analyze how meanings as held are used by people in shaping social relationships. But analytic sociologists are as blind as other scientists to taking values in themselves seriously. Such blindness is an analytic virtue which helps to sustain focus on social processes related to values as held. When we ask the synthetic questions about how the engagement of values in themselves reveals human truth, we have stepped outside analytic science. It is one thing to disregard values in themselves to sustain analytic focus, but it is sociological essentialism to deny the reality and significance of values in themselves. We cannot stand in God's place and see any larger whole, but we can see the creation that we live within, and we can see the effects of value choices in social relationships. Furthermore, in ecstatic moments, we can feel ourselves to be at one with the eternals, with God—the source of the eternals. We can sense the eternals—goodness, truth, beauty, love, justice—even though we do not define them. They define us. What we can do is *appreciate* the eternals and *use* them to guide our relations to each other and our environments. [20] But we do not stand above or outside our participation in creation. Birth and death help remind us of this.

The virtue of a synthetic approach to the sciences for interfacing with theology is that focusing on human awareness of values in themselves as potentials released by the conscious participation of human beings in social relationships and environments, makes the discourse of theology reasonable even though the analytic method is no longer relevant. A synthetic stance sensitizes us to the questions we can ask as people who are part of larger wholes, not merely to express the range of possibilities released by the physiological, psychological, and social integrations of our parts, but also by taking seriously the eternals we can sense but not grasp. Such synthetic awareness does not posit any teleological arguments, any appeals to a hidden design. [21] I merely implore my readers to join me in trying to recognize and engage the best of the potentials in our lives, to welcome each other into the common enterprise of trying to create the best possible social relationships, the best possible standards and laws, the best possible societies and cultures.

Good natural theology begins with an appreciation not only of the Creator who has given us the manifest world, but also of the Creator who has given us the opportunity to experience the eternals. We honor the Creator when we celebrate these gifts and use them to guide our participation in giving life and shape to the eternals. Our artistic creations, our scientific understanding, our civilizations, our sexual sharing and gender relationships can express the eternals. The intrinsic goodness in being born as creatures who sometimes want to engage in sexual sharing and who construct gender relationships lies in the possibility of experiencing and expressing love, beauty, responsibility, and mutuality in sexual sharing and in gender relationships. Taking seriously the possibility of such goodness is one channel to awe of the Creator. For many of us, our engagement comes first and reflection comes later. Seen in this light, faith is our unarticulated thankfulness coming to consciousness. This is good news for transgender people when we learn we can embody the eternals in our sexual expression and gender relationships. When nontransgender people come to understand this transgender truth, it can be good news for them as well; it can lure them into thinking about the eternals as a challenge to their sexual sharing and gender relationships.

*Natural Theology and Christianity*

All Christian theologies hold that creation, in itself, is a good gift from God. However, Roman Catholic and Protestant theologies quickly put this theme aside by arguing that human sin ("the Fall") has corrupted creation. Drawing upon Greek dualism and Roman stoicism, Roman Catholic theology has asserted that things of the body are bad and that Christians should focus on things of the spirit. Protestant theologies have mostly affirmed this element of Roman Catholic theology but have modified or qualified it in various ways. Christine Gudorf points out that "Augustine taught that intercourse was, even in marriage, at least venially sinful because it was virtually impossible to have intercourse without pleasure."[22] This line of thought comes from Greek and Roman sources and is also supported by Jewish and Christian ascetic and apocalyptic traditions, as found in the Essenes of Jesus's time and in several biblical writings.[23] Such theology transformed the life-affirming witness of Jesus into a life-denying focus on going to heaven after death or after the end of the world. Life on earth was to be endured. Fortunately for contemporary Christians, the life-affirming witness of Jesus keeps breaking through our limited constructions.

The Roman Catholic version of natural theology emphasizes that *the* function of genital sexual activity is the reproduction of children. An example of this position can be found in the words of Cardinal Ratzinger concerning homosexuals:

> Although the particular inclination of the homosexual person is not a sin, it is more or less a strong tendency ordered toward an intrinsic moral evil. . . . It is only in the marital relationship that the use of sexual faculty can be morally good. . . . A person engaging in homosexual behavior therefore acts immorally. . . . Homosexual union is not a complementary union, able to transmit life, and so it thwarts the call to a life to that form of self-giving which the Gospel says is the essence of Christian living. This does not mean that homosexual persons are not often generous and giving of themselves, but when they engage in homosexual activity they confirm within themselves a disordered sexual inclination which is essentially self-indulgent.[24]

Ratzinger regards homosexual inclination as inborn, therefore natural, and therefore not sinful in itself, but he still claims that it produces a strong tendency to evil. The defense of such an incredible position is that human sin, "the Fall," has corrupted not only our human constructions within creation but creation itself. This position, as Garry Wills points out in his book *Papal Sins*, takes these parts of Roman Catholic teaching outside the realm of reasonable discourse. For those who are interested, Wills provides a detailed analysis of how Pius XI backed into the foolish sexual assertions found in the encyclical *Casti Connubi* in 1930 and why these mistakes were repeated by Paul VI in the encyclical *Humanae Vitae* in 1968. [25] These encyclicals focused on opposition to contraception, but the supporting arguments reemphasized the principle that the only acceptable purpose for intercourse was procreation. Gudorf spells out several negative implications of the Roman Catholic emphasis on procreation.[26] Here we need only note that Ratzinger asserts that the only virtuous expression of sex is within marriage. Since the Roman Catholic hierarchy denies marriage to same-sex couples, they have placed themselves in the position of trying to block the possibility of loving and responsible erotic sharing between people of the same sex. To cap the irony, Ratzinger says it is homosexuals who are disordered. It seems to me that a theology that tries to block the possibility of loving and responsible sexual sharing is disordered. [27]

Ratzinger's assertion that gay and lesbian sexual activity is not self-giving because it cannot transmit life is a travesty and an outrage, not only for gay and lesbian people, but for all people who give deeply of themselves in sexual sharing without trying to create a new life. It is an offense against the Gospel, as well as common experience, to assert that self-giving is defined as physiological procreation. Nothing could be further from the spirit of Jesus, who focused his words about salvation on giving and loving and never said a recorded word about procreation. Ratzinger tries to escape the horrid implication of his statement by tossing a bone to homosexuals, allowing that homosexuals might have a generous intent but that their erotic expression is nonetheless sinful because it cannot produce children. This kind of natural theology cannot be set right with a few nuances, exceptions, or compromises. The correct natural theology question is whether erotic expression between two people with the same kind of genitals has the possibility of expressing the eternals of love, beauty, and responsibility. There is a parallel question for sexual sharing between people of the same gender, whatever their genital makeup. That is what is important, and the Roman Catholic hierarchy needs to confess its error and seek forgiveness for all the damage it has done by denying and hiding from this Christian truth.

Perhaps Ratzinger realizes the unattractiveness of his position. In any case, he offers one more argument that is not part of historical Roman Catholic thinking. He asserts that the homosexual inclination is "disordered." In this society, such a word is most fairly heard as an appeal to the pathologizing perspectives of the clinical establishment. First the clinical establishment said homosexuality was abnormal because it didn't meet cultural norms, meaning primarily Christian norms. Now, Ratzinger appeals to psychology to buttress his unattractive theological position.

The most telling exposure of Ratzinger's smallness of spirit is his condemnation of all homosexual sexual expression as self-indulgent. But, before my homosexual friends stoke their anger any higher, it is important to remember that Ratzinger feels this way about all sexual expression that is not intended for procreation within marriage. Celibacy is the standard of Roman Catholic sexual spirituality, and anything less is worldly or self-indulgent.

Given the comments above, it is time to assert that Ratzinger's comments, and all that they reflect in Roman Catholic teaching, should no longer be called natural theology. There are two basic reasons that such theology is not natural. The first is that many people—straight, gay, bisexual, lesbian, transgender, and those "under construction"—actually engage in a lot of genital sexual sharing in pursuit of pleasure rather than to create children. Pleasure is a common and natural function of sexual expression. Ratzinger and other Roman Catholics may not like pleasure, but to deny that it is a natural function of genital sexual expression is to deny the truth available from observation and experience.[28] When pressed, we shall see that Roman Catholics actually back off from claiming their "natural" theology is grounded in the observation or experience of nature.

The second reason that Roman Catholic sexual theology isn't natural is tragic. Roman Catholics emphasize the importance of marriage because marriage links the power of sexual appetites to the obligation to care for children. Yet once a child is born, there is no good Roman Catholic reason to have any more sexual expression which further links couples together emotionally. What is good is the bonding of love between people who share parenthood. It is the loving that makes the sexual exchange good. Such bonding is not an assertion of will. It is a discovery that can come with the experience of sexual sharing. The failure to celebrate the potential for directly experiencing love as part of sexual expression denies one of the most precious gifts of creation. This denial is one of the most damaging results of antinatural Roman Catholic sexual theology.

A group of Roman Catholics, organized through the Pope John XXIII Medical-Moral Research and Education Center, created a dialogue between themselves and leading researchers. The consultation was held in 1982, and a book based on it was published in 1983. The book, *Sex and Gender: A Theological and Scientific Inquiry*, consisted of papers by the scientists about homosexuality and transsexuality with rejoinders from theologians asserting the scientists were wrong.[29] Some of the theological criticisms were appropriate recognitions of the points where the scientists had overstepped the boundaries of their disciplines and inserted their values into their conclusions. Although several of the theological respondents were clearly trying to reach out to sexual minorities, they repeatedly came back to positions as ugly and outrageous as those of Cardinal Ratzinger. For example, Benedict Ashley, after once again explaining that sexual expression by people with the same kinds of genitals is a mortal sin because it doesn't produce children, clarified that his use of the word *natural* did not mean "things as they are" but really meant "healthy."[30] Ashley is claiming a revelation-based knowledge of health, calling it nature, then trying to force the truth about nature through his sieve. The truths that don't make it through this sieve are discarded. There could hardly be a better example of the breakdown of dialogue between theology and science because of the hubris of the involved theologians. It is a sad story, because Ashley started off so well, doing his best to lift up the importance of love as a proper measure of sexuality. Albert Moraczewski, in the same book, is more blunt when defining the word *nature*. For scientists, he says, natural is "what a population of a species actually does," while for Catholic theologians natural "is that which is in accord with God's revelation. "[31] This is not natural theology in the sense of trying to draw close to the Creator by contemplating the creation.

Though a poor understanding of biology may have influenced historical Roman Catholic positions on sexual sharing, contemporary advocates who are very skilled in the biological sciences are still focused on defending the sacredness of human life from the moment of conception. They are unwilling to distinguish between human life and a human person. This position gives no weight to the emergence of the human person through a developmental process for which conception is a necessary but not sufficient condition. [32] No degree of scientific sophistication can cover up for an ascetic distortion that lifts up the sacredness of undeveloped potential at the cost of the sacredness of fully formed people seeking to embody the highest Christian values in their sexual sharing and gender expressions.

The pathologizing of transgender experience and expression by the clinical establishment is a strong support for those who see transgender experience and expression as abnormal. Transposed into theological language, this becomes "Transgender experience is not part of God's natural order. "The earlier chapters that deal with the issues of how transgender experience and expression came to be pathologized are offered in rebuttal of this assertion. As noted before, the clinical establishment often refers to the religious basis of contemporary cultural tradition as part of their arguments that transgender experience and expression are abnormal. George Rekers was quoted earlier in this regard. Timothy and Joseph Costello, in their chapter on sexual disorders in their textbook *Abnormal Psychology*, write, "In that part of the world which is influenced by the Judeo-Christian traditions, normal sex, as prescribed in their religious writing and moral codes, is sex in which the goal is penile/vaginal intercourse (coitus). "[33] Despite sparring on other issues, the religious establishment and the clinical establishment have powerfully supported each other, and circularly quoted each other to defend traditional sexual ethics.

The second line of thought that intrinsically challenges the naturalness of Roman Catholic theology has to do with the overlap of characteristics, such as height, that are supposedly distinctly distributed by sex. Saying that males are taller than females is true as a statement of average but fails to convey that a lot of females are taller than a lot of males. The failure to appreciate overlap is a major grounding for the argument that the sexes are opposite and therefore need each other to be complete. My concern is not merely that such assertions are used to justify patriarchal oppression but also the larger concern that it leads heterosexual partners to misunderstand each other and suggests to gay or lesbian couples that there might be some fundamental incompleteness to their loving relationships. Instead, I suggest that all couples consider whether they are different or similar on any particular point, and then consider how to deal with the pluses and minuses of either relational truth. The point for Roman Catholic theology is that if males and females, men and women, are substantially similar then there is no natural argument for treating them so differently, as, for example, being unwilling to ordain women to the role and status of priests.

In Chapters 2, 3, and 4, attention was given to studies of sexual differences between males and females as they relate to gender differences between men and women. The review found more similarities than differences. Following the review I argued that it would be helpful to give up the use of the word *opposite* for describing or identifying the sexes. Indeed, if we define sex-linked characteristics as broadly as do writers who are seeking to show sexual differentiation, then the fairest conclusion would be that most people are at least partly intersexual. I do not favor such a broad definition, because I do not think research shows that most of the factors studied are meaningfully differentiated by sex. Adopting a narrower focus means recognizing more similarity between males and females, men and women.

In showing that cultural stereotypes of masculinity and femininity are not natural or neutral expressions of an underlying physiological order, Chapters 2, 3, and 4, lay the groundwork for alternative ways of thinking about gender. The urges of people that do not fit traditional gender role expectations, such as a man's urge to nurture, create discomfort with assigned sex roles and enculturated images. In Chapter 6 I developed the theory that transgender experience and expression can be seen as *one* outcome of a human search for interior congruence and social responsibility.

Although earlier chapters challenge the view that "anatomy is destiny," I continue to affirm that bodies matter. Human beings are not disembodied spirits. Our bodies contain resources and limits, predispositions and opportunities. We all have to work out our lives with what we have been given in our individual creation, with what we gain and lose in interactions with all our environments. Natural theology, at its best, notices the embeddedness of the theological quest. Embedded theology brings an incarnational understanding of individuals into interaction with the createdness of other people and our many environments.

*A Desirable Natural Theology*

The most fundamental beginning point for all Christian natural theologies is that we are all created by God. We do not know life as disembodied souls, whatever our capacity for imagination, but as human creatures. The most fundamental celebration of God is thanksgiving for our most precious gift from God, our life. Part of our experience as human creatures is awareness of the eternals. Even so simple an eternal as the mathematical concept of unity cannot be reduced to perceptions of phenomena. Rather, mathematics is used as one aspect of seeing order in our perceptions of phenomena. Brains make it possible to bring together awareness of the eternals with perceptions of the manifest world and the result is usually called mind. [34] When we use our minds to become self-aware and guide our social relationships, we are releasing the possibilities that are invisible in the carbon, oxygen, and other physical elements integrated into our bodies. We shape concepts in our minds and interchange the concepts through the use of language. In this process we synthesize some of the potentials made possible by our physiological integration with some of our direct experience of the eternals. Gender concepts are such constructions. We can discuss how our gender concepts relate to physiological factors and we can discuss how our gender concepts relate to our awareness of the eternals. This way of describing human reality reminds us that we do our experiencing and thinking as creatures and not as God.

The first core truth pointed to by natural theology is thankfulness for being alive, for being able to participate in creation as aware human beings who can choose not merely how we want to meet our physiological needs but also what we want to do with our lives beyond merely existing until we die. This first truth makes possible the innumerable questions about how we might relate to, and incorporate, justice, beauty, and passionate love in our lives. One such question is about how we want to shape our gender images and activities. What values shall we emphasize? The good news in this book, whether you are gender-conforming or transgender, is that, even though you are not used to reflecting on your gender choices, you can indeed reflect on them. However you take advantage of such reflective distance, you can choose to change your gender commitments to more adequately reflect the values you respect and cherish.

In taking seriously the opportunity to become intentional about gender choices, some of us turn to guidance from Christianity. Christianity offers paths and conversations by which individuals can offer their personal contributions, and engage the contributions of others, to create and share in a larger community and story. Sadly, not all Christian communities are attractive, and not every telling of the Christian story is well grounded or spiritually inspired. Embodying transgender truth, just as the embodying of other important truths, serves the Christian community by pointing out helpful reforms so that the best of Christianity may be more clearly seen and appreciated. A payoff for transgender people for continuing to share conversation with Christian communities is that we contribute to building a spiritual home for ourselves and others.

I have already pointed out that Roman Catholic antinatural theology on sexuality is wrong because it recognizes only the function of procreation while denying the function of pleasure. Here I argue that it is more profoundly wrong because it is functionally constructed. Roman Catholic theology affirmed the function of procreation to moderate the ascetic denial of any goodness in sexual interaction for married people, while continuing to affirm ascetic denial as a standard for priests, the hierarchically appointed leaders of the Roman Catholic Church. Choosing self-denial to achieve a personal or social purpose such as saving money or donating to charity, is one thing, but to make self-denial an end in itself is life-denying and violates the great commandment to love one's neighbor as oneself.

Roman Catholic theologians used the same kind of functional thinking to justify slavery. They argued, in the tradition of Aristotle and with appeals to Scripture, that slavery is a natural form of human relationships based on the obvious fact that some people are able to dominate others, then asserted that those who dominated did so because they were naturally superior. The assertion of Aquinas that men should dominate women because they are naturally superior has been quoted earlier in this book. The functional evidence of such superiority is that men did dominate women. The error of all of this kind of functional thinking is the underlying essentialism discussed earlier. This kind of functional thinking argues that if it exists it must be naturally caused, meaning that it is not caused by human motives. Misunderstanding a social pattern as natural rather than constructed creates the mistaken idea that it is unchangeable. [35] Such presumed unchangeability has then been used to dodge the question of whether a social institution or norm is *just*. Such functional thinking has been used to argue that slavery and patriarchy are not unjust but only the inevitable playing out of forces beyond human control. The truth is that slavery and patriarchy are social constructions within human control. Christians commonly see all human constructions as likely to contain sin and thus likely to be in need of reform, using justice as one criterion. [36] Seeing gender standards and concepts as social constructions invites such reevaluation. [37] In contrast to functional thinking, the natural theology I offer is grounded in our best understanding of synthetically summarized scientific truth with attention to the emergence of possibility.

The kind of Christian natural theology I have been presenting can be useful as a guide to ethical issues. Oliver O'Donovan discusses the case of *Corbett v. Corbett* in his book, *Transsexualism and Christian Marriage*. The case resulted in transsexuals' being denied the right to marry in Great Britain. [38] O'Donovan argues that transsexuals should not be allowed to marry because the marriage would not be between a male and a female, because the transsexual partner lacks biological integrity. The lack of integrity, according to O'Donovan, is that the sexual parts were made by humans and not by God.

What is missing in O'Donovan, and in the more recent homophobic political effort by fundamentalist Christians to make marriage laws explicitly heterosexist, is an appreciation of what marriage is supposed to enable in secular law and celebrate in Christian community. O'Donovan and the fundamentalists emphasize a physiological essentialism that causes them to deny and oppose the observable reality of deep spiritual engagement and bonding, the formation and sustaining of families, and the loving and responsible support of children. The appeal to functionalism is wrong not only because of its refusal to recognize other natural functions but also because functionalism refuses to affirm the potentials for human relationships that are part of God's creation that can sometimes express the eternal values that Christians affirm. One of those possibilities is that people can change their bodies to affirm their self-understanding and value commitments. Failure to consider transgender experience and expression as one more human channel for God's love to enter the world makes O'Donovan and others blind to this activity of God in the world—an activity that shines forth in the good gifts that are exchanged within transgender families, in the children who have been well-raised, in the emotional and relational health that prepares people for their positive contributions to society. It is fair to apply Christian values and standards to all sexual and gender activity in order to see it for what it is, the good and the bad. It is ironic and tragic—it breaks my heart—to watch my brothers and sisters who are Christians block the release and engagement of the highest values that Christians affirm.

Not all transgender relationships are filled with Christian virtues, as is true of traditional heterosexual relationships. In all cases, the purpose of the Christian community should be to celebrate relationships that are loving and life-affirming and to help everyone further improve relationships in the expression of love, responsibility, beauty, and justice. Good Christian natural theology helps us to recognize that human life is a good and precious gift, even though it is a sexually transmitted and terminal condition, because it contains the possibility of embodying the love of God. One of those possibilities is loving relationships that include transgender experience and expression.

Another important application of good Christian natural theology for the creation of Christian transgender ethics has to do with "corrective" surgery for intersexual infants. The surgery is done to fit a bipolar conception of human sexuality and gender. The motive is not the affirmation of what God has given at birth but rather the bipolar constructions of gender carried by parents and/or medical personnel. [39] Some intersexual people are protesting against the damage done to them by infant surgery, particularly the loss of capacity for genital arousal, and argue that such routine surgery flows from intrinsic prejudice against their bodies, which were made and loved by God. [40] Phyllis Burke quotes Anne Fausto-Sterling's review of a substantial group of case histories of intersexual people, compiled between 1930 and 1960 before infant corrective surgery became common. "Almost without exception, those reports describe children who grew up knowing they were intersexual... and adjusted to their unusual status.... there is not a psychotic or a suicide in the lot."[41] Getting clear about natural theology will help us understand that an intersexual birth may be a cultural emergency for parents but that God's grace can flow through an intersexual person just as much as through anyone else. Taking away the intersexuality of these children is taking away part of the specialness, part of the gift of their birth. If a child were to show substantial discomfort with an intersexual status, some form of sexual reconstruction surgery (SRS) might be appropriate at that point. [42] The other side of this coin is that discomfort with one's assignment of gender as an infant is the primary justification for SRS for transsexuals. The difference is that the discomfort is felt by the transsexual person rather than by parents or medical personnel. The issue is not naturalness but the valuation of some body changes rather than others by those in authority.

The basic Christian question to ask about transgender physiological alterations is whether those alterations help the person to more completely experience and express their best gifts—to participate in human interaction in loving, caring, and responsible ways. It seems like a highly specialized question when applied to transgender transformations, but the question is only different in focus, not in kind, from other questions of body changes.

To help obtain a little reflective distance from the medical and legal technicalities concerning body alterations made possible by recent improvements in medical practice, it may help us to remember that since the beginnings of recorded history people have been changing their bodies in small or large ways to pursue psychological or social goals. To add one more example to previous discussions of history and culture, we might notice that in many cultures men have shaved their faces to present an appearance they felt was desirable, even though it approximates a female appearance. Is it wrong to desire a hair-free face because one is aware that it approximates a female appearance but acceptable so long as such awareness is lacking? Is it okay for a male to shave one's face, which produces a more feminine appearance, but wrong to shave one's legs? The issue is intent rather than a matter of physiology or technology.

## What Can We Learn from Scripture?

I understand the Bible as Scripture. That is, I have learned saving truth from the Bible, and it is precious to me. My understanding of transgender experience and expression as one channel of God's grace is grounded, in part, in my understanding of the Bible.

The most important work of biblical theology is pointing to saving truth that can be engaged by becoming aware that the writings of the multiple biblical authors and editors points to an emergent understanding of God. The biblical path to increased awareness of God involves two interwoven challenges: seeing key themes that emerge over the centuries as the Bible was written, and separating the saving truth from its cultural context. I look to Jesus, as we may most reasonably know him, for primary guidance. I value Jesus as my savior not merely for his teaching, but because he showed that embracing the love of God is worth whatever it costs.

It is intriguing to me that over the course of the Bible so little attention was given to sexual expression as sin. Though sexual sin is a large concern in church doctrine, it seems to have been of little interest to most of the biblical writers. Where sexual sin is discussed in the Bible, it is almost always heterosexual sin. In reflecting on the overall place of sex in the Bible, it is interesting to me that the most intense biblical writing about sex and sexual attraction, the Song of Songs, treats sexual pleasure as a good thing.

Others have written extensively about the Bible and homosexuality. I particularly recommend the work of L. William Countryman, *Dirt, Greed and Sex*; the work of Daniel Helminiak, *What the Bible Really Says about Homosexuality*; and Chapter 8 of James Nelson's *Embodiment*. I am particularly indebted to Countryman for much of the detailed analysis in this section, and his book is well worth reading for a more complete development of numerous issues. Countryman, Nelson, Virginia Ramey Mollenkott, John Spong, and others have offered extensive responses to those who would use the Bible to denigrate gay, lesbian and bisexual people. [43] For a more fundamentalist but transgender-friendly reading of Scripture, Julie Ann Johnson has edited the writings of Lee Frances Heller and friends that were published in the newsletters edited by Heller between 1989 and 2000. [44]

The scriptural reference most used to oppose transgender expression is Deuteronomy 22:5. It reads as follows in the Revised English Bible (REB).

> No woman may wear an article of man's clothing, nor may a man put on woman's dress; for those who do these things are abominable to the Lord your God. [0]

This is unequivocal. There is no doubt that the biblical author of this passage meant to stop men and women from cross-dressing. Several transgender writers have picked up on the interpretation offered in the *HarperCollins Study Bible* and in the *Harper's Bible Commentary* that the rule against cross-dressing is based on opposition to the followers of Ishtar, who apparently cross-dressed as part of their ritual observances. [46] Danielle Webster has offered an extended argument in this vein with references to conservative biblical commentators. This kind of interpretation makes sense to me, since opposition to surrounding religions is a major part of the Hebrew scripture. [47] It is easy to understand the need of the Hebrews to differentiate themselves. As they began to have more success establishing themselves in the Promised Land, and particularly as they were able to move down from the hills and their lives as herders to establish themselves as crop agriculturalists, they became far more exposed to foreign religion and culture. The world of crops, planting, and harvesting had different gods, a different sense of seasons. God creates the sun and the moon in the first creation story in Genesis, making it clear that the Hebrews understood their God to be superior to the gods of the seasons.

Although it is reasonable to read the rule against cross dressing in Deuteronomy 22:5 as a rule against becoming involved in foreign religion, it seems more compelling to me to face up to the rejection of cross-dressing in Deuteronomy as a freestanding rule. Instead of looking for a special exemption from this rule by referring to differentiation from foreign religions, although that is probably justified, it seems better to me to consider how the kerygma at stake here is related to the many lists of Hebrew rules.

The rule against cross-dressing in Deuteronomy 22:5 is part of a long list of rules. Following are several of the other rules in this particular list:

- If you find a bird's nest, you must let the mother bird go free and take only the young birds.
- When you build a new house, you must build a parapet to avoid the guilt of bloodshed if anyone falls off your roof.
- You shall not plow with an ox and an ass yoked together.
- You shall not wear clothes with two kinds of yarn in them.
- You shall not make twisted tassels of the four corners of your cloak. (I'm doing pretty well with this one.)

There are a lot of rules in the Torah (Genesis to Deuteronomy). Some are good safety rules, like the building code for roofs. Others of the rules could be read as fashion statements of that day and time. All readers bring interpretive principles to the Bible, and one result is that it is common to give more weight to some rules than others. Sadly, most Christians dismiss most of the rules in the Torah as irrelevant expressions of a different culture that carry no saving truth. Fundamentalist interpreters, and those who call themselves biblical literalists, are selectively dismissive as well.

One positive way for Christians to work with the rules in the Torah is to see them as small pictures of Hebrew culture as that culture evolved over two thousand years. For example, the rule of an eye for an eye moderates the escalation of violence that is part of blood feuds. In turn, Jesus takes this concern a step further when he urged his followers to turn the other cheek and to love their enemies.

In the case of Deuteronomy 22:5, we learn that at least one writer thought it was important to write a rule against cross-dressing. One learning from this fact is that there was apparently enough cross-dressing that someone felt a need to make a rule against it. Many of the rules in Hebrew Scripture, especially the rules related to fashion and eating, seem aimed at creating a distinctive cultural appearance and practice so that those standing in the tradition of Moses could be distinguished at a glance. This felt need to distinguish the Hebrew people leads to some of the harshest stories in Hebrew Scripture: genocide, slavery, treachery, rape, divorce of foreign wives and war after war after war. In this context, the rules of appearance don't seem so trivial.

The felt need to be a distinct people becomes visible in the varied circumstances that influence different books of Hebrew Scripture: escape from Egypt, wandering in the wilderness, guerrilla warfare, a time of judges and then kings, of empire and dissolution, of diaspora and periodic regathering. The function of law as it relates to culture is very different when the context is competing tribes, empire, and learning to serve God when your culture is oppressed. The diverse challenges faced by the Hebrew people forced them to repeatedly reconsider the meaning of their laws and how they can best be followed. In such rethinking we get to see another of the major themes of Hebrew Scripture, the quest for what is universal in God's revelation, true in all circumstances. The Hebrew people lived in a creative dialectic, trying to remain distinct while also trying to serve a nonparochial God. Any specific expression of the law in Hebrew Scripture deserves to be evaluated in this dialectic context. The ongoingness of this dialectic as it relates to appearance and gender standards is visible in our day in the contrasts between Orthodox and Reform Jews.

Traditional Jewish interpretation of Deuteronomy 22:5 is that it is a rule against homosexuality rather than transgender expression, probably specific opposition to the cult prostitutes *(kadesh)* mentioned in Deuteronomy 23:18 as a foreign influence on temple worship. [48] There is debate about who the kadesh (or qaddesh) were, but, whatever the original meaning of this passage, it seems reasonable to understand its later importance as part of the strong patriarchal theme in Jewish culture, which separated the lives of men and women and limited women's education and participation in ritual practices. [49]

In the time of Jesus, the Pharisees, Sadducees, and Essenes were taking paths that emphasized cultural distinctness in the midst of the Roman Empire. [50] Jesus, in sharp distinction, challenged the cultural laws of Judaism that had no saving power. Jesus continuously placed himself in opposition to the distractions of the purity laws. One example is found in Luke 11:37-42.

When he had finished speaking, a Pharisee invited him to a meal, and he came in and sat down. The Pharisee noticed with surprise that he had not begun by washing before the meal. But the Lord said to him,

> You Pharisees clean the outside of cup and plate; but inside you are full of greed and wickedness. You fools! Did not he who made the outside make the inside too? But let what is inside be given in charity, and all is clean. Alas for you Pharisees! You pay tithes of mint and rue and every garden herb, but neglect justice and the love of God. It is these you should have practiced, without overlooking the others. [51]

Some may point out that the Luke 11 passage is about eating rather than cross-dressing. True, but the Luke 11 passage is a far stronger rejection of the purity laws in the Torah than would be found in a remark about cross-dressing. The Torah is loaded with rules about eating whereas only Deuteronomy 22:5 refers to cross-dressing. Instead of appearance, Jesus emphasizes intent. Such a radical position contributed to the enmity that hastened his death. Following Jesus, I suggest that the core ethical standard for assessing transgender experience and expression is whether it expresses Christian virtues.

The closest Jesus comes to directly referring to transgender experience is his words about eunuchs. In Deuteronomy 23:1-2, eunuchs were barred from the assembly of Israel. This was probably for the same reason that cripples were barred. Cripples were seen as impure or incomplete. Furthermore, a eunuch could not reproduce and had no place in the traditional families of the day. But Jesus welcomed eunuchs into the community. In Matthew 19:12 we find the following words:

> For while some are incapable of marriage because they were born
> so, or were made so by men, there are others who have renounced
> marriage for the sake of the kingdom of Heaven. Let those accept it
> who can. [52]

This Revised English Bible translation, like other common translations,
suppresses the word *eunuch*, although the underlying text is plain. [53] In the
Scholars Translation of the same passage, however, the underlying text comes
clear.

> After all, there are castrated men who were born that way, and there
> are castrated men who were castrated by others, and there are
> castrated men who castrated themselves because of Heaven's
> imperial rule. If you are able to accept this advice, do so. [54]

Several biblical commentaries play down the castration theme in favor of
an ascetic, nonsurgical affirmation of sexual abstinence. [55] Although we can
never know whether Matthew's third usage of the language of castration was
metaphorical, one early Christian theologian, Origen, took the language literally
and was voluntarily castrated. [56] Another, Tertullian, declared the Kingdom of
Heaven to be open to eunuchs and encouraged many to castrate themselves. [57]
Like Matthew, rabbinic and Roman commentators at about the time of Jesus also
made distinctions between kinds of eunuchs. They included noncastrated
eunuchs, so it might be fair to interpret celibates as voluntary eunuchs. [58]
Although this distinction may matter to some contemporary transsexuals, the
larger point for a transgender reading of Matthew 19:12 is that some men
apparently felt it was important to turn away from some classical masculine
expectations to more perfectly follow Jesus. [59] Whatever the details of
transgender meanings, the basic point for theology today is that Jesus both
recognized eunuchs and welcomed them into the household of faith. Furthermore, he praised some of them for their dedication, which included rejecting
some of the traditional gender expectations of that day. This saying of Jesus
is aligned with the second author of Isaiah, who wrote the following in
Chapter 56:

> The eunuch must not say, "I am naught but a barren tree." These are
> the words of the Lord: The eunuchs who keep my Sabbaths, who
> choose to do my will and hold fast to my covenant, will receive from
> me something better than sons and daughters, a memorial and a
> name in my own house and within my walls; I shall give them
> everlasting renown, an imperishable name. [60]

Most Christians who attack gay, lesbian, bisexual, and transgender people
on New Testament grounds skip right over Jesus and go to Paul. I find Paul a
complex figure who tried to bridge two cultures. For me, the two greatest

contributions of Paul are his inspiring mystical poetry and his missionary activity to make Christianity available to the Gentiles. [61] Paul's missionary work was critical to establishing Christianity as a separate religion. He broke out of the restrictions of other interpreters of Jesus by making it easier for Gentiles to become Christians because he asserted that Gentiles did not need to conform to the details of the Law, as found in the Torah, but rather should conform to the spirit of the Law. This is a prominent theme in many of Paul's letters, and especially in Paul's letter to the Romans. For example, in the second and third chapters of Romans, Paul offers an extended comment on the Jewish law of circumcision. The core of his argument is that if an uncircumcised man keeps the spirit of the Law, he should be counted as circumcised. [62] I find Paul's approach to the Law closely in keeping with the teaching of Jesus as discussed above, in my comments about Luke's understanding of Jesus's position on eating laws and Matthew's understanding of Jesus's position on eunuchs.

Christians who oppose homosexuality on biblical grounds often turn to Romans 1:13–32, since it contains the only extended comment on the subject in the New Testament. Although the issue in Romans is homosexuality rather than transgender expression, the key is a proper Christian understanding of purity standards, and that is important because transgender expression could be viewed as impure because it mixes activities assigned to different genders. It is also important as a practical matter, since many opponents of homosexuality blur the distinctions between homosexuality and transgender activity.

My analysis of Romans 1 is heavily dependent on the work of William Countryman as extended by Daniel Helminiak, and I suggest that readers who wish to argue the fine points of biblical interpretation refer directly to their work, which is far more extensive and well-grounded. [63] Romans 1 needs to be placed in perspective so that the comments on homosexuality will make sense. Paul wrote in anticipation of a trip to Rome, and, as in most of his writing, he directs his energy to the pastoral needs of the emerging Christian community there and to proclaiming the Gospel that can help his readers deepen their faith. Paul wrote to a Roman Christian community that he believed to be contentiously divided between Jews and Gentiles. It is a carefully crafted letter in keeping with the skilled rhetoric found in the Roman Empire. He begins by praising the Christians for the strength of their faith and then writes of his eagerness to come and see them and his desire to proclaim the Gospel.

In verses 18–23 Paul launches into his first sermon by attacking idol worshipers. This beginning point is most strategic, since it would appeal to a common understanding of both Jews and Greeks in the Christian community in Rome. [64] Verses 24–27 take the critique of idol worshipers a step further—using the language of social disreputability to describe the homosexual acts of the idol worshipers. To the extent that Paul is referring to homosexual prostitution as part of the activity of worshiping idols, it is easy to understand his aversion as a Jew to such practice. (In Job 36:4, for example, cult prostitutes were considered the lowest of the low. [65] ) Paul considers homosexuality to be disgusting and asserts that such activity is punishment for idol worship.

In verses 24–27, Paul does not use the language of sin to describe homosexuality, a language he commonly used to describe other activity. [66] For example, in verse 26 the Greek word translated as *degrading passion* is *atimia*. Paul later uses the same word to describe how others evaluate his commitment to Christ. [67] Similarly, in verse 27, the Greek word translated as *shameless act*, *aschemosyne*, is a word also used to describe a father who refuses to release his daughter for marriage. [68] The primary point is that it is idol worship which is sinful and that homosexuality related to such idol worship is socially disreputable. However, Paul probably did not like homosexuality outside the context of idol worship either. It offended his Jewish attachment to purity. Although we don't have a comment from Paul on his feelings about homosexual erotic sharing when that is an expression of love and leads to bonded and responsible family formation, it is certainly easy to see that Paul's overall commitment to keeping the spirit of the Law should lead us to focusing on the virtues of love and responsibility, and other eternals, as our primary guide to understanding Paul's proclamation of the Gospel.

There is more to be gained from this passage in Romans. Paul provides a point of view that is relevant to the previous section on natural theology. Paul uses the Greek term *para physin,* which is commonly translated as *unnatural*. Verse 26 uses the term to describe intercourse between women. It is easy, but mistaken, to conclude that Paul means that homosexual intercourse is wrong because God created sexual intercourse to produce babies and that therefore it is natural only between males and females. Helminiak argues forcefully that the real meaning of *para physin* is *untraditional* and is not language about morality.[69] The term *para physin* was a common phrase of the Roman Stoic philosophers, and it seems likely that Paul was seeking to appeal to Stoics to notice how well their philosophy fit with a Jewish sense of a single invisible Creator rather than with the Greek cults, which were confused by idolatry. Stoics attempted to live ethically according to their ascetic principles. To offer a bridge to the Stoics, Paul emphasizes his agreement with Stoic opposition to living by undisciplined passion, as modeled by the prostitution associated with idol worship.

Paul was not a Stoic. Rather, his religious understanding turns on his experience of the Christ as risen and alive. Paul never knew the incarnate Jesus, and this limit to his perspective shows up here. Paul is cutting his ties to the world of experience in favor of the world of contemplation. Paul's contemplation differs from that of the Stoics because it is grounded not merely in an ascetic philosophy but in mystical vision. He ends his writing to the Romans with the following benediction:

> To the One who is able to keep you firm in your faith, according to
> my gospel and the proclamation of Jesus Christ, based on the

revelation of the divine secret kept silent for long ages but now
made clear by the commands of eternal God to all nations to bring
them to faith and obedience, as recorded in prophetic scriptures—
to the only God of wisdom, made known through Jesus as our Christ,
be glory for endless ages! Amen. [70]

For Paul, what is unnatural is to be apart from God. Thus the best question
about sexual expression to be derived from the first chapter of Romans is
whether such expression connects one with God. Instead of trying to reduce
questions about sex and gender to opinions about God's revelation through
physiological functions, we would do well to follow Paul, who grounded his
understanding in a right relationship to God. I join the Roman Catholic hierarchy and others when they assert that revelation, rather than scientific analysis, is
needed to guide sexual and gender activities. [71] As I pointed out in the section
on natural theology, the basic debate is about whether asceticism, or what kind
of asceticism, is a Christian virtue. Paul contributed to asceticism when he
emphasized desires of the spirit as being in opposition to desires of the body,
but he trumps any tendency to a life-denying asceticism with his mystical
poetry, which encourages Christians to embody the eternal virtues within this
life and with his emphasis on the spirit of the Law for the guidance of everyday
life.

With the above understanding of Paul in mind, it is easy to respond to the
New Testament passage most commonly used to criticize transgender people—
I Corinthians 11:13–15. It reads as follows.

> Judge for yourselves: is it fitting for a woman to pray to God bare-
> headed? Does not nature herself teach you that while long hair
> disgraces a man, it is a woman's glory? For her hair was given as a
> covering. [72]

The context of these verses is a discussion of the proper behavior of men and
women at prayer. Verses 4–8 set up verses 13–15 and read as follows.

> A man who keeps his head covered when he prays or prophesies
> brings shame on his head; but a woman brings shame on her head if
> she prays or prophesies bareheaded; it is as bad as if her head was
> shaved. If a woman does not cover her head she might as well have
> her hair cut off; but if it is a disgrace for her to be cropped and
> shaved, then she should cover her head. A man must not cover his
> head, because man is the image of God, and the mirror of his glory,
> whereas a woman reflects the glory of man. [73]

This confused patriarchal declaration leads to verse 10, which extends the
hair covering issue to "and therefore a woman must have the sign of her authority on her head. "Paul tries to recover his balance in verse 11. He asserts that, in
the Lord's fellowship, woman is as essential to man as man is to woman. (Essential perhaps, but properly subordinate. )

Paul's comment on masculine hair style has something to do with the dominant position of men in Paul's church. The Greek word for *nature* in this instance is *physis*. *Physis* is a common word with several possible meanings. The most relevant is *native disposition* in the sense of what is expected. [74] The physiological reality is that the hair of a male will grow long unless it is cut. It is cut hair that Paul is concerned about so the native disposition meaning is clearly Paul's intent. The context makes it clear that Paul is defending patriarchal culture in this passage. Paul may have liked short hair cuts for men, but even if he had preferred long hair for men he was willing to support the patriarchal oppression of women, just as he was at least willing to tolerate slavery, because his attention was focused not on public policy but on keeping peace in the congregation while waiting for the end of the world. If the purpose of biblical theology is separating out the kerygma from its cultural context, you could hardly have a better test case. Prayer is important because it lets a person draw close to God. The patriarchal misogyny of Jewish culture, including its appearance code, is exactly the kind of cultural purity rule that Jesus opposed and that Paul, at other points, also vigorously opposed.

It is important to place any dissension over the value of Hebrew cultural standards in the larger context of the emergent message of saving truth begun in Hebrew Scripture, clarified in the teaching of Jesus, and celebrated in Paul's greatest visions. The vision statement of Paul that bears most directly on transgender concerns is probably Galatians 3:28:

> There is no such thing as Jew or Greek, slave and freeman, male and female; for you are all one person in Christ Jesus. [75]

Galatians 3:28 makes no sense as scientific observation. It makes perfect liberating sense by pointing out that what is important is love and justice, truth and beauty. The main theme of Galatians is that people are saved not by conforming to legal detail but by the direct experience of grace. Paul tells us to follow what is life-giving, and we are challenged to work out holy truth in our situation as Paul tried to work it out in his. We can best honor Paul and God by focusing on the saving truth Paul pointed to and leaving the rest behind.

The second story of creation, the story of Adam and Eve, deserves attention in this section because it is referenced in several places in Hebrew and Christian Scripture, because it is prominently referenced in two thousand years of Christian history, and because it is heavily referenced in current biblically grounded discussions of gay and lesbian people and has been applied to transgender people. A first-level reading of this passage certainly supports a bipolar understanding of sex and gender. If the story of Adam and Eve were a divinely inspired physiology text, it would weigh against an appreciation of transgender people.

If we read the story of Adam and Eve with a concern for spiritual truths instead of physiological truths, we see that the passage is about the relationship between human beings and God and about how that relationship changes when humans become aware of the difference between good and evil. This is a story about humans engaging eternal truth. We learn that such engagement can be hazardous for spiritual health—can lead us not to trust God but to rely on ourselves. We learn that relying on ourselves can lead to separation from God and that such separation has profound consequences. As many Christian writers have emphasized, this is a story about sin entering the world.

The setting of this story is a second creation myth in Genesis. [76] The story line talks about the creation of people. Adam is created as an undifferentiated human being. The Hebrew word *adamah* means simply ground or dust. Perhaps the author meant that Adam was a man or masculine. It was, after all, written in a patriarchal culture. If this argument is made it must follow that Adam was not adequately made because Adam was lonely, incomplete. The story tells us that to reduce the loneliness of Adam (sexually undifferentiated or incomplete male), God completed the creation of human beings by creating a woman from the *tzela* of Adam. This word is usually translated accurately as meaning *rib*. Another equally accurate translation of *tzela* is *side*. [77] If you read *tzela* as side, then, instead of seeing Eve as made out of merely a small part of Adam, you see the creation of Eve as a differentiation of Adam into two sexes and as creating the possibility of social partnership and an end to loneliness. [78] This story is an affirmation of life possibilities, even in the midst of our mortality and difficult circumstances, made possible by the emergence of human beings who can become partners in engaging the eternal truths God sets before us. Growing awareness can lead us into mistakes and can lead us to separate ourselves from God, but we are still a wonderful creation, and we have access to the understanding of good and evil to help guide us toward better social partnerships.

In all the ways that males, females and intersexual humans become men, women and transgender people, all the similarities and all the differences can be drawn together into partnerships that show forth the best or worst of what God hopes for us, what God has made possible for us. Jesus helps us understand what good choices might look like.

### What Can We Learn from Christian Doctrine?

I was baptized a Presbyterian and first learned about doctrine in the Calvinist tradition. The concept of doctrine is that a single statement can capture some essence of the Christian faith. Christians who are interested in doctrinal theology spend a lot of time considering how their doctrines should be written, how their doctrines fit together, and how they contrast with the doctrines of other denominations. One of the larger problems of doctrinal thinking is that the meanings of words change over time and so do the larger envelopes of meaning within which words and doctrines fit. This means that once a doctrine has been articulated, a great deal of maintenance is required as language and cultural contexts change.

Whether Calvinist, Anglican, Lutheran, fundamentalist, or Roman Catholic, a primary goal of a doctrine is identifying sin. We Christians are against sin. A few million arguments later, we may confess some disagreements about what constitutes sin as a concept, about how we know what sin is, and about a list of particular sins. Other books that are solely devoted to doctrinal theology can assist you in the joys of such reflection. For this book, I merely direct your attention to three areas of consensus across most doctrinal lines that can guide responses to transgender experience and expression.

First, sin is a violation of the law of God, a concept that may be applied to, but not reduced to, social roles and expectations. A Christian understanding of sin makes us aware of the ways in which people's attitudes and practices are not in accord with the eternal values of love and justice.

Second, idolatry is a particularly bad sin, a direct insult to God. The essence of idolatry is to assign ultimate value to something that is less than God. Any time we give our ultimate loyalty to something less than God, that something stands in the way of seeing God, of being in right relationship with God.

Third, Christians believe that the eternal values, such as love, beauty, and justice, can be directly experienced. We experience love with excitement and appreciation, beauty with awe and heightened sensitivity, and justice as conscience—a sense of correctness.

Awareness that God's laws are not equivalent to human laws, not equivalent to social and cultural expectations, creates space for principled reflection about such human constructions. As with all human constructions, we can reflect on gender. In earlier chapters I make use of this reflective space to reconsider the *accuracy* of scientific, clinical, and common concepts about gender as a preparation for considering transgender experience and expression. In this section it is appropriate to reconsider the *desirability* of traditionally constructed roles of man and woman.

As developed in the second chapter, we are physiologically created as male, female, and intersexual animals. Earlier chapters emphasized the concepts of *emergence* and *synthesis* to link together and give proper weight to the contributions of physiological, psychological and social factors. Taking account of similarities and differences in our bodies—both direct implications and metaphorical potentials—human cultures have constructed varying roles of man and woman, and such roles have changed within cultures over time. Different cultures have made more or less room for people to play specific transgender roles of one kind or another. The doctrinal point to be made here is based on the perspective that there is nothing about transgender experience and expression that justifies some kind of special-case doctrine. Transgender behavior can be evaluated by the usual Christian values of love, responsibility, truth and fairness, and the like.

We make idols of gender roles when we become more committed to defending these human constructions than to asking what God wants from each of us. When we refuse to deepen our spiritual reflection below our understanding of ourselves as man or woman, we have turned gender roles into an idol. Unless we can gain a little reflective distance, reconsider how our experience fits and doesn't fit with our understanding of the roles of man and woman, it may be difficult to be open to what God is about in this part of our lives. The good news of transgender experience and expression for straight people is that it may help to open up such reflective distance.

Does it seem radical or impossible to you to suggest that the roles of man and woman should be evaluated in terms of such values as love and justice? Merely asking this question points out that we don't need to spend any more time on debating whether other gender constructions are possible. It changes everything to realize one is assessing current cultural definitions rather than divine natural order.

What is good, true, beautiful, just, or loving in your conception of the roles man or woman? If you're interested in such exercises, you might stop reading for a minute and write a few key words or phrases under the headings *man* and *woman*. Then pause and ask yourself, are there any virtues of men or women that should not be expectations for everyone? If a man is nurturing to a child, really nurturing as you best understand that word, is this bad or sinful? Maybe it feels uncomfortable or uncommon, but would you say it is sinful? If a woman aggressively defends what is right, using behavior considered masculine, is this bad or sinful? Maybe it is uncomfortable or uncommon, but would you say it is sinful? To be doctrinally elemental, I can't think of a single Christian virtue that is not virtuous for everyone.

Even if we agree to pursue Christian virtues as best we understand them, confessing our sins and shortcomings as we fail, there are still multiple questions about how, or with what style, such virtues should be pursued. Some may argue that both men and women may be nurturing but that there are desirable gender differences in the style or content of such nurturing. Those arguing for gender differences in the style or content of nurturing have a tough argument to make. Whatever the situation, the goal is to provide the most effective nurturance possible. Whether nurturance in a particular situation requires strength or tenderness, whether individuals have been well or poorly prepared by their history of gender socialization, those facing the situation are still constrained to do the best they can with what they've got. Furthermore, we are all challenged to grow so that we may be more effective in more situations. Developing self-honesty and fostering sensitivity to the needs of others are the kinds of Christian habits that empower whatever there is of conscience within us. If our gender habits limit such awareness and commitment, our consciences are injured and our actions are less likely to be ethical.

People team up in many ways and for many goals, including seeking better understanding and the enjoyment of working together. Part of such teamwork often includes a division of labor. Some may argue that it is efficient, and therefore desirable, that men and women should divide various tasks along traditional cultural lines. For example, two parents may play some version of good-cop and bad-cop roles in raising children. Both roles would be conceived as having the child's best interest at heart. The roles would merely be different. Beyond arguing about the desirability of this particular example of role differentiation, and beyond arguing about who gets to be the good cop, there is the question of whether dividing any role or task by gender is a good idea. In following out this concern, we can begin by noting that some tasks are more physiologically based than others, breast feeding being a good example.[79] On the other hand, for most physiologically influenced tasks, there is more flexibility and potential for sharing than is commonly noted by writers who emphasize the physiological dimension. Even though it is rare for males to be able to breast-feed, there is no reason males cannot actively participate in feeding infants.

When it comes to evaluating the effectiveness and efficiency of a particular division of labor, a whole host of considerations come to mind. If one thinks it is effective and efficient for the best- prepared person to take on a particular role or task, shouldn't "best-prepared" trump the categories of male, female, or intersexual or of man, woman, or transgender? Perhaps most men would often, in this society, be better at playing the bad cop than most women. But if a mother happens to be a better bad cop than the father, is there any Christian reason she shouldn't do it? If parents need to back each other up on occasion, or if it makes sense to take turns, is there anything sinful about men and women learning multiple skills and developing their created potentials?

This way of thinking is just as relevant for discussing explicitly sexual activity as it is for discussing nurturance. We might, for example, ask whether any particular sexual act was joyous, responsible, and loving. Merely picking up this topic may seem pretty radical for some doctrinally oriented Christians, but I'm hoping it is becoming apparent that the emotional heat about transgender expressions of sexuality has not changed the basic doctrinal conversation. Inadequate and destructive doctrinal thinking cuts off conversation before reflection has even begun. Helpful doctrinal theology aids and encourages reflection about the relevance of Christian virtues to experience and expression.

Turning aside for the moment from the list of "Thou shalt nots" that stops so much Christian doctrinal conversation about sex before it has even begun, let's focus for a moment on what can be good about sharing sexual passion. Passion is good if lets the love of God in. Respecting people's needs and vulnerabilities is good. Giving and taking is good as long as what is given and taken is good. Feeling one's feelings is good, especially if space is made for God-given ecstasy.[80] Conceiving a child is good if the couple is ready to take responsibility for such a child. Not conceiving a child is good if a child is not sought. This line of thinking builds on the understanding that Jesus threw away a long list of culturally oriented Jewish laws by asking about intent.

Transgender sexual sharing, like other sexual sharing, can be all of the good things just listed, or none of them,. If the sharing is good for both partners, if both feel loved and affirmed, if both give and take, if both are responsible, then where is the sin? If transgender awareness increases expressive flexibility, increases appreciation of the partner, increases access to feelings locked away behind rigid cultural stereotypes, then transgender sharing has made love all the more real, all the more present, all the more revealing of the mysterious presence of God in all human loving.

Assuming that Christians should oppose exploitative sexuality in all its forms, is there anything intrinsically exploitive about transgender sexual sharing? The answer is interactional. If a transgender person demands or forces an unwanted sexual interaction, it is just as exploitive as such force or demand in a traditional gender pattern. It is surely true that some potential sexual partners are not willing to engage in transgender sexual sharing. Force or manipulation in such a context would be sinful. But there are couples who are quite pleased with transgender sexual sharing. Perhaps more important, there are couples who are in between, who are working things out. A Christian guide to such working out calls attention to what is really important. Is it loving? Is it respectful? Are the needs and desires of both partners taken into account? Is the communication honest?

As in natural theology and biblical theology, this section shows there is nothing intrinsic to Christian doctrine that opposes the sharing of transgender experience, including sexual sharing. In fact, Christian doctrine should hold that when transgender expression, including transgender sexual expression, is loving, responsible, mutual, and creative, the marks of God's good gifts are present, and we should celebrate such relationships. This understanding is the most important thing that Christians can contribute to our current cultural debate about transgender expression.

Earlier chapters made it clear that there is no scientific basis for pathologizing transgender relationships. This chapter makes it clear that a Christian understanding of nature, a Christian understanding of the Bible, and doctrinal affirmation of all loving and responsible transgender relationships eliminate any Christian grounding for the claim that transgender experience and expression are intrinsically sinful. Since some psychiatric and psychological leaders claim that their assertions of pathology are based, at least in part, on the current normative culture of the United States, which has been influenced by the Judeo-Christian tradition, there is a direct responsibility for the church to help correct the errors done in its name.

I realize that there will be some within the transgender community, as well as some within the bisexual, lesbian, and gay communities, who will find it alarming to start discussions of theological grounding for social standards from an affirmation of the *choice* of loving and responsible transgender expression. Earlier chapters, and an earlier part of this chapter, dealt with the issue of choice as a complex question and concluded that whereas some people have little sense of choice about their gender expressions, others do have choices to make—choices that respond to varying psychological and social costs and

benefits. Christians are expected to use Christian understanding and perspectives to guide their personal and social lives. This leads Christians to ask how
best to confront destructive and oppressive social realities. I believe that it is
both right, and also the best political choice, to focus on holding up the fact that
transgender expression can be loving, responsible, and desirable. There are
special-case arguments that can be made for those who have little choice about
their gender orientation, including their choice of sexual partner, but there will
be no cultural or social room for many of us until we are prepared to affirm the
goodness of our choices, claim ourselves more deeply, offer our love and responsibility to other individuals and society more honestly, and seek the acceptance
of others for our good choices.

The great 20th century challenge to doctrinal thinking came from Paul
Tillich, who championed dialectic thinking. He pointed out that two truths can
be in tension with each other and yet be true at the same time. For example,
any person is both existing and changing (being and becoming) at the same
time. The last section of this chapter, "A New Wineskin to Hold All the Life-
Giving Truth," works from a dialectic perspective, and it is also responsive to the
next section, on liberation theology.

## Liberating Sex and Gender

The Chevalier(e) d'Eon, the most famous transgender person in Western
Civilization who lived in the 18th century, upon becoming a woman in middle
age became a Christian feminist, and tried hard to open up privileged masculine
positions in French culture to the participation of women. She wanted access
to the same kind of interesting life she had known as a man. Unfortunately,
"libertine" France was moving in the opposite direction, and her life ended in
poverty in London. [81] Stories of d'Eon often emphasize his prowess as a spy and
a swordsman. But, both before and after becoming a woman, s/he wrote prolifi-
cally on many subjects. The Chevalier(e) also collected books and had one of
the most complete collections of feminist writing in her day. Although it is easy
to think of feminism as coming to full flower in the 20th century in the United
States, it is interesting to remember that feminism had multiple sources. This
section follows in the tradition of d'Eon and is aimed at providing a helpful
word from a transgender perspective. [82]

The word *liberation* usually carries the meaning of *freedom-from*. In the
Latin American context, liberation theology begins with a concern for freedom
from economic and political oppression. Although not often held up in this way,
Christian theology provides a grounding for science by valuing a liberation from
ignorance and error. In the United States, feminist theology has emphasized
liberation from patriarchy. In the context of Hebrew Scripture, liberation is
commonly linked to the story of Moses and the escape from oppression in
Egypt. The Hebrew prophetic tradition holds up the theme of liberation from
oppressive kings. Jesus points to the liberation theme in a time of diaspora—

the possibility of liberation in place, of liberation before the political world is made right.

Liberation theology also carries some themes of *freedom-for*. In Latin America, part of the liberating vision is about democracy and the transformation of economic structures. In feminist theology, part of the vision is about sister-hood and interpersonal wholeness. In addition, liberation theologies carry transcendent themes such as love and justice. It is transcendent themes that allow people walking one path of liberation to create bridges to people walking others. It is critical to note this, even though some expressions of liberation theology give transcendence relatively little attention. Without a transcendent element, liberation becomes a new parochialism, and one liberation can be played off against another. If liberation is only for me and people like me, what has been liberated has to be defended by walls of one kind or another. If the vision is one of liberation for all, we have to find ways to join hands against all injustice and oppression.

The contrasting of *freedom-from* and *freedom-for* is also an issue for transgender people. It is easy for speakers to cry out for freedom from gender oppression. But too often our speeches have little sense of positive direction other than that everybody should be free to do their own thing. Some transgender leaders have created a "Declaration of Gender Liberty. "[83] The Declaration has gone through several drafts and been distributed at transgender conferences. It asserts rights to identity, to gender expression, to participate in sexual activity, to parenting, and the like. But, in the referenced draft of the Declaration, there is nothing of a transcendent theme, such as "justice for all. " From my point of view, the Declaration is best understood as taking the first step by naming what had previously been unnamed. Fortunately, a larger affirmation of liberation shows up in the comments of some transgender lead-ers and in the guiding documents of such transgender groups as GenderPac.

Vanessa Sheridan calls for a Christian theology of liberation for transgender people. [84] Her book shares her own story and several other moving stories of transgender people. She criticizes institutional churches for hostility toward transgender people and encourages individual transgender people to look past the rejection of pastors and congregations to the liberation stories in the Bible and particularly to Jesus and the uncompromising love of God.

### Liberation and Movement

If doctrinal theology is static in the sense of attempting once-and-for-all statements about right and wrong, liberation theology is active in the sense of seeking to undergird social change. To empower such change, liberation theol-ogy has the double task of freeing people from being locked into the limits of their own traditions and of projecting a believable future in which things can be truly different. I aim here at the liberation tasks of helping transgender people gain freedom from oppression, and of creating space for transgender experience and expression in the larger common culture. Chapter 7 and 8 discuss many of the legal and cultural challenges facing transgender liberation.

In Chapter 8, no claim is made for a specific transgender lifestyle. Instead, the great variety among transgender people is emphasized over the course of this book. This point bears repeating, because the radical Christian right mistakenly attacks a gay "lifestyle" as if there were only one way of being gay. The ugly name-calling attacks of the radical Christian right then misconstrues the lives of those who most meet their stereotypes of a gay lifestyle. [85] In contrast, this chapter names some Christian concerns that are grounded in the saving truth of Jesus and asks freshly, "What is loving, what is responsible?"

As a start toward a liberation theology of transgender experience and expression it is fairly easy to name the freedom-from element. The social roles *man* and *woman*, and the cultural themes *masculine* and *feminine*, are flawed human constructions in need of reform. Since feminist theologians agree with this starting point, it should be easy to build a bridge between a feminist and a transgender perspective. Virginia Ramey Mollenkott offers such a bridge in her book *Omnigender*. She writes, "I wish I could believe that as soon as religious people learn in detail the plight of intersexuals, transsexuals, and other transgender people, they will repent of their oppressive attitudes and open their hearts to transformation. That's really all this book is asking for. "[86]

Sympathy is a start, but I'm hoping for a stronger foundation based on appreciation. Unfortunately, some feminists are neither appreciative nor sympathetic, so there is work to do to create a better-grounded conversation. Transgender people can build their end of the bridge by going deeper into their personal transformation work and realizing that their energy for escaping gender restrictions points to a larger cultural truth and not just to personal needs for an identity change. We transgender people also need to apply to our goal genders the same quality of critique we apply to our assigned genders.

I hope some of the bridge building by feminists will include revisiting their stereotypes about transgender people and reconsidering the complexity of the relationships between sex and gender. I'm aware that gender images projected by some transgender people are painful to many feminists. Perhaps earlier chapters in this book will help feminists appreciate why some transgender people express gender caricatures. Many transgender people who are seen (read) in public have not had much experience in public settings, have not had a lot of time or support for creative reflection. Conversely, many of those most accomplished in transgender expression become invisible. Although I'm aware that some transgender people have caused pain for feminists, I must also testify to the pain some feminists have caused for transgender people. Hopefully we can get beyond reliving our pains and come to a fresh meeting.

*An Enemy Picture*

The most total and unrelenting feminist challenge to transgender people was drawn by Janice Raymond. As the author of the first feminist book to respond to transsexual expression, she had a decidedly negative effect on conversation between feminist, lesbian, and transgender communities. Although I don't see Raymond as a dominant figure in the current feminist intellectual world, I see that she is not alone.

It is a bit unfair to focus on Raymond, because she started writing in 1973 and her book, *The Transsexual Empire: The Making of the She-Male*, was published in 1979. By 1979, transgender people had not been able to claim much public voice other than in a few autobiographies.

Raymond created an "enemy picture" of transsexuals. She noted no positive or neutral aspects and came close to exhausting the English language in her negative comments. On the basis of 15 interviews with transsexuals, Raymond tells us only that most transsexuals had stereotypic understanding of gender and that some practiced prostitution as their source of income. [87] In discussing a news story of Paula Grossman, a transsexual who lost a court case in which she was trying to keep her job as a schoolteacher, we learn only that she looked pretty in a traditional way but had big feet. [88]

For Raymond, transsexualism attempts to "wrest from women the power inherent in female biology" and is attempting to "make biological women obsolete by the creation of man-made she-males." [89] In response to female-to-male transsexuals she writes, "in a transition period during which the biological woman is in the process of being made obsolete by bio-medicine, the aim would be to assimilate (thus eliminate) those women who do not conform to male standards of femininity." [90]

While Raymond is highly critical of those transsexuals who play stereotypic gender roles, she is even more hostile toward transsexuals who claim to be feminists. Such transsexual feminists try to be women, she asserts, but betray themselves by the typical masculine gestures of possessiveness and by typically masculine obtrusiveness. This masculine obtrusiveness occurs when male-to-female transsexuals participate in women's meetings and even dare to take leadership positions. In addition to betraying themselves, transsexuals are also deceptive, because women would never accept them if they knew they were men. She paints a picture of Olivia Records, an all-woman organization that knowingly accepted a transsexual recording engineer, as betraying the women's movement. [91] She compares transsexually constructed lesbian-feminists to the pseudolesbians found in *Playboy* magazine. [92]

At several points Raymond uses the word *rape* to describe transsexuals. For example, "All transsexuals rape women's bodies by reducing the real female form to an artifact, appropriating the body for themselves." Furthermore, they "violate women's sexuality and spirit as well." [93] And again, "The transsexually constructed lesbian-feminist, having castrated himself, turns his whole body and behavior into a phallus that can rape in many ways, all the time. In this sense he performs total rape. . . . "[94] Following up the language of rape, she accuses women who accept transsexuals of being traitors because such acceptance "mutilates" lesbian-feminist reality. [95]

Raymond attacks the decisions made by males to undergo SRS because, she asserts, no real choice is involved. This is because transsexuals can choose only between patriarchally defined alternatives. Furthermore, transsexuals cannot offer informed consent, because they are in the prison of patriarchy. She further attacks the choice of transsexuals by comparing it to addiction to heroin which people seek to ease their pain. [96]

Raymond is as hostile to the medical establishment that provides transsexual services as she is to transsexuals. She asserts that SRS is part of the tradition of unnecessary surgery in the United States, that the experimental aspects of SRS are hidden, and that the doctors probably don't tell the transsexuals of the physical hazards. She further compares SRS to the surgery performed in Nazi death camps against Jews and others. [97] She compares transsexual surgery to lobotomies and clitoridectomies used by some to control unwanted behavior such as masturbation.[98] She denies even elementary humanity to transsexuals when she writes, "Instead of developing genuine integrity, the transsexual becomes a synthetic product."[99] And again, transsexuals are guilty of "reducing the quest for the vital forces of selfhood to the artifacts of hormones and surgical appendages."[100]

Perhaps Raymond's greatest insult comes at the end when she writes, "It is my deepest hope that this book will not be viewed as an unsympathetic treatment of the anguish and existential plight of the transsexual. "[101] The source of her "sympathy" is her appreciation as a woman of the suffering caused by patriarchy, including hatred of the body.[102] Her "sympathy," however, does not lead to tolerance. The cost of tolerance would be the continuation of more medical casualties; and, far more importantly, "sympathetic tolerance will only strengthen a society in which sex roles are the norm. . . ." Tolerance of what is "radically evil" makes it seem good, and that radical evil is the "control of women."[103]

Lack of tolerance is one thing; oppression is another. Raymond writes, "I contend that the problem of transsexualism would best be served by morally mandating it out of existence."[104] Fortunately, she doesn't have murder or imprisonment in mind. Unfortunately, she does have in mind the equivalent of the religious tradition of banning, where deviants were thrust out of the community and abandoned to starvation or suicide. She writes, "Transsexuals are not women. They are *deviant males* and their particular manifestation of gender deviancy needs it own unique context of peer support."[105] The path to transcendence for transsexuals, according to Raymond, is to reject being either a man or a woman.[106] She writes a whole chapter about why women should not accept transsexuals into their midst and repeats her points at the end of her book. Realizing that her strategy of banning transsexuals from the company of women might be thought of as cruel, she writes that transsexuals should simply suffer because even people in severe pain or suffering from deformity have learned to transcend their condition.[107]

As one might guess from these quotes, reading Raymond felt as toxic to me as reading the works of the establishment psychiatrists and psychologists who name us sick and of some theologians who name us sinful. Despite all Raymond's negativity, however, there are a few things to be gained from working with her ideas. But first of all a bit of analysis and response is needed.

Why does Raymond hate transsexuals so much? Is she really afraid that transsexuals will make females obsolete? Her reference for that charge boils down to the written comments of one transsexual named Angela Douglas and one biologist named John Postgate. Was she merely being politically competitive because she was in a feminist group that accepted leadership from a transsexual? The point of greatest distress, as named in her book, came at the point where she was fighting for a lesbian-feminist definition of who women most truly are. "It is a critical time for woman-identified women. The best response women can make to this is to see clearly just what is at stake for us with respect to transsexualism and to assert our own power of naming who we are."[108]

Raymond's construction of "who women really are" is fundamentally mythic. She writes about having a direct intuition of be-ing which is the source of all integrity. She writes about such intuition as a kind of "mystical grace."[109] Her claim, written in secular terms, is essentially the same as a claim of direct revelation from God, written in Christian terms. What is Raymond's intuition? "The real mytho-historical memory may have been that of an original psychosocial integrity where men were not masculine nor women feminine."[110] This revelation leads her to assert that the "real Fall" was not the creation of male and female but patriarchy's creation of masculine and feminine.[111] This claiming of revelation is an attempt by Raymond to assert a deeper grounding for her gender definitions than patriarchy can claim. Her myth is that creation is distinctly male and female and that she has intuited what it is to be female. For Raymond, *female* involves such things as multidimensional creativity, whereas patriarchy has imposed false categories of masculinity and femininity in the interests of oppression. That is, Raymond sees her categories as not mere social constructions but as the expression of the really-real, which she knows as directly intuited mythic truth. Following Mary Daly, she asserts that this is a far better picture than Christian theology, which has an anthropomorphic understanding of God that is hopelessly attached to patriarchy.[112] For a more holistic feminist engagement of the same mythic material, readers may wish to refer to Elaine Pagels' *The Gnostic Gospels*.

By claiming an intrinsic valuable femaleness, Raymond attempts to place her position above feminist deconstruction techniques, which have been used to analyze patriarchy as an oppressive social construction. I'm hopeful that other feminists will work with all gender constructions as social constructions that can be evaluated with reference to the eternal values. Here we need only note that transsexualism is a threat to Raymond's mythic claim because transsexuals assert that males can become women.

We learn a bit more about the mythic threat of transsexuals when we consider Raymond's favored version of feminism: "lesbian-feminism."[113] Lesbian-feminism is "a total perspective on life in a patriarchal society representing a primal commitment to women on all levels of existence and challenging the bulwark of a sexist society—that is heterosexism. "[114] The presumed superiority of lesbian-feminism, as compared to other kinds of feminism, is shown in the quote, "if female spirit, mind, creativity, and sexuality exist anywhere in a powerful way, it is here, among lesbian-feminists."[115] Lesbian-feminists, in Raymond's view, have the advantage of being more free from the intrusions of patriarchy. In the quest for such purity, any taint of males is unacceptable. And, in Raymond's view, male-to-female transsexuals are intruders and female-to-male transsexuals are "lost women. "

Despite her criticism of lingering masculine traits in male-to-female transsexuals, her more basic posture seems to be that "Medicalized transsexualism creates male-to-constructed-females who are more feminine (in action, speech, and self-definition) than most biological women."[116] She inserts the word "constructed" in her formulary to indicate that she doesn't concede that they are real females. Raymond attempts an argument of genetic essentialism by emphasizing that transsexuals are not chromosomal females. She names this particular facet with full awareness that there are other physiological sources of definition: "while transsexuals are in every way masculine or feminine, they are not fundamentally male or female. Maleness and femaleness are governed by certain chromosomes, and the subsequent history of being a chromosomal male or female."[117] To justify her myth of a distinctive femaleness that is not socially constructed, Raymond needs a definition of maleness or femaleness that cannot be modified. The earlier chapters of this book suggest the shortcomings of Raymond's arguments about genetics.

Raymond does not settle for a merely chromosomal argument. She adds a psychological essentialism as well. She claims the argument of John Money that early socialization is what is critical.[118] Although she relies heavily on Money for her clinical view of transsexualism and explains his theory, she fails to respond to Money's main point, that transsexualism is caused by something in socialization during the first 18 months of life. Her mythic needs lead Raymond to write as if gender socialization is always consistent with birth-assigned sexual categories. She simply skips a major theory of transsexualism that she knows about.

Raymond, in addition to saying that chromosomes are basic, and then saying that mind rather than brain is basic, completes the confusion by saying that social factors are basic: "the issue of transsexualism is basically one of social ontology—that is, an issue of what society allows and encourages its constituency to be."[119] The problem is not that she includes factors of physiology, psychology, and social interaction. So do other theorists, and so does this book.

Her problems are that she forgets disciplinary distinctions when she discusses one or another facet of transgender questions and that she is inconsistent in presenting the causal implications of various factors.

### Grounded Criticism

Annie Woodhouse offers a different kind of feminist critique than does Raymond. She is a British psychiatrist who did some participant observation and interview studies with transvestites and their wives who are part of the Beaumont Society, a well-known transgender support group in England. Her book, *Fantastic Women*, was published in 1989. Woodhouse, despite being a psychiatrist, found little explanatory value in psychiatric or psychological theory for explaining transgender activity. Her primary interest, like Raymond's, is in the implications of transgender activity for changing gender standards in favor of a feminist position in gender politics. Woodhouse writes with far greater consistency than Raymond and uses definitions similar to those found in this book. She considers only male-to-female transgender activity.

Woodhouse offers a good deal of individual case study information, which shows a great deal of diversity in the transgender population. Her comments indicate awareness of further diversity. Some of her reports show transvestites struggling with their lives, while other reports show successful and highly functional people. She reports on all five of her interviews with wives. She found the wives to be critical of, or unhappy with, their spouses. (It seemed to me, however, that two of the reports from the wives could have been summarized more positively.) In any case, it is her sympathy for the wives that leads Woodhouse to the conclusion that transvestism should not be thought of as harmless. As a positive recommendation, she calls for support groups for transvestites and for their wives.

I agree with Woodhouse that ethics should consider relationships and not merely individuals. I do not know much about the one group she studied in Great Britain in the 1980's, but the relevance of her discussion is qualified by her lack of awareness that in the United States, transgender support groups and conventions, including an annual specialized convention for spouses, commonly work with the concerns of spouses and significant others. Some common themes are honesty and rebuilding trust, improving communication, giving space and time for growth, improving negotiations over practical issues, and consideration of family and social contexts. Peggy Rudd has published several books aimed at improving relationships between transgender people and their spouses or significant others.[120] For those interested in reading autobiographical stories written by the spouses and other family members of transgender people, I recommend Mary Boehnke's *Trans Forming Families*. Altough there is always room for improvement, my experience has been that organized transgender activity in the United States has been quite responsive to the kind of critique that Woodhouse raises from the point of view of wives.

Woodhouse is critical of Raymond for trying to have it both ways in her book: that gender should be changed and that there is something about gender that cannot be changed.[121] For the most part, Woodhouse argues the social constructionist position and critiques transvestites from that point of view: "Transvestism is a form of fractured behavior which compartmentalizes masculinity and femininity; thus the possession of two wardrobes does not make for a more complete self, any more than it makes for greater sexual equality."[122] Taking this sentence seriously points to the limits of Woodhouse's insight. Her observations are cross-sectional in time and show little awareness of growth and change in individual transvestites. Of course owning two wardrobes isn't of itself healing or transforming. It is what transvestites do with those wardrobes—the reflective inner work and the social engagement, that generates any wholeness.

Woodhouse observed transgender people at early points in their social emergence. The organized transgender community is still mostly in its infancy and was even more a work of beginners in the 1980s. Support groups, like the Beaumont Society, are often focused on the stress and strain of transgender people who are just coming out to themselves, with people who are wrestling with the challenging step of cross-dressing in a protected social setting. Such support groups listen to many tales of who and when to tell, consider strategies for handling rejection and loss, and help beginners learn the props and scripts of cross-gender presentations. More experienced transgender people talk about their challenges in being out in larger social settings, starting with selected bars and restaurants. For myself, I find it harder and harder to get to my local Transgender Education Association monthly meetings because I have so many competing family, church, and professional responsibilities and interests. But I well remember how important it was for me to go the first few times. To her credit, Woodhouse qualifies her critique of the "fractured" reality she saw by noting that some transvestites were holding up standards of integration. I just wish she had shown a bit more awareness of how hard that work is, both individually and collectively.

The most substantial negation of transgender people that Woodhouse presents is the charge that "Whether the situation is a club, a bar or a drag ball the thread running through and linking them together is that of dissembling—people pretending both to themselves and others, that they are something other than what they really are." And again, "Transvestism involves switching roles and identity, not only from masculine to feminine but also from reality to fantasy."[123] And again, "Transvestism does not mean becoming a woman. It does not even mean becoming a woman on a temporary basis. It relies on contrived appearance and a masquerade which bears little relation to most women's experience of daily life."[124] This charge is much like Raymond's assertion of duplicity and is aimed at justifying a social response that rejects the gender identity being offered when transgender people cross-dress.

The charge of dissembling seriously misunderstands the subjectivity of transgender experience. An earlier chapter of transgender people's stories in this book and numerous autobiographies of transgender people do not point to dissembling. The section in Chapter 4 on social construction, my theorization and comments in Chapter 6, and the extended analyses of clinical studies in Chapters 3 and 7 all point away from the charge of dissembling. Certainly some cross-dressing is pretending, or at least claims to be pretending, as modeled by the drag balls Woodhouse mentions. But, from the social constructionist view that Woodhouse affirms, much of the expression she responds to as dissembling can better be seen as exploration, play, and claiming. By play I mean the social growth and development activity that is usually thought of as existing in the realm of childhood. Play, as one approach to exploration, can be a very important source of growth for adults as well. For example, several kinds of psychotherapy can be thought of as very expensive play, of trying out feeling and expressions. For transvestites, many of whom were denied childhood play that allowed exploration of both gender roles, adult gender play may be regarded as an attempt at recovering lost learning. One part of that learning is the adolescent work of developing skill for making an attractive gender presentation.

Woodhouse was allowed "backstage," where many of the transvestites she observed were just *beginning* their social learning, just beginning their socially based self-acceptance, which generates and supports the possibility of a deeper and more coherent personal integration. It is not surprising that much of what she saw was not believable to her when matched against fully developed women.

All of us who work with developing transgender aspects of ourselves start with our socialized attitudes, reinforced by the responses of people like Woodhouse and Raymond, that what we are attempting is impossible and doesn't make sense. Coping with the resulting confusion, anomie, and anonymity is tough. The early steps out into the world, for those who take such steps, can be pretty scary. Such steps are not merely psychologically challenging. There are the social threats of losing jobs, families, and friends and of exclusion from churches and other groups. Beginning from the bipolar concept that man and woman are discrete realities, it is not surprising that self-understanding and self-esteem are huge challenges for many transgender people.

Scary or not, part of transgender growth work is the process of coming out—of telling and showing people the transgender aspects of oneself. Transgender support groups spend a lot of time on the motives, goals, and strategies for coming out. My process of telling family, friends, church and colleagues took several years. It is fair to criticize me as a beginner, as an inexperienced explorer, but it is not fair to criticize me for pretending or deception. I'm not hiding anything from anyone. Furthermore, in those moments when my feminine presentation is accepted and people respond to me as a woman, they are responding to the aspect of myself that is best imaged as a woman, given the constraints of a bipolar understanding of gender. They are seeing that truth in me.

The basic problem with Woodhouse's critique is that she sometimes slips from her social constructionist perspectives as a feminist to an essentialist view that is in keeping with her training as a psychiatrist. Her language of "masquerade" may be appropriate for describing a drag ball, but her own case studies show there is more to transgender expression than such entertainments. The idea that gender is a social construction includes the understanding that everyone's appearance is "contrived" to include gender messages. The shape of her study leads Woodhouse to deny the reality that some male-to-female transgender people complete a cross-gender social construction and live their lives as women with great integrity and believability.

One telling example of Woodhouse's lack of understanding can be seen in her response to a claim by Virginia Prince that transvestites are significantly motivated by the desire to receive the attitudes and behavior accorded to women: "Prince would appear to be unaware of the disadvantages accruing to women in sexist society."[125] It is Woodhouse's mistake, not Prince's. Although it may not make sense to Woodhouse's feminist and psychiatric consciousness, many transgender people act with the subjective awareness that their alternative gender presentations are authentic, that they are expressing an inner truth by using the common cultural symbols for expressing such truth. Such claiming is sufficiently important for numerous male-to-female transgender people that they not only take on the disadvantages of living full-time in women's roles but additionally accept negative sanctions from those who reject their efforts.

Personally, my sense of self is not limited to my sense of self as a man. At the current moment in my delayed development, it seems most accurate to say that my sense of self as a woman is under construction, known fully in moments and partially at other times. I'm thankful for the modeling of transgender brothers and sisters who have spent more time and energy on their transgender growth.

Woodhouse ends her analysis with a relatively mild dismissal of transgender experience and expression as being irrelevant to a feminist agenda, because transgender people often choose to express feminine imagery that is used to oppress women; and as unhelpful because transgender people don't confront the patriarchal power structures on issues such as jobs.[126]

In contrast to Raymond and Woodhouse, Janice Irvine notes that other feminists have opposed rigid gender definitions and argues that "feminism needed to respect the myriad forms of gender struggle that individuals experience in this culture."[127] Alice Echols names feminists who reject transsexuals "cultural feminists" who are arguing for the superiority of women.[128] In the United States, the National Organization of Women, The National Gay and Lesbian Task Force, and other feminist-conscious groups are beginning to forge alliances or working relationships with transgender people through groups such as Gender PAC. It should also be noted that numerous transgender writers have explicitly challenged patriarchal gender concepts; these include Martine Rothblatt, Kate Bornstein, and Leslie Feinberg. This is a very different picture from the one drawn by Woodhouse, who apparently found no feminist consciousness at all among the transgender people she studied.

*Are Transgender Experience and Expression a Challenge to Patriarchy?*

Despite the problematic ways in which Raymond and Woodhouse did their research and developed their ideas, their core concern deserves an answer that is more substantial than showing the limits of its development by these two authors. Does transgender expression support or challenge patriarchy? This is a different question from, "Does transgender expression support feminism?" For those who think the only possible challenge to patriarchy is feminism, it may be easy to miss this distinction. This section considers three issues that are relevant to the question of whether transgender expression supports or opposes patriarchy: the relevance of service providers, the activities of transgender people, and cultural responses to the increasing visibility of transgender reality in the United States.

Both Raymond and Woodhouse give a great deal of weight to the power of clinical definitions for shaping both the self-concepts of transgender people and popular opinions about transgender people. Both criticize the patriarchal distortions of clinical definitions and perspectives. Although transgender people have widely varying relationships with clinicians and other helping professionals, and although the larger society is hardly unified in its perspectives on the validity of psychiatric thought, I nonetheless agree that clinical opinion is an important factor in creating language about transgender phenomena and strongly influences the opinions of transgender people and the larger society.

How harshly should the pioneer clinical figures be judged for their patriarchy? Even though I am very unhappy with the damage done by people working within a clinical perspective, including the damage that flows from patriarchal bias, my unhappiness is tempered by my awareness that in the 1950s, when much of the pioneering clinical work was done, feminism was hardly a well-developed movement. Whatever their patriarchal commitments, it seems fair to recognize that the founding clinicians had the political task of creating enough legal and social space that they could explore and develop their services to people who were in great need of help. The founding clinicians certainly did not experience the patriarchal society of that time as welcoming their innovations.

Writing in the same period as Janice Raymond, Deborah Feinbloom names herself a feminist. Feinbloom was the director of a gender identify clinic that screened and prepared people for SRS. Although her writing is problematic on several grounds, including the nonrecognition of intersexuality, her existence denies Raymond's claim that the "transsexual empire" was totally run by men. More importantly, Feinbloom became more opposed to patriarchy because of her experience and research. She wrote, "I am much more aware of the need for new definitions of masculinity and femininity, free of the stereotypic definitions so long applied.[129]

Feinbloom was able to see the general positive effects of cross-dressing in overall human terms. "What was remarkable that evening was that Phil, who had been a rather unimpressive male, tentative, nervous, and difficult to relate to, appeared as Helen, well-groomed, poised, articulate, and sensitive."[130] When she brings a symbolic interactionist perspective to bear, she is willing to entertain the possibility that transvestite behavior might really be an "expression of the dual gender potential of us all. . . a harbinger of the 'new' and unstereotyped society to come."[131] She links this last comment to her observation that women have already gained great flexibility in appearance expression. Whatever the reality of the 1970s, by the 1990s a host of clinicians show sensitivities feminists would commonly applaud. Such friendly clinical writers include: Vern and Bonnie Bullough, Mildred Brown and Chloe Rounsley, Gianna Israel and Donald Tarver.[132] Feminists may also be interested to know that some of the favorite speakers at transgender conventions are women therapists who model and speak for an appreciation of womanhood that is hardly stereotypical. For a counseling perspective that includes feminist awareness, readers would do well to start with Niela Miller's *Counseling in Genderland*.

One of the reasons that the times are changing for clinicians is that the transgender community is becoming more organized and is beginning to express itself more effectively. The justification for any clinical involvement is help. Slowly, people with transgender experience are beginning to claim more of a say in the consideration of what help looks like. That is, transgender people are more focused on getting help to understand their transgender experience and cope with the challenges that come when they engage in transgender expression instead of trying to fix their gender identities. For example, dealing with transgender issues may be part of an individual's commitment to being a better parent.

Turning to the question of the relevance of transgender expression in itself as a challenge to patriarchy, I begin by noting that as the decades unfold, transgender people in the United States have become more likely to live outside the clinical story lines projected on them. For example, more transgender people are interested in using hormones without choosing surgery. Others are choosing different kinds of cosmetic surgeries without doing hormones or SRS. Hair transplants lead to less dependence on wigs, and electrolysis allows man-to-woman transgender people to use less makeup. These developments create the possibility, which I and others enjoy, of presenting a face and general presentation more in keeping with feminist style standards.

When a transgender person gets all the way out into general social interaction, not just in the protected bars and clubs Woodhouse writes about, man-to-woman transgender people get the double experience of transgender oppression and the oppression of women. Some, like d'Eon or Jan Morris, grow into fighting for women's rights because of an awareness of what they have lost. How likely is it that such awareness will expand?

Transgender people who spend large parts of their lives presenting themselves as men, and occasionally present themselves as women, are largely motivated by the urge to claim what is feminine in themselves, to claim feelings and interests that are not so easily claimed while making a masculine presentation.[133] It is more accurate to describe some cross-dressing as males claiming the feminine aspect of themselves rather than as their claiming the whole role of woman. It is when the feminine presentation is made to the larger society that the whole role of woman must be at least provisionally claimed. Claiming a feminine appearance in open social presentations requires a man-to-woman transgender person to experience being evaluated by audiences that use bipolar gender concepts. This is a lot different than presenting oneself in the safe space of a support group that makes room for transgender exploration. Worrying about passing, and about being harassed for not passing, is common for newly out transgender people. In this light it is not surprising that man-to-woman cross-dressers want all the props they can get to strengthen their feminine presentations.

Rachel Miller is one of several transgender voices arguing for the importance of personal integration and wholeness as the most important transgender goal. "We can create greater balance in our lives by integrating the dual aspects of our nature. . . . Can only women be appreciative, caring, compassionate, considerate, gentle, gracious, sensitive, soft and sympathetic. Rather than defining the differences between men and women, these qualities should simply be considered human."[134] Yvonne Sinclair, writing with regard to the population of British transgender people discussed by Woodhouse, focused on the spousal relations that so troubled Woodhouse. She has advice for improving spousal relationships while including many positive reports from wives. One of her pieces of advice is that man-to-woman transgender people should do more work with the whole experience of women. "Putting on a frock is not being a woman. Most of the time, for the average woman, the routine is pretty boring, and housework is a drudge."[135] This seems like good advice to me, but I'm aware that to share a broader experience of being a woman requires more welcome access into women's spaces and more woman-to-woman interaction.

In my own life, I was committed to a feminist assessment of gender politics before it had begun to be popular. In my first career line I repeatedly expressed a feminist commitment in my research as a sociologist.[136] As a pastor I used inclusive language and sought to empower more up-front leadership of women in the church. Now, as a policy advocate, I sustain a feminist perspective in my work on welfare reform, child care, the Family and Medical Leave Act, and more.[137] My feminist commitments grew at a time in my life when I hardly had enough transgender consciousness to realize I was in a closet. Instead, my growing feminist consciousness was closely related to my commitment to racial equality as an activist in the civil rights movement of the 1960s. Part of that time I was in seminary or working as a pastor in Essex Community Church, which included sharing in community organizing activities with The Woodlawn Organization. For me, it was a time of intellectual reflection as much as direct action, and I was gifted with a wife who was working to claim her independent identity. I supported that in several ways, and I thought about it. The parallel of her struggle to the struggle of those resisting the impacts of racism was clear to me.

An assessment of the level of feminist consciousness claimed by man-to-woman transgender people needs an appropriate study. Anyone attempting such a study should pay attention to the various stages in the development of an individual's transgender career. Deeply closeted transgender people have little to work with other than their own imagination. As they gain social experience, more of the challenges facing women in a patriarchal culture are likely to become of greater concern. Distinctly feminist presentations at transgender conventions and support groups may improve feminist consciousness.[138] Whatever the level of feminist consciousness in man-to-woman transgender people, many of their stories are filled with distress about not meeting patriarchal expectations. Although I lived a fairly standard boy childhood and made my high school varsity teams in baseball and basketball, many of my transgender brothers and sisters tell of the multiple ways they did not fit in. Whatever the level of consciousness, whatever the shape and intensity of intention, all transgender experience and expression challenge patriarchy for the simple reason that they say that the patriarchal understanding of gender reality is not accurate.

Part of the distress between man-to-woman transgender people and feminists concerns the images that transgender people present. For the many transgender people who pass, this is not much of an issue. Some transgender people do not manage very attractive presentations, and some transgender people present themselves in traditional stereotypical images. Some even present images that could fairly be called caricatures. Not surprisingly, some of the least appropriate presentations are most easily remembered. The most common activities in transgender support groups, and popular workshops at transgender conventions, concern image presentation. There is a general emphasis in the groups and conventions on appropriateness and good manners.[139]

Whatever the issues raised by less attractive or less appropriate feminine presentations of transgender people, it seems fair to me to ask feminists about their standards for assessing the great majority of transgender presentations, which are respectful and appropriate and include the many transgender people who pass in their goal genders. Are *feminine* as well as *feminist* virtues to be affirmed? Are *feminine* as well as *feminist* images and styles to be affirmed as presentations that claim and celebrate the contributions traditional women have carried in society? Realizing that there has been pain in the feminist community over this subject, I hope it will help to ask these questions from a slightly different angle. Is it possible to affirm what has been symbolized in this culture as distinctly feminine without having that be understood as giving in to a patriarchal definition of what is feminine? Assuming that for many feminists the answer is at least partly yes, and assuming that a great deal of the mythic reconstruction of "what it means to be a woman" involves including what is feminine, the transgender question becomes "Is such a reconstructed feminine aspect of self good for everyone?" If the answer is yes to that question as well, the transgender question is "How should people who were defined as male at birth, and who nonetheless desire to participate in such goodness, express themselves?"

The response of the general culture to transgender expression is so complex as to require a book for just that purpose. Fortunately, Marjorie Garber's book *Vested Interests* does a good job of analyzing transgender roles in the arts and literature of recent Western civilization, and argues that transgender images have played a critical role in breaking open locked-up gender stereotypes. Phyllis Burke is a wonderful example of a lesbian mother who was trying to figure out how to raise her son in a sexist and patriarchal world and wrote *Gender Shock* as a powerful critique of gender roles, informed by transgender examples. My personal and lightly grounded assessment of what I've seen in popular culture and entertainment is that audiences seem confused, sometimes angry, but *engaged* by the emergence of more visible transgender experience and expression. Apart from any analysis I might offer, watching culture respond to transgender expression makes me feel like a canary sent into the gender mines to find the poisonous gender gas.

When transgender people try out their subjective sense of self in action, society gets a glimpse of the fact that current gender constructions are not automatic, natural, or universal. At a minimum, such transgender expression opens up the conversation about gender beyond discussions of mere reform of the bipolar concepts. Transgender expression that is not dismissed as some kind of disease changes gender conversations more deeply. Whether the contribution of transgender expression to a societal and cultural reconstruction of gender concepts is helpful or not helpful depends in part on what transgender people say and also depends on the readiness to listen and respond of those who are intentional participants in the gender debates.

In addition to consideration of current changes, some feminists may find it interesting to reflect on the intertwined history of feminist and transgender consciousness. As mentioned in Chapter 7, feminist expression was once lumped with transgender expression as a kind of mental illness. Furthermore, historical and literary feminist models often included a transgender element, including a resistance to the feminine dress standards of that day. One might consider such figures as Joan of Arc, d'Eon, or the then well-known fictional "female mariner" of the war of 1812 in the United States.[140] Despite her modeling of traditional femininity, Christine Jorgenson derided the sexism of the press for being more interested in what she slept in than what she believed in.[141]

The hope for a more solidly based bridge for feminist and transgender conversation also depends on a reconsideration of the goals of gender transformation. If the feminist goal is transcendent—to get beyond bipolar thinking about gender—then we can build a solid bridge and have a lot of fun dancing on it. Do feminists want to develop their potential apart from the rest of the world or in engagement with the world? The metaphor of breathing in and breathing out suggests my hoped-for answer. When you go deep into conscious breathing, the sense of what is in and what is out changes.

My concern at this point is not to "balance" feminist theology with masculine concerns. Rather, it is to lift up the idea that the very name *feminist* theology may have unintended consequences for strengthening bipolar thinking. The name lends itself to oppositional rather than transcendent understandings. Feminism is just the right name for the freedom-from aspect of the liberation agenda. It claims the right to a space to stand in on one's own. Claiming space *as women* means differentiating from, and in some cases standing against, men. Claiming space has been about rejecting restrictive definitions of *women* and *feminine* as defined by patriarchy. Claiming space as women supports the political work of claiming interests and power that have been reserved to men.

For some women, claiming feminist space has meant at least a period of time of rejecting what is called feminine. But feminism has also been about claiming a woman-constructed understanding of things feminine. In doing this kind of work, it is handy to have a sense that there are core differences between men and women. Then one can claim a new and free identity as a woman, the way women were really meant to be. When feminist theology takes this remythologizing path it is choosing a bipolar path.

Transgender experience suggests a deconstruction of the concept of gender, not just of the role and identity of woman or man. Such a deconstruction has already been initiated by some feminists. This larger deconstruction makes room for a reconstruction that directs everyone to all the virtues. The dancing on the bridge part comes when we find our rhythms, when we see that our gender constructions are ways we make available true things about ourselves. This is not an argument for androgyny but for all that is true and life-giving within the matrices of sexuality and gender.

Women's liberation has had at least two core tasks. One has been for women to claim some of the virtues, strengths, and resources controlled by men. This has amounted to recognizing and claiming the power women found in themselves, which had been falsely called masculine. "If I'm a woman and I do it, it must be feminine." This kind of claiming is very much like transgender claiming, but with different naming and modes of expression. The second core task has been to create revised versions of what a good woman is. In effect, this second task is the revision of the role concept woman and a revision of what counts as *feminine*. Transgender people who are becoming women, in whole or in part, are seeking to become good women as well, and there is a rich opportunity for conversation—conversation for which many trangender people are most hungry.[142]

Mary Coombs, a Latina feminist and lesbian, summarizes much of the above conversation within the feminist community as a debate between "Liberal Feminists," who are interested in legal changes that minimize the differences between men and women, and "Cultural Feminists," who are more insistent that men and women are different. Then she writes,

> All the schools of feminism, however, have tended to leave sex untheorized. There simply were biological differences between men and women. The focus of analysis and political protest was gender. In this sense, feminism, like traditionalism, historically assumed that sex was a natural phenomenon to which gender had unfortunately been attached. "[143]

Coombs has become interested in the transgender community because of its potential contribution to the consideration of the relationship between physiological status and gender construction. She goes on to make two points with implications for the future of the gender conversation. She embraces some kind of multigenderal future where gender lines are not drawn so clearly, or at least where more alternatives exist. She also argues a legal point. Unless room is made for transgender expression, rules of appearance will be used to oppress women. In this sense she sees the transgender community as fighting a major battle on behalf of feminism.

Coombs makes an additional point based on what she has learned from the transgender community: that people who affirm both genders in their own lives are more of a challenge to traditional gender stereotypes than are assimilating transsexuals. She goes on to envision a society in which gender is multitudinous and delinked from sex.

I'm hopeful that transgender people can have more mutually beneficial conversations with feminists. As a person who values the best things about myself that are called masculine or feminine in this society, it is pretty hard to be treated as suspicious by traditional men and women, by substantial elements of the gay and lesbian community, and by many feminists. There is a temptation to try to create an apparently well-protected transgender community. But I feel stuck in the middle. We may be an embarrassment to a range of agendas, but we exist just the same. My hope is that wrestling with the theological issues at stake will be unifying, even if political agendas leave us at occasional cross-purposes.

*Freedom for Gender Development*

The liberating word from transgender experience is that anyone can claim all that is good that has been carried by men and women in our culture, can claim all the virtues that have been named as masculine or feminine. This claiming of a freedom for development makes possible a transcendent bridge between feminist theology and transgender theology. Suppose we were free of patriarchy, what would we do? Such a question points to rich possibilities for feminist and transgender collaboration. I hope that all schools of feminism will come to affirm the potential to grow as a person who embodies everything good that was once called masculine and everything good that was once called feminine. Then we can ask of every gender choice, "Is it loving, responsible, courageous, generous?"

To claim all the virtues doesn't mean you have to claim a style or culture of androgyny. I will be sad if the hard-won transgender word becomes a call to a new singular conformity. (This seems highly unlikely to me, for reasons discussed earlier.) I like wearing my earrings. I like claiming both my sensitivity and my assertiveness. But men shouldn't feel any pressure to wear earrings in search of some new political correctness. The liberation point is that I shouldn't have to give up my earrings in conformity to an old bipolar political correctness.

I am aware that my transgender journey has happened within a subculture and a particular generation in the United States. People from different subcultures and different generations, people from outside the United States, will walk transgender journeys different from mine. Maybe wearing earrings won't matter much to other transgender people, but getting my ears pierced was a rite of passage for me.

The prefix *trans* has to do with moving between. It is usual to think of transsexual people as moving from one sex and gender to another, then making their life in the new place. As presented in earlier chapters, transgender reality is more complex than that. I'm one of the myriad of transgender people who move back and forth between roles. Like Leslie Feinberg, I resent being defined by appearance alone, and I report that my subjective sense of self doesn't "move around." I'm the same person all the time. I just choose to show and emphasize different aspects of myself in different settings and from time to time. From this point of view, liberation does not mean merely freedom from masculine role conformity or merely freedom to appropriate feminine appearance aspects or feminine subjectivity. Most fundamentally it means the freedom to be me, to express myself as creatively, as responsibly, as lovingly as I wish. This means that I can claim such liberation when I'm sitting around in jeans and my Chicago Bears sweatshirt, drinking beer, and watching the Bears crush the Packers.[144] As a modified physiological male, traditionally socialized to be a man, it takes a lot more consciousness, a lot more work, a lot more courage to claim and express myself by dressing out of my feminine subjectivity and going to a hotel for a Christmas banquet, but the point is the same. Embracing liberation encourages me to embrace my growing edge as part of knowing and showing all that is true about me.

### A New Wineskin to Hold All the Life-Giving Truth

Liberation theology provides space for new truths to emerge by deconstructing established points of view and emphasizing the humility that comes with remembering that our points of view are influenced by our life experiences and circumstances. Dialectic theology tries to hold all truths in tension. Holding truths in tension is the synergistic work of theology, which is comparable to the synergistic summary of the sciences offered in Chapters 2, 3, and 4. Holding truths in tension reveals potentials that are not clear when truths are looked at one at a time. The revealing of potentials, especially the potentials for transformative embodiment of the eternals in human settings, complements the freedom-from aspect of liberation theology.

Done well, dialectic theology has a double relation to science. Dialectic theology seeks to ground itself in the best possible assessment of scientific facts while supporting good science in the correction of scientism. Scientism subverts science to political or religious goals. It shows its face when science is used to create rationalizations to prop up, or to attack, existing cultural standards. It's bad enough when scientific findings are used like proof texts of biblical passages – to prop up political or religious opinions. The most prominent example of such scientism reviewed in this book was *Brain Sex* by Anne Moir and David Jessel. But even Chandler Burr's excellent book, *A Separate Creation*, was critiqued for its commitment to the premise that homosexuality is not a matter of choice, leading to the book's resulting blind spots. Scientism is worse when political or religious motives creep into the reporting of the basic science itself. Several physiological and clinical studies were challenged earlier for such bias.

Well-done dialectic theology, while wanting to be well grounded in science, is clear that its theological work is to engage the presence of the eternals that we can touch but not hold: love, truth, beauty, justice, and more. I assume that others will correct any scientific mistakes I have made and reground my theological work as more becomes known. Although I care about offering a good scientific grounding for this enterprise, I am confident that those who are reaching for the eternals will keep on reaching whatever the darkness of the scientific glass I hold up. I take comfort in Paul's mystical humility.

> At present we see only puzzling reflections in a mirror, but one day we shall see face to face. My knowledge now is partial; then it will be whole, like God's knowledge of me.[145]

Paul's words seem to me to echo the Psalmist who wrote:

> You it was who fashioned my inward parts;
> you knitted me together in my mother's womb.
> I praise you, for you fill me with awe;
> wonderful you are, and wonderful your works.

You know me through and through:
my body was no mystery to you,
when I was formed in secret,
woven in the depths of the earth.[146]

A *passion* for truth is one of the marks of the Holy Spirit welling up into individual and shared lives, a welcoming of consciousness to help form our minds. For those who dare drink from this stream, other questions soon arise: What shall I do with my understanding of the truth? What is beautiful and fulfilling? How will this truth affect the ways I lovingly relate to others? What does this mean for fairness and justice in social institutions? Such questions and answers are larger than the questions and answers of science. We can learn a lot from Scripture and from other stories that bear saving truth, but there is still the embodiment and work of making any guidance live here and now. Dialectic theology rubs liberating truths together in the pursuit of a holistic vision that cares about not only what is true but what is most important: the release and engagement of love.

Paul finishes his mystical poem as follows:

There are three things that last forever: faith, hope and love; and the greatest of these is love.[147]

What is loving, healing, beautiful, responsible, and fun in our gender expressions? Affirming all that is life-giving in masculinity and femininity allows us to respect and explore the best potentials made available to us in creation and encourages us to build bridges so that we can more deeply discover and appreciate each other.

Transgender consciousness reminds us that even if we were to stretch the roles of man and woman so that both affirmed all that is human and good, the work would not be done. Why would we want to divide the world up into two "teams," as if our primary purpose were to play against each other? Rubbing masculine and feminine truths together releases the pungency of shared similarities and differences. When we ask "What is just and life-giving for everyone?" we move beyond a world divided into teams, a world where your win is my loss. I am not holding up an androgynous vision, although androgyny can be creative and life-affirming, but an *engaged* vision, where caring for each other is more important than defending our boundaries.

*Complementarity*

In Protestant and Roman Catholic theological traditions about sexuality, a great deal of attention has been given to the desirability of complementarity. Anne Gilson traces the development of this doctrine of sexuality nicely in *Eros Breaking Free: Interpreting Sexual Theo-Ethics*. Gilson identifies her task by writing, "I will engage in the feminist liberation theo-ethical task of moving from an alienated and despised eros toward an erotic mutuality grounded in justice. . ."[148] I particularly affirm Gilson as a feminist theologian because she claims a freedom-for element of feminism and Christianity.

Gilson quotes Helmut Thielicke as a major proponent of complementarity. Thielicke argues that to be an appropriate partner for sexual sharing, the "neighbor," as in "love your neighbor as yourself," has to meet several conditions: "he belongs to the opposite sex, that his age be in proper relation to mine, that he be my 'type' in physique, character and mind. . . and thus be in a highly specialized complementary relationship to me."[149] It seems very funny to me that Thielicke said that a partner has to be "my type" to be complementary when the point of complementarity is difference. Furthermore, captured by his use of patriarchal language, we see Thielicke naming himself in a gay relationship when he meant to affirm the opposite. He makes a second anticomplementary comment in asserting that "his age must be in proper relation to mine." Were women of the same age too threatening to Thielicke so that he wanted to prop up shaky patriarchy with maturity versus innocence? After laughing about Thielicke's packing so much self-contradiction into a brief quote, we must seriously consider Thielicke's commitment to complementarity. Thielicke wants the comfort of a staked-out territory of superiority and is willing to balance it by allowing the partner her own areas of superiority. Instead of mutuality, we have a vision of territorial truce.

Gilson points out that the principle of complementarity has been used as a basis for attempting to tame eros. Thielicke thinks marriage would be more stable if it were based on a reciprocal need for each other, based on his belief that men and women feel incomplete without the other. To me, it seems more healthy, and more stable, to form passionate relationships that claim all of oneself and affirms all that the other is. Thielicke's doctrine of complementarity leads us to limit ourselves to culturally defined roles and to specialization. That may be fine for some kinds of societal work. But passionate bonding seems to me to intrinsically include the whole self rather than just a role. Fully erotic sexual experience engages the whole body, commands the whole attention. That is its greatest power, its greatest gift, its sacramental potential. The transgender message to "be all that you can be" is well matched to such a potential for full erotic engagement.[150] I do not mean, however, that one has to embrace nontradional gender roles to be all that one can be.

Celia Hahn diverges from Gilson by offering a contemporary Christian feminist argument for complementarity.[151] While acknowledging the limits of bipolar thinking and noting areas of overlap between men and women, she comes down on the side of emphasizing differences. Her announced concern is intrinsically political. She fears that if similarity is emphasized, masculinity will be the normative standard and women will be judged against it. A transgender perspective challenges masculinity as a normative standard without creating the contentiousness that comes from posing femininity as a better or equal standard. Instead, from a transgender perspective one can affirm and express all that is good that is named masculine and feminine.

The core problem with complementarity thinking is that it makes a virtue out of individual incompleteness and substitutes power for love as the fundamental reality of partnership relations. I love it that Gilson, a woman, celebrates the wildness of eros, including its chaotic impact on social conventions. Such a hymn to wildness converges with the Robert Bly wing of the men's mythopoetic movement. But from a Christian perspective, wildness is a provisional virtue. Jesus goes to the wilderness to grow up, but he doesn't stay there. In the midst of experiencing the freedom that arises from knowing that life is a sexually transmitted terminal condition, and in the hope that arises from touching things that are not bounded by our limited lives, we are enabled to choose what is life-giving.

Transgender experience has helped me appreciate the saving truth that each of us can be whole human beings. We can choose each other for the full range of the images of God that shines forth: all that is beautiful, loving, just, and truthful; all that is courageous and nurturing, all that is hungry and searching and growing; all that is affirming, accepting, and engaging; all that is generous and rigorous and committed. By whole I do not mean finished or unchanging. I mean a fully aware, fully caring person who engages life's challenges as growth agenda and as opportunities to express one's gifts and one's love. As a gender statement, wholeness means that a person is engaged with the full range of human subjectivity and is willing to use the full palette of color, the full creativity of substance and shadow, to draw life pictures.

In contrast, the traditional bipolar approach to gender presentations is an appeal to the limiting conformity of two culturally stylized scripts. My affirmation of the fullness of each person, every particular mix of gifts and developmental challenges, is the opposite of forcing everyone into some kind of androgynous sameness. It is important to say this, because the proponents of traditional gender differentiation continue to assert that their opponents want to blur the differences between men and women. In contrast, transgender experience and expression affirm the differences that are blurred by pretending that men are all alike, that women are all alike. To sharpen the point further, some transgender people may be fairly criticized for expressing unrealistic stereotypes of the other gender. I've done some of that myself as I was first breaking out from the world inside my head into interactive experience in my feminine appearance. But, seen at its best, the crossing of gender lines sweeps away the false distinctions of sharply differentiated sexes and genders and makes room for the full potential of each individual. With understanding and affirmation, every human relationship is given room to shine brightly in its distinctness.

An equality based on eros and agape (passionate love and deep friendship) can only mean giving each other everything we have, everything we are. With spiritual awareness, such vulnerability makes room for the ecstatic expression of God's love, made momentarily manifest in ego transcending passionate identity. When there is similarity of strengths between two people, such similarity can be celebrated as an easy bridge to mutuality and understanding. When there is a similarity of weaknesses, such similarity defines a growth agenda for the passionate partners, an area for exploration, an opportunity for bonding by meeting at the points of mutual need. When one partner has a strength or gift the other lacks, the advantages of complementarity are present, as well as the opportunity for one partner to learn from the other. All these alternatives can be explored, lived through, without the socially and culturally imposed burdens of judgment as to what my strengths and weaknesses are supposed to be. Whatever my gifts and needs, the saving truth is that I can always start from where I am and meet people where they are. This understanding trumps the argument of complementarity by affirming sameness *and* difference and by freeing growth agendas from artificially imposed role restrictions.

### Remythologizing Masculinity

I have criticized some feminists in this book for their attempts to remythologize femininity and "what it means to be a woman," as an effort deriving from a politics of separatism. To further explore the distortions of remythologizing, I turn to addressing the remythologizing effort as applied to men by a man, James Nelson. Lest anyone think that I do not value his contributions, I share with you that James Nelson is my favorite theologian with regard to sexual issues. I find his writing to be generally insightful and courageous, but not well-developed with regard to the specific agenda of transgender issues.[152]

Nelson embraces many of the spiritual goals affirmed previously in this section, but instead of affirming anything *named* feminine for men, he offers a remythologized and expanded masculinity for males, which includes softness and vulnerability.[153] He intentionally restricts his remarks to males in a chapter entitled "Embracing Masculinity" because he wants to do for men what feminists did for women.

Nelson's solution calls on males to affirm their metaphoric penis, which is limp, vulnerable, mostly unconscious, hidden, and dark, as a balance to a personality dominated by the metaphoric phallus, which is strong, demands attention, is penetrating and generative, and rises to the light of fulfilment and logos. His proposed plan of transformation is for Christians (and others) to embrace the "Via Negativa" spiritual path, a path of emptying and silence. He asserts that Jesus taught both the "Via Positiva" and the "Via Negativa. "

In developing his proposed remythologizing of masculinity, Nelson repeatedly attacks the concept of androgyny. He notes that he still affirms much about androgyny, as found in his earlier book *Embodiment*, but is now inclined to "move beyond the concept. "[154]

Nelson, after initially affirming the androgynous theology/philosophy of Nicolas Berdiaev in the early 20th century, attacks androgyny in several ways. Nelson's challenge has two primary aspects. First, he sets up the concept of androgyny as a straw man by defining the term as a "combination" of masculine and feminine traits. By combination he means an unintegrated group of traits. Then he attacks androgyny for all the faults of the complementarity approach, even though he also assaults complementarity as "a giant step backward from androgyny."[155] Nelson claims that the core assumption of androgyny is that there are "two distinct and primordial sets of personality characteristics—one 'masculine' and the other 'feminine.'"

In rejoinder to Nelson's approach to androgyny, I would first point out that the several creation myths of androgyny affirm intrinsic unity, not a combination. For example, Genesis 2:21-22 tells the creation story in which Eve is made from one of Adam's ribs. Usually overlooked is the fact that the Hebrew word *tzela* usually translated as *rib* also means *side*.[156] Read this way, men and women are viewed as arising from a common creation that is merely differentiated and not two separate creations. Second, this unity concept was at the heart of Berdiaev's theological androgyny, which Nelson names as the model of Christian theology on this subject. Third, the best known psychological work on androgyny was done by Sandra Bem and those who worked with her research method. As pointed out in Chapter 3, Bem's research does not find everyone to be androgynous and recognizes that different people have different mixes of characteristics labeled masculine, feminine, or common. Finally, although Nelson comments on the shortcomings of Carl Jung's work, he does not mention the Jungian Carol Singer, who specifically worked with androgyny as a fundamental archetype. Singer also emphasizes a unified rather than a combinationist approach.

Nelson's second fundamental critique of androgyny is that asking men to affirm their feminine is to ask them to learn a burdensome second language.[157] Nelson wants men to affirm many of the same virtues I have supported, but only when named as a masculine penis element of personality. For me, Nelson's program seems a convoluted and unattractive response aimed at building a separate men's team for social and cultural interaction because some feminists have called for building a separate woman's team.

Nelson's solution is unattractive to me for four reasons. First, it is a reductionistic understanding of human experience. For example, he speaks of sexual interaction as a phallic experience for men, while I see the phallus/penis as only one element of sexual and erotic experience. I agree with those who think of the brain as the primary erotic organ. Without relevant brain involvement, the "penis" does not become a "phallus." One of his given reasons for this reductionism might be taken as an insult to women: "We men traditionally have identified women with their biology and neglected our own. It is time that we inquire about ourselves."[158] On the other hand, if he is not really interested in reducing women to their biology—and his other writing makes it clear that he is not so interested—it draws attention to his larger confusion of the difference between physiology in itself and a metaphoric response to the phallus/penis.

Second, Nelson drifts in and out of claiming a physiological essentialism by suggesting, but not naming, what is distinctive for males. Anything he names as distinctive he quickly gives away to a feminist critique of patriarchal oppression. His "earthy" and "solar" phallus imagery is a hymn to physicality and to logos (the eternal "word"), and surely that is as available to females as to males.

Third, I have argued that both males and females learn the imagery of masculinity and femininity in our culture, although females are supposed to choose femininity for themselves and males masculinity. For males, *feminine* is not so much a foreign language as a forbidden language. The core growth task for men who wish to affirm softness and vulnerability is to integrate what they have already learned and taken in, the values and imagery that have been named and imaged in our culture as feminine. Whether or not men choose to affirm explicitly feminine symbolism, it is more honest for most men to pay attention to the fact that they are working with material that our society calls feminine. Knowing the name will also help to build a bridge to mutuality, as opposed to divisive team building.

My fourth and most fundamental rejoinder to Nelson, but also our best point of meeting, is to pay attention to the core deconstruction tasks attempted in the earlier chapters of this book.[159] A fair picture of the social, psychological, and biological facts emphasizes overlap, complexity, flexibility, and interactiveness. Bipolar language does not point to the truth of our common humanity. For any specific individual, the story is that just as we are not all alike in our physiology, we have stronger and weaker predispositions and gifts along many continua. Freedom and responsibility come most deeply from claiming all that we are doing, all that we are exploring—all the virtues, whatever our culture names them. Such claiming for men is truer to physiology and more holistic and integrative than can be seen through the mythology of phallus and penis.[160] Instead of following a via negativa with a wrinkled penis as my symbolic guide, I propose a path of naming and claiming the whole self. To men I say, "Claim all that you are whether others like it or not."[161] This is not the same as claiming unearned privilege. Pursue all the positive virtues and affirm the eternals of love, truth, humility, beauty, and justice. Build relationships that affirm all that is true and beautiful in your partner. And I add, for those with the inclination, have fun playing with all the imagery as a fresh path to exploring and experiencing forbidden realities. For me, at least, it has been a wellspring of integration and healing, a channel of grace.

*Honoring Diversity*

There is a lot more to sex and gender than sexual sharing, sexual passion; a lot more to life than creating passionate relationships. To help us look at the wider horizon we can learn from Virginia Mollenkott who names 10 biblical themes that honor and affirm human diversity.[162] A condensed version of her 10 points is the biblical image of God as a single (monotheistic) person or reality that knows everything, loves everyone, is everywhere, and is solely worthy of worship and ultimate commitment. Mollenkott enjoins us to express our deepest freedom by giving it away in love for others as one expression of thankfulness for God's love for us.

The concept of a single loving creator is the core presupposition of Christian natural theology. For transgender people it is a powerful reminder that the same God has created everyone and not only those who fit the traditional images of one culture in one time period. One critical implication for the transgender community is that we do not need to appeal to any versions of sickness theory to justify our existence. We need recognition more than we need sympathy. When transgender people are seen for the good things we have done with the lives God has given us, we will no longer have to argue that transgender expression is beyond our control. From the point of view of well done Christian theology, what we as transgender people offer to others is good in so far as our expression embodies the eternals. Such good expression affirms our common humanity and our particular predispositions, gifts, and callings. Whether one, a few, or all of our interests and gifts are labeled masculine or feminine, we are each called to make the best life we can: loving others, taking responsibility, developing our gifts, following our callings, and spending our lives for what is true, beautiful, and life-affirming. The diversity affirmed by transgender experience and expression has nothing to fear from being grounded in the good gifts of a single creator God. It is only when we limit our understanding of God by distracting ourselves with single-gender attributions of God's reality, calling God exclusively father or mother, that we develop perspectives insensitive to the best that has been carried by men and women in this or any other culture.

### Drinking In All the Life-Giving Truth

The pleading of Jesus that we should love everyone, even our enemies, directs us to clear all the wellsprings of love and affirmation. Our theological grounding gives us a basis for viewing all roles and cultural standards as human creations that need ongoing reform and transformation to bring them more closely into harmony with what is true and beautiful. Although this may be surprising to some, a Judeo-Christian understanding of sin is a significant grounding for the social construction theory that has played such a prominent role in this book and in feminist theory. It reminds us that although we have been given good gifts by God, all that we have done with these gifts should constantly be reviewed to see how the things we have created embody the eternal values we have been shown.

There is more to dialectic theology for transgender people than holding the truths carried by women and the truths carried by men in tension. Paul Tillich reminds us that each of us is at the same time the person we have been formed to *be* and also the person we are *becoming*.[163] As individuals, and as part of relationships and institutions, we need to work at understanding our true *unity* (center) while engaging our *diversity* (extension). Transgender experience and expression are examples of living out truth in tension.

Despite my disagreements with Celia Hahn's feminist version of complementarity thinking, I find myself heading toward a convergence with her when she talks about paradox. She wants to affirm a human unity in the midst of the differences that she thinks are important between men and women.

> The word paradox points to a transcendent resolution that cannot be explained logically. . . . When I give up my simple answers, I consent to fall between the poles of the tension. This consent is a free fall in space where I must trust in God. "[164]

This speaks to my self-understanding that I need more than reason to achieve a transgender resolution to my apparently conflicting desires. Beyond all the science, all the theology, and all the other conversations, I can testify to the peace that comes from feeling directly accepted by God. But Hahn seems to me to use the concept of paradox as an escape hatch that stops the conversation in the midst of ongoing dialectic tensions. Even though I am subjectively comfortable with my transgender sense of self, I still have to keep on working with all the truths carried by men and women, with all the pressures in each decisional moment.

Dialectic theology suggests that every moment in life can be a moment of new beginnings and that every moment has tensions. The goal of dialectic theology is not transformation as a mystical resolution of tensions in some other time, or place, or a resolution after death. Dialectic theology celebrates life, with all its tensions, here and now. Instead of falling between the poles of masculine and feminine, as Hahn's bipolar language frames gender dilemmas, people can move from one place to the other or choose to stand in both places and claim everything that is good. The faith to take a step that is grounded in hope as well as logic is partly the willingness to take the risk of standing where even sensitized and caring people like Hahn may not be affirming, partly the hope that there is some kind of wholeness that makes sense and is healing, and mostly the willingness to claim what is life-giving as seen from wherever you start and to follow wherever authenticity and honesty lead.

A dialectic understanding of sex and gender is not interested in blurring distinctions. Neither is it interested in sharpening distinctions into a false complementarity by denying the reality of overlap, flexibility, and interactiveness. All points in the gender matrix can be starting points where individuals and groups can get on with the work of love and justice. When the role expectations of man and woman and the cultural images of masculine and feminine are considered, Christian dialectic standards are not conformity and adjustment. Neither are they rebellion and resistance. Christian dialectic theology values what is good, loving, responsible, fair.

Instead of merely living out gender roles—even newly reformed and revised gender roles such as Nelson's remythologized masculinity or Raymond's woman-identified woman—a dialectic approach to life asks how one can live well within the physiological, psychological, relational, and institutional contingencies one faces. For example, in working out masculine liberation theology, as my friend Jesse Palidofsky has taught me, one can ask how men can reject patriarchy without giving up the best of masculinity. The good news of transgender experience and expression is that it is possible to affirm the best in masculine and feminist liberation theology and try to embody all of it in one life. To affirm a transgender alternative does not mean one has to oppose or belittle a life choice of gender conformity. One can live well within the best of either masculine or feminine understandings and expectations. The key to good news for people who choose a version of the masculine gender role, or a version of the feminine gender role, is to make such choices with the consciousness that it is one choice among many and to bear respect and caring for people who make other choices. In working through a life career it can be helpful to remember that most lives offer more than one moment of choosing.

We transgender people exist. God's love can flow through us as much as it can flow through anybody else. Part of the good news of the mere fact that we exist is the intrinsic invitation to everyone to play with and explore gender images, ideas, and values. Such an invitation may be scary for some, but, if the invitation feels vital or touches some resonance within you, you can know that you are not crazy, not alone. I'm not trying to recruit anyone to transgender experience or expression. I do hope that more people will freshly and creatively explore their own gender understandings and commitments. A woman doesn't have to get a crew cut or shave her head to explore toughness and risk taking. But if a woman wants to explore what it feels like to walk down the street with a crew cut or a shaved head, that can be informative, a growth experience.

For those who have claimed transgender exploration as a right path in their life's journey, a dialectic understanding encourages an embracing of, a living with, every eternal value and holding in tension all the concepts and images that arise in your spirit for embodying such values. You can push against your old bad habits, let go of old pains, and exit from dysfunctional relationships without turning away from all your personal history. If a transgender subculture ever becomes strongly developed in the United States, people can explore it without making it a new numbing conformity. If you keep asking yourself what is honest, what is life-giving, what is loving, what is responsible, you can know you are walking a path that was pointed to by Jesus at great cost. On such a path there are Christian brothers and sisters who can support you and hold you accountable despite the rejection of many Christian churches.

Apart from claiming all the truths in one's own gender journey, transgender consciousness can help one affirm everything that is good, true, and beautiful in others. Transgender seeing is just as valuable as transgender claiming. This may be the intrinsic reason why several cultures have drawn transgender people into shaman (healing) roles. The saving truth presented and lived out by Jesus helps us know our names, help us find a purpose and a home instead of wandering in confusion, and helps us move from alienation to affirmation. To the extent that old gender boxes keep us from knowing who we truly are (knowing our names), keep us from finding our gifts and callings and comrades to create a meaningful life (finding a home), or leave us alienated from ourselves and each other, then those old gender boxes are barriers to the free flowing of God's love and acceptance, barriers to embodying the eternals that make life more than existence, and barriers to creating social relationships that are channels of grace, joy, and meaningful work. Transgender consciousness can help to heal us from our gender hurts. The good news of the breaking in of the love of God is that nothing else has to be accomplished before you can start loving and caring and risking and healing.

## Notes

1. Phyllis Burke (1996), Chandler Burr (1996), Anne Fausto-Sterling (2000).
2. I present an extended discussion of psychological strategies used by people who have transgender experience in Chapter 6.
3. Garry Wills (2000). See particularly his comment on page 9, which points out Thomas Aquinas's condemnation of willful ignorance.
4. Wesley Granberg-Michaelson (1999). This article holds up the value of peace in the church and the declaration of a cease-fire after 25 years of discussion of homosexuality in The Reformed Church in America (RCA), rather than taking on the pain of confessing homophobia and seeking reconciliation. At least the RCA is still debating the issue and seeking spiritual guidance.
5. Gil Alexander-Moegerle (1998). The confession quoted is part of a larger and thoughtful confession, including an apology to other Christians.
6. Vanessa S. (1996), Kathryn Helms (1997), Karen Kroll (1997), Frances Cormier (1995), Dana Cole and Dianna (1992). Vanessa Sheridan has recently updated and expanded her offering in *Crossing Over* (2001).
7. Chris Paige (2001). Paige writes, "I appear to live on the cusp of indecision. But only because we are all taught to demand a decision." page 34.
8. David Horton (1994), page 23.
9. John Talamini (1982), page 57.
10. Bob Dylan, "With God on Our Side" (song), (1964).
11. Vern and Bonnie Bullough (1977), page 78.
12. Ibid.
13. Ibid., page 77.
14. Ibid., page 78.
15. Kathryn M. Ringrose (1996), pages 100–108. Ringrose points our in some detail that eunuchs rose to high position in the Byzantine church in the 12th century and that Theophylaktos, Archbishop of Ohrid, wrote an extended tract, *Defense of Eunuchs*. The theological turning point of this defense is that the church had held up the value of celibacy as key to spiritual growth and that therefore it was no

longer necessary to have procreative capacity to achieve the church's version of the masculine ideal.

16. "TS Minister's Ordination Upheld," 1996.

17. United Church of Christ Revised By–Laws (1998).

18. Two transgender authors addressed their feeling of rejection by Christian churches and denominations in *Transgender Tapestry* 95, Fall 2001. Vanessa Sheridan wrote the following in "Transgender Spirituality and Activism," page 54: "the spiritual lives and concerns of the transgendered have traditionally been relegated to the back burner or, even worse, to the trash heap by most mainstream religious denominations. " Sara Herwig wrote the following in "The More Light Presbyterian Annual Conference," page 56: "And for each of us that has left her or his faith community because we know our transgenderness or our transsexuality would not be accepted or tolerated, there are many others who see the established Christian churches and denominations as enemies and want nothing to do with such closed minded hateful people. "

19. Another way of saying this is that when analytic scientists reason from parts to a whole, they reason in terms of the manifest aspects of the parts which are amenable to observation and disregard the potentials of the parts which are not accessible to observation.

20. Appreciating the eternals is at the heart of worship. Using the eternals as guides is at the heart of ethics.

21. Teleology is the study of intrinsic design as a form of causation, a causal concept brought into Western thought by Aristotle. One popular version of such teleological thinking is a belief in the inevitability of progress; another is the fatalistic belief that people cannot change their destinies.

22. Christine E. Gudorf (1994), page 82.

23. See Daniel and other prophetic writings in Hebrew scripture, the end of Matthew, Paul's epistles, and the book of Revelation.

24. Cardinal Ratzinger (1968), quoted in Douglas Haldeman (1996).

25. Garry Wills (2000), Chapters 5 and 6.

26. Christine E. Gudorf (1994), Chapter 2.

27. I am not arguing that one needs to be married to engage in loving and responsible sexual sharing. Instead, I am arguing that if you believe that marriage encourages, or is necessary for, loving and responsible sexual sharing, it is reasonable to allow, even encourage, everyone who desires such a relationship to marry.

28. Because of my strong ecumenical commitments I have been uncomfortable in focusing so much of my criticism on the sexual positions of the Roman Catholic hierarchy. I have been delighted to work alongside representatives of the hierarchy and with representatives of Roman Catholic organizations in advocating for numerous issues of social and economic justice. I fully realize that many of the faults I identify with the Roman Catholic hierarchy are shared by many other Christians. One of the reasons I have focused on the Roman Catholic hierarchy is that they have made their official positions so clear and direct in their official *Catechism of the Catholic Church* (1994). In sections 2331, 2333, 2334, and 2335 on pages 619-620 they clearly state an unqualified commitment to a bipolar understanding of sex and gender and support for complementarity as a guide to marital relations. The language of the *Catechism* concerning homosexuality (section 2357, page 625) closely parallels the language of Cardinal Ratzinger discussed in the text. The

condemnation is clear:"Basing itself on Sacred Scripture, which presents homosexual acts as acts of grave depravity, tradition has always declared that homosexual acts are intrinsically disordered. They are contrary to the natural law. They close the sexual act to the gift of life. They do not proceed from a genuine affective and sexual complementarity. Under no circumstances can they be approved. "

29. Mark F. Schwartz (1983).

30. Benedict Ashley (1983), page 25.

31. Albert Moraczewski (1983), page xiii.

32. Richard M. Doerflinger (1999). Doerflinger's essay on the rights of the human embryo shows excellent awareness of the relevant physiological and legal issues in stem cell research and makes many ethical points I agree with. Nonetheless, it is an essay that defends the perspective that an embryo at the point of conception has as much right to recognition and protection as do people who are suffering from Parkinson's and other diseases and who might benefit from research on embryonic stem cells. The essay therefore opposes any embryonic stem cell research.

33. Timothy and Joseph Costello (1992), page 260.

34. James B. Ashbrook and Carol Rausch Albright (1997). Ashbrook and Albright present a well-developed presentation of the Brain and its functions. They use scientific descriptions of brain activity—left-brain versus right-brain processes, for example—to suggest that different people use their brains differently and have different images of God as a result. The authors develop a perspective that emphasizes the themes of complexity, interactivity, and flexibility. They also emphasize the theme of emergence, partly by pointing out the evolution of brain capacities and the distinctiveness of human cognition. Although the authors are clear that the emergence of mind is critical to a natural theology that points to God, it is not so clear to me that they appreciate the whole-self knowing of eternals. It is when the brain integrates an awareness of the eternals with perceptual inputs from the senses that a mind is created. Said alternatively, mind is created from the potentials released by the integration of physiological brain functions.

35. I do not mean to suggest that psychological or social causes are unnatural. I am responding to the use of the word *natural* to mean physically or physiologically caused without human mediation. I have noted several times that I regard psychological and social causes as grounded in the release of hidden potentials in the objects studied in the physical and physiological sciences. I have also noted that the social constructions of human beings can be evaluated against the eternals, which, though often spoken of as spiritual, are also part of God's creation and therefore natural as well.

36. In this context, sin is a failure to properly incorporate the eternals into personal expressions and social constructions.

37. Cf. Kathryn M. Ringrose (1998), pages 100–108.

38. Oliver O'Donovan (1982).

39. I am not trying to make parents feel guilty. I believe that most parents who choose SRS for their intersexual children have concern for their children as an important motive. I am urging parents and surgeons to reevaluate their positions. I am also urging parents who do not want SRS for their infants to defy any pressure from surgeons to have the surgery.

40. Cheryl Chase, leader of the Intersexual Society of America, is a leading proponent of this view.

41. Anne Fausto-Sterling (1995), quoted in Phyllis Burke (1996), pages 220–221.

42. If there is no physiological problem in a case of infant intersexuality, there is a good reason to wait for any individually chosen SRS until puberty, or close to puberty, when the genitals are more developed and easier to work with surgically.

43. Virginia Mollenkott's *Sensuous Spirituality: Out From Fundamentalism* and John Spong's *Living in Sin: A Bishop Rethinks Human Sexuality* were important contributions.

44. Julie Ann Johnson (2000).

0.428. M. Jack Suggs et al. (editors). *The Oxford Study Bible: Revised English Bible With the Apocrypha.* Hereafter in this book this version of the Bible will be cited as REB.

46. *Open Hands* (1996), page 21.

47. Danielle Webster (2000), pages 30–36.

48. Louis Epstein (1948/1968), pages 64–66.

49. Ibid., Chapters II, III.

50. The Pharisees were a group of Jews who emphasized the keeping of the law, including the ritual law. They worshiped together in synagogues, the forerunners in style of early Christian congregations. Although they valued the Temple, their focus on synagogues allowed them to thrive while dispersed, and they became the primary link to Judaism as it has grown over the last 2,000 years. The Sadducees were a group primarily focused on ritual practice in the temple. The Essenes were an ascetic and apocalyptic group that withdrew to live in desert communities, with as much purity as they could create, while waiting for the Messiah to come. The Dead Sea Scrolls were used by an Essene community.

51. REB.

52. REB.

53. My computerized Bible found 49 biblical references to eunuchs without counting the several descriptive phrases for *eunuch* that do not use the specific Hebrew or Greek words. The King James Bible uses the word *eunuch* 7 times, and modern translations use the word about a dozen times.

54. Robert Funk and Roy Hoover (1993), page 220. The Scholars Translation is the work of the Jesus Seminar, which jointly created a new Greek translation of the New Testament, then translated their Greek translation into English. The Scholars Translation is found in *The Five Gospels*, edited by Robert Funk and Roy Hoover (1993).

55. Paul J. Achtemeier (1996), pages 313–314; Geoffrey W. Bromley (1982), pages 200–202; George A. Buttrick (1951); The Holman Bible Dictionary for Windows (1995), based on the Holman Bible Dictionary (1991); The Interpreter's Dictionary of the Bible (1962), pages 179–180.

56. *Oxford Paperback Encyclopedia* (1998). Also see Kathryn M. Ringrose, page 100.

57. Alev L. Croutier (1989), page 128.

58. http://gendertree.com/eunuch (2001). The anonymous author of this posting quotes Ulpian, a Roman jurist, who allowed the marriage of a eunuch to a woman because the eunuch was capable of penetration. For an extended discussion of kinds of eunuchs and the numerous roles of eunuchs, see Kathryn M. Ringrose's "Living in the Shadows: Eunuchs and Gender in Byzantium."

59. Kathryn M. Ringrose (1996), pages 100–108. Ringrose provides a historical analysis of how Byzantine Christians in the 12th century built on Matthew 19:12 to argue

that becoming a castrated eunuch could be an exemplification of a Christian affirmation of manliness.

60. Isaiah:56:3b-5 (REB).

61. My favorite examples of Paul's mystical poetry are found in I Corinthians:12-13. Paul's extolling of the eternals—unity, truth, faith, hope, and love—are just the right guidelines to apply to all gender images and activities, including transgender experience and expression.

62. See particularly Romans 2:26.

63. L. William Countryman (1988), Daniel Helminiak (2000).

64. Although many Greeks and Romans did believe in idol worship, Stoics and others did not. Since he was writing to Gentile Christians as part of the Roman community, it is reasonable to assume he was writing to Gentiles who were not idolaters.

65. If, as seems likely to me, Deuteronomy 22:5 indicates a similar concern about using prostitutes to worship idols, there is a very similar concern at stake in Romans 1:24-27.

66. For example, in Romans 1:18-19 he uses the word *adikia,* translated as *wickedness,* to describe the activity of people who suppress truth. In verses 28-32 Paul returns to the language of sin to condemn a list of nonsexual activities. See Daniel Helminiak (2000), page 93.

67. II Corinthians 6:8, 11:21. Daniel Helminiak describes the word *atimia* as meaning *socially unacceptable.* See Daniel Helminiak (2000), page 90. In I Corinthians Paul uses *atimia* to describe a man wearing long hair.

68. I Corinthians 7:36. See Daniel Helminiak (2000), page 91.

69. Daniel Helminiak (2000), pages 86-87.

70. Romans 16:25-27. I offer these words as a transliteration of the verses in the Revised English Bible in an attempt to make the mystical power of Paul's words more accessible to readers not used to biblical phrasing.

71. For example, see the section on natural theology in this chapter for comments by Benedict Ashley and Albert Moraczewski. I should also repeat that my understanding of revelation is not magical or supernatural. For me, revelation is about becoming sensitized to the reality of the eternals we participate in but do not grasp, that we know from the inside out. The Bible is Scripture for me because it helps me become attuned to the eternals, and the active presence of God's spirit, by showing how people in the Hebrew and Christian lineage grew in their awareness. I show my Christian faith and commitment, in part, by holding up my transgender experience and expression to the light of the radical demands of the Gospel—to love my neighbor and myself. Faith is not so much believing in, but seeing and living within (embodying), the eternals - God's best gifts.

72. REB.

73. REB.

74. Daniel Helminiak (2000), pages 78-79.

75. REB. Paul echoes this theme in the 2nd chapter of Ephesians when he writes of reconciling Gentiles and Jews into one body. Such use of body imagery to express the theme of overcoming alienation has particular appeal for me as I work with my body imagery as an expression of overcoming alienation from those aspects of myself that I was taught to deny.

76. Genesis 2:4-3:24.

77. Arthur O. Waskow (1996), page 76.

78. Seen this way, the author of Genesis could be said to have a prescientific understanding of emergence and possibility that fits with a synthetic understanding of the sciences.

79. It is now possible for males to transform their bodies with hormones and provide human milk to babies.

80. I don't mean God-given as a special act, but the gift of God, made available to those who explore and give themselves to this possibility of ecstatic momentary bonding of whole selves, that is one of the possibilities that emerges with full human consciousness.

81. Gary Kates (1995), pages 255–257.

82. I'm aware that one of my limitations for doing liberation theology work is that I have not considered womanist perspectives.

83. The Declaration referred to here is one of several such efforts by transgender leaders. This one was affirmed and celebrated on July 4, 1996, at the 5th gathering of the International Conference on Transgender Law and Employment Policy in Houston, Texas. Sharon Stewart was the major author.

84. Vanessa Sheridan (2001).

85. Lou Chibarro Jr. wrote a story in *The Washington Blade* on Thursday, September 13, 2001, that tops anything else I've read from the radical Christian right. It was about remarks made by Jerry Falwell on Pat Robertson's 700 Club on television on September 12. He writes, "The Rev. Jerry Falwell said gays, feminists, 'pagans' and a host of liberal advocacy groups made 'God mad' and must bear some of the responsibility for the thousands of Americans killed in the bombing of the World Trade Center and the Pentagon. Quoting Falwell directly: "I really believe that the pagans, and the abortionists, and the feminists, and the gays and lesbians who are actively trying to make that an alternative lifestyle, the ACLU and People For the American Way—all of them who have tried to secularize America— point the finger in their face and say, 'You helped this happen.' "

86. Virginia Ramey Mollenkott (2001), page 82.

87. Janice Raymond (1979), page 79.

88. Ibid.

89. Ibid., pages xvi and xvii.

90. Ibid., page xxiii.

91. Ibid., pages 100–104.

92. Ibid., page 119.

93. Ibid., page 104.

94. Ibid., page 112.

95. Ibid., page 119.

96. Ibid., pages 127–135.

97. Ibid., pages 138–152.

98. Ibid., page 131.

99. Ibid., page 165.

100. Ibid., page 155.

101. Ibid., page 175.

102. Ibid., pages 175–176.

103. Ibid., page 176.

104. Ibid., page 178.

105. Ibid., page 183.

106. Ibid., pages 174-175.

107. Ibid., page 168.

108. Ibid., page 177.

109. Ibid., page 174.

110. Ibid., page 164.

111. Ibid., page 164.

112. Ibid., page 173.

113. Ibid., page 100.

114. Ibid., page 101.

115. Ibid., page 108.

116. Ibid., page xvii.

117. Ibid., page 4.

118. Ibid., pages 6-8.

119. Ibid., page 16.

120. Peggy Rudd. See References for a list of titles and access information.

121. Annie Woodhouse (1989), page 80.

122. Ibid., page xv.

123. Ibid., pages 25, 138.

124. Ibid., page 144.

125. Ibid., page 74.

126. Ibid., pages 143-145.

127. Janice M. Irvine (1990), page 270.

128. Alice Echols (1984). Quoted in Janice M. Irvine (1990), page 269.

129. Deborah Feinbloom (1976, acknowledgments dated 1974), page 56.

130. Ibid., page 189.

131. Ibid., page 249.

132. Vern and Bonnie Bullough (1993, 1997), Mildred Brown and Chloe Ann Rounsley (1996), and Gianna Israel and Donald Tarver (1997).

133. See earlier relevant references in Chapters 4 and 6, and particularly the survey work of Richard Docter.

134. Rachel Miller (1996), pages 62-63.

135. Yvonne Sinclair (1984), pages 21-26, 35.

136. Patrick Conover (1975).

137. The Family and Medical Leave Act is a federal law that provides the right to workers to take unpaid leave from their jobs when they are sick, when they are caring for someone in their immediate family who is sick, or upon the birth or adoption of a child.

138. Miqqi Gilbert offered such a workshop at the 2001 convention of the International Foundation for Gender Education in Arlington Heights, IL.

139. I have no personal experience with the entertainment scene of drag kings and queens, but I suggest that the resulting presentations should be evaluated in entertainment terms rather than in terms of general social interaction. I also have no experience with sadomasochist groups, which often include transgender themes, but I suggest that these groups also deserve an independent analysis and response. The vast majority of transgender people are neither entertainers nor sadomasochists.

140. Daniel Cohen (1997).

141. From *Christine Jorgenson* (1967), noted by Pat Califia (1997), page 25.

142. What is *good* in the concept of a *good woman* calls for contemplation of the eternal value of goodness, an intrinsically theological task. I make this comment here to point to Christian theology as a better grounding for such work than remythologizing presented as new revelation. I do not mean that Christianity has the only access to such wisdom, and I do not mean that there is no room for innovation and creativity. I do mean that Christianity has a lot to contribute at this point. I also hope this book contributes to additional grounding for Christian reflection on this issue. I care equally about what is *good* in a *good man*.

143. Mary Coombs (1996), page 5. I find this point of view to be very close to my own concepts, which I develop in Chapter 6 and describe as grounded social construction theory.

144. At least I can fantasize that the Bears crush the Packers.

145. I Corinthians 13:12 as found in the REB.

146. Psalm 139:13-15 as found in the REB.

147. I Corinthians 13:13 as found in the REB.

148. Anne Gilson (1995), page 3.

149. Ibid., page 23.

150. Please pardon my playing with a U. S. Army advertising slogan. It has just constantly made me laugh when I hold it up to a transgender mirror, and I hope you can share the laugh with me.

151. Celia Hahn (1991).

152. After writing my comments on Nelson, I read that he has conceded in a Foreword to Vanessa Sheridan's book *Crossing Over* (2001) that his writing about transgender issues needs reconsideration.

153. James Nelson (1994), pages 195-215.

154. Ibid., page 214.

155. Ibid., page 203.

156. Arthur Waskow (1996), page 76.

157. James Nelson (1994), page 204.

158. Ibid., page 197.

159. In the foreword to Vanessa Sheridan's book *Crossing Over (2001)*, James Nelson mentions that his thinking about sex and gender have continued to evolve: "In recent years I have come to appreciate how important social construction is not only to our genders but also to our sex itself, our maleness and femaleness" (page vii). I would say that social construction theory is important to our understanding of sex but that there are physiological factors that influence our constructions, an idea I have discussed in chapters 2, 3, 4, and 6.

160. One consideration that makes this point clear is that men who have penises with little or no capacity to be phalluses can still participate in satisfying and loving sexual relationships.

161. Claiming all that you are is an affirmation of your very being as a gift from God. As a guide to the meditative and interactional work of such claiming, this book suggests breaking free of the limits of traditional roles and concepts, even if you invest such freedom in new commitments to a deepened understanding of traditional gender concepts. This chapter also emphasizes the good news of Jesus as a guide.

162. Virginia Mollenkott (1992), page 61.

163. Paul Tillich develops his dialectic thinking most completely in Volumes 1, 2, and 3 of *Systematic Theology,* (1951), (1957), and (1963). I particularly recommend his sections on self-actualization, self-integration, self-creativity, and self-transcendence in Volume 3, pages 30-110.
164. Celia Hahn (1991), page 9.

*The Christian ideal has not been tried and found wanting;*
*it has been found difficult and left untried.* [1] G. K. Chesterton

# Appendix: Pastoral Advice for Individuals and Congregations

This appendix contains only an outline of pastoral advice. Fully developed, this appendix could become a book in itself. It seems to me that far more experience of transgender individuals in interaction with their congregations is needed before such a book could be well written. Here is a start.

## Pastoral Advice for Individuals

This section is derived from a sermon I preached for Seekers Church, December 8, 1996. The sermon was not focused on transgender issues, but it was prepared with transgender concerns in mind. The theme was moving from fear to hope.

I began the sermon by noting that the first creation story in Genesis includes the creation of a sea monster, as found in verse 21. Even the scariest of creatures have a place in God's design. Even the chaos of ocean depths and sea monsters comes from God. A lot of things are genuinely scary, but, if you face such things, you are not alone. As an example of boldness in the face of real fear, I discussed the example of Nathan the prophet challenging David the king, as found in II Samuel 7:1-6. I also discussed the similar boldness of the *Magnificat*, the recounting of the prophetic expectation of the coming of Jesus, as found in Luke 1:23-45. It was such boldness and hope that led the authorities to kill Jesus, because such hope is dangerous. This pastoral advice is about moving from fear to hope. It is not the same as advice for an easy passage.

First of all, *know your fears*. What would be hardest to lose? If we cover up our fears with security props, whether practical or psychological, we will not deepen beneath our fears, and we are likely to defend our props and avoid a lot of life.

Second, *we can't defeat our fears with a game plan* that makes us feel as if we are in charge of our destinies. Relying on plans and strategies can mean not trusting that God will be available when needed.

Third, anyone who wants to follow Jesus has to *embrace risks and conflicts* as a normal part of life. If you follow Jesus by embracing what is life-giving, particularly when that includes challenging gender expectations, you will be embracing risk. (You get a different mix of risks and conflicts if you don't want to follow Jesus. ) Embracing risks and conflicts includes giving up the romantic notion that heroism will make everything come out all right.

Fourth, if we can *give away everything we do in life as a gift,* then we can let anything go when the hard moments come. This is not so much a counsel of safety as of satisfaction. Even if things turn out badly for us as individuals, if we have given good gifts, they will live on, whether remembered in our names or not.

Fifth, if we *celebrate in every moment,* if we notice what God is doing with us and in the world around us, we can live with full awareness and feeling in the present and not worry too much about the past or the future.

Sixth, we must develop our gifts, accept our diminishments, and *follow our calls.* Each of us has internal work to do to find our gifts and discern our calls. Being able to hold gender expectations at a reflective distance may help to clear the wellspring of spirit in your life, whatever you do about your gender choices. When a calling is daunting, it can help to remember that Jesus didn't have to win or be successful relative to the social standards of his time in order to incarnate saving truth.

Seventh, it helps a lot if you can *find a place in a Christian community.* This is easier said than done. The next section of advice responds to the reality that many churches are not welcoming to transgender people. Everyone has personal contingencies, but it is pretty hard to be a Christian, and especially a transgender Christian, when you feel you are carrying the eternals by yourself. It is easy to start feeling crazy when no one else understands.

Finally, in the end, we have no choice other than to *trust the mystery,* to follow what we know in part but do not fully understand. We do not stand where God stands and cannot know what God knows. What we can do is follow the leadership of Jesus and embrace all that is life-giving. Saving truth is not a declaration about the unknowable. Saving truth embraces without reservation whatever is loving, just, true, and beautiful—enough of a link to God to last a lifetime.

## Pastoral Advice for Congregations

It isn't easy for many transgender people to approach local congregations, and it isn't easy for many local congregations to open their hearts to known transgender people. Since congregations are so different from one another, and since transgender people are so different from one another, there can be no simple recipe for smooth relationships. Hopefully, with some thoughtfulness on all sides and good communication, more congregations can become fully welcoming and more transgender Christians can find a spiritual home. It has happened, so we know it can be done.

First of all, it is important to acknowledge that many congregations have transgender participants and don't know it. Some transgender people pass so well that they are not identified and assimilate within the gender identity of choice. Others are in the closet, not ready to take the risk of being known. So one task for congregations is to welcome the unknown transgender person. The welcoming agenda should thus be important to all churches.

Some denominations are more welcoming than others. Many Unitarian Universalists churches, which include persons of Christian orientation, have provided space for many transgender support groups and are open about welcoming transgender people. The Universal Fellowship of Metropolitan Community Churches (UFMCC) welcomes everyone, but their congregations are primarily made up of gay, lesbian, bisexual, and transgender people. Victoria Kolakowski is a transgender writer among several UFMCC writers in *Take Back the Word: A Queer Reading of the Bible.* [2] Other Protestant denominations either have made welcoming statements as denominations or have individual congregations that have named themselves as welcoming. *Open Hands* magazine prints an ecumenical list of congregations that welcome gay and lesbian people and a list of denominational groups that support welcoming congregations. [3]

Although quite a few congregations have begun to welcome gay and lesbian people and may be theoretically welcoming to bisexual and transgender people, not very many have thought much about what it means to welcome a transgender person. Judith Wray and Maurine Waun have written books about welcoming gay, lesbian, bisexual, and transgender people into congregations, and they exhibit warm pastoral hearts. [4] They also work a bit with Scripture in ways that are compatible with the scriptural section of this book. Waun includes two transgender stories among the many stories told in her book. [5] Neither author, however, deals with the gender challenges posed by including a known transgender person in a congregation.

Melanie Morrison is one of the people who has named the challenge of including transsexual women in the life of the church. In 1993, 2000 women gathered in Minneapolis for a now famous Re-Imagining Conference. The conference was sponsored by several churches in recognition of the World Council of Churches' "Ecumenical Decade: Churches in Solidarity with Women." This conference has been bitterly attacked by Pat Robertson and other radical-right Christians. Morrison reports that the conference was rich in many ways but that she and other lesbian women felt that there needed to be an out-lesbian voice in one of the plenary sessions. She was given a few minutes to speak as co-chair of CLOUT (Christian Lesbians OUT Together). As part of her remarks she said,

> We are keenly, painfully aware that the world is not safe for lesbian women and that often the least safe place is the church. We call upon all of you—whatever your sexual orientation—not to leave this holy place without wrestling with these questions: what does it mean for us to be in solidarity with lesbian, bisexual and transsexual women in this decade, and how can we together reimagine our

> churches so that **every** woman may claim her voice, her gifts, her loves, and her wholeness?. . . I invite every lesbian, bisexual, and transsexual woman who is willing and able to come forward and join hands, encircling this platform, facing out. [6]

Morrison reports that her invitation created a glorious pandemonium, with 150 women coming down to circle the stage and the rest applauding. I include the report here because it recognizes transsexual women as women. I could wish that she had included other transgender people like me who long for acceptance as women, even though our circumstances are not as clear as those of transsexual women. But Morrison nailed the spiritual issue of accepting transgender people—the recognition and acceptance of people in the gender they present. This is far more important than practicing mere tolerance as long as the transgender person isn't too disruptive.

For many straight, gay, and lesbian people the concept of changing sex and gender just doesn't make sense. This book is my best effort to address "making sense" concerns. But it is my sense that a great many people are not really moved by intellectual presentations. For many people, such issues come down to what feels real in direct personal interaction. Many transgender people are at a severe disadvantage in interpersonal interactions because they are not as convincing as they would like to be, because of having been known in the other gender, or because of the energy-consuming challenges of becoming comfortable with transgender experience and expression. Gender transitions are socially constructed, and that requires two-way interaction. Yes, it is at such points that appearance and manner become critical, and transgender beginners are used to being criticized against mature gender standards of appearance and interactive style. Although transgender people can offer their best presentations, it is critical whether the people of their target gender draw them in or not. And that, in turn, depends on whether those people in the target gender respond defensively or welcome the exploration and becoming of a new woman or man, or of a person who stands in both places. Will you recognize that we exist, even if we are not attractive, well practiced, or comfortable with ourselves? Will you give us the benefit of the doubt and a helping hand along the way? Will you reach out in solidarity, even if your understanding is lagging behind?

Part of many people's discomfort with transgender people is that it stimulates long-unarticulated discomforts with one's own gender experience and expression. For example, which of the several appearance styles visible in a congregation shall a transgender person choose when presenting to a congregation? No matter what choice is made, others will feel a lack of congruity and fit. When I started presenting as a woman to my local congregation, several women made it clear to me that I wasn't very observant of how women in this congregation dressed, even though I was choosing styles that fit with how some of the women in the congregation presented themselves. Of course I wasn't as accomplished in my presentations as the women who matched my style choices. I bring up this point because my presentation suddenly created discussion about how the women in my congregation dress.

It is pretty hard for many transgender people to meet appearance standards. Man-to-woman transgender people can compensate for beards and baldness, but wigs and heavier makeup may not be in style in a local congregation.

Some people have reached out to me by focusing on loving and accepting me as a person, by essentially overlooking my discordant (for them) gender presentation. Such acceptance is a wonderful gift, but it doesn't accept all of me. My gender exploration and claiming is an important part of me. While I've had some disappointments in not being accepted in all the ways I want acceptance, I treasure the deep acceptance I've had from my brothers and sisters in Seekers Church. [7]

Although there are many things a local congregation can do to welcome transgender people into their midst, there is a lot transgender people can do to improve relationships. Just as transgender people need local congregations to give them space and time for development, it is also true that congregations need some space and time as well. Assuming good will, not always a reasonable assumption, churches can grow their hearts to make room they didn't know they had. As in so many relationship-building challenges, nonjudgmental communication has to be a two-way street.

Some of the specific things a congregation can do to welcome transgender people include the following:

1. Create non-gender-designated bathrooms or make it clear that people should use the bathrooms of their presenting gender.
2. Create liturgies in which respondents are not divided by gender except in special circumstances.
3. Invite people to activities without designating them as men's or women's events.
4. Create the gender-specific activities and invitations that have a gender-related purpose, then reach out to known transgender people with specific welcome.
5. Use the transgender word in sermons or other worship settings in an affirming way. If you can't think of anything to build on, you might look again at some of the stories in this book or in Mary Boenke's book.
6. Create a prayer group or a support group for people carrying a special burden and make sure it is a safe space for everyone.
7. Sponsor a lecture or discussion on transgender concerns in your church, or include an announcement about such events, or list the access information for the nearest transgender support group in your church newsletter. [8]
8. Place an advertisement in your nearest gay and lesbian newspaper that lists your congregation as a church that welcomes gay, lesbian, bisexual, and

transgender people. You may find some wonderful new members, but, at a minimum, this is a welcoming sign for those you already have, known or unknown.

9. Do some teacher training with your youth leaders so that they can understand how critical it can be to welcome those who are exploring their gender issues. [9]

Perhaps the most important thing some congregations could do would be to create an appropriate adult Christian education program and encourage participation by anyone who wants to explore how their gender self-understandings are related to their faith. If people are doing their own gender work, it won't seem so strange to learn that transgender people are doing a special kind of gender work. Kevin Ogle included the following thoughts in a sermon responding to my presentation of myself as a woman to Seekers Church. After some kind words about me, he said,

> What does it mean to be in community? Community is the place where we learn, little by little, to relinquish control over what we let into our lives. We covenant with each other to share lives – joys and sorrows, failures and triumphs, confusion and vision. We do this because of our faith that this way of being is how we are meant to be, how God created us.
>
> Community is the place where each of us learns, little by little, that our well-being as an individual is inextricably linked to a widening circle of others. We don't learn this intellectually, we *experience* it. And it is only in our commitment to hang in when disagreements or controversies arise – a commitment that I believe is a gift of grace, not something that we engineer by ourselves – that we know in new ways what really matters in life.

Then Kevin called for ongoing engagement and conversation.

> My first hope is that we might learn something about the complexity of, and uncertainty around, the development and definition of human sexuality, because our understanding of human sexuality in all its dimensions affects (often unconsciously) how we judge ourselves and others, as individuals and as groups or classes.
>
> . . . I would hope that engaging in such an examination would help us understand the constricting roles that cultural expectations often assign us and free us up to be more fully the people God created us to be. We have struggled with this issue of culturally defined roles since our beginnings as a church 25 years ago: throughout our life together we have addressed, with varying degrees of intensity, questions about men's and women's roles and realities. We've seen how simplistic distinctions don't hold, how stereotyping

distances us rather than brings us together, how efforts by some of our men to be more "manly" and our women to be more "ladylike" have distracted us from our real work in the world.

... My second hope is that how we learn to see differences within the community will change how we live in this world and how we bear witness to the One who calls us both to celebrate and to transcend our differences. [10]

For other congregations the most important source of welcoming might be the creation of a prayer group where everyone can be safe and all concerns can be brought to God. For any individual who wants to help a congregation become more welcoming, starting with prayer is probably a good idea. In the end, we truly and most deeply meet each other in church as we acknowledge how much we need the saving presence of God in our lives, a presence deeper and more affirming than any social limitations of anonymity, confusion, or alienation. Thanks be to God for always being ready when we open our hearts and awareness. Thanks be to God for waiting for us when we are blocked. Thanks be to God for the ecstasy that comes with the deepest meeting.

---

## Notes:

1. G. K. Chesterton (1910/1994).
2. Victoria Kolakowski (2000), pp. 103-114.
3. Open Hands, 3801 N. Keeler Ave., Chicago, IL 60641; telephone 773-736-5526.
4. Judith Hoch Wray (1998), Maurine C. Waun (1999). Both are part of the Christian Church (Disciples of Christ).
5. Waun, ibid., pages 81 ff.
6. Melanie Morrison (1995), page 94.
7. Seekers Church is an independent Christian community in the tradition of the Church of the Savior. Our web site is www.seekerschurch.org, and it includes some of my sermons. More importantly, it includes a lot of creative worship material and our core documents, which point to our special way of doing Christianity. You can read about Seekers in *Excellent Protestant Congregations*, edited by Paul Wilkes (2001).
8. The most up-to-date list of transgender organizations is in *Transgender Tapestry* which is available from the International Foundation for Gender Education, P. O. Box 540229, Waltham, MA: 02454-0229; telephone 781-899-2212; web site www.ifge.org.
9. A good resource for exploring youth is *Coming Out Young and Faithful*, edited by Leanne McCall Tigert and Timothy Brown (2001). Another is *Life or Death: Resources for Communities of Faith Addressing the Issue of Lesbian, Gay, Bisexual and Transgender Youth Suicide*, edited by Timothy Brown (2001).
10. Kevin Ogle 2000. "A Sermon: Learning From our Differences." This sermon is available on the Seekers Church website: www.seekerschurch.org.

# Glossary

**assigned sex**      The sexual designation attached to one at birth and entered on a birth certificate.

**androgyne**      A person who presents an appearance that is mixed or neutral in terms of gender association. A specialized research definition is offered in terms of the Bem Sex Role Inventory.

**bigender**      A person who chooses to affirm and express both masculine and feminine qualities and images.

**bisexual**      A person who chooses partners for sexual activity of either sex. This term is used very differently for different purposes. Researchers may attach this term to people even though it makes no sense to the person so labeled. See Ruth Colker's book *Hybrids* for an excellent discussion of this issue.

**butch**      A masculine-appearing female.

**cross-dresser**      A common term for people who like to take on an appearance associated with their nonassigned sex.

**deviant**      In this book the term is used as a technical sociological term meaning a person or act that violates a social expectation.

**drag king**      A female who presents a highly stylized image of a man, often in the context of an entertainment performance.

**drag queen**      A male who presents a highly stylized image of a woman, often in the context of an entertainment performance.

**dysphoria**      A psychiatric term meaning a feeling of upset or angry. *Gender Dysphoria* means feelings of unhappiness or upset about conforming to the expectations of one's gender that is supposed to be based on one's assigned sex. The word is in the realm of pathology, since it is used in the context of mental disorder. Psychiatrists introduced this word to get away from the phrase *mental disease* or *mental illness* while still claiming authority for transgender experience as some kind of pathology.

**dystonic**      Negative feelings toward oneself because one has introjected (accepted) negative images about oneself from the society.

| | |
|---|---|
| **f2m** | A term referring to female to male transsexuals. |
| **female** | A person who meets the physiological standards of a female. See the section on legal identity in Chapter 8 for a discussion of such physiological standards. |
| **femme** | A feminine appearing female, usually so named because of relationship with a butch. |
| **feminine** | The qualities of cultural images and symbols usually associated with women. |
| **gay** | This term sometimes refers to the whole homosexual community, as in the *gay community*. Sometimes it refers only to homosexual men, as in *gay men*. |
| **gender** | The social roles of man and woman. Often misused as a synonym for sex. |
| **gender identity disorder (GID)** | A mental disorder invented by psychiatrists in the 1980's to compensate for loss of business when homosexuality was declared to not be a disease. The phrase is constantly being redefined, and lacks a scientific basis, but it presumably means something about transgender expression. |
| **hermaphrodite** | An older term for *intersexual*. Less used now because it suggests a half- and-half concept of intersexuality. |
| **heterosexual** | A clinical term referring to anyone who chooses a partner for sexual activity who is not of one's sex category as assigned at birth. |
| **homosexual** | A clinical term referring to anyone who chooses a partner for sexual activity who is of the same sexual category as assigned at birth. For consideration of many definitional fine points the section on sample survey research in Chapter 4 lists several considerations. This book takes the position that "homosexuals" are one kind of transgender person because their choice of sexual partner does not conform to the socially traditional expectation for their assigned sex and for their presented gender. |
| **intersexual** | A person with male and female physiological characteristics. For a more complete understanding read the section on intersexuality in Chapter 2. |
| **lesbian** | A term referring to homosexual women. |
| **m2f** | A term referring to male to female transsexuals. |

| | |
|---|---|
| **male** | A person who meets the physiological standards of a male. |
| **man** | In psychological terms, a person who thinks of himself as a man. In sociological terms, a person who interacts in social situations in the role of a man. |
| **masculine** | The qualities of cultural images and symbols usually associated with men. |
| **paraphilia** | A psychiatric term meaning the obtaining of some kind of sexual satisfaction from an object or person in a way that psychiatrists, echoing the culture, disapprove of. This is one of many terms that have emerged in recent decades to get away from old definitions while sustaining psychiatric control of the agenda by using unfamiliar words. |
| **pathology** | This term means disease. The official brokers of the meaning of this term as it applies to transgender experience and expression are the American Psychiatric Association and the American Psychological Association. |
| **sexual orientation** | This term refers to choice of partners for sexual activity in relation to whether the partner is of the same sex or not. |
| **transgender** | A term referring to anyone who has the experience of, or adopts the expression of men or women, when they were not respectively, assigned as males or females at birth. |
| **transphobia** | This term means fear of, or hostility toward, transgender people or transgender activity. |
| **transsexual** | A person who has completed sexual reconstructive surgery. It is common to refer to people who are planning toward or preparing for this surgery as *pre-operative transsexuals*. Some refer to people who are living full time in the gender role that is not usual for their assigned sex as *non-operative transsexuals*. For a fuller understanding of the range and complexity of transgender alternatives, the reader may review the We Exist section in Chapter 1. |
| **transvestite** | Clinical term for someone who enjoys taking on the appearance of their nonassigned sex. |
| **woman** | In psychological terms, a person who thinks of herself as a woman. In sociological terms, a person who interacts in social situations in the role of a woman. |

# References

Achtemeier, Paul J., et al., eds. *The Harper Collins Bible Dictionary, Revised*. San Francisco: HarperCollins, 1996.

Allen, J. J. *The Man in the Red Velvet Dress: Inside the World of Crossdressing*. New York: Carol Publishing, 1996.

Allen, Laura. "Sex Differences in the Corpus Callosum of the Living Human Being." *Journal of Neuroscience* 11 (1991): 933–942.

Allen, Mariette P. *Transformations: Crossdressers and Those Who Love Them*. New York: E. P. Dutton, 1989.

Allen, Mariette P. "The Changing Face of the Transgender Community." In *Gender Blending*, edited by Bonnie Bullough et al. Amherst, NY: Prometheus Books, 1997.

Alexander-Moegerle, Gil. "A Public Apology." *Open Hands*. 14 (1998): 15.

American Psychiatric Association. *Diagnostic and Statistical Manual of Mental Disorders,* 4th Edition. Washington, DC: American Psychiatric Association, 1994.

Ashbrook, James B., and Carol Rauch Albright. *The Humanizing Brain: Where Religion and Neuroscience Meet*. Cleveland: Pilgrim Press, 1997.

Bakker, A. et al. "The Prevalence of Transsexualism in the Netherlands." *Acta Psychiatrica Scandinavia*. 87 (1993), 237–238

Becker, Judith. "Sexual Dysfunctions and Disorders." Chapter 11 in *The Columbia University College of Physicians and Surgeons Complete Home Guide to Mental Health*. New York: Henry Holt, 1992.

Bem, Sandra. "The Measurement of Psychological Androgyny." *Journal of Consulting and Clinical Psychology*. 42 (1974): 155–162.

Bem, Sandra. *The Lenses of Gender: Transforming the Debate on Sexual Inequality*. New Haven: Yale University Press, 1993.

Berger, Peter and Thomas Luckmann. *The Social Construction of Reality*. New York: Doubleday, 1963

Bergstedt, Spencer. *Translegalities: A Legal Guide for Male to Female Transsexuals*. Waltham, MA: International Foundation for Gender Education [IFGE], 1997. Available from IFGE, P. O. Box 540229, Waltham, MA, 02454-540229; telephone 978-443-0044, web site, www.ifge.org.

Biber, Stanley H. "Current State of Transsexual Surgery: A Brief Overview," in *Gender Blending*. Bonnie Bullough, et al., eds. Amherst, NY: Prometheus Books, 1997.

Billings, Dwight and Thomas Urban. "The Socio-Medical Construction of Transsexualism." *Social Problems*, 29 (1982): 266–282.

Blanchard, Ray. "Typology of Male-To-Female Transsexualism." *Archives of Sexual Behavior* 14 (1985).

Blodgett, Bonnie. "Daughter John: One of My Little Girls Insists She Wants to Be a Boy. Shouldn't I be Worried?" *Health*. 4 (1990): 26 ff.

Bloom, Amy. "The Body Lies." *The New Yorker*. 70 (1994): 38 ff.

Bochting, Walter O. and Eli Coleman. eds. *Gender Dysphoria: Interdisciplinary Approaches in Clinical Management*. New York, Haworth Press, 1992.

Boenke, Mary. ed. *Trans Forming Families: Real Stories About Transgendered Loved Ones*. Imperial Beach, CA Walter Trook Publishing, 1999. Available from Walter Trook Publishing, 276 Date Street, Imperial Beach, CA, 91932.

Bolin, Anne. "Transcending and Transgendering." In *Third Sex, Third Gender: Beyond Sexual Dimorphism in Culture and History*, edited by Gilbert Herdt. New York: Zone Books, 1996.

Bornstein, Kate. *Gender Outlaw: On Men, Women, and the Rest of Us*. New York: Routledge, 1994.

Bradley, Susan, et al. "Experiment of Nature: Ablative Penis at Age 2 months, Sex Reassignment at 7 months, and a Psychological Followup In Young Adulthood." *Pediatrics* 102 (1998): E9.

Bromley, George W. *The International Standard Bible Encyclopedia,* Vol 2. Grand Rapids, MI: Eerdmans, 1982.

Brooks, David. "The Organization Kid." *Atlantic Monthly*. 287 (2001): 40–54.

Brown, Mildred and Chloe Ann Rounsley. *True Selves: Understanding Transsexualism*. San Francisco: Jossey Bass Publishers, 1996.

Brown, Timothy. ed. *Life or Death: Resources for Communities of Faith Addressing the Issues of Lesbian, Gay, Bisexual and Transgender Youth Suicide*. Holden, MA: The United Church of Christ Coalition for Lesbian, Gay, Bisexual and Transgender Concerns, 2001. Available from The Coalition, P. O. Box 403, Holden, MA, 01520-0403.

Bullough, Vern. "Transvestites in the Middle Ages." *American Journal of Sociology*. 79 (1974): 1381–1394.

Bullough, Bonnie, et al., eds. *Gender Blending*:Amherst, NY: Prometheus Books, 1997.

Bullough, Bonnie, et al., eds. *How I Got Into Sex: Personal Stories of Leading Researchers, Sex Therapists, Educators, Prostitutes, Sex Toy Designers, Sex Surrogates, Transsexuals, Criminologists, Clergy, and More*.Amherst, NY: Prometheus Books, 1997.

Bullough, Vern and Bonnie Bullough. *Crossdressing, Sex and Gender*. Philadelphia: University of Pennsylvania Press, 1993.

Bullough, Vern and Bonnie Bullough. *Sin, Sickness and Society:A History of Sexual Attitudes*. (Particularly, Chapter 6: Sex vs. Gender). New York: New American Library, 1977.

Burke, Phyllis. *Gender Shock*. New York: Doubleday (Anchor), 1996.

Burr, Chandler. *A Separate Creation:The Search for the Biological Origins of Sexual Orientation*. New York: Hyperion, 1996.

Buttrick, George A., et al., eds. *The Interpreter's Bible,* Volume VII. New York: Abingdon, 1951.

Cabaj, Robert J. and Terry S. Stein. eds. *Textbook of Homosexuality and Mental Health*.Washington, DC:American Psychiatric Press, 1996.

Califia, Pat. *Sex Changes:The Politics of Transgenderism*. San Francisco: Cleis, 1997.

Caplan, Paula J. and Jeremy B. Caplan. *Thinking Critically About Research on Sex and Gender*. New York: HarperCollins, 1994.

Carey, Benedict. "Therapists Fail Sex Role Test." *Health*. 4 (1990): 11 ff.

Carlisle, David B. *Human Sex Change and Role Reversal*. Lewiston, NY: Edward Mellen, 1998.

Carpenter, William. *Principles of Human Physiology:With Their Chief Applications to Pathology, Hygiene and Forensic Medicine*. London: Churchill, 1842.

Castle, Stephanie. *The Dual Alliance*.Vancouver, BC: Perceptions Press, 1995.

*Catechism of the Catholic Church*. New York: Doubleday, 1994.

Chesterton, G. K. Chapter 5, *What's Wrong With the World*. 1910. Reprint, San Francisco: Ignatius Press, 1994.

Cicotello, Dianna. *The Employer's Guide to Gender Transition*.Aurora, CO: Transition Press, 1992.Available from Transition Press, 1740 S. Buckley Rd #6-178,Aurora, CO 80017.

Cicotello, Dianna. *Six Stages of Development*. (Unpublished Draft) The Phoenix Project.

Cloud, John. "Trans Across America." *Time*. 152(3) (July 20, 1998).

Clough, Abigail S. "The Illusion of Protection: Transsexual Employment Discrimination." *The Georgetown Journal of Gender and the Law*. 1 (2000): 849–886.

Coates, Susan and Sabrina Wolfe. "Gender Identity Disorder in Boys: The Interface of Constitution and Early Experience." *Psychoanalytic Inquiry*. 15 (1995).

Cohen, Daniel A. ed. *The Female Mariner and Related Works*. Amherst, Massachusetts: University of Massachusetts Press, 1997.

Colapinto, John. "The True Story of John/Joan." <u>*Rolling Stone*</u>. December 11, 1997.

Cole, Dana and Dianna. *Ambi-Gendered: God's Special Gift*. Aurora, CO: Transition Press, 1992. Available from Transition Press, 1740 S. Buckley Rd. #6-178, Aurora, CO, 80017.

Colker, Ruth. *Hybrid: Bisexuals, Multiracials, and Other Misfits Under American Law*. New York: New York University Press, 1996.

Conover, Patrick W. *Necessity and Conflict: A Systematic Theory of Sociology*, Ph. D. Dissertation. Tallahassee, FL: Florida State University, 1971.

Conover, Patrick W. "An Analysis of Communes and Intentional Communities with Particular Attention to Sexual and Genderal Relations." *The Family Coordinator*. 24 (1975): 453–464.

Conover, Patrick W. "A Reassessment of Labeling Theory: A Constructive Response to Criticism." In *The Uses of Controversy in Sociology*, edited by Lewis A. Coser and Otto N. Larsen. New York: Free Press, 1976

Coombs, Mary. "Gender and Transgender." The reference is a pre-publication draft of a paper offered at the 1996 meetings of the International Conference on Law and Employment Policy in Houston, Texas. Quoted by permission of Mary Coombs, University of Miami, School of Law.

Cormier, Frances O. *Frances With an 'e' Our Story*. Moose Creek, Ontario, Canada: Pilgrim Publications, 1995.

Costello, Timothy and Joseph Costello. *Abnormal Psychology: Second Edition*. New York: HarperCollins College Outline, 1992. (Particularly Chapter 15)

Countryman, L. William. *Dirt Greed and Sex: Sexual Implications in the New Testament and Their Implications for Today*. Philadelphia: Fortress Press, 1988.

Croutier, Alev L. *Harem: The World Behind the Veil*. New York: Abbeville Press, 1989.

Dabbs, James Jr. "Salivary Testosterone Measurements in Behavioral Studies." *Annals of the New York Academy of Sciences*: 694 (1993): 177-83.

De Motier, Beren. "The Transgender Craze." *New York Blade*. June 26, 1998.

D'Emilio, John. *Sexual Politics, Sexual Communities: The Making of a Homosexual Minority in the United States 1940-1970*. Chicago: University of Chicago Press, 1983.

D'Emilio, John and Estelle Freedman. *Intimate Matters: A History of Sexuality in America*. New York: Harper and Row, 1988.

Denny, Dallas. "Transgender: Some Historical, Cross-Cultural, and Contemporary Models and Methods of Coping and Treatment." In *Gender Blending*, edited by Bonnie Bullough, et al. Amherst, NY: Prometheus Books, 1997, Pages 33-42.

Denny, Dallas. ed. *Current Concepts in Transgender Identity*. New York: Garland, 1998.

Devor, Holly. *Gender Blending: Confronting the Limits of Duality*. Bloomington, IN: Indiana University Press, 1994.

Devor, Holly. *FTM: Female-to-Male Transsexuals in Society*. Bloomington, IN: Indiana University Press, 1997.

Dimen, Muriel. "The Third Step: Freud, the Feminists, and Postmodernism." *The American Journal of Psychoanalysis*. 55 (1995): 303 ff.

Dines, Gail and Jean M. Humez. *Gender, Race and Class in Media*. Thousand Oaks, CA: Sage, 1995.

Doctor, Richard F. *Transvestites and Transsexuals: Toward a Theory of Cross-Genderal Behavior*. New York: Plenum, 1988.

Docter, Richard F. and Virginia Prince. "Transvestism: A Survey of 1032 Cross-Dressers." *Archives of Sexual Behavior* 26 (1997): 589-605.

Doerflinger, Richard M. "The Ethics of Funding Embryonic Stem Cell Research: A Catholic Viewpoint." *Kennedy Institute of Ethics Journal* 9 (1999): 137—150.

Dragoin, William. "The Gynemimetic Shaman: Evolutionary Origins of Male Sexual Inversion and Associated Talents." In *Gender Blending*, edited by Bonnie Bullough, et al. Amherst, NY: Prometheus Books, 1997.

Driscoll, J.P., et al. "Transsexuals." *Transaction* (1971) pp. 28-31.

Dubos, Rene. *Mirage of Health*. Garden City, NY: Doubleday (Anchor), 1959.

Dylan, Bob. *"With God on Our Side"* (song). Columbia Records, 1964.

Dylan, Bob. *"Desolation Row"* (song). Columbia Records, 1965.

Echols, Alice. "The Taming of the Id: Feminist Sexual Politics 1968-1983." In *Pleasure and Danger: Exploring Female Sexuality,* edited by Carole S. Vance. Boston: Routledge and Kegan Paul, 1984.

Ehrhardt, Anke. "Gender." In *Researching Sexual Behavior,* edited by John Bancroft. Bloomington, IN: Indiana University Press, 1997.

Eilts, Mitzi. "Let's work toward 'Both-And'," *Waves.* September, 2000. Waves is a newsletter of the United Church of Christ Coalition for Gay, Lesbian, Bisexual and Transgender Concerns and is available from: The Coalition, PMB 230, 800 Village Walk, Guilford, CT 06437-2740

Elizabeth, Sister Mary. *Legal Aspects of Transsexualism*. San Juan Capistrano, CA: Educational Resources, 1990.

Elkins, Richard. *Male Femaling: A Grounded Theory Approach to Cross-Dressing and Sex-Changing*. New York, NY: Routledge, 1997.

Epstein, Louis. *Sex Laws and Customs in Judaism*. 1948. Reprint, New York, NY: KTAV Publishing House, 1968.

Ettner, Randi. *Confessions of a Gender Defender*. Evanston, IL: Chicago Spectrum Press, 1996.

Faulkner, William. *As I Lay Dying*. 1930. Reprint, New York: Vintage, 1987.

Fausto-Sterling, Anne. *Myths of Gender*. New York: Basic Books, 1985.

Fausto-Sterling, Anne. "Focus on Only Two Sexes is Narrow," *The Sciences*. (March-April, 1993)

Fausto-Sterling, Anne. "The Five Sexes," a paper giver to the CLAGS Public Forum, New York City, February 10, 1995.

Fausto-Sterling, Anne. *Sexing the Body: Gender Politics and the Construction of Sexuality*. New York: Basic Books, 2000.

Feinberg, Leslie. *Stone Butch Blues*. Ithaca, NY: Firebrand Books, 1993.

Feinberg, Leslie. *Transgender Warriors*. Boston: Beacon Press, 1996.

Feinbloom, Deborah H. *Transvestites and Transsexuals: Mixed Views*. Delacorte Press, 1976.

Feldblum, Chai. "Gay People, Trans People, Women: Is It All About Gender," *Journal of Human Rights Symposium*. October 14, 2000.

Firestein, Beth A. *Bisexuality: The Psychology and Politics of an Invisible Minority*. Sage Publications, 1996.

Fisk, N. And J. VanMaasdam. "A Retrospective Review and Analysis of Gender Reassignment Programs and Professionals over the 1970's," Paper, Seventh International Gender Dysphoria Symposium, 1981.

Fleming, Michael. "Questioning Current Definitions of Gender Identity: Implications of the Bem Sex Role Inventory for Transsexuals," *Archives of Sexual Behavior* 9(1980): 13-26.

Fleming, Michael, et al. "Methodological Problems in Assessing Sex Reassignment Surgery," *Archives of Sexual Behavior*. 9: 451-456, 1980.

Fox, Ronald. "Bisexuality in Perspective: A Review of Theory and Research." In *Bisexuality: the Psychology and Politics of an Invisible Minority*. Edited by Beth A. Firestein. Thousand Oaks, California: Sage Publications, 1996.

Francoeur, Robert T. and Anna K. *The Future of Sexual Relations*. Englewood Cliffs, NJ: Prentice-Hall, 1974.

Funk, Robert and Roy Hoover, eds. *The Five Gospels*. New York: Macmillan, 1993.

Garber, Marjorie. *Vested Interests: Cross Dressing and Cultural Anxiety*. New York: HarperCollins, 1992.

General Accounting Office. *Testimony of the Office of the General Counsel Regarding the Defense of Marriage Act*. Washington, DC: United States General Accounting Office (January 31, 1997): GAO/OGC-97-16.

Gilson, Anne B. *Eros Breaking Free*. Cleveland: Pilgrim, 1995.

Glausiusz, Josie. "Transsexual Brains." *Discover*. 17 (1995): 83.

Goffman, Erving. *The Presentation of Self in Everyday Life*. Garden City, NY: Doubleday (Anchor), 1959.

Goffman, Erving. *Stigma: Notes on the Management of Spoiled Identity*. Englewood Cliffs, NJ: Prentice-Hall, 1963.

Goldstein, Irwin. "Male Sexual Circuitry." *Scientific American*. 283 (August, 2000): 70–75.

Goode, Erich and Richard Troiden. *Sexual Deviance and Sexual Deviants*. New York: Morrow, 1974.

Gordon, Lesley. *Aspects of Gender: A Study Of Cross-Dressing*. Waltham, MA: International Foundation for Gender Education (IFGE) 1994 (1997). Available from IFGE, P. O. Box 540229, Waltham, MA 02454, web site www.ifge.org.

Gordon, Rachel. "New Health Benefits for Sex-Change Surgery Will Help One City Administrator on Journey to Life as a Woman." *San Francisco Chronicle*. May 14, 2001.

Gorski, Roger. "Evidence for a Morphological Difference Within the Medial Preoptic Areas of the Rat Brain." *Brain Research*. 148 (1978): 333–346.

Gorski, Roger. "Sexual Differentiation of the Endocrine Brain and its Control." In *Brain Endocrinology, 2nd Edition,* edited by Marcella Motta. New York: Raven Press, 1991.

Green, Richard. *Sexual Identity Conflict in Children and Adults*. Baltimore: Penguin, 1974.

Green, Richard. "Spelling 'Relief' for Transsexuals: Employment Discrimination and the Criteria of Sex." *Yale Law and Policy Review*. 125 (1985).

Green, Richard. *The "Sissy Boy Syndrome" and the Development of Homosexuality*. New Haven: Yale University Press, 1987.

Greenspan, Francis. *Basic and Clinical Endocrinology: Third Edition*. Norwalk, CT: Appleton and Lange 1991.

Greenspan, Stanley I., and Jacqueline Salmon. *Playground Politics*. Reading, MA: Addison-Wesley, 1993.

Hahn, Celia A. *Sexual Paradox*. New York: Pilgrim, 1991.

Haldeman, Douglas. "Spirituality and Religion in the Lives of Lesbians and Gay Men." In

*Textbook of Homosexuality and Mental Health,* edited by Robert J Cabaj and Terry S. Stein. Washington, DC: American Psychiatric Press, 1996.

Hamer, Dean, et al. "A Linkage Between DNA Markers on the X Chromosome and Male Sexual Orientation." *Science*. 261 (1993): pages 321-327.

Harris, Marvin. *Culture, People, Nature, Fourth Edition: An Introduction to General Anthropology*. New York: Harper and Row, 1985.

Harry, Joseph. *Gay Children Grown Up: Gender Culture and Gender Deviance*. New York: Praeger, 1982.

Hausman, Bernice L. *Changing Sex: Transsexualism, Technology and the Idea of Gender*. Durham, NC: Duke University Press, 1995.

Haval, Vaclav. *Summer Meditations*. New York: Knopf, 1992.

"Health Law Standards of Care for Transsexualism." *Second International Conference on Transgender Law and Employment Policy*. 1993. Available from 5707 Fiorenza Street, Houston, Texas, 77035-5515.

Helminiak, Daniel A. *What the Bible Really Says About Homosexuality, Millennium Edition*. Tajique, New Mexico: Alamo Square Press, 2000. Available from Alamo Square Distributors, P. O. Box 2510, Novato, CA 94948.

Helms, Kathryn J. "Religion and Cross-Gender Behavior." In *Gender Blending*, edited by Bonnie Bullough, et al. Amherst, NY: Prometheus Books, 1997.

Herdt, Gilbert, ed. *Third Sex, Third Gender: Beyond Sexual Dimorphism in Culture and History*. New York: Zone Books, 1996.

Hill, Darryl B. "Three Transgender Perspectives on Gender Categories: Either/Or, Both/And, Neither/Nor." Workshop at International Foundation for Gender Education Conference, Toronto, Ontario, Canada, March, 1998.

Hirschfeld, Magnus. Translated by Michael A. Lombard-Nash. *Transvestites: The Erotic Drive to Cross-Dress*. Originally published 1910. Buffalo, NY: Prometheus Books, 1991.

Hofstadter, Richard. *Social Darwinism in American Thought*. Boston: Beacon Press, 1955.

Hooker, Evelyn. "The Adjustment of the Male Overt Homosexual." *Journal of Projective Techniques*. Volume 21 (1957): 18-31.

Horrocks, Roger. *An Introduction to the Study of Sexuality*. New York: St Martin's Press, 1997.

Horton, David. *Changing Channels?: A Christian Response to the Transvestite and Transsexual*. Bramcote, England: Grove Books Limited, 1994 (Grove Ethical Studies No. 92)

Howey, Noelle and Ellen Samuels eds. *Out of the Ordinary: Essays on Growing Up with Gay, Lesbian and Transgender Parents*. New York: St. Martin's Press, 2000.

*Human Sexuality: A Preliminary Study*. The United Church of Christ. New York: United Church Press, 1977.

Hyde, Janet. *Understanding Human Sexuality, 3rd Edition*. New York: McGraw Hill, 1986.

Imperato-McGinley, Julianne, et al. "Steroid 5 alpha-reductase Deficiency in Man: An Inherited Form of Male Pseudohermaphroditism." *Science*. 186 (1974): 1213-1215.

Irvine, Janice M. *Disorders of Desire: Sex and Gender in Modern American Sexology*. Philadelphia, PA: Temple University Press, 1990.

Israel, Gianna and Donald E. Tarver II. *Transgender Care: Recommended Guidelines, Practical Information and Personal Accounts*. Philadelphia: Temple University Press, 1997.

Johnson, Julie Ann. ed. *By the Grace of God: Lee Frances Heller and Friends*. Wheaton, IL: SSP Publications, 2000. Available from SSP Publications, P. O. Box 1405, Wheaton, IL 60189

Johnson, Katherine and Stephanie Castle. *Prisoner of Gender: A Transsexual and the System*. Vancouver, BC: Perceptions Press, 1997.

Jones, J. R. "Plasma Testosterone Concentrations in Female Transsexuals: Effects of Estrogen Therapy." *Archives of Sexual Behavior*. 2 (1972).

Jorgenson, Christine. *Christine Jorgenson: A Personal Autobiography*. Paul S. Erickson, Inc., (1967). A Reprint is available from the International Foundation for Gender Education, P. O. Box 540229, Waltham, MA, 02454, web site, www.ifge.org.

Jung, Carl G. *The Undiscovered Self.* 1957. Reprint, New York: Penguin, 1997.

Kates, Gary. *Monsieur d'Eon is a Woman*. New York: HarperCollins (Basic Books), 1995.

Kelly, Phaedra. E-Mail transmission. (1997). For follow up contact International Gender Transient Affinity, 1, Banks Building, School Green Road, Freshwater PO40 9AJ Isle of Wight, U.K.

Kinsey, Alfred, et al. *Sexual Behavior in the Human Male*. Philadelphia: W. B. Saunders, 1948

Kinsey, Alfred, et al. *Sexual Behavior in the Human Female*. Philadelphia: W. B. Saunders, 1953

Kirk, Sheila M.D. and Martine Rothblatt J.D. *Medical, Legal and Workplace Issues for the Transsexual: A Guide for Successful Transformation*. Watertown, MA: Together Lifeworks, 1995.

Kirk, Sheila. Private Letter. 1997.

Kolakowski, Victoria. "Throwing a Party: Patriarchy, Gender, and the Death of Jezebel." In *Take Back the Word: A Queer Reading of the Bible*, edited by Robert Goss and Mona West. Cleveland, OH: Pilgrim Press, 2000.

Kolata, Gina. "Man's World, Women's World: Brain Studies Point to Differences," *New York Times, Section B*. February 28, 1995.

Krajecki, James. "Homosexuality and the Mental Health Professions." In *Textbook of Homosexuality and Mental Health,* edited by Robert J. Cabaj and Terry S. Stein. Washington, DC: American Psychiatric Press, 1996.

Kreuger, Lesley. "Brainstorm: Differences Between Men's and Women's Brains." *Chatelaine*. 68 (1995): 72 ff.

Kroll, Karen. "Transsexuality and Religion: A Personal Journey." In *Gender Blending*, edited by Bonnie Bullough, et al. Amherst, NY: Prometheus Books, 1997.

Laing, Alison. "TG Culture: The Last Ten Years and the Next." *Transgender Tapestry*. 77 (1996): 48.

Laing, R.D. and Aaron Esterson. *Sanity, Madness and the Family*. Baltimore: Penguin, 1964.

Laing, R. D. *The Politics of Experience*. New York: Ballantine, 1967.

Laumann, E. O. *The Social Organization of Sexuality*. Chicago: University of Chicago Press, 1994.

Laura, Roberto. "Issues in Diagnosis and Treatment of Transsexualism." *Archives of Sexual Behavior*. 12 (1983): 445-473.

Lawrence, Anne. "Men Trapped in Men's Bodies." *Transgender Tapestry*. 85 (1998): 65-68.

Lawrence, Anne. "The New Standards of Care for Gender Identity Disorder," a workshop presentation at the International Foundation for Gender Education annual conference, Arlington Heights, IL, 2001.

LeDoux, Joseph. *The Emotional Brain: The Mysterious Underpinnings of Emotional Life*. New York: Simon and Schuster, 1996.

Lemert, Edwin. *Human Deviance, Social Problems and Social Control, Second Edition*. Englewood Cliffs, NJ: Prentice-Hall, 1972.

Leiby, Richard. "Clothed in Controversy." *The Washington Post*. September 7, 1994, pages C1 ff.

Lewis, Nolan. *Outlines for Psychiatric Examinations*. (Includes reprint of the 1942 Standard Nomenclature of Disease as approved by the American Psychiatric Association and the American Medical Association.) Utica, NY: State Hospital Press, 1943.

Lofland, John. *Deviance and Identity*. Englewood Cliffs, Prentice Hall, 1969.

Mallon, Gary. "On the Stroll." *In the Family*, 5(2) (1999): 8-13.

Mallon, Gary, ed. *Social Services with Transgendered Youth*. (Co-published simultaneously as Journal of Gay and Lesbian Social Services, 10(3/4), 1999. New York: Haworth Press (Harrington Park Press), 1999.

Margolies, Eva. *Undressing the American Male: Men with Sexual Problems and What You Can Do to Help Them*. New York: Penguin, 1994.

Masters, Roger. "From Inclusive Fitness to Neuroscience: Proximate Mechanisms, Feminism, and the Politics of Gender." *Politics and the Life Sciences*. 14 (1995): 180 ff.

Matus, Jill. *Unstable Bodies: Victorian Representations of Sexuality and Maternity*. Manchester, MI: Manchester University Press, 1995.

Mayr, Ernst. "Darwin's Influence on Modern Thought." *Scientific American*. 283(1) (2000): 79–83.

Meyer, J. and D. Reter. "Sex Reassignment: Follow-up." *Archives of General Psychiatry*. 36 (1979): 1010–1015.

Meyer-Bahlburg, Heino. "Psychoendocrine Research on Sexual Orientation: Current Status and Future Options." *Progress in Brain Research*. 61 (1984): 375–398.

Michael, Robert, et al. *Sex in America: A Definitive Survey*. Boston: Little Brown, 1994.

Michaels, Stuart. "The Prevalence of Homosexuality in the United States." In *Textbook of Homosexuality and Mental Health,* edited by Robert J. Cabaj and Terry S. Stein. Washington, DC: American Psychiatric Press, 1996.

Migeon, C.J., et al. "Studies of Androgens in Transsexual Subjects: Effects of Estrogen Therapy." *Johns Hopkins Medical Journal*. 123 (1968), 128–133.

Miller, Niela. *Counseling in Genderland: A Guide for You and Your Transgendered Client*. Boston: Different Path Press, 1996.

Miller, Rachel. *The Bliss of Becoming One: Integrating 'Feminine' Feelings into the Male Psyche, Mainstreaming the Gender Community*. Highland City, FL: Rainbow Books, 1996.

Mills, Kim. "Mission Impossible: Why Reparative Therapy and Ex-Gay Ministries Fail." Paper by Human Rights Campaign, Washington, DC, 1998.

Mollenkott, Virginia. *Sensuous Spirituality: Out from Fundamentalism*. New York: Crossroads, 1992.

Mollenkott, Virginia. *Omnigender: A Trans-Religious Approach.* Cleveland: Pilgrim, 2001.

Money, John, et al. "Adult Erotosexual Status and Fetal Hormone Masculinization and Demasculinization." *Psychoneuroendocrinology*. 9 (1984): 405–415.

Money, John. *Lovemaps*. New York: Irvington, 1986.

Monteleone, James. "Problems Associated with the Determination of Sex of Rearing in the Presence of Ambiguous Genitalia." In *Sex and Gender: A Theological and Scientific Inquiry*, edited by Mark F. Schwartz. St. Louis, MO: Pope John XXIII Medical-Moral Research and Education Center, 1983.

Morrison, Melanie. *The Grace of Coming Home*. Cleveland, OH: Pilgrim, 1995.

Nangeroni, Nancy. "Transgenderism, Challenging the Binary," *Open Hands*. 12(2) (1996): 4–6.

Nangeroni, Nancy. "SRS Tomorrow: The Physical Continuum." In *Gender Blending*, edited by Bonnie Bullough, et al. Amherst, NY: Prometheus Books, 1997.

Nash, Graham. *Teach Your Children*. (song) New York: Atlantic Recording Co., 1970.

Nash, Madeleine. "Fertile Minds." *Time*. 149(5), (1997): 48–56.

Nelson, James B. *Embodiment: An Approach to Sexuality and Christian Theology*. Minneapolis, MN: Augusberg, 1978.

Nelson, James B. *Between Two Gardens: Reflections on Sexuality and Religious Experience*. New York: Pilgrim Press, 1983.

Nelson, James B. "Embracing Masculinity." In *Sexuality and the Sacred: Sources for Theological Reflection*, edited by James B. Nelson and Sandra P. Longfellow. Louisville, Kentucky: Westminster/John Knox Press, 1994.

Nelson, James B. *Humanly Speaking*. Cleveland, OH: United Church Board for Homeland Ministries, 700 Prospect Ave., 1995.

Nemore, Trish. "More than 'Standing by my Trans'." In *Trans Forming Families*, edited by Mary Boenke. Imperial Beach, CA: Walter Trook Publishing, 1999. Available from Walter Trook Publishing, 276 Dale Street, Imperial Beach, CA 91932.

Nieves, Evelyn. "Another Minority Flexes its Muscle in San Francisco." *New York Times*. (February 24, 2001): A6.

O'Donovan, Oliver. *Transsexualism and Christian Marriage*. Bromcotte, Notts: Grove Books, 1982. Reviewed in *Gender Dysphoria: A Guide to Research*. Dallas Denny. New York: Garland, 1994.

O'Keefe, Tracie and Katrina Fox. *Trans-X-U-All: The Naked Difference*. London, England: Extraordinary People Press, 1997.

Ordinance 983, City of Santa Cruz. *Proceedings From the First International Conference on Transgender Law and Employment Policy.* (1992), page 209. Available from 5707 Fiorenza Street, Houston, TX, 77035-5515.

Offerman-Zuckerberg, Joan. *Gender in Transition: A New Frontier.* New York: Plenum, 1989.

Osterman, Mary Jo, ed. "Transgender Realities" *Open Hands.* 12(2), 1996.

Paddock, Richard. "San Francisco Targets Anti-Transgender Bias." *Los Angeles Times.* 114 (December 26, 1994): A3.

Pagels, Elaine. *The Gnostic Gospels.* New York: Random House (Vintage), 1979.

Paige, Chris. "Other Wise." *The Other Side.* 37 (May-June, 2001): 33-35.

Pauly, I. B. "Female Transsexualism." In *Proceeding of the Second Interdisciplinary Symposium on Gender Dysphoria Syndrome,* edited by D. Laub and P. Gandy. Palo Alto, California: Stanford University Medical Center, 1973.

Parsons, Talcott. "Definitions of Health and Illness in the Light of American Values and Social Structures." In *The Patient and the Mental Hospital,* edited by Milton Greenblatt, et al. New York: Free Press, 1957. Reprinted in E. Gartley Jaco. *Patients, Physicians and Illness, Second Edition.* New York: Macmillian, 1972.

Penny, Robert. "Ambiguous Genitalia." *American Journal of Diseases of Children.* 144: (1990): 753.

Pillard, Richard C. and James D. Weinrich, "The Periodic Table of the Gender Transpositions: Part 1. A Theory Based on Masculinization and Defeminization of the Brain." *Journal of Sex Research.* 23 (1987): 425-54.

Pool, Robert. *Eve's Rib: Searching for the Biological Basis of Sex Differences.* New York: Crown, 1994.

Potter, Lillian. "Man-Woman": Anti-Gay Peer Harassment of Straight High School Activists." *The Georgetown Journal of Gender and the Law.* 1 (1999): 173-179.

Prince, C.V. and P. Bentler. "Survey of 504 cases of Transvestism." *Psychological Reports.* 31 (1972): 903-917.

*Proceedings: International Conference on Transgender Law and Employment Policy,* Volumes 1-5, 1992-1996. Available from 5707 Fiorenza Street, Houston, Texas 77035-5515.

Rako, Susan. *The Hormone of Desire.* New York: Harmony, 1996.

Ramet, Sabrina P. ed. *Gender Reversals and Gender Cultures: Anthropological and Historic Perspectives*. New York: Routledge, 1996.

Ramsey, Gerald. *Transsexuals: Candid Answers to Private Questions*. Freedom, CA: The Crossing Press, 1996.

Raymond, Janice. *The Transsexual Empire: The Making of the She-Male*. Boston: Beacon Press, 1979.

Rekers, George A. *Growing Up Straight: What Every Family Should Know About Homosexuality*. Chicago: Moody Press, 1982.

Rekers, George A. and Shasta Morey. "The Relationship of Measures of Sex-Typed Play With Clinician Ratings On Degree of Gender Disturbance." *Journal of Clinical Psychology*. 46: (1990): 28–34.

Rekers, George A. *Handbook of Child and Adolescent Sexual Problems*. New York: Lexington Books, 1995.

Reisman, Judith A. and Edward W. Eichel. *Kinsey, Sex and Fraud*. Lafayette, LA: Huntington House, 1990.

*Religion and Transvestism* (A collection of writings from Transgender Tapestry). Waltham MA: International Foundation for Gender Education (IFGE), 1996. Available from IFGE, P. O. Box 540229, Waltham, MA 02454.

Rilke, R. M. "A Walk." (Originally published in 1924.) In *Selected Poems of Rainer Maria Rilke*, translated by Robert Bly, New York: Harper and Row, 1981.

Ringrose, Kathryn M. "Living in the Shadows: Eunuchs and Gender in Byzantium" In *Third Sex, Third Gender: Beyond Sexual Dimorphism in Culture and History*, edited by Gilbert Herdt. New York: Zone Books, 1996.

Rothblatt, Martine. *The Apartheid of Sex*. New York: Crown, 1995.

Rowe, Robert J. (Forward by Vern Bullough.) *Bert and Lori: The Autobiography of a Crossdresser*. Amherst, NY: Prometheus Books, 1997.

Rudd, Peggy. *Crossdressers and Those Who Share Their Lives* (1995). *Who's Really From Venus* (1998). *CrossDressing with Dignity* (1990). *My Husband Wears My Clothes* (1999). All four books are PM Publications (P. O. Box 5304, Katy, TX 77491-5304) and are available from The International Foundation for Gender Education (IFGE), P. O. Box 540299, Waltham, MA 02454, web site, www.ifge.org.

Rushing, William A., ed. *Deviant Behavior and Social Processes: Second Edition*. New York: Rand McNally, 1975.

Satin, Barbara. Presentation to the 1998 Annual Conference of the United Church of Christ Coalition for Gay, Lesbian, Bisexual and Transgender Concerns in Chicago, IL.

Scholinski, Daphne with Jane Meredith Adams. *The Last Time I Wore a Dress*. New York: Riverhead Books (Penguin Putnam), 1997.

Schroeder, Gerald. *The Science of God: The Convergence of Scientific and Biblical Wisdom*. New York: The Free Press (Simon and Schuster), 1997.

Schwartz, Mark F. ed. *Sex and Gender: A Theological and Scientific Inquiry*. St Louis, MO: Pope John XXIII Medical-Moral Research and Education Center, 1983.

Scott, William A. "Attitude Measurement." In *Handbook of Social Psychology, Second Edition,* Vol. 2, edited by Gardner Lindzey and Elliot Aronson. Reading, MA: Addison-Wesley, 1968.

Seil, David. "Transsexuals: The Boundaries of Sexual Identity and Gender." In *Textbook of Homosexuality and Mental Health,* edited by Robert J. Cabaj and Terry S. Stein. Washington, DC: American Psychiatric Press, 1996.

Sheff, Thomas. "The Role of the Mentally Ill and the Dynamics of Mental Disorder." *Sociometry.* 26 (1963): 436–453. Reprinted in *The Mental Patient: Studies in the Sociology of Deviance,* edited by Stephen Spitzer and Norman Denzin. New York: McGraw Hill, 1968.

Sheridan, Vanessa. *CReferencesrossing Over: Liberating the Transgendered Christian.* Cleveland: Pilgrim Press, 2001.

Sherman, Suzanne, ed. *Lesbian and Gay Marriage*. Philadelphia: Temple University Press, 1992.

Silverstein, Charles. "History of Treatment." In *Textbook of Homosexuality and Mental Health*, edited by Robert J. Cabaj and Terry S. Stein. Washington, DC: American Psychiatric Press, 1996.

Sinclair, Yvonne. *Transvestism Within a Partnership of Marriage and Families*. London, England: TV/TS Group, 1984.

Singer, June. *Androgyny: Toward a New Theory of Sexuality*. New York: Anchor Press - Doubleday, 1976.

Spahr, Jane Adams, et al. eds. *Called Out: The Voices and Gifts of Lesbian, Gay, Bisexual and Transgendered Presbyterians*. Gaithersburg, MD: Chi Rho Press, 1995.

Spitzer, Stephan and Norman Denzin, eds. *The Mental Patient: Studies in the Sociology of Deviance*. New York: McGraw Hill, 1968.

Spong, John. *Living in Sin: A Bishop Rethinks Human Sexuality*. San Francisco: Harper and Row, 1988.

St. Pierre, Tracy. Press Conference, National Press Club, Washington, DC, August 12, 1998.

Steiner, Betty W., ed. *Gender Dysphoria:Development, Research, Management.* New York: Plenum, 1985.

Stoller, Robert J. and I.S. Levine. *Coming Attractions:The Making of an X-Rated Video.* New Haven, CT:Yale University Press, 1993.

Suggs, M. Jack, et al., eds. *The Oxford Study Bible: Revised English Bible With The Apocrypha.* New York: Oxford University Press, 1989.

Swan, Wallace, ed. *Gay/Lesbian/Bisexual/Transgender Public Policy Issues:A Citizen's and Administrator's Guide to the New Cultural Struggle.* Binghampton, NY: Haworth Press (Harrington Park Press), 1997.

Szasz, Thomas. *Ideology and Insanity.* Garden City, NY: Doubleday (Anchor), 1970.

Tafoya, Terry. "Nature of Two-Spirit People." In *Textbook of Homosexuality and Mental Health,* edited by Robert J. Cabaj and Terry S. Stein. Washington, DC: American Psychiatric Press, 1996.

Talamini, John. *Boys Will Be Girls:The Hidden World of the Heterosexual Male Transvestite.* Washington, DC: University Press of America, 1982.

Tigert, Leanne M. and Timothy Brown, eds. *Coming Out Young and Faithful.* Cleveland, OH: Pilgrim, 2001.

Tillich, Paul. *Systematic Theology,* Vol.1, 2, 3. Chicago: University of Chicago Press, 1951, 1957, 1963.

Tiryakin, Edward. "The Existential Self and the Person." In *The Self in Social Interaction,* edited by Chad Gordon and Kenneth Gergen. New York: John Wiley and Sons, 1968.

*Transgender Tapestry.* Available from the International Foundation for Gender Education, P. O. Box 540229, Waltham, MA 02254.

"TS Minister's Ordination Upheld," *Aegis News.* 9 (1996): 8. Available from P. O. Box 33724, Decatur, GA 30033-0724.

Vanessa S. *Cross Purposes: On Being Christian and Transgendered.* Decatur, GA: Sullivan Press, P. O. Box, 33724, 1996.

Vera, Veronica. *Miss Vera's Finishing School For Boys Who Want to be Girls.* New York: Doubleday (Main Street), 1997.

Von Mahlsdorf, Charlotte. *I Am My Own Woman:The Outlaw Life of Charlotte von Mahlsdorf, Berlin's Most Distinguished Cross-Dresser*. Pittsburgh, PA: Cleis Press, 1995.

Walker, Paul A. "A Contemporary Perspective on Gender Dysphoria." In *Sex and Gender:A Theological and Scientific Inquiry,* edited by Mark F. Schwartz. St. Louis, MO: Pope John XXIII Medical-Moral Research and Education Center, 1983.

Waskow, Arthur O. *Godwrestling: Round 2:Ancient Wisdom, Future Paths*. Woodstock, VT: Jewish Lights Publications, 1996.

Waun, Maurine C. *More than Welcome: Learning to Embrace Gay, Lesbian, Bisexual and Transgendered Persons in the Church*. St. Louis, MO: Chalice Press, 1999.

Weber, Max. *Economy and Society,* Vol. 3. New York: Bedminster Press, 1968.

Webster, Danielle E. "Dealing With Deuteronomy." *Transgender Tapestry*. 92 (2000): 30-36.

Wechsler, David. *The Measurement and Appraisal of Adult Intelligence*. (See particularly the section on "Sex Difference in Intelligence.) Baltimore: Williams and Wilking, 1958.

Westheimer, Ruth. *Dr. Ruth's Encyclopedia of Sex*. New York: Continuum, 1994.

Wilchins, Riki Anne. *Read My Lips: Sexual Subversion and the End of Gender*. Ithaca, NY: Firebrand Books, 1997.

Wilkes, Paul, ed. *Excellent Protestant Congregations*. Louisville, KY: Westminster John Knox Press, 2001.

Williams, Walter L. *The Spirit and the Flesh: Sexual Diversity in American Indian Culture*. Boston: Beacon Press, 1986.

Wilson, Edward. *Sociobiology*. Cambridge, Massachusetts: Belknap Press, 1980.

Wills, Garry. *Papal Sin: Structures of Deceit*. New York: Doubleday, 2000.

Woodhouse, Annie. *Fantastic Women: Sex, Gender and Transvestism*. New Brunswick, NJ: Rutgers University Press, 1989.

Wray, Judith Hoch. *Gay, Lesbian,Bisexual and Transgendered Christians in the Church: Reflections for Disciples of Christ Who Seek to Discern God's Will*. Available from: web site, www.sacredplaces.com/discern.

Wyden, Peter and Barbara. *Growing Up Straight:What Every Thoughtful Parent Should Know About Homosexuality*. New York: Stein and Day, 1986.

Yen, S.S.C. and R. B. Jaffe. *Reproductive Endocrinology*. Philadelphia: W.B. Saunders, 1991.

Zucker, Kenneth, et al. "Prenatal Gender Preferences of Mothers of Feminine and Masculine Boys: Relation to Sibling Sex Composition and Birth Order." *Journal of Abnormal Child Psychology*. 22 (1994):1 ff.

Richard M. Zuckerberg. "From John Wayne to Tootsie: The Masculine Struggle with Psychological Integration." *Gender in Transition: A New Frontier*. New York: Plenum, 1989.

# Order Additional copies

Copies of Transgender Good News are available from:

New Wineskins Press
12 Wessex Road
Silver Spring, MD 20910-5437

To order:
Send the address where you want the book(s) to be sent

Enclose a check for $19.00 ($15 for the book, plus $4 for shipping and handling) for each book.

Please help to spread the word about Transgender Good News. Encourage people to review the book on the internet at www.newwineskinspress.com